Huntington Library Publications

The Cattle
on a Thousand Hills

SOUTHERN CALIFORNIA · 1850-1880

by Robert Glass Cleland

The Huntington Library

SAN MARINO, CALIFORNIA

Henry E. Huntington Library and Art Gallery
1151 Oxford Road, San Marino, California 91108
www.huntington.org

Library of Congress Cataloging-in-Publication Data
Cleland, Robert Glass, 1885–1957
The Cattle on a thousand hills: southern California,
1850–1880 / by Robert Glass Cleland. — 2nd ed.
    365 p. 24 cm.
Includes bibliographical references.
1. California, Southern—History. 2. Cattle trade—
California, Southern—History—19th century. 3. Ranch
life—California, Southern—History—19th century.
I. Title.
[F867C6 1951b]
979.4'904—dc20   89-49490

ISBN: 0-87328-097-0

TO BARBARA

WHOSE LIFE HAD IN IT

THE BEAUTY AND FRAGRANCE OF

RED ROSES ON A SUNLIT WALL

Table of Contents

List of Illustrations

(FROM DRAWINGS AND PHOTOGRAPHS IN THE
HUNTINGTON LIBRARY)

Preface to the Second Edition

THE PUBLICATION of a second edition of *The Cattle on a Thousand Hills* has given me opportunity to add a new chapter on the development of southern California between 1870 and 1880, correct a number of errors which appeared in the former printing, revise the style and phraseology of the volume in certain places, transfer the footnotes to the end of the text, and provide a bibliography and numerous additional illustrations. The Appendix has been expanded by the addition of a contemporary newspaper account of the activities of the noted bandit Tiburcio Vasquez.

The supplemental chapter brings the book down to the beginning of Dr. Glenn S. Dumke's significant study *The Boom of the Eighties in Southern California*, a Huntington Library publication of 1944. Taken together the two works span almost half a century in the formative period of the making of the southern California of today.

I am especially indebted to my secretary Miss Norma Jones for careful reading both of the text and proof of this new volume, assistance in compiling the bibliography, and preparation of the index. Mr. Carey Bliss, Mr. William Parish, and Mr. Erwin F. Morkisch have been of great assistance in the selection of the illustrations. I am also under obligation to Miss Haydée Noya for her advice on manuscript material and to Mr. Edwin Carpenter for critical reading of the proof.

ROBERT G. CLELAND

Huntington Library
May, 1951

Preface to the First Edition

BECAUSE of rich and varied resources, certain distinctive industries, and a vigorous though as yet amorphous culture, the southern California of today plays no mean part in the life and thought and making of the world. But men still living can recall when the region, now so populous, highly developed, and renowned, was only an isolated cattle frontier, without an exact counterpart among the other frontiers of the Old West.

This book is an economic and social history of the southern California of those half-forgotten, formative years. It is chiefly concerned with the impact of Anglo-Saxon customs and institutions upon the pastoral life of the Spanish-Californians, with the conversion of great grazing ranchos into farms and settlements, with the gradual displacement of frontier violence and instability by a more restrained, law-abiding society, and with the transformation of the so-called "Cow Counties" of the post-Gold Rush era into the small beginnings of the southern California of our own time.

Although complete in itself, the book was originally designed to serve as the introductory volume in a series of kindred studies, covering the whole field of southern California's economic and social development, from the time of the American conquest down to the present day. It is hoped that the plan, though now in abeyance, may eventually be carried to completion.

With the exception of the first two chapters, devoted to an account of the Spanish-Mexican land-grant system, the study is chiefly confined to the period which lay between the Gold Rush of 1849-51 and the completion of the Pacific Railroad, some two decades later. The field is one through which the familiar trails of California history do not run; rather, from the standpoint of historical research, it is more analogous to those fascinating areas on the older maps of the Sierra Nevada Mountains, across which was written the laconic legend, "Unexplored."

In the preparation of the volume, I have sought to interpret, as well as to describe; to catch the authentic color and spirit of the period; and to deal with factors of fundamental significance rather than with events of only petty local interest.

Much of the material for the volume has come from primary sources in the Huntington Library, especially from the extraordinary collection known as the Gaffey Manuscripts. Indeed, without access to that extensive and varied storehouse of Californiana, the book could not have been written. The collection consists of some 15,000 items, representing private letters, documents, accounts, memoranda, and business records of Abel Stearns—a man whose interests and activities touched every phase of southern California life from 1829 to 1871. Unfortunately, though filed in chronological order, the materials in the Gaffey collection are not as yet systematically catalogued.

As the footnotes indicate, extensive use has also been made of a number of other manuscript collections, both in the Huntington Library and elsewhere. The records of the federal district courts of California, which contain the proceedings of the cases heard by the Commissioners appointed under the Act of 1851 "to ascertain and settle the Private Land Claims in California," furnish almost inexhaustible material on the early histories of individual ranchos, as well as on the provisions of the Spanish-Mexican land-grant system itself.

County archives have supplied the records of deeds and mortgages and early assessment and tax returns. The files of contemporary newspapers, such as the Los Angeles *Star*, the *Southern Vineyard*, and the *Semi-weekly News*, have furnished a wealth of illustrative and descriptive material. All such primary sources have been supplemented by full use of important secondary works.

A large part of the study is devoted to the so-called Los Angeles basin—a territory roughly defined as extending from the southern limit of Ventura County to the San Jacinto Mountains —but such emphasis is not out of proportion to the dominant position that area occupied in the early life of southern California. The history of the region, moreover, except in incident and detail, is in the main the history of the entire pastoral south.

In the preparation of the volume, I have been placed under obligation to many persons. Dr. John Walton Caughey enabled the Huntington Library to obtain photostats of a considerable body of Abel Stearns' correspondence; Mr. Cave Couts, of San Diego County, permitted me to have access to his large manuscript collection; Mr. Palmer Conner, of San Gabriel, offered the use of his extensive private files; Mr. Terry Stevenson called my attention to a number of important items in Orange County; and my son, Dr. Robert Stewart Cleland, supplied certain interesting side lights on the early history of medicine in Los Angeles County. Other material was placed in my hands by Mr. J. Gregg Layne, Mr. William W. Vannier, and Mr. David Davies. I have also profited greatly from Mr. William W. Clary's precise legal knowledge of early California land titles.

Without exception, the members of the Huntington Library staff have been helpful, courteous, and co-operative. Because of their special interest in California history, and their ready assistance at all times, I am particularly indebted to Mr. Leslie Bliss and Mr. Lindley Bynum. Miss Haydée Noya generously assumed responsibility for the translation of certain documents, and Miss Phyllis Rigney placed at my disposal her extensive knowledge of the Library's California manuscript material. Mr. Merrill H. Crissey has gone even beyond the second mile in his meticulous reading of the manuscript and of the proof. I owe to him the elimination of many errors. Miss Ethel Holton has also been most helpful in many matters of detail, and to Miss Edith

Klotz I am especially indebted for the preparation of the index.

Dr. Max Farrand, the Director, and Professors Louis B. Wright, Edwin F. Gay, and Godfrey Davies, members of the research staff of the Library, have given me both of their counsel and friendship.

My secretary, Miss Margery Bowen, merits and receives my grateful appreciation. Lastly, to Dan Hammack, lifelong friend and generous critic; to my ever patient wife; and to my sons, Robert and George, whose interest was at times a badly needed spur, I acknowledge a debt far greater than I am ever likely to repay.

ROBERT G. CLELAND

Occidental College
January 16, 1941

The Cattle on a Thousand Hills

CHAPTER I

The Land Concessions of 1784

F OR more than three-quarters of a century after the coming of the Spaniards, California remained a sparsely populated outpost on the long rim of the Mexican frontier. Its inhabitants enjoyed only a limited contact with the outside world, possessed a pleasing, but definitely restricted culture, and engaged almost exclusively in the ancient vocation of cattle raising.

Annexation by the United States in 1848 had little immediate effect upon the prevailing social and economic institutions of California and scarcely touched the pastoral traditions and habits of its people. But what the Treaty of Guadalupe Hidalgo failed to accomplish, James Marshall's investigation of a curious substance in the tail race of a Sierra Nevada sawmill quickly and dramatically brought about. For that chance discovery of gold set in motion one of the most spectacular migrations the world has ever seen—a migration that swept over much of California like a turbulent spring-time flood and obliterated the old order, the old culture, the old customs and way of life.

The Gold Rush in effect created two Californias. North of Monterey, the huge immigration overwhelmed the native population, transformed drowsy adobe pueblos into sprawling, cosmopolitan cities, and supplanted the simple agrarian life of the Spanish-Californians with a frontier society of the most explosive type.

To this California—the true California of the Gold Rush, a California of tumultous mining camps, feverish economic activity, and polyglot cities, one of which presently came to be recognized as a "financial competitor of New York and a cultural rival to Boston"[1]—the southern half of the state offered a striking and arresting contrast. Between Monterey and the Mexican border lay some five hundred miles of grazing land. Here the Gold Rush, contrary to its revolutionary effects in the north, destroyed little that was old, created little that was new. It brought about almost no increase in population, built neither villages nor cities, and left the established life and customs of the Spanish-Californians almost undisturbed.

In 1850, two years after Marshall's epochal discovery, the total white population of the six southern California counties was less than 8,000, and the social and economic life of the people was still that of a typical Mexican cattle frontier.[2] East of the Coast Range extended an isolated hinterland of savage mountains, rich but uncultivated plains, and almost illimitable deserts. Adjacent to the coast lay a land of captivating beauty, diversified by ranges of low foothills, infrequent watercourses, and pleasant valleys opening out upon the sea. Here the traveler encountered a few despoiled, half-abandoned missions and an occasional unpretentious pueblo, or presidial town, founded by Spanish colonists before the century began. For the most part, however, the coastal area was occupied by a succession of enormous private estates, called ranchos, which were primarily devoted to cattle raising and served as California's counterpart of the more familiar Mexican hacienda.[3]

At the time of the American conquest, these great landholdings were the dominant feature of California life. They remained the controlling factor in much of the state's settlement and agricultural development for nearly half a century, and their gradual conversion into cities, towns, and farming communities served in large measure to bring into being the southern California we know today. The ranchos thus constituted one of the few enduring legacies that California inherited from Mexico and Spain.

The system of land tenure, out of which the ranchos evolved, was based upon an ancient principle of Spanish law which recognized the king as owner in fee simple of all the colonial possessions in the Americas and vested in him exclusive title to the fabulous resources of a continent. "We give, grant and assign forever to you and to your heirs and successors, Kings of Castile and Leon," ran the famous bull of Alexander VI in 1493, "all and singular the aforesaid countries and islands thus unknown and hitherto discovered by your envoys and to be discovered hereafter, together with all their dominions, cities, camps, places, and towns as well as all rights, jurisdictions, and appurtenances of the same whereon they may be found."[4]

Successive Spanish sovereigns used the land thus placed at their disposal in a great variety of ways. Upon conquistadores and other royal favorites they bestowed estates "of lands and villages . . . meadows, waters and streams," sometimes as large as provinces. Land constituted the basis for the encomienda and *mita* systems of the early Spanish colonists, provided royal endowments for the church, and furnished the economic basis for the permanent occupation of New Spain's outlying territories, including the vast, little-known wilderness called Alta California.

The Spanish colonial system, with its genius for method and uniformity, used three highly specialized institutions — the presidio, mission, and pueblo — to colonize the wilderness and expand the frontier. California, like all other border provinces, owed its settlement to these three institutions, each of which, in turn, depended upon a royal land grant for its foundation and existence.

The presidio was a military post designed both for the defense of the province against foreign invasion and for the preservation of internal order. It received sufficient land to supply the garrison with food and furnish pasture for the king's cattle, horses, and other livestock. To aid in the settlement of California, presidios were established at San Diego, Santa Barbara, Monterey, and San Francisco.

The pueblo, or town, was founded by civilian colonists. Its land holdings usually contained four square leagues, or about 17,500 acres, and the boundaries of the grant ran a league distant, "North, South, East and West from the center of the church door."[5] Each pueblo grant made provision for a plaza, a church, and one or more public buildings, and allocated a building site, with its orchard and garden, to each colonist or settler. The remainder of the tract became a communal pasture. Los Angeles and San José were the two principal pueblos in California, though the short-lived Branciforte, or Santa Cruz, originally enjoyed the same status.[6]

Upon the missions, "a conspicuous example of Spain's frontiering genius," rested the responsibility of converting the Indians to Christianity and of transforming them into loyal and industrious subjects of the crown. To accomplish this many-sided, herculean task, the Franciscan establishments in California undertook not only to Christianize but also to feed, clothe, train, instruct, and discipline the hundreds of natives over whom they exercised paternal but rigorous control.

In addition to fulfilling their ecclesiastical functions, the friars accordingly taught the Indians necessary handicrafts, developed a surprising variety of industries, built dams and canals for irrigation, planted orchards, gardens, and field crops, and raised immense herds of cattle, sheep, and horses.[7] To enable the friars to carry on such multiple responsibilities, the crown placed enormous tracts of land at the disposal of the missions; but such concessions were only temporary in character and carried with them neither title in fee simple nor the permanent right of use. This restricted form of grant worked little hardship at the time, but a generation later the government used it to terminate the land concessions to the missions and thus bring about their economic ruin.[8]

Governor Pedro Fages, who marched to San Diego as captain of the "leather jacket" troops, or *soldados de cuero*, in the Portolá expedition of 1769, authorized the first private grants of land in California and thus inaugurated the all-important rancho system.[9] In 1784 three or four members of his old command, who looked forward to becoming rancheros when they retired from the army, petitioned Fages for certain unoccupied grazing lands in the vicinity of the Mission San Gabriel.

In submitting the request to his superior officers in Mexico, Fages wrote:

The cattle are increasing in such manner, that it is necessary in the case of several owners to give them additional lands; they have asked me for some *sitios* which I have granted provisionally, namely to Juan José Domínguez who was a soldier in the presidio of San Diego and who at this moment has four herds of mares and about 200 head of cattle on the river below San Gabriel, to Manuel Nieto for a similar reason that of la Zanja on the highway from said Mission along by the oak tree, and to the sons of the widow Ignacio Carrillo that on the deep creek contiguous to the foregoing. . . .[10]

At the end of two years—by no means an abnormal delay in the conduct of Mexican-California business — Fages received formal approval for his action, provided the tracts in question did not encroach upon the four square leagues of "water and pastures, wood and timber" allotted to a pueblo, or upon the holdings of a mission, or upon any Indian rancheria.[11] Fages was also reminded that one of the fixed conditions of a land grant required the recipient to build a stone house, stock the ranch with at least 2,000 head of cattle, and provide enough *vaqueros* and sheepherders to prevent his stock from wandering.[12]

Of the three beneficiaries of Governor Fages' liberality,

Manuel Nieto profited the most.[13] The San Gabriel River, which then emptied into the ocean near the present Long Beach-Wilmington boundary line, defined the western extent of the Nieto grant; twenty-five miles down the coast the Santa Ana River marked its limits on the east; and from the lonely shore line of the Pacific its unfenced leagues of grazing lands spread away to the north to meet "the main road leading from San Diego along the hills to San Gabriel."[14] As thus defined, the grant included nearly 300,000 acres; but at the insistence of the San Gabriel Mission, upon whose concession Nieto's holdings seriously overlapped, the latter were eventually reduced to about half their original extent.[15]

Manuel Nieto retired from the army in 1795 and spent his declining years on that part of the grant known as the Rancho Santa Gertrudes, where he had an "adobe house and corrals and cultivated land." When he died in 1804, his extensive land holdings and enormous herds of horses and "black cattle" made him the wealthiest man in California.[16]

In accordance with the custom of the time, each of Nieto's four children, Juan José, Manuela, Antonio María, and José Antonio, received an undivided interest in his father's estate. The huge Nieto grant was thus kept intact for nearly thirty years longer; but in 1833 the heirs petitioned Governor José Figueroa for a partition and distribution of the property, and the latter divided the original concession into six great ranchos — Los Alamitos, Los Cerritos, Los Coyotes, Las Bolsas, Palo Alto, and Santa Gertrudes.[17] The land included in the Nieto grant is now occupied by the cities of Long Beach, Huntington Beach, Norwalk, Downey, and all the intermediate communities; by five or six large oil fields, including Signal Hill, Santa Fé Springs, and Huntington Beach; and by thousands of acres of citrus groves, walnut orchards, truck gardens, and bean fields.

Although smaller than the Nieto grant, the concession obtained by Juan José Domínguez was also a principality. The San Gabriel River furnished a natural eastern boundary for the rancho, and the Pacific Ocean served the same purpose on the south and west. The northern limit of the grant, as defined in 1817 by a monument of stones, extended westward from the San Gabriel River to certain well-known salines, or salt pits, on Redondo Bay. The area thus included in the Domínguez sitios was over 16 square leagues, or about 75,000 acres. In later years the grant came to be called by many names; but usually it was known as the Rancho de Domínguez, or the Rancho of San Pedro of the Cove.[18]

For many years after receiving the grant, Juan José remained at the presidio in San Diego and left the management of the property to a *mayordomo;* and when finally he went to the ranch to live, he was "too old and lazy" to put much energy or interest into its development. A livestock census taken in 1805 showed that he owned "3,000 mares, 1,000 fillies, 1,000 colts, 700 cows, 200 heifers, and 260 bulls."[19]

Juan José's ranch house on the San Pedro was a crude adobe structure, altogether typical of the period, with earthen floor and a "wooded top covered with pitch." Relations between the aging corporal and his neighbors apparently were none too friendly; and a quarrel with Manuel Nieto over the ownership of cattle lasted the greater part of a decade.[20] As Domínguez grew more infirm with the advancing years, he neglected his ranch, permitted his cattle to go unbranded, and did "not properly herd his brood mares, and they became wild and many horses of the San Gabriel joined them so that . . . there were thousands of wild horses on the plains, to the great detriment of the Mission and other owners of stock."[21]

Ninety years old, bedridden, and blind, Juan José died at the Mission of San Juan Capistrano in 1809.[22] Upon his death, Manuel Gutiérrez, to whom Domínguez and his estate were heavily indebted, was made administrator of the Rancho San Pedro. Under the new management, the ranch enjoyed unusual prosperity, and the rapid increase of its herds led people to say that "every cow was followed by five calves of the Gutiérrez brand and every mare by three colts."[23]

Some years after his uncle's death, Cristóbal Domínguez, nephew and heir of Juan José, sought to establish title to the Rancho San Pedro in his own name; but Gutiérrez flatly refused to surrender possession of the property. To add fuel to the flames, he permitted his friend, José Dolores Sepúlveda, to graze several hundred cattle on the western part of the original Domínguez grant, a tract known as the Rancho de Los Palos Verdes, and disregarded Cristóbal's heated protest against the intrusion of a third party, who "had no right to mix himself up in the affairs of the Rancho."

After pasturing from 800 to 1,000 head of stock on the Palos Verdes for several years, Sepúlveda petitioned to have the land bestowed upon him as a separate grant; but while the proceedings were still in progress, he was killed in an Indian massacre at the Mission La Purísima. The governor then provisionally granted the Palos Verdes to Sepúlveda's minor heirs.[24]

The quarrel between the Domínguez family, on the one side, and Gutiérrez and the Sepúlvedas, on the other, smoldered along for another decade. Still entangled in difficulties, Cristóbal Domínguez died at San Diego on January 6, 1825, "at four o'clock in the morning." His will, made only the preceding day, provided that his heirs should be placed in peaceful possession of the "Rancho called San Pedro which I inherited from my deceased Uncle Juan José Domínguez," and that a division of the personal property should be made among his six children, "the preference being always with the youngest."

In 1834 the various claimants for the Domínguez and Palos Verdes ranchos finally submitted the dispute to Governor José

"DISEÑO" OF THE NIETO GRANT (1834)

Figueroa for arbitration. Figueroa decided that Gutiérrez should be allowed to pasture cattle on the Rancho San Pedro for the remainder of his life, provided he renounced all further interest in the property; that the Domínguez heirs should be recognized as legal owners of the San Pedro and given full possession of the ranch when Gutiérrez died; and finally that the Sepúlvedas had legitimate title to the Rancho Los Palos Verdes and might expand its boundaries to include a further portion of the San Pedro grant.[25]

The loss of the Palos Verdes reduced the original Domínguez concession to slightly more than half its initial area; but even under such diminished boundaries the Place of the Domínguez still remained an estate of royal size. In 1854 the United States Land Commission fixed its area at approximately 38,000 acres, or "8½ leagues, a little more or less."[26]

During the decades since the Land Commission rendered its decision, the pasture lands of Juan José Domínguez have undergone miraculous transformation; and the sitios granted in 1784 to an illiterate corporal who had "4 herds of mares and about 200 head of cattle on the river below San Gabriel" today constitute one of California's most important petroleum, industrial, and shipping centers.[27]

Like Domínguez and Nieto, José María Verdugo was a corporal of the royal presidio of San Diego and a member of the company of *soldados de cuero* commanded by Pedro Fages in 1769. Since military service at the San Gabriel Mission, to which he had been assigned, rarely proved exacting, Verdugo undertook to supplement his meager and precarious salary by grazing horses and cattle on the fertile lowlands through which the San Gabriel River found its way to the sea. Unfortunately for Verdugo, the land was already pre-empted by Nieto and Domínguez, and he was finally compelled to move his stock to another range.

To avoid trespassing upon either mission or pueblo lands, Verdugo chose an unoccupied tract west of the watercourse called indiscriminately the Arroyo Hondo and the Arroyo Seco. The land lay about a league and a half from the San Gabriel Mission, on the old "Road to Monterey."[28] From the junction of the road and the arroyo, the tract extended "to the river of the Pueblo de la Reina de Los Angeles as far as the Saca de Agua (or water dam) and north to the Sierra."

To Verdugo's petition for this tract, Fages replied: "I concede to the petitioner the permission which he solicits to keep his cattle & Horses at the 'Arroyo Hondo' . . . provided that he does not prejudice the . . . Mission, nor the inhabitants of the Reina de Los Angeles, & having some one in charge, without being exposed to the gentile Indians, nor in any manner injuring them."[29]

Since Verdugo himself could not live on the ranch, because of military duties at the mission, he sent his brother to manage its affairs. In due time the brother built a crude "house of sticks," planted a garden, and set out a vineyard.[30] Four years later, Governor Fages gave Verdugo the right to use his own cattle brand, thus indicating that José María's livestock had become sufficiently numerous to raise him to the status of a true ranchero.[31] For "it was not the custom of the Spanish government to give a brand to a man unless he had one hundred and fifty head of breeding cattle." The owner of a smaller herd, though not entitled to a brand, could use a "mark for cattle on the Cheek."[32]

As the years went by, Verdugo became a victim of dropsy and found himself unable to endure the hardships of army life. He suffered, too, from the great misfortune, as he somewhat ambiguously declared, of having "five daughters and one small male child, but no son to assist me."[33] Provincial regulations required a soldier incapacitated by illness for further military service to live in one of the pueblos; but Verdugo, vigorously protesting against the application of this rule to his own case, pointed out that in a pueblo he would "have to suffer the various fatigues which all persons, although for good, share in common," and then added, "I know that I am already incapable. I require some greater ease."[34]

The leisure-seeking corporal accordingly petitioned Governor Diego Borica, who had assumed office in 1794, for a confirmation of the grant which "Colonel Don Pedro Fages" had originally approved in 1784, and asked permission to retire from the army and make his home on "the tract of the Zanja." Verdugo added that the ranch was already supporting perhaps "two hundred head of horned cattle, three hundred horses and one hundred and fifty sheep."[35]

Governor Borica submitted Verdugo's petition to Lieutenant Antonio Grajera for verification and comment. On December 13, after the required investigation, Grajera wrote: "I consider the petitioner in the same circumstances relative to his solicitation as Don Manuel Nieto. He has already a considerable number of cattle, horses and sheep Stock, cleared fields in which he sows, and his 'Saca de aqua.' . . . The tract which he describes makes a triangle with the Mission and the Pueblo, its bordering locations."[36]

Upon receipt of Grajera's reply, Borica formally approved Verdugo's petition, and at the same time commended him for having fulfilled the conditions of the earlier Fages' concession which required him to stock the grant with cattle, cultivate part of the land, and build dams and ditches for irrigation. In conclusion, the governor counseled Verdugo "to increase the breed of his sheep and not to prejudice the neighboring Missions and to treat well the Indians both Christians and Gentiles that live near the Rancho, with that love and charity so much recommended by the laws, but not on this account to forbear living with the proper precaution so as to avoid all insult."[37]

Having obtained an honorable discharge from the army in

1799, Verdugo went to live upon the grant which he had been awarded fifteen years before. With him he took his numerous daughters, his "one small male child," and his lingering dropsy. In the course of the years, the "Invalid with the Grade of Corporal," and the relatives who came to live with him, cultivated some of the most fertile parts of the Rancho San Rafael and brought a considerable area under irrigation. By 1817 the ranch was pasturing 1,800 head of large cattle, 1,000 calves, 600 unbroken horses, 70 tame horses, and 70 mules. Twelve years later the number of cattle had almost doubled.[38]

As his flocks and herds increased, Verdugo became involved in occasional difficulties with his neighbors over grazing rights and boundary lines. On one occasion, the *mayordomo* of the Mission San Gabriel attempted to pasture sheep west of the Arroyo Seco, on land included in Verdugo's grant; but the old ranchero protested so vigorously and to such good purpose that the governor peremptorily "ordered the sheep to be taken away, and they were taken away."[39]

West and northwest of the Rancho San Rafael lay the vast holdings of the Mission San Fernando. The boundary line between the mission properties and Verdugo's grant was only vaguely defined, and Verdugo protested that the friars constantly pastured their cattle on his ranges and harvested crops of beans and corn produced on his land. Instead of taking action himself, however, the governor referred Verdugo's complaint to the Los Angeles pueblo officials. A deputation, consisting of an alcalde and representatives of the two contesting parties, thereupon made a personal inspection of the disputed ground and established a definite boundary line between the Rancho San Rafael and the mission grant, using "sycamores, hollow oaks, and mounds of stones for markers."[40]

Despite the dropsy and frequent bleedings (which, according to common report, constituted an excellent remedy "for a pain in the side, with fresh drinks taken moderately"), José María Verdugo lived more than thirty years after his retirement as an invalid from the army. In 1828, when death at last seemed imminent, he gathered his failing strength, summoned the appropriate officials, and made his will.[41]

The document, like all wills of the old Spanish-Californians, was striking naïve, intimate, and detailed. It began with the usual affirmation of faith:

In the name of God and his Most holy Mother, Our Lady conceived in Grace, and without any original sin . . . considering that men have to die and that such may take place at any hour, without knowing when, firmly believing as I do in the Mystery of the Most Holy Trinity, the Father, Son, and the Holy Ghost, three persons distinct, and one only true God & in all and everything that our Holy Mother Church believes and acknowledges. The Most Holy Mary being my intercessor and advocate, . . . as she has been my whole life, I order and make my testament in the following form.

Thereafter, item by item, came the bequests, large and small, and the list of debts, down to the last fraction of a peso, which the testator owed to others, as well as those which others owed to him. Like the will of Juan José Domínguez, that of José María Verdugo clearly reflected the psychology and simple social background of the early Californians. The following clauses are typical:

Item: I declare that José Ma Aguillas owes me, as is proved by a memorandum bearing date 13th August of this year, the sum of $172.

Item. Teodócio José owes me the sum of $170 and a tame Mule, the money is for Aguardiente.

Item. Teodoro Silvas owes me $9—for a horse.

Item. The sergeant Ing Siseno owes me $34 for three fat cows, 1 ox and a calf.

Item. José Ant Tapia owes me for 2 cows and 1 large bull.

Item. The Commissary Department of San Diego owes to my

credit since the year 1825 the sum of $1550⅞ and besides what will become due in the present year.

As the last item to his testament, Verdugo declared, "It is my will that the Rancho which the Nation granted to me, called San Rafael, be left to my son Júlio and to Catalina, in order that they may enjoy the same with the blessing of God."[42]

For nearly forty years, José María's dying wish was fulfilled. In 1855 title to the San Rafael was confirmed to his children, Júlio and Catalina, by the federal Land Commission, and six years later the great ranch was divided between the two heirs. But in 1869 Júlio lost his share, the more desirable southern half, through mortgage foreclosures; and in 1871 Catalina's Rancho La Cañada was also broken up.[43]

The Rancho San Rafael, or Rancho La Zanja, even though only 36,000 acres in extent and thus the smallest of the three famous Fages grants of 1784, was large enough to furnish sites for ten or twelve modern metropolitan communities.[44] In the inexact but picturesque language of the grant its boundary lines were defined as follows:

Beginning at a place on the river called Porciuncula, about ten miles up the said River from the city, where the water for the city is taken from the river, thence following up the river Northerly to the point of the Mountain, thence easterly passing by a swamp to the steep Mountain, thence in a Southern direction to a dry creek, thence along said dry creek to the Place of beginning.

The mountain which is reached following up the river is where the principal head waters of the river take their rise. From this Mountain the line runs in an Easterly or North Easterly course & strikes the place called Cerrito Colorado. From this place the line runs in a direct course to the Arroyo Seco, or dry Creek, leaving the Canada within the boundary. The cross that is above the swamp is the boundary.[45]

The later history of the Verdugo, Domínguez, and Nieto

grants lies beyond the scope of the present volume. A glance at a modern map of the Los Angeles basin, however, will show to what an enormous extent the conversion of the original Fages concessions into cities, towns, factories, oil fields, and farming communities entered into the making of the southern California of today.

CHAPTER II

The Era of the Ranchos

F ROM the time of the accession of Governor Fages, in 1782, to the close of Spanish rule forty years later, less than twenty private rancho concessions were made in California. This conservative land-grant policy was due, in the main, to the lack of responsible citizens in the province and the preemption of a large part of the desirable land by the missions.

Most of the important grants of the Spanish period were situated in southern California; and at least half of the total number lay within a hundred miles of the pueblo of Los Angeles.[1] In addition to the original grants to Nieto, Verdugo, and Domínguez, the Topanga Malibu, of 13,000 acres, granted to José Bartolomé Tapia; the Rancho Santiago de Santa Ana, of 62,000 acres, awarded to Antonio Yorba; the Rancho Simí, of 93,000 acres, jointly owned by Patricio Xavier and Miguel Pico; and the Rancho San Antonio, of 30,000 acres, belonging to Antonio María Lugo, were among the earliest of these concessions.[2]

After the overthrow of Spanish rule and the collapse of the short-lived empire of Iturbide, the Mexican Republic came into possession of the public domain and exercised all the rights previously vested in the Spanish crown. Almost immediately the national congress undertook to liberalize the nation's land policy, stimulate agricultural development, and encourage the settlement of the frontier by the important Colonization Act of 1824.

The Colonization Act, together with its important supplementary *Reglamento* of 1828, furnished the legal pattern for subsequent land grants in the Mexican border provinces and "established a principle which, with slight modifications, remained in force down to the enactment of the Constitution of 1917."[3]

So far as California was concerned, however, neither the change from Spanish to Mexican sovereignty nor the new legislation had any appreciable effect upon the existing land situation.[4] The governors sent by successive Mexican presidents to Monterey made no effort to annul the concessions approved by their Spanish predecessors or to change the conservative land-grant policy under which the province had lived for fifty years. But in 1826 a group of influential Californians, led by Governor José María Echeandía, "a tall, thin, juiceless man," began to demand the restoration of the mission lands to the public domain and the opening of their enormous holdings to the right of private denouncement or pre-emption. The movement found enthusiastic support both in Mexico and California and finally culminated in the revolutionary Secularization Act of 1833—a law which brought the mission era to a dramatic close in California and ushered in the golden age of the ranchos.[5]

To understand the nature and full significance of the Secularization Act, it is necessary to review both the theory and practice of mission land grants under Spanish law. As previously indicated, the mission was distinctly a frontier institution. It had no place in a settled, well-ordered society and ceased to fulfill its original purpose whenever the wilderness in which it was situated became adequately civilized.[6]

Land grants were therefore never made in perpetuity or fee simple to California missions, and the friars were looked upon merely as custodians, or trustees, for the Indian neophytes over whom for a time they exercised spiritual and temporal jurisdiction. According to Bancroft, "Neither mission, church, nor religious order, owned any land. The Missionaries had only the use of the land needed for mission purposes, namely, to prepare the Indians that they might in time take possession as individuals of the land they were then holding in commonalty. This purpose once accomplished, the missions were to be secularized and made pueblos. . . ."[7]

The ownership of mission lands, said the United States Land Commission,

was always regarded as existing in the crown or government. They did not become the property of the missions or of the church or of the priests having charge of them, or of the Neophytes who, while they lived in the Mission community, enjoyed the benefit of their use. We have nothing in Mexican or Spanish laws, decrees or regulations which recognizes any of these as owners of the soil. . . . After the secularization law of 1833 was passed and the breaking up of the community system succeeded it, these lands were uniformly treated by the government as subject to the granting power.[8]

But if the California missions were denied perpetual rights of ownership in public lands, they at least enjoyed provisional grants of Gargantuan size. Prior to secularization, the pastures of the Mission San Fernando embraced over fifty square leagues, or nearly 350 square miles. A much larger area was included in the original holdings of the Mission San Juan Capistrano. In 1822 the Mission San Diego reported that its lands extended to the south thirteen leagues, to the east seventeen leagues, and to the north seven leagues. In the same year the Mission Santa Barbara estimated its land holdings at about twenty-eight square leagues, or close to 122,000 acres.[9]

According to Father José Bernardo Sánchez, the lands of the Mission San Gabriel extended west a league and a half to the Arroyo Seco and the limits of the pueblo of Los Angeles; six leagues southwest to the Rancho San Pedro, and south, three leagues, to the Nieto ranch of Santa Gertrudes.[10] East and southeast, to quote verbatim from the report, they ran "along the Cañon towards the Colorado some 20 odd leagues; in which confines are found the Ranchos La Puente, a little more than 4 leagues—Santa Ana, distant about 10 leagues; at the distance of 15 leagues another called 'Jurupit', and to the San Bernardino it is about 20 leagues, all belonging to the Mission; and following the same line about 27 leagues, a Rancho called San Gorgonio."

On this immense tract, as well as on Juan José Nieto's ranchos of Los Cerritos and Las Bolsas, the mission kept large numbers of horses and black cattle. Sheep and hogs were also pastured along the banks of the Rio San Gabriel and on the "Green Cañada of the Coyotes."[11]

A large amount of irrigable land adjoined the mission, and similar tracts were to be found in the "Puente," at Santa Ana, and on the Rancho San Bernardino. Water conduits were made from tile manufactured on the ranchos and at the mission. Extensive tracts of moist ground along the rivers were adapted to cultivation, while other lands were suitable for dry farming. The mission had jurisdiction over the San Gabriel and Santa Ana rivers, and cut wood and timber in the lofty mountains from which the streams flowed.[12]

The land holdings of all the other missions in California were comparable in size to those just mentioned. Extending from Sonoma to San Diego, enjoying usufructuary title to millions of acres of the richest pasture and tillable land in the province, possessing flocks and herds almost without number, and exercising jurisdiction over thousands of Indian neophytes, the Franciscan foundations, in 1833, were the most flourishing institutions in California. A few years later, thanks to the sequestration of their grants by the government, the missions were little more than rapidly decaying, melancholy ruins.

The Secularization Act, mentioned previously, was ostensibly designed to benefit the Indians and make them a self-sustaining people.[13] Actually, it led to the rapid disintegration of the mission-controlled communities, scattered the partly civilized neophytes like sheep without a shepherd, ushered in half a century's tragic aftermath of wretchedness and poverty, brought about the virtual extinction of the mission system in the province, and, by throwing open millions of acres to private denouncement, revolutionized the departmental land system and made the rancho the dominant economic and social institution in the province.[14]

With the adoption of the Secularization Act, the provincial government completely abandoned the cautious land-grant policy previously followed in California, and distributed the national domain to private petitioners with lavish generosity. "The public land was granted not by the acre, as in the American states," wrote John Hittell,

but by the square league ... The government granted away its land willingly, and without compensation; no pay was required; the only condition of the grant was, that the grantee should occupy the land, build a house on it, and put several hundred head of cattle on it. Whenever he promised to comply with these conditions, he could get a grant of any piece of public land, of eleven square leagues or less, for which he might petition. It was a grand Mexican homestead law; and the chief complaint made about it was by the government, that the number of applicants for grants was not greater.[15]

The new land policy was in fact so liberal that California governors issued fully seven hundred concessions to private claimants between the Secularization Act of 1833 and the American occupation thirteen years later.[16] The number and enormous extent of such grants, as already indicated, made them the controlling factor in southern California's economic life for upwards of half a century, and gave critical and lasting significance to every phase of their development.

Because the uncertain titles and vaguely defined boundaries of many of these early California land grants led to persistent and widespread evils in later years, it is essential to understand the legal formalities and procedures under which the grants were acquired, and the methods employed in defining and measuring their boundaries.

The applicant for a ranch first filed a formal petition with the governor. The document contained a description of the desired grant, declared that no part of the land was included in a prior concession, and gave assurance that the petitioner was a Mexican citizen by birth or naturalization. A *diseño*, or map, showing the area, location, natural boundaries, and landmarks of the grant and giving the names of the contiguous ranches, accompanied the petition.[17]

When the governor had examined the petition and *diseño*, he forwarded them to a local official of the district in which the land was located for verification. If this official reported favorably on the application, the governor approved the petition and ordered that a formal grant, bearing his signature, should be given to the petitioner. The governor's office retained a blotter copy, or *borrador* of the document, and a clerk entered a minute of the transaction in a record book, called the *toma de razón*. The petition, *diseño*, and *borrador* were then assembled in a file called an *expediente* and placed in the provincial archives.[18]

The procedure outlined above, though always followed in essential particulars, was sometimes subject to minor variations. Thus, when Mariano B. Roldan applied for the Rancho La Habra, a former San Gabriel Mission grant lying between the present cities of Whittier and Santa Ana, he addressed the petition to Antonio Machado, *prefect ad interim*, instead of to the governor. Machado sent the request to the *ayuntamiento* of Los Angeles—a body which then had jurisdiction in civil, criminal, and municipal matters "from the limits of San Juan Capistrano on the south to San Fernando on the north, and eastward to the San Bernardino mountains . . . an area now comprised in four counties and . . . as large as the state of Massachusetts," and the *ayuntamiento* referred the petition to its committee on vacant lands.[19] The latter, after consulting the *administrador* of the mission, made a favorable report on the grant and the *ayuntamiento* unanimously concurred. The petition, indorsed by Machado, was then sent to Manuel Jimeno, the acting governor of the province. Jimeno transmitted the document to the departmental assembly where it was first acted upon by the committee on agriculture and then ratified by the assembly as a whole. Governor Juan B. Alvarado brought this phase of the proceedings to a close by signing the grant, on June 10, 1840.[20]

Theoretically, as in the case of the Rancho La Habra, the approval of the assembly was required to validate a grant, but often that formality was ignored and the title rested on the governor's signature alone.[21] The final step in the procedure incident to a grant consisted of an official survey of the land and the award of formal or juridical possession to the claimant. The latter was an ancient, picturesque, vividly symbolic ceremony. In the presence of a magistrate and official witnesses, the new owner "entered upon and walked over said lands, pulled up grass, scattered handsful of earth, broke off branches of trees, and performed other acts and demonstrations of possession as signs of the possession which he said he took of said lands. And the aforementioned magistrate ordered that from that time he should be held and recognized as the true owner and possessor of them."[22]

The official survey, which immediately preceded the grant of juridical possession, was conducted with a startling absence of that accuracy and precision so necessary under modern law. To the California land owner of that day, meticulously defined boundary lines had in fact little practical significance. Since there were no fenced ranches in the province to keep the herds from intermingling, it was customary for the cattle of neighboring rancheros to use the open ranges almost as a common pasture.

In a country, moreover, where the square league was the customary unit of measurement and even the smallest ranches embraced many thousands of acres, land was so abundant and had so little value that disputes over boundary lines, unless watering places or some other unusual feature was involved, became altogether pointless. The description of virtually every Mexican grant contained the familiar words, *más o menos*—more or less —and if, as in many cases, the expression affected the ownership of some hundreds of acres of land, no one gave the matter a second thought. Certainly no better phrase could be found to express the common attitude of the early Californians toward metes and bounds.

But though indefinite and carelessly defined boundary lines caused few complications during the Spanish-Mexican period, they became a perennial source of difficulty and dispute when the American legal system was introduced, and proved responsible for many of the most serious social and economic ills from which the state suffered for a long generation.

The location of a California grant, as illustrated by the typical case of the Rancho Sespe in the Santa Clara Valley, was carried out with tolerant disregard for anything remotely resembling an accurate survey. On the appointed day, the grantee, Carlos Antonio Carrillo, the magistrate in charge of the proceedings, and "the assisting witnesses," went to the "Place Called Sespe," to measure and mark the boundary lines. According to the grant, the rancho lay between the lands of the Mission San Buenaventura and those of the Mission San Fernando, and between the "mountains on the north and the high hills on the south."

As the first step in the proceeding, two *vaqueros* from nearby ranchos were appointed to "the office of surveyor and made oath by God our Lord and a sign of the cross, to use it faithfully and legally to the best of their knowledge and understanding without deceit or fraud against any person." A fifty-vara *reata,* tied at either end to a long stake, was brought before the magistrate and officially measured. Using this in lieu of a surveyor's chain, the *vaqueros* began the actual measurement of the land. While one of the mounted "surveyors" held his stake at the starting place, the other rode at a gallop along the indicated boundary line for the full length of the *reata.* Then he in turn thrust his stake into the ground and held it in place until his companion measured the next length of the cord.[23]

In this way two well-mounted *vaqueros* could run mile after mile of boundary line in the course of a single day; but such surveys were little more than rough-and-ready approximations and made no pretense to accurate measurement.

In the use of boundary monuments, the Californians also showed themselves naïvely unmindful of the future. Boundary corners were marked by anything that happened to be at hand, and naturally many of these casually chosen objects were so transient or destructible that, in a few decades, they either lost their identity or entirely disappeared.

After American annexation, the inexact California surveys and lack of boundary monuments thus made it impossible to identify the original boundary lines of many ranches and the resultant confusion and uncertainty gave rise to innumerable squatter controversies and wholesale litigation. The following examples of the haphazard and temporary character of early California monuments and landmarks will illustrate this point.

The boundary line of the ten-square-league Rancho San Juan, or Cajón de Santa Ana, was officially described as "beginning at the River Santa Ana and running out on to the hills where there is an oak, near the Valley of the Elders, which line is contiguous to the property of Bernardo Yorba, from the oak to a stone which is permanent and another one resting upon it. From the stone to the Pillar which is now fallen, from the Pillar to the Sycamore tree, from the Sycamore to the Lake and from there to the river."[24]

In the survey of the Rancho La Bolsa Chica, the line ran from a willow tree on the seashore to the borders of an inlet. When the mounted surveyors found it impossible to cross the water-filled channel and continue the line on the other side, Cristóbal Aguilar, who was directing the survey, called upon his "experts" to determine the distance from the inlet to the top of a high hill, or mesa, beyond the channel. They "estimated" that the distance was 2,400 varas, or about a mile and a half. That figure was accordingly entered on the official record and a boundary marker erected on the hilltop.[25]

"Commencing at the *Camino Viejo*," ran the description of the boundaries of the Rancho La Habra,

and running in a right line 500 varas more or less distant from a small corral of the tuna plant that forms the boundary of the Rancho of Don Juan Perez, at which place was taken as a land mark the aforesaid corral of tuna, thence in a direction West by South & running along the *Camino Viejo* 18,200 varas, terminating in front of a small hill which is the boundary of Don Juan Pacífico Ontiveras, at which place was fixed as a land mark the head of a steer. From thence East by North passing by a "Cuchilla" 11,000 varas terminating on a Hill that is in a direct line with another much higher, that has three large oaks upon it: at which small hill a stone land mark is placed, being the boundary line of the Rancho of La Puente & formerly belonging to the Mission of San Gabriel; thence North by East 2,000 varas terminating at the right line of the small corral of tunas of the aforesaid boundary of Don Juan Perez . . .[26]

Commenting upon this description, J. M. Guinn humorously wrote: "In the course of time the *camino viejo* was made to take a shorter cut across the valley, the corral of tunas disappeared, a coyote or some other beast carried away the steer's head, the three oaks were cut down and carted away for firewood, the small stone was lost, the *cuchillo* was reclaimed from the desert and the La Habra was left without landmarks or boundary lines."[27]

The boundary lines of the Rancho San Antonio, far-famed home of the Lugos adjoining the Pueblo of Los Angeles, were marked by equally transitory monuments—a bullock's head on a bluff, a place where two roads crossed, a spot "between the hills at the head of running water," a spring surrounded by some little willows, a brush hut on the bank of the San Gabriel River, a clump of trees on the same stream, a large sycamore, a ditch of running water, and an elder tree blazed in several places with a hatchet.[28] Although such landmarks were sufficient for the simple conditions of the time, they failed lamentably to meet the demands of a more complicated society or of a more exacting legal system.

A California land grant, like every other *concesión* recognized in Mexican law, depended for its validity upon the fulfilment of certain specified conditions.[29] The requirements were set forth in a conventional formula in every deed, and read substantially as follows:

1st. He [i.e., the grantee] may enclose it without prejudice to the cross roads and servitudes, enjoy it freely and exclusively, using it or cultivating it in the manner most agreeable to himself, but within one year he shall build a house upon it and have it inhabited.

2nd. He shall request the proper judge to give him juridical possession in virtue of this instrument by whom shall be marked the boundaries, on whose limits shall be placed at the proper points for land marks, some fruit or forest trees of some utility.

3rd. The land of which mention has been made is of *sitios de ganado mayor* as explained by the plan or design annexed to the respective *expediente*.

4th. If he contravenes these conditions, he shall lose his right to the land, which may be denounced by another.[30]

Although the drastic penalty mentioned in Article 4 was seldom imposed by California officials, the Rancho San Pasqual, on a portion of which the city of Pasadena now stands, was twice successfully "denounced" on the ground that former grantees had failed to carry out the provisions of their concessions.[31] After annexation, when American courts were called upon to decide the validity of California titles, the fulfilment or non-fulfilment of the conditions set forth in a grant often proved a deciding factor in the approval or rejection of the claim.[32]

The carefree life of the California ranchero has been the theme of many earlier descriptions, some of which no doubt exaggerated its color and romance, and requires little further comment. From an economic and social standpoint, the great ranches of the period had much in common with the medieval English manor. Except for a few luxuries obtained from trading vessels on the coast, each estate was virtually self-sustaining. In return for simple but abundant food, primitive shelter, and a scant supply of clothing, scores of Indians, recruited chiefly from the fast-decaying mission communities, served as *vaqueros*. Many of these native families lived in the *Indiada*, a cluster of primitive huts built near the main adobe *casa*, while others dwelt in small villages, called rancherias, widely scattered over the estate.[33]

The deference shown to a California ranchero by members of his own family, as well as by his retainers, was like the homage rendered by his vassals to a feudal lord. The members of a typical California household were numbered by the score. The ranchero provided a home for a host of poor relatives, entertained strangers, as well as friends, with unwearying hospitality, and begat as many sons and daughters as one of the ancient Hebrew patriarchs.[34]

On large estates an army of Indian women was required for domestic service. "Each child (of whom there were sixteen) has a personal attendant," said Señora Vallejo of her household staff, "while I have two for my own needs; four or five are occupied in grinding corn for tortillas, for so many visitors come here that three grinders do not suffice; six or seven serve in the kitchen, and five or six are always washing clothes for the children and other servants; and, finally, nearly a dozen are employed at sewing and spinning."[35]

The chronic dearth of money, characteristic of the entire Spanish-Mexican period, forced the Californians to resort to barter in virtually all of their domestic business dealings, and trade between the ranchers and foreign vessels, portrayed so vividly by Richard Henry Dana in his *Two Years Before the Mast*, depended almost exclusively on this method of exchange. Contracts and promissory notes were usually made payable in cattle, hides, or tallow; judges levied fines and judgments in the same commodities; and even the smallest amount of merchandise —a few yards of cloth, a pound of sugar, a box of raisins, a handful of cigars—was purchased with the standard currency of the province, the ubiquitous cattle hide, known from Alaska to Peru as the "California bank note."[36]

Free from the pressure of economic competition, ignorant of the wretchedness and poverty indigenous to other lands, amply supplied with the means of satisfying their simple wants, devoted to "the grand and primary business of the enjoyment of life," the Californians enjoyed a pastoral, patriarchal, almost Arcadian existence, until a more complicated and efficient civilization invaded their "demiparadise." One who knew by experience the simplicity and contentment of California ranch life a hundred years ago drew, for less fortunate generations, the following picture of its serenity and charm:

The *rancho* lay beyond the mountain range and extended over rolling hills and little valleys. A creek flowed through it, and on the banks were many sycamores. Shaded by oaks was the long, low adobe house, with its red tiled roof and wide veranda. Behind the fence of chaparral was the orchard and the melon patch, and beyond the orchard was the meadow, golden with buttercups in the early spring. In the open fields, dotted with oaks, the rich alfilerilla grew, and on the hillsides were the wild grasses which waved like billows as the breezes from the distant ocean blew across them. The sameness of recurring events of each succeeding year never seemed monotonous, but brought repose, contentment and peace. When the dew was still on the grass, we would mount our horses and herd the cattle if any had strayed beyond the pasture. In the wooded cañons where the cool brooks flowed, and where the wild blackberries grew, we ate our noon day meal and rested. And as the hills began to glow with the light of the setting sun we journeyed homeward. When the long days of summer came, we ate our evening meal beneath the oaks, and in the twilight we listened to the guitar and the songs of our people. In the autumn we harvested the corn and gathered the olives and the grapes.

Those were the days of long ago. Now all is changed by modern progress; but in the simple ranch life of the older time there was a contented happiness which an alien race with different temperament can never understand.[37]

LOS ANGELES, 1848

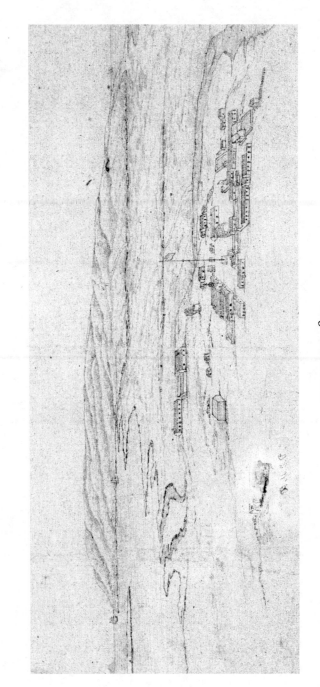

SAN DIEGO, 1850

CHAPTER III

The Land Act and Its Aftermath

B Y the time of the American occupation, a large part of
the accessible public lands of California, including all
but a meager remnant of the former mission grants, were
in the hands of private owners, and the rancho system dominated every phase of provincial life. California was then at the
height of its pre-American prosperity. In 1845-46 the province
exported 80,000 hides, 1,500,000 pounds of tallow, 10,000 fa-
negas of wheat; 1,000,000 feet of lumber, staves, and shingles; a
thousand barrels of wine and brandy; beaver, sea otter, and other
skins valued at $20,000; ten thousand dollars worth of soap and
two hundred ounces of gold.[1]

But despite such economic progress, the more thoughtful Californians viewed the political future of the province with justi-
fiable misgivings. Since the early thirties the country had been
afflicted with a succession of revolutions and lived in a chronic
state of instability and turmoil; and the provincial government,
having lost the ability to command either the respect or the obedience of its subjects, was rapidly degenerating into political
impotence. Visiting California in 1842, Commodore Charles
Wilkes found "a state of anarchy and confusion," "a total absence" of all authority, and even the "forms and ceremonies" of
government thrown aside.[2] Between 1831 and 1841 the government changed hands on an average of once a year; in 1836 a fac-
tion declared the province independent of Mexico; and a few
years before American annexation, as J. M. Guinn aptly remarked, the country was "blessed with two governors at the
same time and once with triplets."[3]

Overland communication between Mexico and California
was both hazardous and difficult; and Mexico's own threatened

financial and political dissolution prevented the central government from aiding the province in the solution of its domestic problems and establishing an adequate system of defense either against internal revolution or the encroachment of other nations. The presidio at Monterey, long the capital and port of entry for the province, sometimes lacked sufficient powder to exchange salutes with foreign naval vessels entering the harbor, and was forced to borrow from the ships themselves to return the courtesy.[4] Guarding the long inland reaches of San Francisco Bay, "where all the navies of the world might ride in safety," Commodore Wilkes found a garrison of one officer and one barefooted private—and the officer was absent when Wilkes visited the port.[5]

Thanks to Mexico's chronic weakness and the growing confusion within the province itself, American influence in California grew rapidly after 1840. New England merchants dominated the all-important hide-and-tallow trade; American fur hunters breached the mountain barriers on the east, and an aggressive vanguard of American settlers pressed overland from the Missouri frontier.

By 1845 a few of the most influential Californians, convinced that the country would never prosper under Mexico's sovereignty, began to advocate annexation to the United States as the only way to insure order, provide political stability, and enhance the value of their immense personal estates.[6] Other Californians, fearing that the American government might challenge the validity of their land titles or even confiscate their properties, opposed the proposed plan of annexation.

On the face of it, however, there was no real basis for such fear, since both official and semi-official spokesmen for the United States repeatedly assured the Californians that the American government would scrupulously safeguard existing land titles and respect all other rights of private property.[7]

"Persons holding title to real-estate or in quiet possession of the lands under color of right shall have their titles and rights guaranteed them," read a clause in Commodore Sloat's famous proclamation to the Californians, of July 7, 1846, after the occupation of Monterey.[8] The Treaty of Guadalupe Hidalgo likewise bound the United States to protect the Californians in the free enjoyment of their liberty, property, and religion, and pledged the Washington government to give recognition to "legitimate titles to every description of property, personal and real, existing in the ceded territories."[9]

In offering these assurances to the Californians, the American officials acted in honesty and good faith; but Congress, later adopting a very different policy, passed a law that challenged the validity of every title in California, reduced many legitimate landowners to bankruptcy, and sowed the seed of injustice and confusion throughout the state. The enactment of this legislation, whose implications congress did not appreciate and whose outcome it could not possibly foresee, was due in the main to the bedlam resulting from the Gold Rush and the creation of a situation in California too complex and bewildering for the remote Washington government to understand.

As explained in earlier pages, the unparalleled migration of the Gold Rush obliterated the old political order and institutions in California and gave no opportunity for the orderly replacement of the simple Spanish-Mexican customs by Anglo-American laws. Officials in Washington knew little of actual conditions in the new territory, and the lack of trans-continental telegraph or railroad prevented them from receiving either accurate or up-to-date information on the rapidly changing scene. Much federal legislation affecting California was therefore harmful and ill-advised.

The confusion in California land titles presented the most difficult question, arising out of the acquisition of Mexican territory, with which congress had to deal. The Spanish-Mexican grants, which covered most of the inhabited areas, included mission lands, pueblo lands, private lands, and public lands; titles technically complete and titles technically faulty; titles granted in good faith and titles granted solely to anticipate American annexation; titles free from any shadow of suspicion and titles obtained through obvious fraud.[10] Unfortunately, many California grants, owing to lost or defective documents, haphazard surveys, poorly defined boundaries, and unfulfilled conditions, were legally subject to forfeiture even under Mexican law.

As already pointed out, the economic and political chaos created by the Gold Rush would not permit this intricate land problem to work itself out in orderly fashion, but stampeded Congress into hasty, ill-considered action.

Two official reports on California land grants were presented in Washington and made available to Congress in the spring of 1850. The first was prepared by Lieutenant Henry W. Halleck, who came to California in 1848 and served as secretary of state under Governor Richard B. Mason.[11] Halleck's report contained an excellent account of the laws and regulations governing the grant of public lands before American annexation; the decrees affecting the holdings of the missions; and the titles to the lands the government might need for fortifications or other military purposes.

Halleck emphasized especially the problems to which, under American law, the carelessly defined Mexican grants would inevitably give rise; cited the failure of many grantees to meet the conditions imposed by the original concessions; and called attention to the existence of large numbers of claims either patently fraudulent or at least suspiciously irregular.

The second report, somewhat more detailed and complete, was prepared by William Carey Jones, a representative of the General Land Office, who had made a special study of Spanish colonial land titles and was thus conversant with their legal and historical background.[12] Jones arrived at Monterey in September, 1849; visited San José, San Francisco, Los Angeles, and San Diego; and, on his return trip to Washington, spent two weeks examining the archives in Mexico City. His report described the operation of the private-land-grant system in California under Spanish-Mexican rule and dealt with the history and status of mission grants, mining concessions, and claims for land of possible military value.[13]

In his estimate of the validity of Spanish-Mexican titles, Jones came to a much more favorable conclusion than that reached by Halleck. "The grants in California, I am bound to say," he wrote, "are mostly *perfect titles*; that is, the holders possess their property by titles, that under the law which created them, were equivalent to patents from our government, and those which are not perfect—have the same equity, as those which are perfect, and were and would have been equally respected under the government which has passed away."[14]

Following the submission of the Halleck and Jones reports, Senator Thomas H. Benton, of Missouri, and the two newly appointed Senators from California—John C. Frémont and William M. Gwin—each offered a bill to clarify and regulate the confused California land situation. Benton's measure sought to maintain the *status quo* of the Spanish-Mexican grants and left to the United States District Attorney, and a specially created officer called the Recorder, the final decision on all doubtful claims.

Frémont's bill proposed the creation of a Board of Land Commissioners to determine the validity of all existing grants, and allowed the claimant the right of appeal from the decision of the Board to the federal courts. The government, however, was denied this right.

On March 3, 1851, the bill sponsored by Senator Gwin, the

professed champion of the settlers' cause in California, was enacted into law and made the basis of the federal government's
subsequent land policy in California. The act constituted one of
the most important legislative measures in the history of the
state.[15]

The bill provided for appointment by the President of three
"Commissioners to ascertain and settle the Private Land Claims
in California"; for submission to this Board of all California titles
held under Spanish or Mexican grants;[16] for outright forfeiture
of claims not presented within two years; and for an appeal,
either by the claimant or the government, from the decisions of
the Board to the federal courts. The Commission was originally
established for three years, but subsequent legislation length-
ened the three years to five.

The Board was formally organized in San Francisco on December 8, 1851, and began regular hearings approximately two
months later.[17] During the next five years it considered over 800
cases, involving title to approximately 12,000,000 acres.[18] It approved some 520 claims, and rejected 273. The remaining claims
were either dismissed by the Commissioners or withdrawn by
the petitioners.[19] Despite occasional charges of bias, sometimes
by large landholders, sometimes by settlers, the Commissioners
apparently performed their difficult and involved task as impartially and expeditiously as circumstances would permit.[20]
Appeal was taken from the Board's decisions to the courts,
either by the government or by the claimant, in nearly every
instance, but in three-fourths of the cases the decrees of the
Commissioners were sustained.

The procedure prescribed for the presentation of a claim, and
the documentary and other forms of proof necessary to validate
a title, were minutely set forth in the following preliminary
statement issued by the Board before it opened formal hearings
in San Francisco:

The mode of bringing the claims specified in the Act of March 3, 1851, before the Commissioners, shall be by petition in writing, signed by the claimant or his counsel, addressed to the Commissioners, and filed with the Secretary of the Board, which petition shall set forth the names of the original and present claimants; the nature of the claim, the dates of the original grant and the several assignments or conveyances, with the names of the parties thereto, through which the present claimant deduces his title; from whom the original grant was derived; the power or authority under which the granting officer acted; the quantity of land claimed; the locality; when surveyed and when certified by the Surveyor General (if thus surveyed and certified); and the nature and extent of every known interfering claim; with a reference to the documentary and other evidence relied upon by the claimant; and said petition shall be accompanied by a copy of the original grant and a translation of the same, or by reasons for not furnishing them.[21]

Compliance with the Board's instructions put the landowners to enormous trouble and expense and placed the Spanish-Californians, especially, at serious disadvantage. Strangers to American laws and legal procedure, ignorant even of the language, they were required to submit to judicial processes in which they were wholly inexperienced, and to defend their rights under proceedings which they could not understand. The validity of many titles rested upon documents long since destroyed or forgotten, or upon the claimant's ability to produce eyewitnesses to events which had happened, in some cases, many years before he was born. Grants held, time out of mind, by succeeding members of the same family were attacked on the ground of technical imperfections, and boundaries recognized by custom and tradition for a generation were arbitrarily challenged by the government.

In the face of such conditions the validation of even the most perfect title presented serious difficulties, frequently involved ruinous expense, and often entailed years of uncertainty and delay. In many instances, legitimate costs were greatly magnified by the imposition of excessive lawyers' fees and other exorbitant charges. Lack of ready money—a characteristic feature of California's economic life throughout the colonial era—compelled many owners of grants to sacrifice land and livestock to meet the costs of defending their titles, or to resort to the much more hazardous expedient of mortgaging their properties.

To most native landowners, the pledge of the American government in the Treaty of Guadalupe Hidalgo to recognize "legitimate titles to every description of property . . . in the ceded territories," thus proved a bitter and costly delusion; and the fact that the clause was written into the treaty in good faith offered little consolation to the California ranchero whose property was stripped from him by the operation of the Land Act of 1851.

Since the Commissioners confined their sittings almost wholly to San Francisco, it was necessary for southern landowners to take their lawyers, witnesses, and documents to the northern city. The additional inconvenience and expense involved in this procedure led some forty or fifty southern rancheros, representing grants covering nearly 1,000,000 acres, to urge the Board to transfer some of its sittings to Los Angeles. Spokesmen for the petitioners estimated that a third of the land in Los Angeles County would be forfeited if its owners were forced to validate their titles in San Francisco, and declared that the impossibility of producing witnesses and documents at so great a distance would result in the loss of "many just and ancient claims."[22]

I. S. K. Ogier was appointed to present the case of the southern landowners to influential leaders in Washington, and a petition was sent to the President to authorize sessions of the Land Commission in Los Angeles. As a result of these efforts, the Board was induced to hold its hearings in Los Angeles during the fall of 1852, but after a brief session the Commissioners returned to San Francisco and declined to go on their travels again.

According to Hittell, one out of every ten of the bona fide

landowners of Los Angeles County was reduced to bankruptcy by the federal land policy, and at least forty per cent of the land legitimately owned under Mexican grants was alienated to meet the costs of complying with the Act of 1851.[23] "The long lists of Sheriffs and mortgage sales in our newspapers," wrote Abel Stearns to John C. Frémont, "the depopulation of flourishing stock Ranches, and the pauperism of Rancheros, but a short time since wealthy, all attest the disastrous consequences of too much litigation and of this unsettled state of titles."[24]

Commenting, in the *Southern Californian* of April 11, 1855, relative to the adverse action of the Board upon certain well-known claims, Don Juan Bandini said:

We were much surprised indeed to hear of such titles being rejected, because being intimately acquainted with the country, and with most of the individual proprietors of the lands, we are well assured of their legality; and it provokes pity to see such unlooked for spoliation committed under pretexts truly puerile, and which in no way ought ever to have affected the just right of property and possession acquired by the owners. Of the lands mentioned, some have been in the quiet possession of the proprietors and their families for forty and fifty years. On them they have reared themselves homes—they have enclosed and cultivated fields—there they and their children were born—and there they lived in peace and comparative plenty. But now,—"Our inheritance is turned to strangers—our houses to aliens. We have drunken our water for money—our wood is sold unto us. Our necks are under persecution—we labor and have no rest."

In the examination of our land titles, no attention has been paid to the usages and customs of the country, nor much less to the investigation of whether defects in some of the requisite forms may have proceeded from bad faith on the part of the grantees, or from want of knowledge on the part of the officers whose business it was to have acted in conformity to the provisions of the laws. It is evident that the colonization laws had for their object the settlement of a country lying waste; and also that the colonist was authorized by the laws to ask for lands to the extent of the maximum established, and to select freely the locality of the same, where most convenient or agreeable to himself; and that the local Government had author- ity to grant the whole or a part of the land applied for, regulating its operations by the reports received, and by the peculiar circum- stances of the individual applicants. There were no surveyors in the country, and fortunately no lawyers; Judges were not professors of law; every transaction was executed in simplicity and good faith; and it should not be considered strange that insignificant mistakes should have occurred in the various capricious conditions annexed by the granting authorities; or that involuntary errors should have been committed by the grantees or others intrusted with the meas- urements, boundaries, maps, etc. In such errors or mistakes, how- ever, nothing can be found which can affect the spirit of the law, which was simply to grant to those persons who wished to devote themselves to the raising of cattle or to the cultivation of the soil, the lands required for these purposes out of the unappropriated lands of the Government.

From the standpoint of the Spanish-California landowners, the situation was, in fact, so desperate that some of the largest rancheros made a direct appeal to the American government and people in the following memorial:

In view of the doleful litigation proposed by the general Govern- ment against all the land owners in California in violation of the Treaty of Guadalupe Hidalgo and the law of nations, which year by year becomes more costly and intolerable, in view of the repeated falsehoods and calumnies circulated by the public press against the validation of our titles and the justice which supports us in this in- terminable litigation and which equally influences the tribunals of justice and prejudices our character and our dearest rights; in view of the injustices which have accumulated against us because of our patience in suffering and our silence in defending ourselves, we, the land owners in the state . . . mutually contract and agree to aid and support each other by every legal means as free men, which we are, to resist every effort made against us to carry out a general confisca- tion of our properties; and especially to adopt the most efficient means to assure the abrogation of the existing law which holds all titles acquired from the former government to be fraudulent and which were guaranteed us by treaty. And we name and authorize Señores D. Abel Stearns, D. Benito D. Wilson, D. Julian Workman, D. Pío Pico, y D. Agustín Olvera, as our representatives in our name and place to secure the services of a printing office and of suitable persons to argue and defend our cause before the people of the United States and to resort to every legal means which appears most effectual to them of bringing about on the part of the United States a prompt recognition of our just and sacred rights.[25]

Resolutions and petitions—the only concerted form of defense the Californians were able to devise against the loss of their properties—had no effect upon the government's land policy or upon the administration of the Act of 1851. "More than one in ten of the victorious claimants," wrote Hittell, "have been ruined by the costliness of the litigation; and of those whose claims have been finally dismissed, a considerable portion have been lost to the claimants merely because they were unable to pay for the costly litigation necessary to defend their rights."[26] Viewed from almost any angle, the results of the federal law were unsatisfactory. In actual practice it violated the spirit of the Treaty of Guadalupe Hidalgo, even though the United States Supreme Court held that it did not contravene the actual terms of that compact. The act did irreparable injury to a great body of legitimate landowners, caused an endless amount of confusion and litigation, and seriously interfered with the economic progress of the state for almost a generation.

By placing the burden of proof upon the Spanish-Mexican grantees, the law also inflamed the minds of land-hungry settlers against the large rancheros and furnished a plausible excuse for squatters to occupy the lands whose titles were clouded or jeopardized by the act. Even without such encouragement, the pioneer settler of the post-Gold Rush era was not likely to pay too much respect either to the titles or the boundaries of Spanish-California owners. For generations the lure of cheap land had stimulated American migration across the continent and determined the course and pattern of westward expansion. Long before the Gold Rush, the inhabitants of the Mississippi and Missouri frontiers had been led to look to California as an agricultural paradise, a region of unsurpassed resources, an illimitable empire, bidding for settlement with leagues of free and fertile land.

Waddy Thompson, the American Minister to Mexico, described California in 1842 as "the richest, the most beautiful, the healthiest country in the world." "When we reflect," said a writer in *Hunt's Merchants' Magazine,*

that this superb region is adequate to the sustaining of twenty millions of people; has for several hundred years been in the possession of an indolent and limited population, incapable from their character of appreciating its resources—that no improvement can be expected under its present control, we cannot but hope that thousands of our fellow countrymen will pour in and accelerate the happy period . . . when Alta California will became part and parcel of our great confederation; and the cry of Oregon is only a precursor to the actual settlement of this more southern, more beautiful and far more valuable region.

"A foreigner," said an authoritative article in the New York *Sun,* "can become a citizen of California by obtaining two signatures to his petition. He then possesses the right to take up vacant land, and may secure as much as eleven square leagues upon the payment of $26 in fees. Many grants held by such owners are 33 miles long and 3 miles wide." "The fertile plains of Oregon and California," said another communication to the same paper, "are resounding with the busy hum of industry; all around us are the germs of empire, prosperity and wealth. Those who would reap a harvest should come out young, secure their lands, and in ten years they will have their fortunes."[27]

To the western pioneer such a picture offered irresistible appeal. Begining with the Bidwell-Bartleson party of 1841, a steady stream of immigrants flowed into California to take advantage of the Mexican government's liberal land policy and avail themselves of the rich agricultural resources of the province. Even in 1849 the expectation of eventually obtaining farms and building homes in El Dorado probably drew the Argonauts westward almost as effectively as the more dramatic lure of gold.

Most of the emigrants who set out for California after Marshall's discovery, with dreams of easy wealth to be gotten from the mines and of millions of acres of virgin farming lands to be had for the asking, suffered two rude awakenings. To a majority of the forty-niners, prospecting proved a hard and disappointing business, and only a favored minority found a bonanza in the mines. Disillusioned by their experience, thousands of gold seekers eventually returned from the mountains, expecting to acquire homesteads on the fertile farming lands near the coast. But in this quest, again, a large majority were disappointed. Only a small fraction of the millions of acres of public domain in California was then accessible to markets or susceptible of cultivation, and most of the land actually adapted to agriculture was held by native Californians—a people for whom the western settler had traditional contempt—under titles which neither the American land seeker nor, seemingly, his government regarded with very great respect.

Under such circumstances conflict between American homeseekers and the great cattle ranchers became inevitable and the state was divided into two hostile camps for a generation. Partisans of the landowners characterized the settlers as ruffians, trespassers, and lawless ne'er-do-wells; supporters of the settlers charged the landowners with occupying land to which they had no right, excluding claimants from the public domain by force, and maintaining their position by legal chicanery and fraud.

Voicing the cause of the landowner, John S. Hittell indignantly wrote:

Cases are known where they [the squatters] fenced in his best land; laid their claims between his house and his garden; threatened to shoot him if he should trespass on their inclosure; killed his cattle if they broke through his sham fences; cut down his valuable shade and fruit trees, and sold them for firewood; made no permanent improvements, and acted generally as tho' they were determined to make all the immediate profit possible out of the ranch. . . . Blood was not infrequently spilled in consequence of the feuds between the land holders and the squatters; the victims in nearly every case, belonging to the former class.[28]

In 1859 a petition to congress from a large body of native California landowners voiced substantially the same complaint. "The discovery of gold attracted an immense immigration to this country," said the address,

and when they perceived that the titles of the old inhabitants were considered doubtful and their validity questionable, they spread themselves over the land as though it were public property, taking possession of the improvements made by the inhabitants, many times seizing even their houses, where they had lived for many years with their families, taking and killing the cattle and destroying their crops so that those who before had owned great quantities of cattle that could have been counted by the thousands, now found themselves without any; and the men who were the owners of many leagues of land now were deprived of the peaceful possession of even one *vara*.[29]

In contrast to such charges against the settlers, a writer in the *Alta California* of December 12, 1853, attacked the landowners in the following bitter paragraph:

Time was when, if a man had a bit of dusty parchment containing an indefinite description of any tract of country which was never occupied, it was considered by some men as rank robbery to trespass upon it. Anything in the shape of a Mexican grant was esteemed sacred, and it was not thought necessary to prove its validity or have it affirmed by the rightfully constituted authority. The man who knew it to be a fraud, and knew that it could not be confirmed, if he settled upon the lands covered by it, was branded as a vagabond and a thief, and the indignation of all law-loving citizens was invoked upon him.[30]

The California land situation was further complicated, and the enforcement of the Act of 1851 rendered still more difficult, by the presentation of scores of spurious claims to the Board of Land Commissioners. Some of the fraudulent claims, representing remarkable ingenuity and months of careful preparation, covered thousands of acres of agricultural lands and city properties worth millions of dollars. The largest of such claims rested upon an incredible number of forged or altered documents and relied for support upon a mass of perjured testimony. The unsettled state of California society, the careless methods employed in drafting and preserving official documents during the Mexican regime, and the vicissitudes through which the California archives passed immediately after American occupation, afforded even the most preposterous of such frauds a reasonable possibility of success.[31]

The most notorious case presented to the Land Commission was that of the so-called Limantour grants.[32] José Y. Limantour, the central figure in the fraud, was a French trader who came to California in 1841 and subsequently gave his support to Governor Manuel Micheltorena—a man who had few friends and encountered many difficulties. In recognition of this assistance, according to Limantour's contention, Micheltorena bestowed upon him six separate grants, amounting in all to 134 square leagues, or about 950 square miles! Although it rejected the greater part of this munificent award, the Land Commission was induced to validate Limantour's richest claim, a tract, four square leagues in extent, embracing a large part of the city of San Francisco, Point Tíburon, and the islands of Yerba Buena, Alcatraz, and the Farralones.

When the Commission's decision was appealed to the Federal

District Court, the trial revealed the spurious nature of Limantour's claims, and the gigantic fraud quickly fell apart. The government's counsel showed that nearly all of the vital evidence offered by Limantour was forged; that the official seals on the documents were counterfeit; and that many of the witnesses who testified in favor of the grant were guilty of the grossest perjury. In his decision denying the validity of the claim, Judge Ogden Hoffman summed up the case with the biting comment, "The proofs of fraud are as conclusive and irresistible as the attempted fraud itself has been flagrant and audacious."[33]

By 1858 land frauds in California had become so alarming that Edwin M. Stanton, better known as the combative Secretary of War in Lincoln's cabinet, was sent to the coast by Jeremiah S. Black, the United States Attorney-General, to protect the interests of the federal government. Stanton's investigations showed that highly organized rings composed, in large part, of well-known officials of the Mexican government, former influential native Californians, and wealthy American and British residents were operating in California.[34] "The archives thus collected," said the Attorney-General, reporting to the President on Stanton's activities,

furnish irresistible proof that there had been an organized system of fabricating land titles carried on for a long time in California by Mexican officials; that forgery and perjury had been reduced to a regular occupation; that the making of false grants with the subornation of false witnesses to prove them, had become a trade and a business. Desolate islands, barren rocks, and projecting promontories, useless to individuals, but of priceless value to the government, had been seized upon under these spurious titles with a view of extorting millions from the United States. . . . The richest part of San Francisco was found to be covered by no less than five different grants, every one of them forged after the conquest; Sacramento, Marysville, Stockton, and Petaluma were claimed by titles no better. . . . The value of the lands claimed under grants ascertained to be

A RODEO

A RECOGIDA

forged is probably not less than $150,000,000. More than two-thirds of them in value have already been exposed and defeated.[35]

At the time of Black's report it was generally believed that the United States was on the point of annexing several of the states of northern Mexico. As evidence of the forehandedness of certain land agents, the Los Angeles *Star* declared that a leading Mexican official was even then in San Francisco, preparing fraudulent claims for grants in Lower California and Sonora which he planned to present to the American government as soon as the territories were acquired.[36]

It is indeed difficult to exaggerate the evil effects of the enormous, far-reaching land frauds initiated in California between 1850 and 1870. By clouding titles, bringing legitimate claims under suspicion, and involving great areas in litigation, they operated, as the Attorney-General pointed out, "like a curse and a scourge upon the most magnificent portions of the American empire."[37] This harmful influence, unfortunately, was not limited to the chaotic period following the Gold Rush. Persistent, widespread, capable of appearing under many forms and in many guises, spurious land claims plagued legitimate landholders and honest settlers alike for at least a generation.[38]

So, whatever may have been the intention of the sponsors of the Land Act of 1851, its enforcement brought to fruition a multitude of evils. It adversely affected the whole economic structure of the state, penalized legitimate landowners, often to the point of ruin, played into the hands of speculators, discouraged settlement and immigration, retarded agricultural progress, and, by creating a resentful and disaffected landless element, served to produce a large measure of social instability.[39]

As William Carey Jones warned in his report, any attack upon established California land titles was an attack upon the economic progress of the country. "A title discredited," he went on, "is not destroyed but everyone is afraid to touch it, or at all events to invest labor and money in improvements that rest on a suspected tenure. . . . The titles not called in question, . . . the pressure of population, and the force of circumstances, will soon operate to break up the existing large tracts into farms of such extent as the nature of the country will allow of, and the wants of the community require."[40]

"If the history of Mexican grants of California is ever written," said Henry George in 1871, "it will be a history of greed, of perjury, of corruption, of spoliation and high-handed robbery, for which it will be difficult to find a parallel. . . . It would have been better, far better, if the American government had agreed to permit these grant holders [i.e., the Spanish-Californians] to retain a certain amount of land around their improvements, and compounded for the rest the grants called for, by the payment of a certain sum per acre, turning it into the public domain." With that verdict, most economic historians would today agree.[41]

CHAPTER IV

Life on the Ranchos

D ESPITE the uncertainty and confusion caused by the Land Act of 1851 and the ultimate absorption of most of the great ranch holdings by Americans, southern California remained a typical cattle frontier for almost twenty years after the Gold Rush, and all the activities of its people took form and color from the traditions of the open range.

"Large quantities of arable and grazing land are held under Mexican or Spanish titles, and occupied by rancheros of the ancient order of shepherds and herdsmen," wrote the assessor of San Diego in 1855, in describing the characteristics of the county and the adherence of its inhabitants to old forms and customs. "Many of them are averse to the changes and innovations brought about by the advent of American rule, and cleave manfully to the time-honored institutions of raw-hide ropes, wooden ploughs, and stumpy wheeled ox-carts. . . . Several thousand cattle of a fierce and savage breed infest the valleys of this whole county."

The assessor added that the presence of the cattle made "the Surveyor's duty of running lines through their range a matter of some personal risk and uncomfortable foreboding," and that he had "had an unsuspecting flag man prostrated once by a charge in the rear from an infuriated bull." In the same report the assessor of San Bernardino County pointed out that in his county there were no "bridge companies, toll bridges, canals, turnpikes, railroads, electro-magnetic telegraphs, Artesian wells, etc."[1]

The dominant influence of the old order was further shown by the survival of Spanish as the common language of the country and by the unconscious incorporation into the American settler's vocabulary of such Spanish words as *vaquero, rodeo, reata, fierro, caballada, paisano, zanja, cañon, arroyo,* and the like. His adoption of a score of simple, commonplace practices employed by the Californians in everyday life showed still further the intermingling of the old culture with the new. This was illustrated by such a simple thing as the use of rawhide as a general "repair all" for farm and household purposes.

A traveler in Texas once wrote: "Rawhide slits the latch string, and the hinges, laces the shoes, lets the bucket down the well, weaves the chairs, darkens one pane, twists the lariats, stretches the bedstead, is glue, nails, pegs and mortises. Rawhide is pegged to the ground to dry, rawhide is stretched across the yard to be oiled, rawhide is nailed across the house to grow pliable."[2]

The description was equally true of the use of rawhide in California. "Peter has repaired the weak wagon wheel," wrote William Brewer in 1861, "with that universal plaster for ailing implements, rawhide, and says it will now go. We will try it. I had no idea of the many uses to which rawhides are put here. I was in a house on a ranch, where a rawhide was spread before the beds as a carpet or mat. Bridle reins and ropes for lassos (riatas) are made, fences are tied—everything is done with rawhide."[3]

On the great ranchos themselves life flowed on in its familiar, long-established channels. Bearing the picturesque name of family, saint, or Indian rancheria, each huge, manorial-like estate supported a population of several hundred people, maintained a variety of household manufactures, produced its own grain, vegetables, and other foodstuffs, grazed thousands of head of cattle, sheep, and "beasts of burden," and constituted an economically independent, self-sustaining community. The following account of the Rancho Cañada de Santa Ana, in what is now the heart of Orange County, presents a vivid picture of the activities and feudal organization of one of these huge estates.

By 1850 the Hacienda de Las Yorbas was the social and business center of the Santa Ana Valley. The master's house became a two story structure of about thirty rooms, not including the school, harness shop, shoemakers room, and other places occupied by dependents. In all there were more than fifty rooms arranged about a court or patio in the rear of the main residence. . . .

According to a descendant of Bernardo Yorba, the tradesmen and people employed about the house were: Four wool-combers, two tanners, one butter and cheeseman who directed every day the milking of from fifty to sixty cows, one harness maker, two shoemakers, one jeweler, one plasterer, one carpenter, one major-domo, two errand boys, one sheep herder, one cook, one baker, two washerwomen, one woman to iron, four sewing women, one dressmaker, two gardeners, a schoolmaster, and a man to make the wine. . . . More than a hundred lesser employees were maintained on the ranch. The Indian peons lived in a little village of their own. . . .

The rancho had two orchards where various types of fruit were grown, and some wheat was raised. . . . Ten steers a month were slaughtered to supply the hacienda.[4]

In 1851 the state legislature passed an act, dealing with almost every phase of the cattle industry, entitled *Laws Concerning Rodeos, and Defining the Duties of Judges of the Plains.*[5] For the most part the law merely recognized the practices already in effect among California rancheros and gave legal sanction to those ancient customs which had been introduced into New Spain from the cattle ranges of Andalusia at least three centuries before.

The act required each ranchero to brand his cattle with three separate brands and to register these in the County Recorder's "Book of Marks and Brands."[6] The brands were called, respectively, the *fierro*, or range brand; the *señal*, or earmark; and the *venta*, or sale brand. The *fierro* was branded on the hip; the *señal* was a slit, notch, or hole cut in the ear; and the *venta*, often called in English the counterbrand, was burned on the shoulder when the animal was sold.

The law also made detailed provision for the conduct of annual stock roundups, or rodeos, so indispensable to the system of open-range pasture. A landowner was required to hold at least one general rodeo each year, and to give neighboring rancheros four days' notice of the time and place of the gathering. In some parts of southern California the rodeo season ran from April 1 to July 31; in other sections it began in March and ended in September.

Because of the difficulty of driving stock from widely separated ranges to a single rodeo, the law permitted large cattle owners to have as many as five or six roundups at as many different places on their ranchos. The Rancho Santa Margarita y Las Flores thus had five rodeo sites—namely, "that of the Valley of Santa Margarita, that of the valley of Las Pulgas, that of Las Flores, that of San Onofre, and that of San Mateo."[7] The use of the same place year after year for the rodeo led the cattle to turn to it instinctively as soon as the roundup began. "When the vacqueros went out to gather in the cattle from the hills and valleys for some miles on every side," wrote Charles Nordhoff of a rodeo on the rancho just mentioned, "they had only to begin driving, when all within sight turned to the big tree in the center of the plain, where they were accustomed to be collected."[8]

Tally sticks, on which each notch represented ten animals, were used to record the number of cattle branded in a rodeo.[9] The size of a herd was roughly estimated at three or four times the number of the branded calves.[10] Mavericks, including calves without mother or brand, were called *orejanos* by the Californians and became the property of the ranchero holding the rodeo.[11]

In one of his many appearances before the Land Commission, Abel Stearns gave the following excellent summary of the laws and customs governing a rodeo:

Each owner of a stock farm collects his cattle together in herds on his own farm in Rodeos. When the farm is large some have two or three Rodeos on the farm at different spots.

The cattle of different owners necessarily get mixed together as there are no fences and it is the custom at certain seasons for the owners of the Ranchos to drive their cattle together within their own limits for the purpose of separating their own cattle from those of their neighbors. When this is done they notify their neighbors to appear and take their cattle away if they choose to do so . . .

When a Rodeo is ordered the servants are sent out in the borders of the Rancho and the cattle are driven in to the place established for the Rodeo, and no owner of a Rancho has a right to go over the line of his Rancho to drive in the Cattle except by special permission of the neighboring land owner. . . .

Orejanos are all unmarked cattle. All unmarked calves that do not follow the mother so that the owners can be recognized by the brand of the Cow are *Orejanos*, and belong to the owner of the land within the limits of which the Rodeo is given.[12]

An official, known as the *Juez de Campo*, or Judge of the Plains, presided over each rodeo, settled disagreements involving the ownership of cattle or the interpretation of rules and customs, and had authority to order the arrest of cattle thieves and of "vagrants, vagabonds, and dangerous and suspicious persons."[13] The office was therefore one of recognized dignity and responsibility. For a time it was filled through appointment by the court of sessions and later by the county board of supervisors.[14]

The management of each rancho, whether the owner lived on the property or not, was in the hands of a trusted employee, called a *mayordomo*. His responsibilities and duties were thus explained by Pío Pico: "My Mayordomo is the person who represents my interests at the rancho and is subject only to the proprietor or owner of the ranch. His business is to take care of the cattle and do whatever is demanded, to deliver or sell cattle when he is commanded, and he arranges the labors of the ranch."[15]

Under the *mayordomo* served a corporal, and from ten to twenty cow hands or *vaqueros*. The California *vaquero*, whether Indian or Mexican, was a superb horseman—perhaps the most skilful the world has ever seen—and had no superior in the use of the lasso or *reata*. A good *vaquero* received from $12 to $15 a month, together with primitive living quarters, simple but abundant food, horses, saddle, *reata*, and other necessary equipment.

Every California ranch had its *caballada*, or band of carefully trained horses, which, in their way, showed as consummate skill as the *vaqueros* themselves in rounding up, roping, or cutting out cattle. California horses, like the Mexican horses from which they sprang, were partly of Moorish or Arab blood, small, finely formed, agile, and capable of almost incredible endurance. Immense herds of wild or unbroken horses, from which the *caballada* was recruited, also grazed on the ranchos, and at times became so numerous that hundreds were slaughtered to save the pasturage for cattle. In his classification and nomenclature of horses, the Californian employed some two hundred names, many of which have no synonym in English, to indicate precise shade of color and variation in markings.[16]

A roundup of horses was generally called a *recogida*. The Los Angeles *Star* of December 3, 1859, contained the following graphic account of one of William Workman's *recogidas* on the Rancho La Puente:

The scene was most exciting. The plain was literally covered with horses; they were driven into the corrals, in bands of from twenty to fifty, and there examined and parted. The proceedings were conducted under the superintendence of Don Felipe Lugo, a Judge of the Plains, but there were several others present—Messrs. Workman, Temple, Rubottom, etc.—There was a very general attendance of the neighboring rancheros, besides farmers from the Monte and vicinity, to all of whom Mr. Workman dispensed his hospitalities in the most liberal and profuse manner. The feats of horsemanship performed by the Californians were astonishing; but the facility and precision with which the "lasso" was thrown could scarcely be credited by those who have not witnessed such experts. The animal aimed at was secured whether in the band or running at full speed over the plain; and that, too, by the neck or limb at the fancy of his pursuer. The proceedings occupied two days.

In addition to the customary rodeos and the usual routine of ranch activities, some landowners found it necessary, at certain seasons of the year, to hold a special drive or roundup, probably unknown in any other part of the world. In southern California the growth of wild mustard was even more remarkable than that mentioned in Christ's striking parable. During the late spring, a sea of yellow bloom flowed over valleys, plains, and foothills; and the thickset stalks, higher than a man's head, made an ideal hiding place for cattle. Even when the bloom and the leaves died, a forest of dry, rustling stalks furnished ample covert for livestock. In badly infested districts, neighboring rancheros and their *vaqueros* consequently united for a few days to carry on what was colloquially known as a "run through the mustard." In a letter to Abel Stearns, the manager of the Rancho Los Alamitos spoke of "a run of two or three days through the mustard" at the Nietos and said that the Lugos and four or five other rancheros had been invited to participate. "The Temples, Manuel Domínguez and the Coyotes will be there sure," he added, "and most likely a sufficient number of people will be brought together to effect some good."[17]

After the enforcement of the Secularization Act, many of the Indian neophytes whom the missions could no longer support found employment on the private ranches and furnished the chief labor supply of southern California throughout the cattle era. They lived and worked under a form of peonage similar in some respects to that so long in effect in Mexico, and rapidly deteriorated, both morally and physically, in their new environment.

Drunkenness was the special curse of the domesticated Indians of southern California, and in Los Angeles, especially, the unrestrained sale of adulterated, and often poisoned, liquor resulted in an appalling amount of misery, viciousness, and crime. Every Saturday night the meaner streets of the city were filled with intoxicated mobs; the next morning's sun rose on scores of sodden wretches lying in alleyways and gutters; and when the police made their morning rounds it was taken for granted that they would find a few stabbed or bullet-ridden corpses among the victims of the night's debauch.[18]

As early as 1850 the *ayuntamiento*, or town council, confronted by the problem of feeding the multitude of Indian prisoners arrested every week — none of whom had enough money to pay even a nominal fine—hit upon the happy expedient of farming out the services of such prisoners to the highest bidders.[19] Landowners, especially those who had large vineyards, quickly took advantage of the opportunity, and soon the use of enforced Indian labor on the ranchos became a matter of common practice.

"I wish you would deputize some one to attend the auction that usually takes place on Mondays and buy me five or six Indians," wrote the *mayordomo* of the Alamitos to Abel Stearns in 1852;[20] and as late as 1869 the Los Angeles *Semi-weekly News* referred to the farming out of Indian prisoners as still a regular weekly occurrence.

The system, as outlined by the *News*, was simplicity itself. "The habits of the Indians," said the editor, are such that decay and extermination has long since marked them for their certain victims. They build no houses, own no lands, pay no taxes and encourage no branch of industry. Their scanty earnings at the end of the week are spent for rum in the lowest *purlieus* of the city where scenes of violence occur, particularly on Saturday and Sunday nights, that would disgrace barbarism itself. . . . They have filled our jails, have contributed largely to the filling of our state prison, and are fast filling our graveyards, where they must either be buried at public expense or be permitted to rot in the streets and highways.

* * *

For years past it has been the practice of those most extensively engaged in the cultivation of the soil, to hang around the Mayor's court on Monday morning and advance the degraded Indian a few dollars with which to pay his nominal fine for having been dragged through the streets to the station house in a state of beastly intoxication, . . . and on Saturday night, after deducting the sum advanced, pay him a couple of dollars, which insures him a place in the station house on the following Monday, should he not lose his miserable life in a drunken brawl before that time—and thus the process goes on.[21]

The *News* condemned the system, not on humanitarian grounds, but because degraded and inefficient Indians, "being brought into competition with that class of labor that would prove most beneficial to the country, checks immigration, and retards the prosperity of the country." Large landowners, the article went on to say, had used the county jail for nearly twenty years as an "intelligence office" from which to recruit their inferior peon labor.[22]

"Los Angeles had its slave mart," wrote Horace Bell,

as well as New Orleans and Constantinople—only the slave at Los Angeles was sold fifty-two times a year as long as he lived, which generally did not exceed one, two, or three years under the new dispensation. They would be sold for a week, and bought up by the vineyard men and others at prices ranging from one to three dollars, one-third of which was to be paid to the peon at the end of the week, which debt due for well performed labor would invariably be paid in *aguardiente*, and the Indian would be happy until the following Monday morning having passed through another Saturday night and Sunday's saturnalia of debauchery and bestiality.[23]

With the notable exception of the skilled *vaquero*, Indian labor was generally regarded as miserably inefficient and unreliable; but, considering the conditions under which the Indians lived, the diseases from which they suffered, and the degenerating effects of vice and liquor, no other result was possible.

If the California landowner was blind to his responsibilities to the hapless Indians, however, he was equally blind to the advantages of a more enlightened policy in other economic and social fields. For two decades southern rancheros made almost no attempt to improve the type of long-horned, slim-bodied cattle with which the early Spanish colonists originally stocked the California ranges. Large landowners, such as Abel Stearns, sometimes bought a few thoroughbred bulls, and the Mormons who settled at San Bernardino sold some of their Utah cattle for breeding purposes; otherwise almost no systematic effort was made at scientific breeding in southern California until the close of the era of the open range.[24]

The Mormon bulls were heavier than California bulls and produced much larger calves when bred to native cows. The meat of such crossbred stock was also considered better than that of the native steer and had a certain appetizing tang not found in the uncrossed American stock.[25]

Early state legislation deliberately favored the interests of the cattlemen at the expense of the small farmers. For a time such discrimination resulted in little real hardship in southern California, because of the lack of immigration; but, as diversified agriculture came increasingly to dispute the monopoly of the grazing interests, the legislature's partiality for the large landowners worked grave hardship upon the settlers.

The chief grievance of the farming class, apart from the perennial conflict between squatters and rancheros over land and water rights, was the so-called Trespass or "No-Fence" Act. Originally passed in 1850, the law remained on the statute books until 1872 and aroused increasing opposition as the number of settlers increased and more and more land was placed under cultivation. The law read as follows:

An Act concerning lawful fences, and animals trespassing in premises lawfully enclosed.

Section 1. Every enclosure shall be deemed a lawful fence, which is four and one half feet high, if made of stone; and if made of rails, five and a half feet high. . . . A hedge fence shall be considered a lawful fence if five feet high and sufficiently close to turn stock.

Section 2. If any horses, mules . . . hogs, sheep . . . or any head of neat cattle shall break into any grounds enclosed by a lawful fence, the owner or manager of such animals shall be liable to the owner of said enclosed premises for all damages sustained by such trespass; . . .

Section 3. If any owner or occupier of any grounds or crops injured by any animals breaking into or entering on grounds not enclosed by a lawful fence, shall kill, maim, materially hurt or injure any animal doing such damage he shall be liable to the owner for all damages. . . .[26]

Enacted when stock raising constituted the state's dominant agricultural interest and the use of the open range was universal, the Trespass Law thus forced settlers either to go to the ruinous expense of fencing their small-income producing farms, or to run the risk of having their orchards, vineyards, and grain fields overrun and destroyed, without recourse for damages. J. W. North, founder of the Riverside colony, thus expressed the settler's hatred of the Trespass Act.

It is a contest between advancing civilization and obsolete barbarism . . . . The development of the latent resources of the State would be twice as rapid if men did not have to expend more than half their capital in making fences for other peoples stock. The owners of Stock that are allowed to graze on our grain fields, do nothing to improve the country, they simply prey upon the products of others. The State ought to see that its true interest is to end this state of things at once.

To show how this works in new settlements like ours. A poor neighbor has put in ten acres of Wheat. He must now expend near three hundred dollars to fence it; to guard against other peoples stock. If others were obliged to take care of their own stock he could put in fifty acres more. In that manner the development of the State is retarded, by those who do nothing to improve the state.[27]

Although North's picture did not exaggerate the settlers' grievances, the Trespass Act was as indispensable to the rancheros during the fifties and sixties as it was unjust and harmful to the small farmers, and its repeal under conditions then prevailing would have demoralized the livestock industry in many parts of the south.

Entirely apart from the historic background of the Spanish-Mexican grants, the semiarid character of most of the range land in southern California made the large ranch an economic necessity. Barbed wire, which later revolutionized the western cattle industry and did away with the open range, had not yet been invented; quick-set hedges of willow, sycamore, or alder, though useful for fences in moist bottom lands, could not be grown on the ranges generally; and the prohibitive cost of lumber in southern California virtually precluded the use of board fencing.[28] From the standpoint of the cattlemen, the inclosure of thousands of acres of grazing land thus became a financial impossibility, and the Trespass Act, so bitterly criticized by the settlers, was a *sine qua non* of the open range.[29]

With the decline of cattle prices in the late fifties and recurring droughts during the next ten years, southern California landowners were often hard pressed to find either pasturage or markets; and many rancheros reverted to the early California practice of slaughtering their cattle for hides, tallow, and dried beef. In addition to the hide, worth perhaps $3.00 or $4.00, each full-grown steer yielded about 200 pounds of tallow, and nearly 50 pounds of dried beef, or *carne seca*. According to the Los Angeles *Star*, a steer marketed in this way yielded a gross return of from $12.00 to $13.00.[30] Figuring wood at $5.00 a cord, and wages at $5.00 a day for a chief butcher, 70 cents a day for each Indian laborer, and $2.00 for the chief who supplied the Indians and supervised their work, Phineas Banning estimated that the cost of slaughtering and skinning a steer and trying out the tallow came to $4.50, leaving a net profit of $7.00 or $8.00 to the ranchero.[31]

Carne seca, or "jerky" as the Americans called it, was made by a very simple process. When a steer was killed the hide was spread out, hair side down, and used as a receptacle for the meat. The latter, cut into strips about an inch thick, five or six inches wide, and from one to three feet long, was dipped in brine, hung on a rope or *reata*, in the hot sun, and turned every twenty-four hours. In four or five days the meat was hard, black, and dry. It was then made into fifty- or sixty-pound bales and bound together with pieces of rawhide. Sometimes the meat, instead of being treated in this fashion, was stripped from the body of the steer and dried in thin sheets.[32]

Though not particularly appetizing in appearance, *carne seca* was well-flavored and full of nourishment. Uncooked, or prepared in any one of many ways, it formed an indispensable part of the diet of the Californians, from the humblest peon to the proudest don. "The mode of cooking dried beef," wrote Stearns, "is to pound it up fine and then put it into a pan with a little hot Lard, stir and Moisten with a little water. A little boiled potato, & onion cut fine, with a little red Chile & Tomato mixed with it makes a very fine dish. Also it is used by boiling in water."[33]

Most of the tallow obtained in a matanza was sent to San Francisco or shipped to the eastern markets, but on some of the larger ranchos part of it was converted into soap. The process used by Isaac Williams on the Rancho Chino, south of the present city of Pomona, was carried on as follows:

Over a furnace was placed a boiler about ten feet deep and the same in diameter, and the upper part made of wood. This was filled with tallow and the fattest of the meat. A little water was also poured into it and then the whole was tried out, after which the grease was dipped into a box about ten or twelve feet square. The meat was then thrown away. Mineral earth was then leached like ashes, the lye obtained from it put with the grease and boiled into soap. The best quality of soap . . . was almost as white as snow. Indians usually did the work.[34]

During the unsettled years after the Gold Rush, southern-California rancheros suffered severely both from Indian forays and the depredations of organized bands of cattle rustlers. Strangely enough, little attention has been paid to this chapter of the region's history, though it is packed full of dramatic, highly colored incidents, and, if presented in detail, would make a noteworthy addition to the literature of the American frontier.

Outlying ranches in Los Angeles and San Bernardino counties were as much exposed to the danger of Indian attack, as well as to the menace of white desperadoes, as almost any part of Arizona, Texas, or the Rocky Mountain West. Coming from the desert by way of the Cajón Pass or the ancient Indian trail farther south, bands of Utes and Mojaves periodically swept across the ranches from San Gorgonio to Los Angeles, killing unprotected cattle, making off with the *caballadas*, and often taking toll of human life.[35]

So serious was the situation that, on September 29, 1849, Stephen C. Foster, son-in-law of Antonio María Lugo and recently appointed prefect of the district of Los Angeles, wrote Governor Bennett Riley:

As Prefect of said District of Los Angeles, I beg leave to state that the District is particularly exposed to the depredations of Indian horse thieves and other evil disposed persons, and at present the inhabitants are badly armed, and powder cannot be procured at any price. Under these circumstances, I would respectfully request that you place at my disposal (for the defence of the lives and property of the citizens of said District) subject to such conditions as you may deem proper the following arms and ammunition, viz

(100) One hundred Flint Lock muskets with corresponding accoutrements.

(10,000) Ten thousand Flint Lock musket *Ball & Buckshot Cartridges*

(500) Five hundred musket Flints

Ranches north of Los Angeles were preyed upon by Indians from the San Joaquin and Owens valleys, especially by members of a small tribe, consisting of only forty or fifty warriors, which inhabited the rugged mountains between the headwaters of the Kern River and Owens Lake. The tribe was apparently divided into two bands, each headed by a capable leader; and with every new moon one or the other of the companies raided the horse herds of the ranchos near the coast.[36]

The southern Indians were especially troublesome during the first six or seven years after the American conquest. In May, 1849, the Rancho Azusa, where the town of Azusa now stands, was so harassed by Indian attacks that its *mayordomo* appealed to the citizens of Los Angeles for assistance.[37] The following month Abel Stearns led a posse in pursuit of a band of Utes which had carried its activities to the very outskirts of the pueblo itself. The company overtook the Indians in the Cajón Pass, killed ten of the raiders, and recaptured the stolen horses, but lost two of its own men in the skirmish.[38]

Early in 1850 another band of Utes (perhaps accompanied by

a few Mormons), under the reputed leadership of Walker, the foremost Indian chief of the Southwest, came down through the Cajón Pass to attack the *caballadas* of Antonio María Lugo and Francisco Alvarado.[39] About a year later, José María Lugo lost seventy-five animals in a similar raid by Ute horse thieves. The Indians were so well organized that they not only repulsed a party of Californians and Sonorans which set out to rescue the stolen horses, but were only prevented by the coming of darkness from wiping out the entire posse. Describing the incident, together with the reputed massacre of the Dalton and Dorsey parties by Tulare Indians, Lewis Granger, of Los Angeles, wrote:

We have three more horse-thieves to try, Simplicio Valdez, Ignacio Belarde & José Rodriguez. It is thought they will get clear. The Utahs have been in the valley within a week past, and drove off all of José Maria Lugos Caballada, amounting to 75 horses. Fifteen men (paisanos and Sonorans) started in pursuit, came upon the Utahs 100 miles from the Cahon Pass, attacked them, but were repulsed with the loss of one man, a Sonoran, who fell at the first fire, pierced with five balls. Had it not been for the darkness of the night, the party in pursuit would have been all killed, as the Utahs were 50 strong, armed with rifles and revolvers. They were on guard and under arms. . . .

News has reached us that the Tulare Indians have killed Dalton's party, and Capt. Dorsey's party. Don Henrique himself was here at the time, after more horses and provisions, as his horses had failed and he was under the necessity of making a coral at the Four Creeks. There seems no doubt of his Vaqueros together with Capt. Dorsey and his party, who coralled with Dalton, or nearby, having all been killed, and the cattle dispersed. French's ranch was attacked by the same Indians, who appear to have been several hundred strong, armed with bows and arrows. Fortunately an emigrating party of 40 Americans were at the ranch at the time. The Indians were repulsed with the loss of about 40 killed. . . . Thirteen men in all are reported to have been massacred at the Four Creeks. Capt. Dorsey is from San José.[40]

In March, 1850, the Los Angeles *Star* reported that a maraud-
ing band of Paiutes had made away with the *caballadas* of several ranchos, including 500 horses belonging to Pío Pico from
the Rancho Santa Margarita y Las Flores, near San Juan Capistrano. "During 1851 and the early part of 1852," wrote J. M.
Guinn,

the mountain and desert Indians were on the warpath. Warner's
ranch had been plundered, emigrant trains attacked, and Antonio
Garrá had boasted he would exterminate the white race in California . . . The *Star* of December 6, 1851, says: "It is supposed that all
the southern Indians are in a plot to massacre the whites." The
Mormons of San Bernardino erected a stockade, of cottonwood
and willow trees, 300 feet wide, 700 feet long, and 12 feet high. In
this fort the settlers lived for nearly a year.[41]

Antonio Garrá, the instigator of the threatened insurrection,
was later captured by Juan Antonio, chief of the Cahuilla Indians, in the upper end of what is now the Coachella Valley.
Juan Antonio surrendered his prisoners to a company of rangers
commanded by General J. H. Bean, and they in turn carried
Garrá to the Rancho Chino and later sent him to San Diego,
where he was tried by a military court and shot. A witness of
Garrá's execution wrote:

The court martial on Antonio closed its proceedings yesterday
about 3 P.M. Sentenced him to be shot, and at sundown the Execution took place. Anto Garra now lies in his grave litterally riddled
with balls. His obstinacy exceeded anything I ever witnessed. The
old Padre asked him not less than 20 times to ask pardon of all
present for his manifold sins & wickedness. He would not say a
word: stood with his hat on, until they were ready to blindfold him
When he remarked, that he would ask pardon of all, if they would
pardon him.[42]

A number of the largest landowners in the south, including
Abel Stearns, Isaac Williams, and B. D. Wilson, subscribed $200,

in cash and goods, as a reward to Juan Antonio for the capture of Garrá.[43]

The editor of the *Star*, in the issue of October 20, 1855, asked:

How many thousands of horses were stolen in the years '50 '51 '52 '53 from the Ranches of San Ysabel, Santa Margarita, Los Flores, El Tamuel, San Jasinto, Agua Caliente and numerous other ranches in San Diego County? Who that has lived in this county, for the past five years, does not recollect the magnificent droves of horses stolen from San Bernardino, San Jose, El Chino, El Rincon, Santa Ana, El Neguil, the Verdugos, Tajunga, San Fernando, Cahuenga and every other exposed Rancho in this county? We well recollect of hearing of the robberies committed on the San Buenaventura and Santa Clara Rivers, in the county of Santa Barbara, the actual capture and spoilation of the Mission of San Buenaventura by the Indians, while Santa Ynez, Santa Rosa, Lompoc, Los Alamos and other exposed Ranchos in the same county were actually stripped of all their horses. The same Indians who would enter this county through Walkers pass to rob, would add novelty to their depredations, by descending through the pass of Buenavista into the exposed county of San Luis Obispo, and would leave only the saddle horses that were tied at the doors of the Rancheros. We are confident we are under the mark, when we estimate the loss of the southern counties, for the five years previous to the establishment of the Tejon Reserve, arising from the depredations of the Indians upon horses alone at 300,000 dollars, and when we add the loss of horned cattle, the insecurity of person and property, and the abandonment of the frontier settlements, this estimate is insignificant in comparison to the material and almost fatal check to the prosperity of these counties.

In the fall of 1853 the Sebastian Reservation was established and in three months thereafter Indians robberies had ceased. Since that time we do not believe that the wild Indians tribes have robbed a single hoof of stock of any kind. The Mission of San Fernando whose owners suffered in the four years previous to the establishment of the Reserve, a loss of between four or five thousand head of horses, now brands in security their yet numerous stock. The Ranchos of San Francisco and Capuntos, from which had been driven all their horses to pasture in the vicinity of this city, pastured last spring upwards of seven hundred horses, while San Cayetano, Tin and La Liebre formerly with out a single horse or beef now have their thousand head upon their thousand hills. Now, safely through the Tejon into the Tulares Valley, and right in to Stockton, the peaceable cattle drover in security passes with his herds, where in '52, two cattle drovers alone lost near two thousand head by a whole sale robbery of the Indians, who also attacked and murdered in their houses, at the Four Creeks six or eight Americans.

Six months after the foregoing article appeared, the Four Creeks region was again the center of an Indian uprising. A letter in the *Star* of May 10, 1856, thus described the gloomy plight, both of the settlers in the district and of the prospectors in the newly opened Kern River mines:

I take this opportunity to inform you that we are all well at present, but not doing as well as we might. Times are squally here.—The Indians have broke out on the Four Creeks, and driven off a great many cattle. They have stolen three or four hundred head of horses from Santa Barbara, and carried them up into the mountains on Tule River. The miners on Kern River have quit work and forted up. There have been two fights on Four Creeks, and the Americans were whipped both times. An Express came in from Kern River this morning. They expect to be attacked in a day or two.

The settlers have all gathered into my house.—We hardly know what to do. I think you had better come up and get your cattle and take them to a more safe place. I am sure that all the stock in this valley will be stolen in a few days. Uncle Davy Smith is going to start for Los Angeles in the morning with a letter from the miners at Kern River to the Sheriff of Los Angeles, to raise a company to come to their assistance. If you come up, I want you to bring me five or six pounds of lead.

Yours most respectfully,
JOHN M. BRIGHT.

After the establishment of the Mormon colony at San Bernardino and the development of the Los Angeles-Salt Lake trade,

Indian forays from the Mojave and Colorado basins gradually declined; but sporadic depredations continued for many years, and even as late as 1866 a party of Indians, armed with bows and arrows, massacred the owner of the Rancho San Pasqual and one of his employees, somewhere within the boundaries of the present city of Pasadena.[44] "The scalp of the famous chief, Joaquin Jim, can be seen at Dick Wilson's new saloon on Main Street," ran an interesting notice in the Los Angeles *News* about this time. "The sunning of his moccasins has been a benefit to the Owens' River travellers."[45]

Much as they suffered from Indian depredations, the rancheros paid far heavier toll to the cattle thieves and other outlaw bands which then infested southern California. As early as 1851 Governor Peter H. Burnett listed stock rustling as one of the state's major economic ills and sought to have it made a capital offense. "The crime of grand larceny, in stealing horses and cattle," ran his message to the legislature, "has become so common in many places as to diminish their value fifty per cent. In some instances whole bands of tame cattle have been stolen, and farmers have lost their teams, and been compelled to abandon their business in consequence."[46]

The conditions portrayed by the state's first governor became more aggravated in southern California as time went on. In April, 1858, more than 150 horses, carrying the brands of various owners, were taken from a band of Mexican and American outlaws near Tujunga Cañon.[47] Within the space of a few weeks, the *Southern News* reported the arrest of a band of 45 cutthroats and horse thieves, with headquarters on the Mojave River; and the apprehension of a similar company, with 46 stolen horses in their possession, at the head of Rock Creek in the Sierra Madre Mountains.[48]

The Los Angeles *Star* also contained frequent accounts of the activities of rustlers near Los Angeles and referred especially to the losses suffered by such large landowners as William Wolfs-kill, Abel Stearns, and Benjamin D. Wilson. According to common report, the outlaws had a rendezvous on the Mojave River, from which the stolen stock was driven to Utah and sold in Salt Lake City and other Mormon settlements.[49]

In the summer of 1862 a nephew of William Wolfskill encountered a band of rustlers rounding up his uncle's *caballada*, and fought a running battle with the outlaws until both he and his horse were wounded. The thieves thereupon drove off the Wolfskill herd and added to it, for good measure, the *caballada* from the Rancho Los Coyotes.[50]

During the same summer a band of "robbers and murderers," led by a desperado named Manuel Marquez, infested the region between San Juan Capistrano and Santa Ana, defying the authorities, raiding the ranchos almost with impunity, and driving off many cattle and horses, including the *caponeras* of Raymundo and Domínguez Yorba.[51] Some months later a gang of masked men, "doing about as they pleased," terrorized the ranches between Los Angeles and San Juan Capistrano.[52] Santa Barbara County also paid heavy toll to highwaymen and stock thieves, especially to the remnant of the notorious Jack Powers band which still held together after its leader had decamped to Lower California. At the close of 1863 the *Star* reported the dissolution of "one of the most formidable bands of horse thieves" in the history of Los Angeles County. Two of the outlaws were killed by a sheriff's posse; one was wounded, and later hanged by a vigilance committee; and a fourth was captured and sentenced to fifteen years' imprisonment.[53] Commenting upon the incident the editor of the *Star* added, "We hope that should there be any others left of the same sort, they will take warning of the fate of their companions and give this county a wide berth."

Despite the grim justice occasionally inflicted by outraged

citizens upon such renegades, cattle rustling and other forms of lawlessness continued to plague the country until the close of the pastoral era. During the early part of 1865, for example, Los Angeles newspapers reported the loss of fifty horses by a ranchero named Andrés Duarte; the "lifting" of a *caballada* of the same size from another ranchero; and successful raids by a band of desperadoes, which had "long hovered about San Bernardino county," upon a number of ranches near the Cajón Pass.[54] Even as late as 1868 southern California newspapers published frequent notices of stolen *caballadas*, continued to deplore the prevalence of lawlessness throughout the country, and cited stock rustling as one of the region's major ills. The editor did not exaggerate. In the course of a single day a traveler saw three separate bands of outlaws near Temécula, with a total of 140 stolen horses in their possession.[55]

Except for the vigilance of their *vaqueros*, the harassed landowners had no defense against the depredations of stock thieves on the open ranges. Sometimes, however, a ranchero protected a few highly prized cattle or horses from *ladrones de caballos y ganados* by surrounding the pasture with an adobe wall surmounted by a *cheveaux de frise* of steers' horns, or by a deep, moat-like ditch, called a *ballado*.

As employed by Abel Stearns in one of his pastures on the Rancho Los Alamitos, the *ballado* was five feet deep, five feet wide, and lined with willow trees to make an almost impenetrable hedge.[56] Even though cattle rustlers or horse thieves gained access to a herd surrounded by such a barrier, they could not drive the animals across it into the open country.

Describing the other method of fencing land commonly used by his fellow countrymen, a Californian of that long-forgotten era wrote: "Sometimes low adobe walls were made high and safe by a row of the skulls of Spanish cattle, with the long curving horns attached. These came from the *Matanzas* or slaughter-

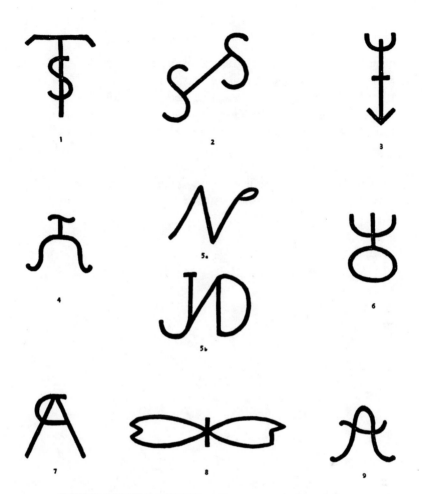

EARLY CATTLE BRANDS OF LOS ANGELES COUNTY

1 Brand of the Mission San Gabriel
2 Brand of José María Verdugo (Rancho San Rafael, 1787)
3 *Venta*, or counterbrand, of Abel Stearns
4 Brand of José and Francisco Sepúlveda
5a and 5b Brands of Juan Bandini
6 Brand of Vicente Lugo
7 Brand of the Compañía Agricultura (Rancho Los Alamitos; Abel Stearns)
8 *Señal*, or earmark of Abel Stearns
9 Brand of Vicente Domínguez

corrals, where there were thousands of them lying in piles, and they could be so used to make one of the strongest and most effective of barriers against man or beast. Set close and deep at various angles, about the gateways and corral ways, these cattle horns helped to protect the inclosure from horse-thieves."[57]

The mischief suffered by rancheros from Indian raids and cattle thieves was merely indicative of the general state of lawlessness then prevailing in the country and of the frontier society from which such conditions sprang.

CHAPTER V

Society in Flux

IR George Simpson wrote in 1842: "The Pueblo of Nuestra Señora contains a population of one thousand five hundred souls, and is the noted abode of the lowest drunkards and gamblers of the country. This den of thieves is situated ... in one of the loveliest and most fertile districts of California."[1] Twenty years later this unflattering description was still true of Los Angeles and the cattle frontier to which the pueblo belonged. Life everywhere throughout southern California, during the fifties and sixties, was still rude and violent; crime remained a normal feature of society; schools and churches found foothold only in a few communities; culture and refinement blossomed like exotic plants in an uncongenial soil.

It is almost impossible to exaggerate the contrast between the civilization of today and the cultural poverty of southern California a hundred years ago. The census of 1850 listed neither newspaper, hospital, college, academy, library, public school, nor Protestant church in Los Angeles County.[2] Three Catholic churches ministered to the religious needs of a region larger than many eastern states; two-thirds of the population could neither read nor write; only nine children were attending school![3]

But despite such a dearth of cultural opportunities, early Los Angeles society had in it a saving element of cultivated, well-educated people whose literary tastes were both catholic and discriminating; and the few newspapers published in southern California, notwithstanding novel and at times almost insurmountable handicaps, maintained a higher standard and reflected a far more cosmopolitan point of view than most small-town newspapers of the East and Middle West.

For the benefit of the native Californians, newspapers published articles and advertisements in Spanish as well as in English. But the widespread illiteracy reduced the "reading public" to a very small percentage of the population; subscriptions and advertisements were few; and all the southern California newspapers eventually died of pernicious financial anemia.[4]

Southern California's isolation from the outside world presented to bedeviled publishers a problem of peculiar difficulty. "The sources of public news are sometimes cut off for three or four weeks . . . ," wrote the editor of the Los Angeles *Star* in 1853. "San Francisco, the nearest place where a newspaper is printed, is more than five hundred miles distant, and the mail between that city and Los Angeles takes an uncertain course, sometimes by sea and sometimes by land, occupying in its transmission from two to six weeks, and in one instance, fifty-two days."[5]

The demand on the part of the educated residents of Los Angeles for books and magazines was clearly indicated by the newspaper advertisements of the time. As early as 1859 I. M. Hellman opened a "Book Department" in his general store, and in connection with it, advertised the establishment of a "Circulating Library."[6] In May of that year a notice in the Los Angeles newspapers invited all interested persons to come together to form a "Library Association."[7]

The regular appearance of the names of many leading American and British magazines in the advertisements of the Los Angeles newspapers of the time indicated a taste and intellectual appreciation not usually found among the inhabitants of a frontier "cow town." *Harper's Weekly*, described as a "Journal of Civilization," *Harper's Magazine*, the *London Quarterly*, the *Edinburgh Review*, the *North British Weekly*, Blackwood's *Edinburgh Magazine*, and the *Westminster Magazine* were all included.[8]

Yet, despite the small group of citizens who read well-known English and American magazines, patronized Hellman's circulating library, and clung tenaciously to their social and cultural traditions, southern California society as a whole was lawless and unlettered—an unstable mixture of the characteristic elements of both the Hispanic borderland and the Anglo-American frontier.

In the field of public health and sanitation, the native inhabitants, or *pobladores*, long resisted every effort of the Americanized *ayuntamiento* to restrict their ancient liberties or change the customs of their fathers. The water used for drinking and other domestic purposes came from the Los Angeles River and flowed through the city in open ditches, called *zanjas*, collecting all manner of filth and refuse in its course.[9] Ordinances designed to change the confirmed habits and long-established practices of the Mexican population in the use of the *zanjas* were much more honored in the breach than in the observance. Housewives persisted in washing soiled clothing at the half-century-old *lavaderos* on the banks of the open ditches; and the city council was forced to content itself with a compromise, in the field of public health, of dubious hygienic value.

"All persons," read an ordinance adopted May 27, 1852, "who may find it necessary to wash articles of any kind near the habitable portions of the city will do it in the little canal that runs from the river, but will be bound to place their board or washer on the outer edge of the border of the canal, by which means, although they use the water, yet the washings from the dirty articles are not permitted, under any pretence, to again mix with the water intended for drinking purposes."[10] How effectual the ordinance proved, may be judged from the following editorial in the Los Angeles *Star*, three years later:

Day after day, from sunrise till evening, groups of females from "snowy white to sooty," can be seen at the daily avocations of wash-

ing clothes through nearly the entire length of our water canals—
and very few of them we are informed take any care to prevent the
filthy rinsing from running back into the stream. A stranger would
be very apt to suppose that our water canals were built for the purpose of carrying off the garbage and foul matter that is continually
accumulating within the precincts of a city, instead of being the
source from which a large portion of the inhabitants are supplied
with water for domestic purposes.[11]

Travelers complained that the fleas of southern California
were as bad as one of the plagues of ancient Egypt, and spoke
with equal bitterness of the Los Angeles hotels. "Winston and
Hodges kept the Bella Union at that time," wrote Horace Bell.

The house was a one-story, flat roofed adobe, with a corral in the
rear, extending to Los Angeles street, with the usual great Spanish
portal. On the north side of the corral, extending from the back-
door of the main building to Los Angeles street, were the numerous
pigeon-holes, or dog-kennels. These were the rooms for the guests
of the Bella Union. In rainy weather the primitive earthen floor was
. . . generally rendered quite muddy by the percolations from the
roof above, which, in height from floor to ceiling was about six or
seven feet. The rooms were not over 6 x 9 in size. Such were the ordinary dormitories of the hotel that advertised as "being the best
hotel south of San Francisco."[12]

Despite a requirement that householders sweep the streets in
front of their premises once a week, and the attempts made
from time to time to collect "all the heads and remains of cattle
and other dead animals . . . that they might be set on fire to be
thoroughly consumed and the air purified," the streets of Los Angeles became pitfalls of filth and mud during a rain, and resembled dusty cowpaths for the remainder of the year.[13] Even
civic pride could not keep an embittered editor from charac-
terizing Alameda Street, then the select residential center of
the city, as a "quagmire and a slough," or from describing the
"rivulets of soap suds and dirty water" which flowed along the
street's squalid surface.[14]

According to the first census, there were eight physicians residing in the pueblo. In 1850 four of these formed the "Los Angeles Medical Faculty" and posted a standard schedule of fees, including $5 for an office prescription or a day visit within the city, $10 for a night visit, $5 for each league traveled on a visit to the country, $5 for bleeding, and $10 for cupping.[15]

One of the sponsors of the "Los Angeles Medical Faculty" was Dr. William Osbourne. It is said that this versatile physician established the first drugstore in Los Angeles, took the first tintypes, dug the first artesian well, exported the first southern California grapes to the East, served as deputy sheriff and postmaster, and imported roses and shrubbery from "the states" to beautify his garden.[16]

In 1854 Dr. John S. Griffin, a brother-in-law of Albert Sidney Johnston and a member of Kearny's California expeditionary force, resigned his commission in the army and opened a private practice in Los Angeles. He soon became widely known, both for professional skill and leadership in community affairs. In the course of time he purchased 2,000 acres of land, in what is now East Los Angeles, for 50 cents an acre; assisted in the organization of various water companies; served as superintendent of schools; and in later years took an active part in the formation of the County Medical Society and the Los Angeles Chamber of Commerce.[17]

Dr. Richard Den, brother of Nicholas Den of Santa Barbara, was one of several arresting persons whom a stranger might encounter on the streets of the small pueblo. "He was seldom seen except on horseback," according to Harris Newmark's *Sixty Years in Southern California,*

in which fashion he visited his patients, and was, all in all, somewhat a man of mystery. He rode a magnificent coal-black charger, and was himself always dressed in black. He wore too, a black felt hat; and beneath the hat there clustered a mass of wavy hair as white as snow. In addition to all this his standing collar was so high that he was compelled to hold his head erect; and as if to offset the immaculate linen, he tied around the collar a large black silk scarf. Thus attired and seated on his richly-caparisoned horse, Dr. Den appeared always dignified and even imposing.[18]

In July 1858, the County Hospital was established "in a quiet and airy part of the City in the house belonging to Cristóbal Aguilar, North of the Church." Here the sick were cared for "by the Sisters of Charity under the direction of the best medical advice in the city." This first hospital, "in the house belonging to Cristóbal Aguilar," contained two wards, one for paying and the other for indigent patients. It was under the control of a Board of Health composed of Stephen C. Foster, Júlian Chavez, and Ralph Emerson.[19]

Although the climate was proverbially mild and the early Californians enjoyed an enviable reputation for longevity, health conditions among the Indians and lower-class mestizos appear to have grown steadily worse after the American conquest. The highest mortality, to judge from the data in newspapers and other contemporary sources, was caused by respiratory and venereal disorders, the destructive effects of cheap, adulterated liquor, and the ravages of diphtheria, smallpox, and similar contagious diseases. Deaths by violence, usually ascribed by coroners' juries to accident, homicide, acute alcoholism, or "visitation of God," were too common to excite more than casual comment.

During the winter of 1863 a virulent epidemic of smallpox swept over southern California and took an appalling toll of life on the ranchos, as well as in the towns. In Los Angeles alone 500 persons were stricken during the first few weeks; deaths in the city for a time ran as high as 15 or 20 a day; and, before the disease subsided, the poorer Mexican quarter, "from the Church to the mill," was almost depopulated.[20]

According to the Los Angeles *Star* of January 31, 1863,

The City Council, last Saturday, adopted an ordinance, instituting a Board of Health for the city. This act became necessary, in consequence of the prevalence of the smallpox. The city, as will be seen by the ordinance which we published today, has been divided into five districts, and a commissioner appointed to inspect each house, and every person therein. The Board resolved to designate the infected premises by affixing a flag to the house—a great many of these are to be seen throughout the town. Dr. Winston, in the second district, made his inspection, and found it in rather a favorable condition. There were only fifteen cases of the disease, of a mild type, and about twenty persons who had not been vaccinated. In the third and fourth districts the disease prevails very extensively, especially in the fourth. But we have not had reports from the commissioners. It is supposed there are at least 200 cases of small-pox within the city limits, and that fully 100 persons have died of the disease.

The Board are to have a meeting today, and will report to the Council. Such further action will be recommended by the Board, as their experience shall dictate, to stay the progress of the plague.

Quack doctors, practicing chiefly in Sacramento and San Francisco, and the makers and vendors of patent medicines advertised extensively in the Los Angeles newspapers and guaranteed a cure for every disease known to suffering humanity. In keeping with its name, for example, a certain "Balsamo de Mil," promised to give teeth an alabaster whiteness, clear the skin of pimples (leaving it smooth and rosy), soften the beard for shaving, and serve as a mouth deodorant. "Many people do not realize," said the sponsors of this preparation of many virtues, in almost the same phraseology now used in the advertisements of a well-known product, "that they have a bad mouth odor, and the subject is so delicate that their friends will not mention it."[21]

A popular liniment was modestly advertised as performing "more cures in shorter time on man and beast, than any article ever discovered." "Will you answer this question?" challenged its sponsors. "Did you ever hear of any ordinary sore, swelling, sprain, or stiffness, either on man or beast, which the Mexican Mustang Liniment would not cure? Did you ever visit any respectable Druggist in any part of the world—in Europe, Asia, or America—who did not say it was the greatest discovery of the Age?"[22]

One of the most widely advertised frauds was a certain "World Famous Specialist lately arrived from Austria," with innumerable honors, degrees, and testimonials, who established himself in Sacramento, opened the "Grand Medical and Surgical Institute for the Permanent Cure of all Private and Chronic Diseases and the Suppression of Quackery," and publicized himself and his "Institute" in many newspapers throughout the state.

This paragon of doctors advertised the cure of "Spermatorrhea, Local Weakness, Nervous Debility, Low Spirits, Lassitude, Weakness of the Limbs and Back, Indisposition and Incapability for Labor and Study, Dullness of Apprehension, Loss of Memory, Aversion to Society, Love of Solitude, Timidity, Self-Distrust, Dizziness, Head-ache, Involuntary Discharges, Pains in the Side, Affections of the Eyes, Pimples on the Face, Sexual and other infirmities in man." He also invited "the attention of sick and afflicted females laboring under any of the various forms of Diseases of the Brain, Lungs, Heart, Stomach, Liver, Womb, Kidneys, Blood, and all diseases, peculiar to their sex." He had, too, an infallible treatment for "Rheumatism and Fever" and "a New and Efficient remedy for Diarrhoea and Dysentery."

Further along in the advertisement the "World Famous Specialist" gathered up a number of other diseases, inadvertently omitted from the earlier lists, and promised cures for them also. Thus he "strove unceasingly for the welfare of afflicted humanity and the suppression of quackery!"

The field of recreation and amusement, though much restricted from the modern point of view, offered more variety than could be found at that time in many an eastern community. Quail, ducks, and rabbits made all southern California a hunter's paradise. Bear and deer abounded in the mountains and foothills; antelope were plentiful on the arid plains; trout filled every mountain stream.

The old Spanish-California tradition of a carefree life, with its delight in music, dancing, fiestas, rodeos, and open-handed hospitality, survived until the close of the era of the ranchos. Bullfights and bear- and bull-baiting constituted popular forms of amusement in Los Angeles until they were banned by ordinance in 1860.[23] By a curious coincidence, the same year bullfighting was abolished, the following item appeared in the Los Angeles *Star*: "The Base Ball Club of this city was duly organized this week, by the election of officers, adoption of constitution, by-laws, etc. On Wednesday afternoon, they had a fine time of it, and on Monday next they will again take the field. The members evince great enthusiasm for the sport." Two weeks later the same newspaper contained a notice of a football game between two Los Angeles teams.[24]

The saloons, gambling dives, and brothels which lined the notorious *Calle de los Negros* in Los Angeles were heavily patronized both by the vicious substratum of the native California population and the hapless Indians whom the new civilization had thoroughly debased.[25]

In more cultured circles, there were frequent card parties, balls, picnics, serenades, "sociables," and suppers. Special celebrations were held on important holidays or in honor of distinguished visitors. Formal funeral invitations were issued by California families of any standing; religious festivals provided occasions for merrymaking, bonfires, and fireworks; weddings were celebrated with all the feasting and hilarity of the pleasure-loving days before the conquest. A *baile*, following the marriage of one of the Yorba daughters, was described by the editor of *El Clamor Público* in the following poetic vein:

On Tuesday of this month, there was solemnized the marriage of Don Juan S. Smythe and Doña Josefa Yorba, and in the evening, a dance was given at the home of Don Manuel Garfias. The salon was decorated very tastefully and simply, and a happy company of young gentlemen and young ladies contributed greatly to the liveliness of the occasion. At about eight o'clock, there commenced to move about the room the lovely and elegant forms of beautiful and charming young ladies following their partners to the harmonious measures of the music so that in an instant that lovely scene was transformed into a veritable Eden.

Never had we attended a more elegant or entertaining dance in this city, and no doubt all the guests will cherish in their memories like a pleasing souvenir, the delightful hours that slipped away so unnoticed as they enjoyed the enchantment of the amusement.

To Señor Smythe and to the gracious Señorita Yorba, we extend a thousand thanks for their marked expression of their appreciation, and at the same time, we wish them long life and happiness.[26]

Political campaigns were carried on to the accompaniment of open-air barbecues and community picnics. These occasions afforded opportunity for the consumption of an enormous amount of home-cooked food, the drinking of endless toasts, and the infliction on the guests of an interminable number of speeches of the florid, spread-eagle style so characteristic of the period. The oratory, however, was generally enlivened by violent diatribes against the candidate of the rival party, and sarcastic comments on his character, ability, and even personal appearance. The more unrestrained and violent his language, the greater the popularity of the speaker; for partisanship ran high and taste in such matters was in no sense subtle or refined. Colonel Edward J. C. Kewen's attack upon J. J. Warner at a Democratic mass meeting and barbecue at El Monte furnishes a typical example of such political invective. During the course of his diatribe Kewen said, "This trifling fellow, Warner, is so notoriously corrupt and villainous, as to wholly exclude him from any consideration except that which prompts a man to kick a snarling cur that intercepts his path. The reptile's teeth have been extracted, there is now no venom in his bite."[27]

In the course of time, schools and churches were built in most of the larger communities of southern California and began to fulfill their customary function of ameliorating the impoverished intellectual, social, and spiritual conditions of the frontier and imperceptibly leavening and invigorating society.[28] But even as late as 1869 the rector of the Episcopal Church in Los Angeles despairingly exclaimed: "In our day people do not wish to be reminded of their faults. A minister to be popular in this place, must be possessed of great eloquence, extensive learning, a handsome face, fine form, excellent teeth, small feet and hands, and possessed of no religion whatever."[29]

By 1855 there were eight public schools in Los Angeles County, with a total enrollment of 180 pupils. Ten years later the number of schools had doubled and enrollment risen to 581. In curriculum, organization, and methods of teaching, the southern California schools followed pretty closely the general pattern of rural schools in eastern states; but both salaries and the requirements for teachers were relatively high.[30] In small country schools, lead pencils were sometimes made by pounding lead bullets into thin sheets and rolling these into the desired shape. Painted redwood boards were used in place of blackboards, and bits of raw sheepskin served as erasers.[31]

In later years the well-known traveler and publicist, Charles Nordhoff, commented at length upon the excellent quality of California schools and the emphasis laid upon education. On a tour through the southern counties, he wrote:

San Bernardino has also, what you would hardly find in a town of its size and character outside of California, a large, well-built and well-kept schoolhouse. The schoolhouses in this State are a constant surprise to an eastern traveller. You will find them everywhere; and if you are interested in education, you will easily discover that the people take great pride and interest in their public schools. The school building at San Bernardino would be creditable to an eastern town of 10,000 inhabitants.[32]

In many communities the school "exhibition" constituted one of the chief occasions of the year; but, curiously enough, conservative parents sometimes condemned such exercises as educationally unsound and hurtful to "the routine of common school studies." The Los Angeles *Star* of March 10, 1860, mentioned a controversy which had arisen in San Bernardino over the matter, gave the teacher's defense of her position, and offered the following naïve description of the exhibition which had called forth the protests of parents and taxpayers. "The exercises commenced with an opening address by Miss Laura Brown," wrote the San Bernardino correspondent.

She stepped on the stage with that timidity natural to one so young, on first appearing before a large audience. Her changing color indicated the inward struggle, and many an anxious heart among the audience beat heavily, lest she should prove unequal to the task. Great was the relief when with unfaltering voice and appropriate gesture, she commenced her address, which she delivered in a most excellent manner, without fault or hesitation, and bowing gracefully, retired amidst great applause.[33]

Theatrical troupes sometimes came down to Los Angeles from San Francisco, and occasionally a traveling circus visited the city. An amusement park, "much frequented by citizens, especially on Sundays," was opened on Main Street below Third, under the name of the "Garden of Paradise." The park reflected the owner's highly original conception of the Garden of Eden, and numbered among its attractions "a frame work containing what are called flying horses for the amusement of the children, and a band of music stationed on the balcony of the house which plays at intervals."[34]

But, of all forms of amusement, horse racing held first place in the affections of every true *hijo del país*. In the glamorous days before the conquest, the Picos, Ávilas, Sepúlvedas, Yorbas, and nearly all of the other great rancheros were devotees of that ancient sport and wagered prodigally on any race in which their favorite horses participated.

Apparently, however, even in that romantic age, the devotees of racing had little confidence in the purity of the turf or the honor of their rivals. At least Isaac Graham, Kentucky-born fur trader, distiller, and potential revolutionist, advised, for one, against taking any chances. On March 23, 1840, Graham wrote from Monterey:

Don Abal Stearns
Sir I have this day seen Don Pio Pico and he requests me to go to the Pueblo below to run a race for you and himself to the am't of one thousand head of Cattle and one Thousand Dlls in Cash, & provided I shall win the race, Pico and yourself are to give me Five Hundred Dlls in Cash for my trouble, and I myself shall go Five hundred Dlls in cash in the race, & in Case I should loose the race yourself and Pico are to give me nothing only my expenses for myself & horse—

Sir on these Conditions you can make the race if you see proper, & furthermore it will be necessary for the parties concerned to leave the time the race shall be run to myself I will run the race btwix this and the Mo of Septr next I shall furnish my rider he being a man & their rider must also be a man—Sir I want you to make the race against Jose Sepulvaros' horse for the distance of Eight Hundred yds or against any horse they Can bring, & Sir, if it is possible for you to get them to come as far as Capt Denn's Rancho, it will be much to your advantage & also to mine—If you make a race please Sir let me know as fast as possible (as it is possible they may poison my horse or hurt him otherwise) & I will come down without delay

Isaac Graham

P.S. Sir be shure you do not call me down unless the race is so made that they cannot back out of it & in case they back out of the race after my coming down I shall look to you for the mony

I G[35]

The rivalry between the Picos and the Sepúlvedas survived long after the coming of the Americans. In 1852 Pío Pico matched his famous horse, "Sarco," against the Australian-born mare, "Black Swan." José Sepúlveda and other members of his family were among the principal backers of "Black Swan." The race, one of the most famous events of its kind in California annals, was run over a nine-mile course and at least $50,000 in money, land, horses, and cattle was wagered on the result. To the great chagrin and impoverishment of the backers of the California-bred horse, the Australian mare won by at least seventy-five yards.[36]

Races such as that between "Sarco" and "Black Swan" (not to mention innumerable minor races between horses of only local reputation) continued to divide southern California into opposing camps until the colorful day of the Spanish-California ranchero came to its close.[37] In 1860, when the sun of that day was already hastening to its setting, the Picos and Ávilas brought their long-standing rivalry to a fitting climax in a series of races between the two most famous horses of the time—Juan Ávila's "Coyote" and Pío Pico's "Azulejo." As the day for a race between these two famous rivals drew near, popular excitement boiled over, rancheros wagered recklessly—and often ruinously; and enthusiastic patrons challenged their opponents, in such newspaper notices as the following, to cover their bets:

"*Advertisement*: $5,000! $5,000! *Challenge to the Backers of the* Coyote. $5,000 (*or* $6,000) *plus 50 horses & mares offered by Desiderio Burnel of Santa Ana and his associates on Azulejo v. Coyote for 1,000 yards. Fernando Sepulveda backer of Coyote.*"[38]

Commenting upon one of these races, the editor of the *Star* remarked: "On Tuesday, 21st inst. a great race came off at San Juan, for $3,000 a side, distance 300 yards, between Don Pío Pico's horse 'Azulejo' and Don Juan Abila's horse 'Coyote.' The race was won by the former. A great deal of money changed hands on the decision." In support of the last statement, the article added that one backer of "Azulejo" won at least $8,000 on the race.[39]

The terms and conditions of a typical California race of the time have been unearthed and preserved by Terry E. Stephenson, of Santa Ana, lover and student of California history. The unusual document, originally written in Spanish, was translated as a court record and read:

Today the 12th day of October, 1852, we José Sepúlveda and Pío Pico, the first in the name of his brother, Fernando Sepúlveda, and the second in the name of his brother, Andrés Pico, empowered by the parties, have determined to adjust and contract the following agreement:

First, José Sepúlveda is bound in the name of his brother, Fernando, to run on the 20th inst. a roan horse which ran with the Martilla horse, and the distance of the race shall be 450 varas.

Second, Pío Pico is bound in the name of his brother, Andrés, to run the race aforesaid with a sorrel horse of Santa Barbara which belongs to the Messrs. Ruices.

Third, this race shall be sported, staking on the issue, each party $1,600 and 300 head of cattle, 200 of three years and upwards and 100 of one year and upwards. These cattle shall not be bulls, but steers and cows.

Fourth, the race shall take place on the day stated above at the door of the cañada of this city, from the place where there are some rocks, departing from said rocks, to 10 varas upon the city limits, start shall be from one to two o'clock p.m. with the word to start "Santiago" the race horses free at one only shriek, and to secure the fulfillment of this contract, both parties obligate themselves that the party that does not run shall forfeit 150 head of cattle, and this obligation which is established by the laws.

In testimony of which we subscribe our names and place our seals, in the city and date above stated.

There is one condition of this contract, that if Don Andrés Pico loses he shall deliver the cattle on the ranch of Santa Margarita the 15th day of November, and if Don Fernando Sepúlveda loses he shall deliver the cattle on the ranch of San Joaquín by the same day, the 15th of November.

The starting word "Santiago" has to be given from behind the horses that run.

Thus we agree date as above. The horses are also staked in the race.[40]

During the fifties and sixties southern California society offered many contradictions; but in lawlessness it found at least one common denominator. Crime was not limited to the horse-stealing, cattle-lifting depredations mentioned in an early chapter; but spread itself with catholic impartiality into every field.[41] In addition to organized bands of cattle thieves, there were desperadoes who preyed indiscriminately upon stagecoaches, freight caravans, and lonely travelers; notorious "bad men" who made wanton murder their avocation; professional gamblers; escaped criminals and fugitives from justice; offscourings of hard-bitten communities below the border; backwash from the mines; and ruffians of every sort whom vigilance committees in the north had encouraged to migrate to other fields. Los Angeles was the natural rendezvous for a large part of this heterogeneous criminal element; and in its characteristically modest way the city boasted of more murders annually, in proportion to its population, than any other community in California.

Crime statistics for the period are not available; but the picture presented by travelers, newspapers, and other contemporary sources justifies the pueblo's right to that undesirable distinction. Since the Law, as represented by the usual machinery of sheriff, jail, judge and jury, was notoriously impotent to deal with the chronic violence from which all southern California suffered, society sought to find a substitute in the organization of so-called citizens' or vigilance committees. But the administration of justice by such sporadic, extra-legal bodies was haphazard in the extreme and furnished at best only casual and ephemeral relief.

Because society was poorly organized and the law powerless to bring them to justice, outlaws and criminals (some of whom attained legendary stature because of the extent and heinousness of their crimes) robbed, pillaged, and murdered, almost unmolested, from Monterey to San Diego, and from the ranches and settlements on the coast to the newly opened mines in the wastelands along the state's eastern border.

Most notorious among the leaders of such bands were Joaquín Murieta, run to earth near the Pacheco Pass in 1853 by Captain Harry Love and his company of rangers; Salomon Pico, dubious offshoot of a famous family, who won distinction as a robber and murderer of unsuspecting gringos; and the nefarious Jack Powers, a former member of Stevenson's California Regiment, who specialized in gambling, highway robbery, and the assassination of cattle buyers, and eventually "retired" to Sonora, where he was stabbed to death by one of his companions.[42]

In 1856 many sections of southern California were terrorized by a band of outlaws led by Pancho Daniel and Juan Flores— "bad men" of the worst type, who climaxed their careers with the massacre of Sheriff James R. Barton and most of the members of his posse. The attack on Barton was made in Santiago Cañon, near Orange, in January, 1857. The entire countryside, from Los Angeles to San Diego, was aroused to a fever pitch of excitement. Detachments of mounted rangers, native Californians, federal troops, and even friendly Indians, set out to bring the murderers to justice. A number of the *bandidos* were shot, some were hanged, and upwards of fifty were brought to Los

Angeles and imprisoned. An interesting side light on the dispersion of the band is found in the following hitherto unpublished letter from Juan Forster:

> San Juan 30th Jany 1857
>
> Dr. Griffin
>
> Dear Sir.
>
> As Don Andres left here yesterday evening acting in concert with the force from the Monte, I take the liberty of answering his letter. . . .
>
> Dn Andres had such information (amounting to a certainty) that the Robbers were hidden in the Mountain of Santiago somewhere about the head of the stream, and after obtaining a fresh supply of horses from Santa Margarita, and joining in concert with the Monte force they left here about dusk last evening, and by this time or this evening I have no doubt that they will have caught either all, or most of them, they have with them men, from this place well acquainted with every nook & corner of the Mountain & I can see no possible chance of their escaping excepting they should take the direction of Los Angeles, as we have a very strong force posted in every pass and Mountain between this place and San Juan, for instance, there is 40 Drugoons, some citizens from San Diego, the Indian Mannelito with upwards of 50 Indians posted on the Mountain, and between that and the Flores, Geronimo is also on the alert in the country about Temecula, so that there is no possible chance of their escaping down South.
>
> It is reported that the Wounded robbers have been sent to Los Angeles, so they must be looked out for. . . .
>
> According to information the Robbers are not by any means as strong as they have been represented.
>
> The bearer has orders that in case of meeting any force from Los Angeles to request their leader to open this so as to obtain what information I can impart, for his government.[42a]

The existence of such outlaw bands as those led by Murieta, Powers, Daniel, and the like, was merely symptomatic; for all southern California was violently in flux. And, as the following extracts from newspapers and other contemporary sources show, lawlessness was looked upon as a normal condition of frontier life, and violence was accepted as an inevitable expression of the rude, masculine society of the time.

"The Deputy Sheriff has handed us a list of forty-four homicides which have been committed in this county within the last fifteen months," wrote the editor of the Los Angeles *Star* in the fall of 1851. ". . . . With very few exceptions, the perpetrators of the murders remain undiscovered. No Person has been convicted, and if we are correctly informed there has been but one person tried for murder since the county was organized, and the defendant was acquitted."[43]

In 1852, according to the same paper, "The Mayor, City Marshall, and jailor of Los Angeles were indicted by the grand jury for selling out the services of Indians arrested for minor offenses and dividing the funds thus received. The jailor . . . was also charged with such negligence that it was altogether a matter of their own choice whether prisoners remained in jail or not. In one case he furnished tools to the prisoner . . . to effect his escape."[44]

Later, according to Horace Bell, the jail was equipped with a unique device to prevent the escape of its inmates. "There was a big pine log extending from end to end of the long room," wrote that vivid if not always veracious chronicler, "with staples driven into it at intervals of three or four feet, to which were chained the prisoners, whose feet were shackled with cross chains, with a center chain about a foot long fastened to the staple and pine log. . . ."[45]

The record of violent crimes committed in Los Angeles during the early fifties is entirely too long to be described here in detail. A few specific instances, however, will perhaps serve to illustrate the general conditions. In February, 1852, John Forster wrote Abel Stearns:

Dear Sir. Having arrived here about six o'clock and taken up my quarters at Dn Teodocio's house shortly the house was taken possession of by a party of deserted volunteers from San Diego demanding to be provided with liquor using the most abusive and threatening language and brandishing their arms, when being on the point of shooting the man in charge of the establishment I offered some words of pacification which they returned (determined to take the life of somebody) with the same abusive and threatening terms and actually went so far as to *toss up* among themselves for the chance as it might occur, as to which of the party should shoot me and during the opperation I have been so fortunate as to escape from the house.

Don Ramon Oscuro with his family being in the house has had to take to the *Campo* [field] until this hour without any of us having any Covering. We are now in Doña Vicenta's house momentarily expecting to be attacked.

This state of things is really intolerable and I have taken the liberty to state the circumstance to you hoping you will circulate it amongst your friends &c so as to see if there can be measures concerted to prevent in future such a dreaded State of affairs.

Don Leandro Serrano's family have also deserted their house and have actually taken to the Guatamotal for protection. (Excuse haste)[46]

On Washington's Birthday, 1853, "El Palacio," the residence of Don Abel Stearns, was the scene of an elaborate and exclusive ball. A crowd of boisterous citizens, resenting the omission of their names from the invitation list, attempted to join in the festivities; but thanks to massive doors and iron-shuttered windows, the interlopers found it impossible to force their way into the house. Securing a small cannon from the Plaza, they placed it close to the house and relieved their feelings by firing off a number of salvos, to the great annoyance of the dancers. Accordingly, when the self-invited guests attempted a second time to crash the door, some of Stearns's friends took matters into their own hands, fired into the mob, killed two of its number, and seriously wounded two others.

In the next issue of the Los Angeles *Star*, the editor described the incident at some length. His work was a masterpiece of its kind and far too perfect to require comment. "There is no brighter sun, no milder clime, no more equable temperature, no scenes more picturesque, no greener valleys, no fairer plains in the wide world, than those we may now look upon," began the account of this multiple homicide. "There is no country where nature is more lavish of her exuberant fullness; and yet with all our natural beauties and advantages, there is no country where human life is of so little account. Men hack one another to pieces with pistols and other cutlery, as if God's image were of no more worth than the life of one of the two or three thousand ownerless dogs that prowl about our streets and make night hideous."[47]

James Woods, a Presbyterian minister, who made the first attempt to organize a Protestant congregation in Los Angeles, was appalled by the murders and homicides in the community. "A person lives a whole life time in a very short period in this country of wonders and of extraordinary and exciting events," he wrote in his Diary on November 12, 1854.

Thus while I have been here in Los Angeles only two weeks, there have been it is said eleven deaths, and only one of them a natural death—all the rest by violence—some killed in quarrels—some in being taken for crimes—some assassinated. . . . Last week a Mexican called upon an Irish woman who kept a drinking establishment and as she was opening the door he shot her in the breast; he then rode around to the Bella Union and snapt his pistol at a man who immediately pursued him on horseback to take him prisoner, but refusing to surrender the man shot him in the groin and took him. He died the next day in the jail yard, the woman whom he had shot died also.[48]

The *Southern Californian* of November 16, 1854, remarked, "The week has been comparatively quiet; four persons have been killed it is true, but it has been considered a poor week for killing; a head or two has been split open, and an occasional case of cutting has occurred, but these are minor matters and create but little feeling."

Travel in all parts of the country was rendered hazardous, both by lone outlaws and by organized bands of highwaymen. The first Protestant Episcopal bishop of California, W. Ingraham Kip, described in vivid detail the lawless country through which he was compelled to pass on his missionary journeys. In 1855 the road between Los Angeles and Fort Miller in the San Joaquin Valley was so dangerous that he wrote:

The country through which we are to pass—scarcely settled—is infested with California and Mexican outlaws, whose trade is robbery, and who will often down a traveller for the sake of the horse on which he is mounted. . . . At . . . times a single Mexican on horseback dashes by the unsuspecting traveller. As he passes within 20 feet, suddenly the lariat, coiled up at his saddle-bow, is whirled around his head, and ere the traveller can put himself on his defense, its circle descends with unerring precision and he is hurled, lifeless, from his horse.[49]

At times, as previously suggested, the orderly, peace-loving element grew tired of bandits and other criminals and set about with grim energy to curb their activities and reduce their number. "In 1854," according to J. M. Guinn,

it is said that Los Angeles averaged a homicide for each day of that year. . . . Then the law-abiding citizens arose in their might and in the shape of vigilance committees and military organization put an end to the saturnalia of crime, and to many of the criminals as well. The gallows tree on Fort Hill bore gruesome fruit and the beams over corral gates sometimes were festooned with the hangman's noose. In less than a year twenty-two criminals, bandits, murderers, and thieves, were hung in accordance with the laws or without law whichever was most convenient or most expeditious; and more than twice that number expatriated themselves for the country's good, and their own.[50]

"MUSIC, DANCING, . . . AND OPEN-HANDED HOSPITALITY"

AT BAY

The vigilante type of law enforcement reached a climax when Stephen C. Foster, mayor of Los Angeles, carried out his promise to resign office and lead a committee to hang a notorious murderer, Dave Brown, who was about to evade the penalty of his crimes because of the court's respect for legal technicalities! But such sudden and effective outbursts by law-abiding citizens, and even the dissolution of well-organized outlaw bands, had little permanent effect in reducing lawlessness or uprooting crime.[51]

Writing to his brother, near the close of 1860, William H. Brewer, the famous geologist and botanist, remarked:

This Southern California is unsettled. We all continually wear arms —each wears both bowie knife and pistol (navy revolver), while we have always for game or otherwise, a Sharp's rifle, Sharp's carbine, and two double-barrel shotguns. Fifty to sixty murders per year have been common here in Los Angeles, and some think it odd that there has been no violent death during the two weeks that we have been here . . . as I write this there are at least six heavily loaded revolvers in the tent, besides bowie knives and other arms. . . .[52]

The homicide record of Los Angeles County during the four or five years after Brewer's visit amply justified the latter's comments. On one occasion, the editor of the Los Angeles *Star* prefaced the account of a shooting affray on one of the principal streets of the pueblo with the caustic remark, "Unfortunately the combatants escaped with their lives but killed a fine horse." One of the principals in the affair protested vigorously to the *Southern Vineyard* against this evidence of the "brutal and fiendish disposition" of the editor.

In the fall of 1862 John Rains, son-in-law of Isaac Williams and owner of the Rancho Cucamonga, was waylaid and murdered near the settlement of Azusa. The Los Angeles *Star* contained the following account of the crime:

On Monday, the 17th inst., John Rains, Esq. of the Cocomongo
Rancho, left home for the purpose of coming to this city, to trans-
act important business, but has not since been heard of.

* * *

On Wednesday, the horses of the wagon returned to the rancho
without harness, one of them having marks of hard riding. Even
this did not at first attract the attention which it deserved, and it was
not until Friday that inquiry was made for the missing gentleman.

Dr. Winston and other gentlemen from the city, on their way to
the Colorado, stopped at the rancho, inquiries were of course made
for Mr. Rains, and the fact of his non-appearance becoming known,
the alarm was at once given.

R. S. Carlisle, Esq. of Chino, commenced the search, and arrived
at the Mission on Friday evening; on Saturday noon word was
brought here, and on Sunday morning Sheriff Sanchez started from
town to commence a search, accompanied by a number of friends.
The citizens of the Monte joined the company, and a large party
was thus organized, who have been unremitting in their exertions
but up to the present time no trace of the missing gentleman has
been discovered.

The melancholy fact that he has been murdered, in broad daylight, on the open highway, can no longer be doubted. The deed
was the result of a deliberate plan, carried out more successfully
than any ever heretofore attempted in this section of the State.

On Monday, or Tuesday of this week, the wagon was discovered
in a deep ravine, a short distance from where it is supposed it was
driven off the road. It was found secreted among bushes, having
been thrown over a steep bank. The harness was afterwards discovered, secreted in a tree; the collars have not yet been discovered. A hat was found, with stains of blood on it, which, it is said,
has been identified as belonging to Mr. Rains; an overcoat was also
found, said to belong to him—Beyond these, no trace has been found
of the murder.

* * *

Yesterday the body of Mr. Rains was discovered. It was lying
about four hundred yards from the main road, in a cactus patch.

The body gave evidence that the unfortunate gentleman had been lassoed, dragged from his wagon by the right arm, which was torn from the socket, and the flesh mangled from the elbow to the wrist; he had been shot twice in the back, also in the left breast and in the right side. His clothes were torn off him, and he lost one boot in the struggle. The body was not far from where the wagon had been concealed. It had been mutilated from the depredations of wild animals.

The funeral will take place to morrow evening, (Sunday), at 10 o'clock from the Bella Union Hotel. Friends are respectfully invited to attend.[53]

A Mexican named Manuel Cerradel, supposedly in the pay of Rains's enemy, Ramón Carrillo, was arrested for complicity in the murder, tried, convicted, and sentenced to ten years' imprisonment. As the prisoner was being ferried across San Pedro Bay to the ship which was to carry him to San Quentin, a company of vigilantes took him from the custody of the sheriff, hung him from the mast, weighted his body with stones, and dropped it overboard into the bay.[54]

Crime reached one of its numerous crests in Los Angeles during the fall of 1863. In November of that year a few ruffians, led by a notorious character known as "Boston" Daimwood, murdered an inoffensive prospector. Daimwood and three of his companions were captured a few days later and lodged in jail to wait trial, but a company of vigilantes relieved the sheriff of his prisoners and summarily hanged them on the porch of the city hall.[55]

A few weeks after this incident, John Sanford, one of the county's foremost citizens, was waylaid and murdered near the Tejon Pass. His assailant, having confessed to the murder of Sanford and eight other persons, was given short shrift by a citizens' committee.[56] Within the same month the vigilantes carried out six additional executions.

The *Semi-weekly Southern News* gave the following account of a typical lynching of the time. A certain Mrs. Leck, wife of a small tradesman in Los Angeles, was attacked and killed during her husband's absence. The woman's throat was cut from ear to ear with a butcher knife, and blood-spattered clothes, together with other circumstantial evidence, pointed to a Californian named Francisco Cota as the murderer. Cota was arrested, brought before the justice of the peace for preliminary hearing, and remanded back to jail. The editor thus described and moralized on the wretched man's fate:

The crowd which by this time had become highly excited made a rush for the prisoner, tore him from the officers, placed a rope around his neck, and failing in their efforts to find a suitable place for hanging him in the vicinity, rushed with him to a tannery, on the corner of Aliso and Alameda streets, where there is a large gateway, and throwing a rope over this, strung the wretch up, and kept him there till life was extinct. . . . Verily the soul of the murderer shall descend with curses to perdition.[57]

During the next few years little progress was made in the establishment of law and order. Commenting upon the murder of a young man named Edward Newman near San Bernardino early in 1864, the editor of the *Semi-weekly News* remarked, "A horde of the worst kind of characters now infest this lower portion of the State, and there is little or no safety for travellers, when a murder like this can be committed in broad daylight, on a frequently travelled road, and within but a short distance of town."[58]

In May of the next year the Los Angeles newspapers published a sensational report of the discovery of a plot, hatched by a band of desperadoes, to seize and sack the town of San Bernardino and carry their loot to the mountains of Lower California. It was said that several hundred men were assembling at a rendezvous on the Mojave Desert for the attack, and that detachments from the main party had already raided ranches near the Tehachapi to obtain horses. The inhabitants of San Bernardino were thrown into a near-panic by the threatened attack, and all able-bodied men gathered under arms to defend the city.[59]

The lawless conditions revealed by the foregoing illustrations were the inevitable result of a backwash from the mines; the bitter resentment of a wild, resentful element among the Spanish-California population, made landless by the passing of the ranchos into other hands; and the coming of large numbers of frontier "bad men" and outlaws to the wild hinterland of southern California.

Increased immigration, the expansion of settlements and small farms, and greatly improved means of communication brought the worst of such evils to an end, except in the isolated interior and the roughest of the mining camps, before the close of the turbulent sixties.[60]

CHAPTER VI

The Rise and Collapse of the Cattle Boom

D URING the period covered by the last two chapters, most
of the great land holdings in southern California passed
from the control of native Californians into the hands
of Americans. The change was inevitable. It was brought about
by the Land Act of 1851, whose harmful and confusing effects upon the old Spanish-Mexican titles have already been
described; by the prodigality, extravagance, and financial in-
eptitude of the native Californians; by inequitable short-term
mortgages and fantastically high interest rates; by a prolonged
depression in the cattle industry, following a period of sky-
rocketing prices produced by the Gold Rush; and, finally, by
the historic drought of the mid-sixties, which caused a widespread revolution in the life and customs of southern California.

The spectacular cattle boom of 1849 and the early fifties was
the natural outgrowth of the Gold Rush. Prior to 1848 California cattle were commercially valuable only for their hides
and tallow; and the average price of full-grown steers seldom
rose above four dollars a head. But the Gold Rush created an
enormous and ever-expanding demand for beef, raised the price
of cattle to levels never before dreamed of in California, destroyed the simple scale of values to which the ranchers had
long been accustomed, and transformed herds of black, slim-
bodied cattle into far richer bonanzas than the gold fields of
the Sierra yielded to a vast majority of the Argonauts.

Because of the urgent demand for livestock in the mining
regions and in such newly created cities as San Francisco,
Stockton, and Sacramento, the long-established custom of
slaughtering cattle for hides and tallow rapidly gave place to

the much more profitable business of selling the animals for beef. Prices began to feel the stimulus of the new market as soon as the first wave of gold seekers reached California. In the spring of 1849, Hugo Reid, the picturesque and capricious Scotsman of San Gabriel, wrote from Monterey to Abel Stearns that dried beef was considered cheap at 20 cents a pound, that tallow was selling for 48 cents a pound in San Francisco, and that there was not a candle for sale in all Monterey. Reid added that "Stinking mould yankee Candles, so soft you cannot handle them" were bringing 30 cents a pound, wholesale, in "the Yerba Buena."[1]

Under such conditions, Reid believed that Stearns could net nearly $20,000 on the sale of a thousand head of steers in northern California. As grounds for his opinion, he estimated that the cattle would yield 2,000 arrobas of *manteca*, or tallow, which could be sold at five dollars an arroba; 2,000 arrobas of *sebo*, or suet, used chiefly in the making of candles, at three dollars an arroba; and 3,000 arrobas of *carne seca* (for which any kind of meat could be used) at two dollars an arroba. The hides and other products would bring at least $1,300, making a gross total of $23,300. It would cost about a dollar a head to kill the steers, and $2,000 to charter a vessel to carry the various products from San Pedro to Monterey or San Francisco.[2]

Instead of following the suggestion outlined by Reid, southern rancheros adopted the much more feasible plan of driving their cattle on the hoof to the northern markets. The practice, begun in the early days of the Gold Rush, quickly developed into one of the essential economic operations of the state, and continued with little interruption until the completion of the Southern Pacific Railroad to Los Angeles more than a quarter of a century later.

During that time tens of thousands of cattle were driven, either along the coast or through the sparsely inhabited San

Joaquin Valley, from the southern ranges to northern California. In economic significance and picturesque detail, the traffic was comparable to the great cattle drives over the Bozeman Trail of Montana or the Abilene Trail of Kansas. But despite its historical importance and adventurous background, the subject has been ignored in both the historical and romantic literature of the state, and material on it, whether statistical or descriptive, is disappointingly meager.[3]

The cattle, which necessarily "lived off the country," usually started north when the grass had reached maturity after the early winter rains; and as they seldom traveled more than ten or fifteen miles a day, a herd was usually a full month on the trail.

The average herd included from 700 to 1,000 animals, though sometimes the number ran as high as 2,000 or 2,500. A trail boss (perhaps a *mayordomo*) and three or more *vaqueros* went with each herd. The cost of "carrying" a drove from Los Angeles to "the upper country" averaged, roughly, from two to four dollars a head. Wholesale stampedes, severe storms, forays by wild Indian tribes, or the depredations of cattle thieves occasionally took heavy and even disastrous toll, but under normal conditions the herd suffered little loss.[4]

Some southern rancheros leased grazing rights in the vicinity of San José, Sacramento, or San Francisco Bay, where the stock fattened after the long drive;[5] other owners sold direct to cattle buyers who came down in large numbers from the north either to purchase on their own account or to serve as agents for butcher shops and meat dealers in the larger cities.[6] Such buyers usually assumed responsibility for delivering the cattle to the purchaser.

The following excerpts from contemporary letters reveal the typical difficulties and vicissitudes experienced on the long drives up the coast.

"The cattle and horses are getting on very well," wrote Cave

Couts to Abel Stearns in the spring of 1852. "The nest of thieves in the Sta Clara did all they knew how to make me lose a lot, if not all. By believing all they told me to be false, and threatening a couple pretty closely, I escaped. I learned that they got about 100 head of Forster, 50 from José Anto Argüello, 70 of Machados, all of Castros, and others in proportion. I have had not had an opportunity of counting since leaving Triumpho Rancho, but have lost very few if any—have had no stampede and no kind of bad luck."[8]

Inefficient *vaqueros*, great fields of mustard (in which some of the stock were lost), heavy fogs in the mountains, a poisonous weed that killed six heifers at one time, lack of grass and intense heat kept the trail boss of a band of 800 cattle belonging to Abel Stearns decidedly on tenterhooks during the early summer of 1862.

"I have had no stampeeds for the past eight nights," he wrote from a camping place above Santa Barbara. " . . . I had an awful time passing the beach at San Buenaventura; it was a matter of impossibility to keep my Stock from running, I had half of my Baqueros ahead with me and I know everything was done to keep them from running but we could not keep them back, the consequences were Some ten or twelve got verry lame and will not be able to travel. . . ."[9]

In the same year, a drover named Blunt also wrote from Santa Barbara: "We arrived here last evening with our number of cattle and horses complete but can't say much for their good condition. The weather has been so cold and disagreeable since we left that it has been almost impossible to keep our stock together day or night. While encamped on the beach at Buenaventura it rained verry hard and the wind blew as hard as I ever saw it, the cattle consequently on the stir all night but we have not had a Stampeed since we left Los Angeles. It is all owing to the cold weather that the stock is reduced in flesh—

two *partidos* just ahead of us Forsters and Lugos both lost cattle between here and San Buenaventura.

"Grass destroyed above San Luis Obispo by frost and cold—3500 head 'have gone up'. Prospects very discouraging—wherever good grass can be found will stay over a day or so."[10]

The rise in cattle prices, which began early in 1849, continued with only temporary setbacks for nearly seven years. During that time, beef cattle were quoted as high as $75 in San Francisco, and small calves brought from $20 to $25 each.[11] Even on the distant southern ranges, the price of full-grown steers, representing an eight- or ten-fold increase over that of the hide-and-tallow days, rose to $30 and $40 a head.[12]

But the seven fat years of inflated prices and treacherous prosperity proved, in the end, the curse of the native landowner. "Curious tales are told of the improvidence of the old Californians in their last days," wrote Charles Nordhoff in 1873.

When the Americans from the East rushed into the country on the discovery of gold, cattle suddenly became valuable for their meat; before then only their hides were sold; and I have myself, in 1847, in Monterey, seen a fat steer sold for three dollars to the ship's butcher, who later sold the hide for a dollar, thus receiving the whole carcass for only two dollars. The Yankee demand for beef made the cattle owners suddenly rich, and they made haste to spend what they so easily got. Saddles trimmed with solid silver, spurs of gold, bridles with silver chains, were among the fancies of the men; and a lady in Santa Barbara amused me by describing the old adobe houses, with earthern floors covered with costly rugs; four-post bedsteads with the costliest lace curtains, and these looped up with lace again; and the *señora* and *señoritas* dragging trains of massive silk and satin over the earthen floor. It must have been an odd mixture of squalor and splendor.[13]

It is interesting to note that Francisco Gamboa, the foremost authority on the mining industry of New Spain, made almost the same comment about the Mexican mine owners of the eighteenth century who suddenly became rich through the opening of a bonanza; and even as early as 1582 the English merchant, Henry Hawks, wrote in the same vein: "The pompe and liberalitie of the owners of the mines is marvelous to beholde; the apparell both of them and of their wives is more to be compared to the apparell of noble persons than otherwise. If their wives go out of their houses, as unto the church, or any other place, they go out with great majesty, and with as many men and maids as though she were the wife of some noble man. . . . They are princes in the keeping of their houses, and bountiful in all manner of things."[14]

Horace Bell, who came to California in the extravagant days of the cattle boom and saw, like Nordhoff, the prodigality and ostentation of the *paisanos*, left the following picture of the Los Angeles of that day:

The streets were thronged throughout the entire day with splendidly mounted and richly dressed *caballeros*, most of whom wore suits of clothes that cost all the way from $500 to $1,000, with saddle and horse trappings that cost even more. . . . Of one of the Lugos, I remember, it was said his horse equipments cost over $2,000. Everybody in Los Angeles seemed rich, everybody *was* rich, and money was more plentiful at that time, than in any other place of like size, I venture to say, in the world.[15]

The improvidence and luxury of which Bell and Nordhoff wrote consumed the income of the Californians so completely that little or nothing was added to their capital, set aside as a prudent reserve against forthcoming years of drought and other disaster, or employed to restore the seriously depleted herds.

In failing to preserve their breeding stock, rancheros were especially shortsighted. Abel Stearns estimated that, during the boom period, from 25,000 to 30,000 cattle annually were sold out of Los Angeles County alone, and that the southern ranges

suffered a yearly loss, over and above the natural increase, of at
least 15,000 head.[16]

Scarcely able at first to comprehend the fictitious prices created by the mining boom, southern rancheros soon came to accept them as a normal and permanent feature of the industry.
But their delusion was short-lived. Due chiefly to large imports
of sheep (especially from New Mexico), the development of
farms devoted to the breeding and fattening of livestock on an
extensive scale, and the introduction of cattle in immense numbers from the Mississippi and Missouri valleys, the demand for
southern California range stock began to decline as early as
1855.

During the Gold Rush thousands of head of livestock were
brought into California from the Middle West, by way of the
overland trails; and early in the fifties the cattle trade between
the Missouri frontier and the Sacramento Valley had developed
into a definite, well-established business. According to an estimate published in the Los Angeles *Star*, over 90,000 head of
cattle and nearly 25,000 sheep en route to California passed Fort
Kearny during the spring and early summer of 1852.[17] The following year Governor Bigler reported that over 24,000 cattle
reached California by way of Beckwith's Pass; 9,000 by way of
the Gila route; 15,000 by way of Sonora Pass; and some 13,000
by way of the Carson River Trail—making a total of nearly
62,000 which entered the state over the main emigrant roads
alone.[18] Thousands of head of Texas longhorns were also driven
to California, and the trade became an important feature of the
Texas cattle business during the middle fifties. Describing the
movement of cattle from the great ranges along the Rio Grande
to the coast, Joseph McCoy wrote:

This journey of fifteen hundred or two thousand miles was the
first really long drive of Texas cattle. Hot winds, dusty trails, and
hostile Apache were among the obstacles encountered. Some cattle

had to be left behind because they were footsore; others died on the way due to the scarcity of water and absence of proper grazing facilities. Hundreds of carcasses were strewn along the trail—mute evidences of the hazardous nature of the long journey. "From end to end it was a trail of dangers and uncertainties—long dry drives that set cattle mad with thirst and drew saddle horses to 'skin and bones'; alkaline lakes that poisoned and killed thirsting herds; *malpais* ridges that cut hoofs to the quick and set the riders afoot; and the eternal threat of loss to white and Indian thieves." Very few drovers arrived in California with their herds intact; hence the high prices they obtained for cattle were essential to compensate them for losses on the long and hazardous drive.[19]

By 1860 the trade in cattle between the Middle West and California had perceptibly declined; but the decrease was more than offset by large imports of sheep from New Mexico. According to one estimate, 100,000 sheep crossed the Colorado River, en route to California, during the fall and early winter of 1858-59.[20] In February of that season, the Los Angeles *Star* reported the arrival of Joaquín Perca, Jesús Luna, and Vincente Otero with 35,000 sheep from New Mexico.[21] The following fall it was said that 46,000 head from the Rio Grande Valley were passing through Arizona, bound for California;[22] and between December 9 and January 21 some 80,000 head arrived at the ferry on the Colorado.[23]

The growth of the sheep industry in California, supplementing other factors already mentioned, led to a decline in cattle prices before the close of 1855. A severe drought, the next season, destroyed at least 10,000 cattle in Los Angeles County alone, and compelled many ranchers to market their herds at sacrifice prices.

The editor of the Los Angeles *Star* of April 26, 1856, wrote:

"Dull times!" says the trader, the mechanic, the farmer,—indeed, everybody echoes the dull sentiment. The teeth of the cattle have this year, been so dull that they have been able scarcely to save themselves from starvation; but buyers are nearly as plenty as cattle, and sharp in proportion to the prospect of starvation. Business is dull—duller this week that it was last; duller today than it was yes-terday. Expenses are scarcely realized; and every hole where a dol-lar or two has heretofore leaked out, must be stopped. The flush times are passed—the days of large prices and full pockets are gone: picayunes, bad liquor, rags, and universal dullness—sometimes too dull to be complained of—have usurped the minds of men, and a common obtuseness prevails. Neither pistol shots nor dying groans have any effect; earthquakes hardly turn men in their beds. It is no use talking—business has stepped out and the people is asleep.

The *Star* of May 3 estimated that 6,000 head of cattle had been driven to the north from Los Angeles County on "owners' accounts," during the year; that 16,000 had been taken by agents or buyers; and that 20,000 had been sent out of the county for pasture. Prices for large cattle had fallen to $16 or $18 a head, and young stock brought only $7 or $8. "The profits on raising cattle at these prices, we are assured," said the editor, "are easily footed up."

The year 1856 may therefore be looked upon as marking the end of the golden age of the cattle business in California. From that time on, the industry suffered one vicissitude after another until the great drought of the mid-sixties subordinated it to other forms of agriculture. By the summer of 1857 cattle dealers found the Los Angeles market "completely gutted";[24] in 1858 drovers purchased only a third as many cattle as they had been accustomed to take in former years.[25] During 1860 the standard price of breeding cows fell to ten dollars a head, and, even at that figure, there was no demand.[26] A special report in the feder-al census gave the following pessimistic account of the industry:

A convention of stock-raisers, composed of intelligent gentlemen met in San Francisco last year. They inform us, from their best source of information that we now have in the state three millions of horned cattle, a number far beyond the wants of consumption;

and there being no market open to us beyond the limits of the State, this branch of the industry has become ... ruinous.[27]

Because there was no market for their stock in the north, Abel Stearns, Don Juan Temple (owner of the Rancho Los Cerritos),[28] and other large rancheros slaughtered some 15,000 cattle in the summer of 1861 and made such profit as they could from the sale of hides, tallow, and dried beef.[29]

In the midst of this acute depression most of the old *paisanos* discovered that they were heavily involved in debt and saddled with interest charges of staggering proportions. As the editor of the San Francisco *Bulletin* pointed out, in the flush days of the early fifties they had contracted debts which they were now compelled to meet by selling cattle on "a dead, heavy, lifeless market."[30]

Easygoing by nature, accustomed to an open-handed credit system under which the debtor was seldom pressed for payment, unfamiliar with the diabolical attributes of compound interest, most of the native rancheros fell easy prey to every financial ill and questionable practice of the time.

Short-term mortgages (secured by property far in excess of the value of the loan), unconscionable interest rates, and deficiency judgments that stripped the defaulting debtor of his last real, eventually took from even the wealthiest and most distinguished of the native California families, first their herds of cattle, then their broad leagues of land, and finally the friendly shelter of their simple adobe *casas*.[31] The columns of contemporary newspapers, as well as the books of deeds and mortgages in country archives, contain the laconic records of scores of such forgotten tragedies.

Innumerable instances might be cited of the fantastic interest rates of the post-Gold Rush decades.[32] In December, 1850, Don Juan Bandini borrowed some $10,000 from a moneylender in San Diego. Interest on the loan was fixed at 4% a month.[33] Benjamin D. Hayes, a well-known southern California judge, paid monthly interest of 5% on a $500 note.[34] In July, 1852, Dolores Valenzuela was in default on two mortgages, totaling about $2,200, on which he had contracted to pay 8% a month.[35]

In 1854 José Ramón Yorba mortgaged 17,000 acres of the Rancho Las Bolsas, together with his home and vineyard, to James P. McFarland and John G. Downey, for $5,500 at 5% a month.[36] In the same year, Joaquín Ruíz borrowed $400 from Abel Stearns, giving in return a mortgage, payable a year from date, with interest at 5% a month, on the 6,600-acre Rancho La Bolsa Chica. Ruíz later borrowed an additional $2,200 at the same rate.[37]

José Sepúlveda, who won romantic distinction for his great landholdings, fast race horses, reckless wagers, open-handed hospitality, and the elegance of his costumes, ran heavily in debt. Among other obligations, he owed $7,000, in varying amounts, to twelve different creditors. Interest rates on these loans ranged from 4% to 7% a month, and in most instances the interest was compounded.[38] In 1861 Júlio Verdugo mortgaged his share of the Rancho San Rafael (which he had received from his father, in 1831, "with the blessing of God") for $3,445.37. Thanks to interest charges of 3% a month, the original debt in eight years increased to $58,750 and Don Júlio found himself a landless man.[39]

One might continue the melancholy tale indefinitely. "They sold out Vicente Lugo," wrote C. R. Johnson of the owner of one part of the famous Rancho San Antonio. "Phillips bought the cattle—cow and calf six dollars and steers six dollars—Vicente has nothing now but his wife's property."[40]

Pío Pico and his brother, Andrés, were once among the largest of the landowners of southern California. Included in their holdings was the huge Rancho Santa Margarita y Las Flores, adjacent to the Mission of San Juan Capistrano, but the ranch

DON ANDRÉS PICO

DON JOSÉ SEPÚLVEDA

was mortgaged to two San Francisco moneylenders, Pioche and Bierque, for some $44,000, with interest at 3% a month. Other notes given by the Picos, according to Don Juan Forster, brother-in-law of Pío and Andrés, "were scattered out all over Los Angeles," so that a deficiency judgment on the mortgage would jeopardize every acre the brothers owned.[41] "Over-flooded with heavy indebtedness," and at his wits' end, Pío Pico offered to surrender the ranch, 5,000 head of cattle, and 500 head of horses in return for the note, but Pioche and Bierque refused the offer.[42]

At great risk to his own solvency, Forster advanced sufficient money to satisfy the mortgage, and in the end became the sole owner of the immense ranch. Pío Pico's remaining holdings passed into the hands of other creditors; and the last of the Mexican governors of California, once the owner of an empire, became dependent for his modest living on the bounty of relatives and friends.

Lemuel Carpenter was a Kentuckian who came to California in 1833 with a fur-trading expedition from Santa Fé. Carpenter married María de Domínguez, and later acquired that portion of the old Nieto grant known as the Rancho Santa Gertrudes. For many years he lived as an adopted "son of the country," prosperous and respected. But in the end a trivial debt, swollen to huge proportions by chicanery and outrageous interest rates, consumed his property and brought him to a suicide's tragic end. On December 16, 1858, the case of Lemuel Carpenter, "an Insolvent Debtor," appeared on the calendar of the court of the First Judicial District of California; and on November 9, 1859, the 22,000-acre Santa Gertrudes ranch, on which the famous Santa Fé oil field is now located, was sold by the sheriff to James P. McFarland and John G. Downey for $2,200! But Don Lemuel was not present at the sale. A few hours earlier he had liquidated debts, wounded pride, and bitter disappointment by the simple expedient of sending a pistol bullet through his head.[43]

The extraordinarily high interest rates, which more than any other factor brought about the ruin of the landowners of the old regime, constitute an economic phenomenon difficult to understand. For twenty years loans of all kinds, irrespective of the security behind them, paid interest charges of the most fantastic character. Such rates were not limited to southern California; borrowers everywhere, whether miners, merchants, shippers, or ranchers, paid substantially the same exorbitant charges and gave the same excessive hostages to fortune for the loans.

The situation arose no doubt, in part, from the uncertainty and confusion incident to the transition from Mexican to American rule, the substitution of Anglo-American institutions for those of Spanish origin, an inadequate supply of money (despite the state's large production of gold), a banking system barely developed to the embryonic stage, a spirit of reckless speculation bred by the Gold Rush and the wild fluctuation of prices during the mining period, and the universal state of economic and social instability from which California suffered during the formative years of statehood.

But after giving these various factors due weight, one still finds no rational explanation for a compound interest rate that frequently ran as high as ten per cent a month and persisted for nearly twenty years.

The situation in California appears all the more abnormal when compared to the status of capital and interest in Australia during the same period. The English economist, Ernest Seyd, called attention to the arresting contrast in the following paragraphs:

California has, for the last three years, received scarcely any addition to her population, which is hardly one-half of that of Australia; capital is scarce, and rates high; so that enterprise is checked, and many advantageous undertakings are thus left unfinished.

Hence the respective differences in the value of both labour and property between the two countries. Rates of labour in California are still at their old standard of five dollars a day, whilst wages in Australia are, as a general rule, scarcely one-third of that amount. Land, in California, can be obtained at rates ruling from fifty cents to one dollar per acre; whilst in Australia nothing can be got for less than £1 per acre. . . . Public banks in Australia are abundant, and money rules at an interest of 6 per cent. per year, whilst California cannot boast of a single public banking institution, and capital is sought after on the best securities, at the high interest of 2 to 3 per cent. per month.[44]

As early as 1851 Governor Peter H. Burnett, seeking to obtain the passage of a law to ameliorate "the extravagant and unlimited rate of interest" in the state, declared that "the idea that competition among lenders would reduce the rate of interest to a fair and just standard . . . seems to be delusive. Our own sad experience in California has conclusively shown, that competition among lenders does not diminish the rate of interest. . . . If the system is permitted to continue for some years longer, the productive industry of the State will be seriously crippled."[45]

Some fifteen years after Burnett's message to the legislature, Edward H. Hall prefaced his popular emigrants' guide and handbook with the remark, "When currency becomes plenty and interest within living rates, we shall have permanent and general prosperity in California; not before."[46]

Whatever the causes for the usurious interest rates in California, they proved an enormous handicap to the state's prosperity and economic development; and the scarcity of capital for productive purposes, like Bunyan's Apollyon, straddled clean across the path of the state's material progress for a generation. In southern California, especially, a complete dearth of capital prevented the development of the region's great natural resources and caused general economic stagnation. Agriculture made little progress, industry advanced only slightly beyond the household stage of Spanish-Mexican culture, and the trickle of immigration was barely large enough to establish three small settlements.

Failure to contend successfully with debts contracted at the prevailing interest, or to adapt themselves to other conditions imposed by the new economic order, compelled the old *paisanos*, one by one, to surrender their vast estates to alien hands and pass, almost unnoticed and forgotten, into the dim twilight of their once-romantic day. In a humorously pathetic way, the following simple newspaper advertisement of Vicente de la Osa, a well-known ranchero of the time, indicates the change that had taken place in a brief decade in the lot of the old Californians. Once given to open-handed hospitality, like his fellow rancheros, and untroubled by any thought of the economic problems of the morrow, Vicente was now face to face with the bewildering and sordid necessity of converting his ranch house into a wayside inn. The implications of the advertisement, even with its delicately phrased suggestion to prospective guests, make all too apparent the unhappy financial expedients to which members of the old order had been reduced:

I have established at my Ranch, known by the name of "The Encino," situated at the distance of twenty-one miles from the city, on the road to Santa Barbara, a place for affording the accomodation to the people traveling on this road. They will find at all times food for themselves, and for their horses, beds at night, etc. I hope those wishing to call at our place will not forget to bring with them what is necessary to defray their expenses.[47]

CHAPTER VII

Taxes, Drought, and Epidemic

Prior to American annexation, the California government derived its meager revenue chiefly from port charges and import duties on foreign vessels, and direct taxes were consequently almost unknown in the province. The establishment of statehood brought this idyllic situation to an abrupt end. Under the Constitution of 1849, the "venerable general property tax," then in universal use throughout the United States, was introduced into California and became the chief source of revenue for state and county governments alike.

Both the census and tax returns, if one may attempt the difficult task of "translating statistics into vitalities," showed the extent to which the land was concentrated in the hands of the large proprietors. In 1850 the distribution in Los Angeles County was as follows:

Numbers of Landowners	Value of Real Estate
2	Under $100
70	$100 to $999
79	$1,000 to $2,499
29	$2,500 to $4,999
27	$5,000 to $9,999
10	$10,000 to $19,999
4	$20,000 to $29,999
1	$30,000
3	$50,000
1	$80,000[1]

In 1852, only fifty landowners in the county paid as much as $100 in taxes.[2] In 1858 the total wealth of the county was estimated for tax purposes at $2,370,523; half of this amount was assessed against the following landowners:

117

Abel Stearns	$186,000
Juan Temple	90,000
William Wolfskill	80,000
Bishop and Beale	48,000
Ricardo Véjar	42,000
Sainstevain Brothers	40,000
Matthew Keller, Andrés Machado, John Rowland, each	35,000
Andrés and Pío Pico	32,000[3]

At that time the state tax ranged from sixty to seventy cents a hundred; and the county tax from a dollar to a dollar and a quarter. In 1858 the Los Angeles County budget was made up as follows: normal county tax, 30 cents; jail tax, 30 cents; interest on funded debt, 25 cents; support of the indigent, 25 cents; school tax, 5 cents.[4]

Assessment and tax records also brought out the striking difference between the wealth of northern California and the comparative poverty of the southern counties. In 1855, for example, the total value of real and personal property in Los Angeles County was slightly over $2,500,000; in the same year Sacramento County was assessed at approximately $9,300,000; San Francisco at $33,000,000; Santa Clara at $5,500,000; Sonoma at $4,000,000; and Yuba at $5,000,000.[5]

Thus, when compared to the more prosperous northern counties, even the most important and populous of the southern counties was economically insignificant. Its relation to the wealth of the state as a whole is shown by the following comparative table:

	Los Angeles County	*Total for the State*
1850	$1,931,403	$ 57,670,689
1855	2,561,359	95,007,440
1859	2,370,529	131,060,279
1863	1,623,370	147,104,955
1870	6,918,074	277,538,134[6]

As previously stated, land and cattle made up the chief resources of the southern counties. In 1850 grazing lands were assessed at 50 cents an acre; but within a year or two the valuation was reduced to 25 cents, and that figure remained a common standard of assessment in southern California until 1863. The following tables, taken from the records of Abel Stearns, wealthiest landowner in the county, furnish a concrete example of the land values and taxes of that time:

1856

Ranches	Acres	Value
Los Alamitos	22,040	$ 5,510
Las Bolsas	8,680	2,170
Los Coyotes	6,510	1,627
Total	37,230	
Los Angeles real estate		500
Improvements		8,000
Personal property (chiefly cattle and other livestock)		65,260
Total		$83,067

On the above property, Stearns paid a state tax of $631.30 and a county tax of $946.96, or a total of $1,578.26.[7]

In 1861 Stearns's properties in Los Angeles County were assessed as follows:

Ranches	Acres	Value
Los Alamitos	26,041	$ 6,570
La Bolsa Chica	8,680	2,170
Interest in La Bolsa Grande	19,000	4,750
Two-thirds interest in Los Coyotes	37,986	9,497
La Laguna de Los Lugos	10,000	2,500
Two-thirds interest in La Habra	4,400	1,100
Interest in Santa Ana	2,000	500
Improvements on the above		6,500
Total	108,107	$ 33,587

Other property

Arcadia Building in Los Angeles	$ 25,000
Lot in Los Angeles	1,500
Lot and residence in Los Angeles	5,000
Note of Pío Pico, secured by mortgage	13,000
Other notes	6,750
County scrip, face value $10,000; actual value	5,005
City scrip, face value $1,224; actual value	612
16,000 cattle of the plain, at $4.50 per head	72,000
1,500 unbroken horses, at $5.00 per head	7,500
250 gentle horses, at $15.00 per head	3,750
Plate, jewels, and furniture	3,000
100 shares of telegraph stock, at $20.00 per share	2,000
Total	$145,117
Grand total	$178,704 [8]

Stearns's personal property was valued at $90,930 in 1862; and his ranchos, on the basis of 25 cents an acre, were assessed at $96,743. On the combined total of $187,673, Stearns paid a state tax of $1,163.57 and a county tax of $3,753.46, or $4,917.03 in all.[9]

As previously stated, land and livestock were assessed in other southern California counties on substantially the same basis as that used in Los Angeles. In 1860 the property of T. Wallace Moore, one of the large rancheros of Santa Barbara County, was assessed as follows:

Ranches	Acres	Value
Rancho de San Cayetana [or Sespe]	26,640	$6,660
Improvements		1,500
Rancho Santa Paula	17,760	4,440
Improvements		1,000
One-half interest in Rancho de Lompoc	24,420	6,105
One-fourth interest in Rancho Mission Viejo	2,200	550
One-fourth interest in Isla de Santa Rosa		3,125

Personal property

3000 head of cattle	18,000
300 horses	3,000
Isla de Santa Rosa	
1,000 head of cattle	3,000
2,000 sheep	1,500
100 horses	500[10]

County assessors were frequently charged with discrimination against the small farmer in favor of the large landowner. Since it was the common practice to appraise orchards, vineyards, and cultivated ground at five dollars an acre—a sum equal to the value of twenty acres of range land—the resentment of the settlers was understandable. It is doubtful, however, if the financial returns from grazing lands, at least after the peak of the cattle boom in 1855, warranted a higher valuation.

The charge was also made that thousands of acres belonging to influential rancheros were deliberately omitted from the assessment lists, and that county boards of equalization customarily granted substantial reductions to large landowners, but ignored the requests of small taxpayers for similar consideration.[11] The lapse of more than three-quarters of a century makes it difficult to determine how far such accusations were founded on fact, and how far they merely reflected the ill will of the settlers in their chronic feud with the rancheros. But whether justified or not, the charges at least produced a widely diffused sense of injustice and served to intensify the tradition that large proprietors enjoyed immunities and privileges from which the small farmer was excluded.

The issue of taxation in the southern counties, however, was much more than a local controversy between settlers and rancheros. In wealth, population, and political influence southern California was hopelessly inferior to the self-assertive mining and commercial regions of the north. The south was traditionally pastoral, and conditioned to a large landholding system. It had no true community of interest with the dominant northern half of the state, and its experience with the federal Land Act of 1851 led it to view all government action with suspicion and alarm.

The leading southern rancheros feared, especially, the imposition of confiscatory taxes by the state legislature, and the enactment of other discriminatory measures designed to break up the large cattle ranges for the benefit of land-hungry settlers, immigrants, and disappointed miners. The attitude of numerous members of the state legislature, and the frankly avowed policies of some of the early California governors, furnished a logical basis for such concern.

In 1849 the chairman of the legislative committee on public lands wrote Abel Stearns that the north "was teetotally and universally against anything Spanish"; that the southern members of the legislature were "only a drop of water in an ocean," compared to the northern delegation; and that the political power of the north could crush the south "like an unresisting insect."[12]

"The overwhelming influence of the north in the legislature," lamented Stephen C. Foster, son-in-law of Antonio María Lugo, "is seen in every act which has been passed within two years. The northern counties are engaged almost entirely in mining and contain very little land liable to taxation. As a consequence the burdens of taxation fall principally upon the south—burdens which our people are poorly able to bear."[13]

In his annual message of January 7, 1851, Governor Peter H. Burnett declared: "The beneficial effects of a system of direct taxation have already been seen in the increased impulse given to our agriculture during the past year. The large tracts of land have, in many cases, been subdivided and small portions sold to agriculturists, who have thus become permanent and prosperous residents."[14]

The position taken by Governor Burnett on the enforced "subdivision of large tracts of land," by means of direct taxation, added greatly to the fears of the southern rancheros. In 1850 a group of prominent Los Angeles citizens addressed a petition to congress seeking to have the counties south of Monterey organized as a territory under the name Central California. In September, 1851, a much larger group issued a call for a convention to divide the state. The address, directed to the citizens of the southern counties, bluntly declared:

It is the plain truth that whatever of good the experiment of a state government may have otherwise led to in California, for us, the southern counties, it has proved only a splendid failure. The bitter fruits of it no county has felt more keenly than Los Angeles. With all her immense and varied and natural resources, her political, social and pecuniary condition at this moment is deplorable in the extreme; her industries paralyzed under the insupportable burden of taxation; her port almost forsaken by commerce; her surplus products of no value on account of the enormous price of freights; her capital flying to other climes; a sense of the utter insecurity of property pervading all classes and everything tending to fasten upon her, in the guise of legislation, a state of actual oppression which will soon exhaust the energies of a population that deserves a better fate.[15]

Nothing was done to give effect to the foregoing petition; but an occasional recommendation that the taxing power of the state be used to break up large landholdings kept southern rancheros in a condition of uncertainty and suspense. The evils of large landholdings, for example, were thus dramatically pictured by Governor Bigler, in 1856:

Of what avail is it that our soil is the most productive, and our climate admirably adapted to the culture of all the necessities and luxuries of life, if flowing vales sleep in native beauty and silence, and expansive plains are but the roaming grounds and rich pasture fields for the unchecked herd? The true wealth of a prolific soil is to be found alone in the hardy and industrious hand which brings it into subjection—which turns the rich sod with the ploughshare, prepares it for the rains of winter and dews at night fall, and which at harvest season, reaps from fields of bending grain the rich recompense of toil.[16]

The geographic, racial, and economic factors which prevented the development of any real bond of interest or mutual understanding between northern and southern California, immediately after the Gold Rush, became intensified as the years went by. Southern landowners were more and more convinced that their interests and economic welfare would never be properly safeguarded under the existing state government. They contended, with a measure of truth, that the legislature looked upon southern California only as a satellite of the north; and they feared that sooner or later all large ranchos would be taxed, or legislated, out of existence.[17]

Shortly before the outbreak of the Civil War, some of the most influential rancheros accordingly made another effort to separate the southern counties from the rest of the state, and to organize them into a federal territory. The movement came to a head in February, 1859, when Andrés Pico of Los Angeles introduced a joint resolution in the state assembly, calling for the withdrawal of the counties of San Luis Obispo, Santa Barbara, Los Angeles, San Bernardino, and San Diego from the state of California, and authorizing them to form a new political division, to be called the "Territory of Colorado." The preamble of the measure read as follows:

Whereas, The present boundaries of the state of California enclose an area of such extent, and so diversified in physical and other features as to preclude, to an unwholesome degree, the possibility of uniform legislation, and render cumbersome and expensive the operation of government,

And Whereas, All of that part of said state, hereinafter described, is so peculiarly situated as to make a longer continuance of its political connection with the remainder of the state alike ruinous to the inhabitants of said part, and burdensome to the said state at large, without any corresponding benefit resulting in any way to either party,

And Whereas, The representatives from the said part unanimously demand, in the names of their respective constituencies, that the aforesaid untoward connection be dissolved . . .

Be it therefore Resolved . . . that all that part of the said state of California . . . composed of the counties of San Luis Obispo, Santa Barbara, Los Angeles, San Diego and San Bernardino, including all the islands lying opposite to its adjacent coast . . . be separated from the said state and organized as a territory of the United States, under the name of the territory of Colorado.[18]

Southern newspapers, which supported the plan of state division, emphasized the irreconcilable differences between the economic interests of the north and south, pointed out the contrasts in social organization between the two sections, and stressed the wrong and injustice inflicted upon the helpless rancheros by the politically dominant mining and commercial counties.

Northern California, as a whole, assumed an apathetic attitude toward the loss of the five backward grazing counties, and both houses of the legislature approved the division bill. A popular vote in the seceding counties subsequently ratified the measure; but because of the controversy over slavery and the threatening cloud of civil war the bill died in congress.

The disappointment of southern landowners over the failure of the plan for state division was soon forgotten in a succession of ever increasing misfortunes, including financial depression, flood, drought, and epidemic, which soon visited the country.

Owing to the prolonged decline in prices, the cattle industry was in the doldrums in the early sixties; rancheros were heavily involved in debt; the northern markets were glutted; many owners were seeking, by the sacrifice sale of stock, to raise enough money to satisfy creditors and meet their taxes; and in some counties swarms of grasshoppers settled on the ranges and devoured the summer and fall pasturage. All in all, conditions were so doleful that one despairing ranchero of Santa Barbara wrote:

Everybody in this Town is Broke not a dollar to be seen, and God bless everyone if things do not change. Cattle can be bought at any price, Real Estate is not worth anything....
The "Chapules" [grasshoppers] have taken possession of this Town, they have eat all the Barley, Wheat &c. &c. there is not a thing left by them, they cleaned me entirely of everything and I expect if I do not move out of this Town soon, they will eat me also. "Dam the Chapules," I have lost about two thousand dollars.[19]

Normally, California was an ideal cattle country; and to the owner of flocks and herds no land could have been kinder or more consistently benign. Year by year the ranges responded to the miracle of the fall rains, and the springing grass spread an inviting carpet over endless miles of valleys and rolling hills. Usually the rains ceased in April; but, throughout the cloudless months of summer, cattle found an abundance of nutritious pasture in the dry alfilaria and bur clover which covered the ranges.

Despite nature's traditionally benevolent rule, however, southern California was not immune to occasional visitations of flood or drought. A succession of such disastrous seasons, each one worse than its predecessor, began in 1862 and continued until the fall of 1865. Never before or since has the country suffered as it suffered during those dry years; but out of the land's misfortunes came a major economic revolution and a new southern California.

The series of ills started with unprecedented floods. A storm set in shortly before Christmas, 1861, and continued almost without cessation for a month. During that time rain fell so continuously and in such tropical proportions, that the editor of the Los Angeles *Star* remarked: "On Tuesday last the sun made its appearance. The phenomenon lasted several minutes and was witnessed by a great number of persons."[20]

The prolonged rains caused floods which paralyzed business everywhere, drowned thousands of head of cattle, and destroyed possibly a fourth of the state's taxable wealth.[21]

The storm's worst effects were felt in the San Joaquin and Sacramento valleys. Inundated both by continuous rainfall on the floor of the valleys, and by an enormous runoff from the Sierra Nevada and Coast Range mountains, the huge central basin became an inland sea, "250 to 300 miles long and 20 to 60 miles wide." "America has never before seen such desolation by flood as this has been and seldom has the old world seen the like," said William H. Brewer, who was then making a geological and botanical survey of California.[22]

In many places the water was deep enough to cover the tops of the telegraph poles. For three months a large part of Sacramento, the state capital, lay submerged. Roads leading into the city were utterly impassable; and streets were blocked with overturned houses, dead animals, household furniture, and all manner of wreckage and debris. The ruin, indeed, was so great that Brewer exclaimed: "Such a desolate scene I hope never to see again. Most of the city is under water, and has been for three months. . . . I don't think the city will ever rise from the shock, I don't see how it can."[23]

Though somewhat more fortunate than the central valleys, many parts of southern California also suffered serious damage from the flood. Scores of adobe buildings became saturated and collapsed; dry washes grew into raging torrents; nearly every stream cut a new channel for itself to the sea; turbid rivers carried away hundreds of acres of vineyards and gardens. "On Saturday last," said the Los Angeles *Star*,

torrents of water were precipitated on the earth—it seemed as if the clouds had been broken through, and the waters over the earth and the waters under the earth were coming into conjunction. The result was, that rivers were formed in every gulch and arroyo, and streams poured down the hillsides. The Los Angeles river, already brimful, overflowed its banks, and became a fierce and destructive flood.

The embankment lately made by the city, for the water works, was swept away—melted before the force of the water. The Arroyo Seco poured an immense volume of water down its rugged course, which, emptying into the river, fretting and boiling, drove the water beyond all control.—On Saturday night the work of destruction began. The vineyard of Mrs. T. J. White was the first to suffer. Almost instantly about 5,000 vines were washed away, besides several acres of land used for pasture. The destruction continued the next and following days, until a great breadth of land was washed away, which had been planted with orange and all other kinds of the most valuable fruit trees.

*   *   *

The roads and rivers were, as a matter of course, impassable. The San Gabriel river had overflowed its banks, preventing travel. It then became dammed up where it enters the plain, but it forced a passage for itself, making its way from the eastward to the westward of El Monte, causing the inundation of those lands.

The road from Tejon, we hear, has been almost washed away. The San Fernando mountain cannot be crossed, except by the old trail which winds round and passes over the top of the mountain. The plain has been cut up into gulches and arroyos, and streams are rushing down every declivity.

*   *   *

A rumour prevailed in town yesterday, that the flourishing settlement of Anaheim has been completely destroyed by the flood. We hope it is not so.

Reports from this city [San Bernardino] inform us, that almost

A RIVER IN FLOOD

LA JORNADA DEL MUERTO—THE MARCH OF DEATH

the entire property in the valley has been destroyed. We hope these are exaggerations, and that it will be found our fellow-citizens there have escaped as lightly as ourselves.

Another report says, that the dead bodies of thirteen Indians had been discovered, drowned by the flood.

* * *

Another week has passed without a mail, making five consecutive weeks, during which we had no communication with the outer world, except by steamer express.[24]

The same issue of the *Star* contained the following account of the destruction of the Mexican communities of Agua Mansa and Placita on the Santa Ana River:

Rev. Mr. Borgatia, of Jurupa, arrived in town from his pastorate, on Thursday. The intelligence he brings is of a most unfortunate character. The flood in the Santa Ana river was so great as to pour into the town, washing away the houses, leaving the people without shelter. The church, fortunately, withstood the flood, and thither the people flocked. Everything, of provisions and clothing, has been destroyed, and the people are left absolutely in a state of starvation. There are now fully 500 persons in the church, without the means of subsistence, or the ability to procure them. This is the most utter and complete destruction which we have heard of, and appeals strongly to the sympathies of the public.

As he viewed the wreckage left by the storm at Agua Mansa, Judge Benjamin Hayes wrote:

A dreary desolation presented itself to my eye, familiar buildings overturned or washed away; here only a chimney, there a mere doorpost or a few scattered stakes of a fence, stout and lofty trees torn up, a mass of drifted branches from the mountain canyons, and a universal waste of sand on both banks of the river, where a few months before all was green and beautiful.[25]

In San Diego County the flood carried off vast quantities of soil and timber, destroyed many vineyards and houses, and drowned large numbers of livestock. At San Luis Rey the water "cut an arroyo fifty feet deep." In Santa Barbara County the disaster reached an extent "unknown to the oldest inhabitant." In Ventura, said a correspondent of the *Star*, "the torrent rushed through the town with such force, as to wash away the street to a depth of fifteen feet, carrying several houses with it. The town was abandoned, the people taking refuge in the Church and other elevated places. In the valley, the grass, timber, and lands have been destroyed, and eight or ten houses knocked to smash."[26]

No estimate can be made of the toll of cattle taken by the floods in the southern counties; but, throughout the state as a whole, it possibly ran as high as 200,000.[27] By way of compensation, the rains transformed thousands of acres of grazing lands into a vast meadow, and produced more luxuriant pasturage than even the oldest *vaquero* could recall.

But in the end this generosity on nature's part merely intensified the woes of the harassed stockman and increased his financial problems. For the abundant supply of grass added greatly to the number and fatness of the herds, and the already glutted markets were wholly unable to absorb the surplus. Prices, accordingly, broke almost to the levels of the pre-Gold Rush era.[28]

The great flood of 1861-62 was followed by two years of unparalleled drought.[29] Almost no rain fell during the ensuing fall or winter; and, by spring, cattle on many of the southern ranges were beginning to be in desperate straits. "We have had no rain yet," wrote Johnson to Stearns, in February, 1863, "there is no grass and the cattle are very poor; your Rancho men report a great many dying. Should we have no rain your cattle buyers will get nothing but hides and bones."[30]

A month later the same correspondent said: "It is the opinion of the rancheros that we shall have the worst year known for a long time. We have had very warm weather; and what little grass we had is all dry and burnt. . . . In consequence of the shortness of grass and scarcity of vaqueros, no one has thought of Recogidas or Rodeos as yet."[31] A few days later Johnson added: "There is absolutely no grass and it is the opinion of the Ranch men, the cattle will commence dying within a month. Everything is dried up. . . . The Caballada is in very bad condition . . . the horses have no strength . . . the loss on the stock must be very heavy this year."[32]

From other counties came the same grim report. In January, Juan Forster of the Rancho Santa Margarita wrote, "We poor Rancheros have had a damned bad string of luck these last two years and if it is going to continue I don't know what will become of us."[33] From the Rancho Guajome, near Mission San Luis Rey in San Diego County, Cave J. Couts sounded the same pessimistic note: "What are the cattle raisers going to do? No rain, no grass, nearly as dry as in the month of August. . . . Not only the want of pasture, but Small-pox allows no general recogidas this spring."[34]

Cattle prices, already affected by the conditions of the preceding fall, dropped lower and lower as the drought continued. In January, 1863, Abel Stearns reluctantly agreed to sell a thousand of his best cattle to Miller and Lux, of San Francisco, for eight dollars a head; a few months later multitudes of starving animals were being slaughtered for the trifling value of their hides and horns.[35]

To make matters worse, the late spring brought a succession of hard, scorching winds from the desert; and millions of grasshoppers swept across the country like a devastating fire. A few rancheros were fortunate enough to find pasturage for portions of their herds in the mountains; one of the Wolfskills sent 3,000 head of stock to the Mojave River; the Yorbas, and some other owners, even drove cattle across the border into Lower California.[36]

But far grimmer and more ruthless than the country's multiplied economic ills, was the virulent epidemic of smallpox which broke out in widely scattered localities and ravaged the whole of southern California. Making its first appearance in the fall of 1862, the plague grew steadily worse throughout the winter. Living conditions among Indians and lower-class Mexicans were deplorable; no attempt was made to enforce adequate quarantine regulations; patients stricken with the plague were often concealed from the authorities and attended secretly by members of their families; and almost nothing could be done to check the spread of the disease.

The country had few physicians, all of whom resided in the larger towns, and consequently most ranch settlements and Indian communities were without medical attendance. Vaccine could be secured only by steamer from San Francisco.[37]

Letters of the time, written by hands long since turned to dust, still speak eloquently of the loathsome terror which stalked the countryside and paralyzed even the routine activities of daily life. "We are all badly scared about small-pox," wrote Cave Couts to Abel Stearns from the remote Rancho Guajome,

and keep a sentinel posted to give notice of the approach of anyone, and have to know all about them before they can come nearer than the corral. Many around do the same thing. . . . Have stop'd my vaqueros from their rounds in the campo. . . . Ysidro Alvarado's family nearly all have it. His wife gave birth to a child Monday last, and was yesterday secretly buried at San Luis—died of Small-pox. Ysidro himself is dangerously ill—only his daughter and a Sonorian to attend five at the same time. No medical aid called.[38]

The effect of the smallpox epidemic in Los Angeles itself has already been mentioned. Deaths in the pueblo were so numerous that the municipal authorities discontinued the tolling of the church bells; the disease, though most virulent in the district north of the Plaza, eventually spread to all parts of the city; and business, already paralyzed by the drought, came to a complete standstill.

All through the long, dry summer, southern California ranchers looked to the coming of the fall rains to save them from ruin;[39] but the fall slipped into winter, and the winter into spring, while the parched earth waited in vain for relief, and the cattle died by the thousands on sun-baked ranges and beside waterless streams and sand-choked springs.

"Do you remember what kind of a season it was in the latter part of the Fall of 1863 and the winter of 1864?" Don Juan Forster was asked in the trial of Forster *vs.* Pico. "The climate was very dry," he replied. "It was a most miserable drought that time. There was no moisture and our cattle died off in great numbers. About that winter the whole country from North to South became almost depopulated of cattle. . . . Before the year 1864 had passed away there was a perfect devastation—such a thing was never before known in California."[40]

Forster's statements were fully borne out by the newspaper reports of the time. "Owing to the unusual drought," said the Los Angeles *Star* of January 23, 1864,

little or no farming has been commenced, while the prospects of the rancheros are gloomy in the extreme. During the present winter only two rains have occurred, one in November, and a slight shower in January, altogether not more than an inch and a half of rain has fallen. The weather is now unusually warm, assuming in the day time, a temperature almost that of summer heat, withering every remnant of vegetation and leaving not a green spot on the whole plain. The hills are now as red and arid as we ever saw them presenting the appearance which characterize them during the summer season.

Although the prospects of the farmers at the present time are exceedingly disheartening, we have every reason to suppose that we will yet have the average amount of rain which annually falls, between this time and the latter part of April.

It is truly melancholy to learn of the great amount of cattle, that have died lately, on different ranches throughout the county. It is admitted, that on some, one half of the stock have perished from hunger and there is great apprehension that many more will yet be lost, if a favorable rain should not shortly come. In passing over the plains, it is sad to see the number of dead cattle; while those that survive, present an appearance, such as to produce sympathy for the suffering of the poor dumb animals. Many of them appear like skeletons, and seem unable to move far from the springs and water courses, from which they receive nearly all that prolongs life.

As the drought continued, the price of cattle was determined solely by the value of the hides. A large hide normally brought about two dollars and a half, but the cost of skinning the animal reduced the net return to the owner by at least twenty-five cents.[41] Many herds were offered for a dollar and a half, or two dollars, a head; but "no one would buy them"; and one Los Angeles newspaper even reported that 5,000 cattle had been sold in Santa Barbara for thirty-seven cents each.[42]

The carcasses of dead cattle lay in heaps about the parched water holes and *cienagas,* and beside creeks and streams from which every trace of moisture had disappeared. A drover described the twenty miles of once rich grazing land between Los Angeles and Wilmington, as "a regular mass of dead cattle,"[43] and the editor of the *Southern News* drew a despairing picture of the great ranchos and their now almost vanished herds. "The cattle of Los Angeles County are dying so fast in many places, for the want of food," he wrote,

that the large rancheros keep their men busily employed in obtaining hides. Thousands of carcasses strew the plains in all directions, a short distance from this city, and the sight is harrowing in the extreme. We believe the stock interest of this county, as well as the adjoining counties, to be "played out" entirely. Famine has done its work, and nothing can now save what few cattle remain on the desert California ranches. . . .

Again, he said:

No wonder there is want in the South, with the dread of famine
and starvation before the spring months.[44]

In mid-February, 1864, the drought was temporarily broken
by a generous rain, leading the editor of the *Southern News*
to exclaim:

At last through hopes and fears, and smiles and tears, we have an
evidence . . . that God has not forgotten us in our needs.[45]

But the day of rejoicing was short-lived. Dry electrical north
winds, unseasonable heat, and desiccating dust storms so completely wiped out the beneficial effects of the rain that the earth
once more became iron and the sky brass. No further precipitation of any consequence occurred until the close of May; and,
with the rainless months of summer already at hand, this relief
came too late to save the luckless cattlemen, many of whom,
indeed, were already long past succor.[46]

It is impossible to determine, even approximately, how many
cattle perished in the Great Drought, or were slaughtered by
the ranchers for the small salvage value of their hides and horns.
In addition to the losses caused directly by the drought, thousands of head of stock, in their weakened condition, fell easy
prey to mountain lions, bears, coyotes, and other predatory
animals. According to the federal census there were nearly
1,234,000 cattle in California in 1860; by 1870 the number had
decreased to 670,000—a drop of close to 46 per cent. During the
same decade the number of cattle in Los Angeles County fell
from 70,000 to 20,000—a loss of over 71 per cent.[47]

The effects of the drought were graphically reflected in the
assessment and tax returns of the period. In 1862 grazing lands
in Los Angeles County, as previously explained, were assessed
at the standard rate of twenty-five cents an acre. During the

first year of the drought, this figure was reduced twelve and a half cents, and cattle were assessed at only three dollars a head. Grapevines, on the other hand, which the drought did not affect, were valued at twenty cents each. For the fiscal year ending March 1, 1863, real property in the county was appraised at only $694,114.70, and personal property at $783,-564.72.[48] The general property tax brought into the county treasury only a little over $22,000 and the state tax yielded less than $9,500.[49]

In 1864 property values throughout southern California declined still further. Range lands were assessed on the basis of ten cents an acre, and ranch cattle at from a dollar to two dollars and a half a head. For the fiscal year ending March 1, land and improvements in Los Angeles County were valued at $457,-001.07, and personal property at $561,475.09—a total of $1,018,-476.16.[50] So hard pressed were the landowners for ready money that taxes on at least five-sixths of the property throughout the county were allowed to become delinquent.[51]

During the next fiscal year the assessed valuation of Los Angeles County declined to the lowest figure on record. Land and improvements were appraised at $454,187.70, and personal property at $379,769.40, or a total of only $833,957.10. Range lands continued to be assessed at ten cents an acre, and cattle at an average of about two dollars a head.[52]

The delinquent-tax list again included most of the prominent landowners of the county.[53] Among the names were those of the few Spanish Californians who had been able to maintain at least a portion of their original holdings until the coming of the drought. Almost none, even of that small number, survived the widespread ruin of the mid-sixties. Reduced by mounting debts and unpaid taxes to the condition of a "devastated grain field," the little that was left of their once lordly estates passed forever into alien hands. On the assessors' books their broad leagues of grazing lands were found under other names, and the princely grants which a prodigal government had made to them or their fathers gave place to tiny milpas of beans, melons, and chili peppers, with barely enough room for the cheapest of frame or adobe houses.

So, too, the thousands of head of "black cattle and beasts of burden," which once carried the familiar brands of the proudest of California families, disappeared forever from the plains and valleys and rolling hills. Reduced to the unromantic realism of assessment lists and tax returns, the story of the passing of the old rancheros is written in the long-forgotten, dust-covered records of every southern California county.

But out of the drastic losses inflicted by the Great Drought came a new economic order. Forbidding heaps of bones and skeletons, everywhere bleaching in the sun, symbolized the ruin of the universal industry of southern California. Thereafter, the "cow counties" lost their distinctive appellation. The day of unfenced ranchos, of enormous herds of half-wild cattle, of manorial estates, and pleasure-loving *paisanos* came to its inevitable close. But, in its passing, something of color and romance faded forever from the California scene.

CHAPTER VIII

Minor Economic Enterprises

THE first federal census of California, as previously indicated, was made in the year 1850. Nearly every item in the report testified to the pioneer aspect of southern California society and to the pastoral character of its culture and economic life. The returns showed, for example, that only 2,648 acres out of a total of some 3,250,000 in Los Angeles County were under cultivation, and that the annual value of orchard and field crops was less than $9,000! By way of contrast, the county's range lands included nearly 1,000,000 acres, and its ranches grazed over 100,000 head of cattle, besides immense numbers of horses and other livestock.[1]

The most arresting feature of the census returns was the contrast between the immense size of the southern counties and their sparse population. The figures for Los Angeles County graphically illustrate this feature. Limited to a beggarly 5,000-square-mile area by the first California legislature, the so-called "Queen of the Cow Counties" almost immediately expanded, in characteristic Los Angeles fashion, to Brobdingnagian dimensions. Under the boundary lines established in 1851, the county sprawled from the Pacific Ocean on the west to the Colorado River on the east, and from the "Tulares," in the San Joaquin Valley on the north, almost as far south as San Juan Capistrano.[2] It thus embraced nearly 35,000 square miles—an area one-sixth larger than the whole of Scotland, almost three times the size of Holland, and seven times that of the state of Connecticut. But despite its immense size, the county had only about 4,000 so-called white inhabitants, many of whom belonged to the mixed racial Mexican-Indian group called mestizos, and a slightly larger number of domesticated Indians.[3]

In contrast to the sparse population of this, the largest of the southern counties, the remote mountain county of El Dorado had 40,000 inhabitants; Calaveras, Yuba, and Nevada counties each had nearly 20,000; San Francisco had slightly over 36,000; and the population of the state as a whole was approximately 260,000.[4]

So long as southern California remained a cattle country and the rancheros held their immense estates intact, a large increase in population was impossible, since, obviously, a region so restricted in economic interests and so limited in opportunity offered no inducement to immigration; but even while range and herd held undisputed mastery, a few new enterprises made their appearance during the fifties and early sixties; and certain older industries, inherited from the prosperous days of the missions, were re-established on a somewhat larger scale.

Sheep raising, successfully carried on both by the Franciscans and the early rancheros, expanded year by year after its revival in the early fifties, and under the stimulus of the Civil War finally usurped the dominant place held by the cattle industry until the drought of 1862-64.

According to the federal census, there were less than 18,000 sheep in California in 1850; a decade later the number had risen to approximately 1,000,000, nearly fifty per cent of which were pastured in the south. Monterey County grazed approximately 200,000 head; Los Angeles and San Luis Obispo counties each had nearly 100,000; Santa Barbara County about 65,000; San Diego County 14,000; and San Bernardino County 5,000.[5] In 1854 the California wool clip amounted to only 175,000 pounds; by 1860 it had risen to 2,000,000 pounds; five years later it came to 6,500,000 pounds; and in 1870 it reached the huge total of 11,400,000 pounds.[6]

San Francisco was the chief wool market on the coast and fixed the scale of prices for the rest of the state. Native California sheep were decidedly inferior to imported varieties, in both wool- and meat-producing qualities, and generally sold at less than a third the price of imported breeds, or so-called "fine sheep." The following prices were quoted in 1863 for the different varieties of wool: merino, 25 to 28 cents a pound; half-merino, 21 to 25 cents; American, 19 to 21 cents; half-American, 17 to 19 cents; Mexican, with crosses, 12 to 17 cents.[7]

California sheepmen followed the time-honored practices that came from Spain into the arid provinces of the Southwest, rather than those brought to the Atlantic seaboard from England. Owners divided their flocks into bands, customarily numbering from 1,000 to 2,000 animals, and put a herder in charge of each band.

Sheepherders as a class were looked upon almost as social outcasts. It was a calling in which a fugitive from society—or equally from himself—could easily conceal his identity and lose all contact with the past, and many broken men took refuge in it. "One of the great shepherds on the *Nacimiento*," said Stephen Powers, traveler and ethnologist, who wrote under the curious pen name of "Mr. Socrates Hyacinth," "told me that during one year, he employed on his *rancho* a bishop's son, a banker, an editor, a civil engineer, and a bookkeeper, all of them college alumni."[8]

By the very nature of his occupation, a sheepherder was called upon to live a life of extreme loneliness and solitude and some elements of danger. Like Moses of old, he led his flock to the backside of the desert and into the remote pastures of the high mountains. Sudden cloudbursts menaced the sheep in summer, and unseasonable snowstorms sometimes blocked their escape in early fall. Predatory animals, such as bears, coyotes, wildcats, and mountain lions, were a constant menace to the flock; and not infrequently the herder's own life might be jeopardized by Indians, grizzly bears, and lawless whites.[9]

Although sheep raising proved highly profitable in California before 1860, the industry experienced its greatest prosperity with the disruption of the cotton trade and the creation of a huge demand for wool during the Civil War. Monterey County was the center of the industry in California—a pre-eminence due primarily to the activities of half a dozen pioneer sheepmen, including the two Hollister brothers; Jotham, Llewelyn, and Marcellus Bixby; Dr. Thomas and Benjamin Flint; and James Irvine.[10]

Soon after the opening of the Civil War, some of the leading Monterey wool producers sought to extend their activities to Los Angeles County and to convert a number of its great cattle ranges into sheep pastures. W. W. Hollister offered to buy Pío Pico's share of the Rancho Los Coyotes for $11,000, and proposed to Abel Stearns to unite the Ranchos Los Coyotes, San Juan Cajón de Santa Ana, La Laguna, and La Ranchita into one enormous sheep ranch, to be operated under a partnership agreement.[11] Hollister and his associates agreed to furnish a hundred thousand dollars in sheep and cash to match Stearns's contribution of land.

If the arrangement had been carried through, Stearns might well have made a fortune during the next few years instead of barely escaping bankruptcy; but Don Abel was primarily a cattle ranchero of the old regime, and declined to enter into the partnership.[12] Although disappointed in their first efforts, the Monterey woolgrowers were able to take advantage of the collapse of the cattle industry after the drought and transformed many of the best-known southern ranches into sheep pastures.

In 1866 Dr. Thomas Flint, in co-operation with the Bixby family, purchased Juan Temple's 26,000-acre Rancho Los Cerritos for $20,000.[13] Subsequently the same group acquired a portion of the neighboring ranch of Los Alamitos; a large part of the Rancho Los Palos Verdes; half of the Ranchos San Joaquin and Las Lomas de Santiago and part of the old Rancho Santiago de Santa Ana.[14] By that time the wool boom was at its height, and throughout the south, sheep were taking the place of cattle as the principal product of the ranchos.[15]

According to Hittell, the annual cost of herding, pasturing, shearing, and providing for the general care of a flock of sheep amounted to only 35 cents per head. Each animal yielded an average of six and a half pounds of wool, which brought the grower from 18 to 35 cents a pound.[16] The profits, even heavily discounting Hittell's figures, thus made the business far more profitable than the proverbial gold mine.

Next to the livestock industry, viticulture was the most important industry in southern California. Wine making in California, primarily for local or household use, began soon after the Spanish occupation and played an important role both in mission and ranch life. Before secularization, the San Gabriel Mission vineyards contained approximately 50,000 vines and in 1844 Hugo Reid had nearly half that number on the Rancho Santa Anita.[17] The Gold Rush created an enormous thirst for California wines and brandies and a lesser demand for fresh grapes. Landowners, large and small, hurriedly planted vineyards to take advantage of the opportunity and the grape industry soon became one of the most important features of California's economic life.

Shortly after 1850, grapes began to be raised extensively in southern California, not only for conversion into wines and brandies, but also for direct shipment to the northern markets. In 1854, according to a report by A. F. Coronel, there were nearly 400,000 vines in Los Angeles County, yielding annually over 3,000,000 pounds of grapes.[18] Before the close of another decade, the Los Angeles vineyards contained more than 2,500,-000 vines; and by 1866 the number had increased to approximately 3,000,000, representing about a sixth of the vineyard acreage of the state.[19] The county was then producing annually some 600,000 gallons of wine and 70,000 gallons of brandy. Large quantities of fresh grapes were also being shipped to San Francisco and other northern cities.[20]

The "paper profits" of a California vineyard were highly attractive, according, at least, to the figures of one enthusiast. "One hundred acres make a very large vineyard," wrote Augustus Bixby in his diary. "50 acres make quite a large one. The average is 1,000 vines to the acre. Each vine yields an average of 10 lbs. of grapes. 12 lbs. are required to make a gallon of wine —which makes the average yield 833 gals. per acre which at 40 cents per gal. amounts to $33.20 or $16,660 from a 50-acre vineyard and $33,320 from 100 acres."[21]

Oranges and other fruits were raised commercially by a few enterprising ranchers; and according to W. C. Bartlett, there were 10,000 bearing orange trees in Los Angeles County in 1868, and 100,000 young stock in nurseries and orchards. Bartlett estimated the annual net profits at $50 a tree, or from $3,000 to $4,000 an acre! The expense and inadequacy of transportation greatly restricted all forms of horticulture, however, until the coming of the Southern Pacific Railroad to Los Angeles in 1876.[22]

Wheat farming, which dominated the Sacramento and San Joaquin valleys after the opening of the Civil War and furnished an epic chapter in the economic and social history of the state second only to that of the Gold Rush, made little progress in southern California until the opening of rail transportation. Corn was grown on a much more extensive scale, especially on the moist bottom lands about El Monte, Anaheim, and Santa Ana.[23] Reliable figures are not available to show the extent to which diversified farming developed at the expense of pasturage in Los Angeles County before the mid-sixties; but it is probable that at least 100,000 acres were under some form of cultivation by 1866.[24]

In contrast to the efficient and scientific methods of today, the farming practices of three-quarters of a century ago seem almost primitive. Oxen were still extensively used for plowing and other field work; power machinery was unknown; irrigation had made no real progress since the days of the missions. Climate and soil, however, to some degree compensated for inefficiency of agricultural implements and methods, and southern California soon acquired a legendary reputation for the phenomenal productivity of its farms.

Mexicans, of the peon class called cholos, and the descendants of the Mission Indians constituted almost the only available source of farm labor. "About San Bernardino the farm laborers are chiefly Indians," wrote Charles Nordhoff, the observant traveler and California publicist. "These people, of whom California has still several thousand, are a very useful class. They trim the vines; they plough; they do the household 'chores'; they are shepherds, and trusty ones too, vacqueros, and helpers generally. Mostly, they live among the whites and are their humble and, I judge, tolerably efficient ministers."

Describing the living conditions of the Indians on one of the large ranches, Nordhoff added:

Beyond the house itself, about fifteen feet distant, was a clay oven for baking bread, covered over with raw bull's hide, the hairy side downward, intended to keep the top dry in case it should rain; and beyond this, a few feet farther off, marking the boundary of what Western people call their "yard," was a range of open shanties, which, on riding up, I had innocently taken for cattle sheds. Here, close to the house, the Indians lived.

* * *

"They are poor creatures," said Senor M., with a shrug of his

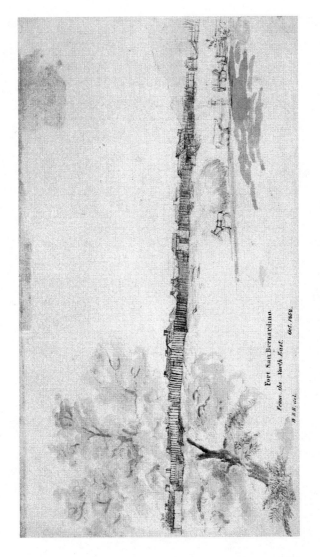

Fort San Bernardino.
From the North East.
Oct. 1852.

FORT SAN BERNARDINO

Rancho de los osos, Oct. 1850
San Francisco — Santa Barbara Profile —

THE RANCHO DE LOS OSOS

shoulders; "poor creatures, but quiet; not good for much, but useful."

"But where do they sleep?" I asked.

He pointed to a door, which opened into a lightly inclosed shed, which I had imagined to be the chicken-house. In the farther end truly, the chickens were at roost, but the larger part was floored with poles, on which barley-straw was spread, and here the Indians slept.[25]

Although agriculture constituted southern California's major industry, mining also filled an important place in the economic life of several counties. All true southern Californians felt that Nature had committed a colossal blunder in locating the state's world-famous gold fields north of the Tehachapi, instead of in the south where God unquestionably intended them to go. But with characteristic spirit Los Angeles newspapers sought to rectify the mistake by magnifying every local mining district into a second Mother Lode.

"Another field of labor is opening up to us," said the Los Angeles *Star* of December 3, 1859,

and that is the development of our mineral resources. In this branch, it has been heretofore considered that we were deficient; it has been supposed, that the deposits of the precious metals, ores, and minerals, were confined to the northern portion of the State; but such is very far from being the case. Lately investigation has directed itself to the mountain ranges of our county and district, and we are glad to say that discoveries have been made which prove them to be rich indeed in all the metals which attract emigrants to the north. Gold, silver, copper, tin, lead, are found, and not in one locality either, but spreading throughout the whole range of mountains which bounds our valley. Gold placers are now being worked, from Fort Tejon to San Bernardino. Rich deposits of this precious metal have lately been discovered in the northern part of the county, and this week we saw a bag of gold dust which had been panned out in that section during the rains, where formerly its existence was not dreamt of.

* * *

Miners are now at work in the San Fernando hills rolling out the gold, and in the hills beyond discoveries have been made which prove the whole district to be one grand gold placer. The mountains abound in gold-bearing quartz; and latterly silver ore has been discovered of almost fabulous richness.

Whatever causes exist to create a scarcity of the circulating medium at the present time, there is no reason to despond for our future. A bright career lies before our people. With propitious seasons, the plains will again be alive with cattle, the fields covered with luxuriant crops, the vineyards yield abundantly of their luscious fruit, the wine presses pour forth their generous liquid; whilst our mountains, gulches and ravines, will contribute their gold and silver, to recompense the toiling miner, and benefit all classes, the mechanic, as well as the merchant and trader.

Many of the deposits, discovered in the mountains and little-known deserts of southern California, were even rich enough to justify a measure of the glowing prophecy of the *Star*, and some of them eventually took their place among the historic bonanzas of the West. Southern California could also claim the site of the first gold discovery in California. Six years before Marshall found the yellow flakes in the tail race of Sutter's mill, California prospectors mined gold in Los Placeritos and Santa Feliciana cañons near the present town of Newhall.[26] "In this pueblo there is nothing new to note," wrote Abel Stearns in April, 1842,

except a few days since a mine of Gold was discovered about twelve leagues from this place which bids fair to be virry rich; the extent of the mine is not known but from the place where it was first discovered it has been followed a distance of three or four leagues and as the few persons employed proceed in washing out the gold in different places they find the grains larger and more abundant. There is here a few persons from Sonora who are acquainted with working mines of this class and are now engaged in this and they pronounce it is virry rich and extensive, we may expect a rich harvest of the precious metal, and many advantages to this place.[27]

Although the San Fernando mines fell short of Stearns's optimistic prediction, they did yield some thousands of dollars in dust and nuggets before the excitement died down in 1845. Five years later, the discovery of small additional deposits started a second short-lived rush to the Placerito field. "The placers at the Rancho de San Francisco are creating much excitement," wrote H. M. Nimmo to Stearns, in February, 1850, "miners are averaging from $11 or $20 a day—Antoine Robideaux has gone out with an assortment of merchandise and thinks the San Fernando mines will prove the equal of any in the south."[28]

In 1855 considerable quantities of gold were found in the Kern River Cañon—a discovery which gave rise to a brief but hectic stampede and enabled the Los Angeles newspapers to publish highly colored reports of the new fields. "Immense ten mule wagons strung out one after another;" said an article in the *Southern Californian*, "long trains of pack mules and men mounted and on foot with pick and shovel; boarding house keepers with their tents and articles of warfare; merchants with their stocks of miners necessities, and gamblers with their 'papers' are constantly leaving and thronging the roads to the mines."[29]

The failure of the Kern River field to yield the anticipated bonanza dampened only momentarily the optimism of the southern California enthusiasts. "We have little news of importance to present to our readers this week, relative to the mines," wrote a correspondent in the *Southern Californian* of March 28:

Parties are at work at the San Fernando and San Gabriel diggings and are *reported* as doing well. No doubt can exist in the minds of those who have paid any attention to the history of the explorations made in different portions of this section of the State, that the precious metals exist to a greater or less extent throughout this country from the Tejon to the Colorado, and thence along the entire borders of the Gila. These explorations it is true thus far have been very superficial, but wherever the pick has been struck in the neighborhood of the mountain ranges the gold has been invariably found.

It is a fact well known that one of the richest Quartz mines in the State exists on the Amagossa, about two hundred and sixty miles from here, which was worked by a company in '51, but owing to the hostility of the Indians, want of good water and grass for animals, and other causes it was found necessary to abandon the enterprise.

The recent discoveries in the county of San Diego is another confirmation of the correctness of our opinions. At no distant day mining will be prosecuted as extensively and with as much success as heretofore characterized the northern portion of the State.

The partial disappointment which has been experienced by those who on the spur of the moment have rushed to Kern River and other points where gold has been developed, is no evidence of their inadequacy to support a larger mining population. As in all excitements of this nature heretofore, the greater portion of those who have flocked to these diggings have been totally unacquainted with the business, entirely incapable of selecting the gold bearing localities, unprovided with the requisite tools and apparatus, destitute in many cases of even the necessaries of life, sporting men, speculators, whisky dealers, loafers and of course a fair sprinkling of thieves. That these classes should fail in their expectations, is no matter of surprise.

It is but the history of the past,—we are glad that it is so. It is infinitely more to the interests of our people that our hidden treasures should be gradually brought into activity by the hardy, industrious and enterprising portion of our people, who, satisfied with moderate winnings will eventually secure to themselves a competency and form a valuable acquisition to the population of this part of the State.

Hundreds of such are now at work, and will so continue, and as the sphere of their labors become extended will open up the golden veins which now remain hidden from the view, attracting thereby the attention of men of capital—who ever ready to invest in any feasible enterprise—will in good time scatter the Quartz crushers along the base of our mountains, pierce their jagged sides and turn the mountain streams from their courses to be rendered auxiliary to man in his pursuit of wealth.

Superlatively selfish men may feel inclined to repine at the sudden curtailments in the hitherto brisk demand for picks and shovels, rum and cigars, but let them husband the profits levied upon those who have recently passed onward to the imaginary goal of their bright hopes—enhanced still further on their return—with as much care and economy as during its acquisition, and they may safely await the realization of the prospect we have adverted to above.

The San Gabriel Cañon, source of the most important river in the Sierra Madre range, became the scene of an unusually rich bonanza in 1859. A short time after the initial discovery, the *Southern Vineyard* reported the location of a gold-bearing vein at least two miles long and said that three hundred prospectors were already working in the cañon.[30] Los Angeles newspapers carried the following advertisement:

San Gabriel Mines Stage Line!

The undersigned have established a line of Stages from this city to the above mines, leaving Los Angeles tri-weekly on Mondays, Wednesdays and Fridays at 7 A.M. Returning leaves Prospect Bar on Tuesdays, Thursdays and Saturdays.

Fare:

To San Gabriel Mission................$1
Santa Anita Mines...................... 2.50
Mouth of Canon....................... 3.00
Through to Prospect Bar............... 6.00

Express and Freight Business attended to on reasonable terms.

Roberts and Williams.[31]

The Los Angeles *Star* of March 10, 1860, stated that eight companies were engaged in bringing water into the camp called Eldoradoville, "so as to ground sluice or hydraulic wash." The article also included a very long and elaborate set of mining laws, embracing some twenty-seven items, and concluded by saying, "The writer of these lines is confident from his experiences in the upper country that . . . the returns of gold dust from the San Gabriel will be second to those of no other river in the state."[32]

During the course of the next few years, the cañon's innumerable bars and gravel beds yielded considerable quantities of gold; and mining camps, similar to those of the northern Sierra, sprang up and died away almost as rapidly as Jonah's celebrated gourd. True to type, such camps had their saloons, gambling houses, periodic shooting affrays, and self-imposed mining codes.

Shortly before the San Gabriel mines came into the spotlight, a company, capitalized at $50,000, was organized to exploit the placers of Santa Anita Cañon, not far from the present town of Sierra Madre. The excitement continued in a mild form for two or three years and a fair amount of gold was taken out of the district.[33] Mines were opened on a much larger scale in Bear and Holcomb valleys, near San Bernardino, leading to the establishment of several flourishing but short-lived mining camps in the regions now traversed by the popular "Rim of the World" highway.[34]

The discovery was made by a group of hunters and prospectors, one of whom, W. F. Holcomb, gave his name to the valley. By the summer of 1860 some 300 miners were at work in the Bear Valley district; and though heavy snows closed the mines during the ensuing winter, the following spring witnessed a typical rush to the new diggings, including a large element of roughs and gamblers, that made the mining districts the most populous sections of the county. Hydraulic mining was carried on successfully in the cañon of Lytle Creek and a number of important discoveries were made in the Colorado and Mojave desert areas.

In the early sixties the gold mining district known as La Paz, on the lower Colorado River, attracted prospectors from every part of the state, and for a time the mines, according to common report, yielded as high as $10,000 a week. A few individuals made a hundred dollars or more a day; and a company of five men cleaned up $2,000 in three days. The price of food and supplies, however, robbed the miner of most of his profits. Freight rates from Los Angeles came to 12 or 15 cents a pound; and speculators who spent two weeks driving cattle from the coast ranges to La Paz received ample compensation for their pains.[35]

Santa Catalina Island was the scene of a mining boom in 1863; two years later copper was found in Soledad Cañon, through which the Southern Pacific Railroad now runs; and for a time the tin deposits of Temescal Cañon, in Riverside County, gave promise of making the region a second Cornwall and attracted a substantial investment of English capital.[36]

Prospectors and members of punitive expeditions sent against the Indians made known both the mineral and agricultural possibilities of the Owens Valley and brought about its settlement in the early sixties. Mines were opened at Coso, Benton, Darwin, Esmeralda, Cerro Gordo, and elsewhere in the inconceivably barren wastes between the Sierra Nevada Mountains and the Colorado River.[37]

The mining camp known as Cerro Gordo became the most famous in the region. It was discovered, probably, in 1865, and produced over $17,000,000 during the next decade. "Transportation of the bullion was a problem," according to W. A. Chalfant,

and it was not unusual for the furnaces to shut down because of being too far ahead of the teams. For a while hauling contracts were made with any and all comers, but this proved unsatisfactory, and the mine owners organized the Cerro Gordo Freighting Company.

They associated Nadeau, a teamster, with them; he took active charge, and made a fortune from the service. The corporation became the dominant factor in Inyo transportation, . . . The line was equipped with huge wagons, each hauled by sixteen to twenty animals. Fifty-six of these outfits were on the road, and still could not move the bullion to tidewater half as fast as it rolled from the furnaces. Some relief was given by the building of the small steamer Bessie Brady, a craft of 85 feet length and 16 feet beam. This vessel plying between Swansea, at the northeastern corner of the lake, Ferguson's Landing, at the northwestern, and Cartago, at the southwestern, took eight days out of the round trips of the teams, yet the increased number of trips of the wagons could not move the bullion fast enough. To see the bullion piled up like cordwood at different points was quite the usual thing.[38]

As already indicated, a considerable part of the business of Los Angeles merchants came from furnishing isolated mining districts with food and supplies, and from the transportation of freight between the mines and the pueblo.[39]

Before the advent of the railroads, inadequate transportation was one of the most serious economic and social problems of the grazing and farming regions as well as of the mines.[40] A region of vast distances, utterly lacking in navigable streams, shut off (except by sea) from outside markets, hemmed in by a back country of rugged mountains and wide deserts, southern California suffered the destructive blight of almost complete cultural and commercial isolation for a generation. Before the coming of the Americans, travel was almost entirely by horseback; shipment of goods and merchandise was by pack train, or in the crude California oxcarts called *carretas*; and roads were little more than bridle paths.

For a long time after the conquest, state legislatures had too little interest in the sparsely populated and politically unimportant "cow counties" to make appropriations for road building and other public works in southern California; and county boards of supervisors, sensitive to the opposition of their constituents to higher taxes, were equally apathetic. The wagon road across the steep San Fernando grade north of Los Angeles furnished an excellent example of this official indifference and neglect.

For many years this principal stage-and-wagon route to northern California used a narrow gap, known as Frémont Pass, to cross the rugged San Fernando Mountains. At one point the pass was so steep that teamsters, reverting to the last resort of overland immigrant trains, were often compelled to use ropes to raise or lower their heavy wagons.

The barrier which thus so seriously retarded the development of Los Angeles County, and indeed of a large part of the remainder of southern California, could have been eliminated at the cost of a few thousand dollars, but nothing was done, either by the state or county governments. Finally, in 1855, a group of private citizens subscribed sufficient funds to change the grade and make the road more suitable for freight and passenger service.[41]

Gradually other wagon roads were constructed or improved; wheeled vehicles came into general use; and in the end, adequately-financed, well-equipped companies undertook the transportation of mail, passengers, and express. The Butterfield Overland Mail Company opened its famous stage service from St. Louis to Los Angeles and San Francisco in 1858; and trains of high-wheeled freight wagons forced their slow way along the desolate Mormon trail from San Bernardino to Salt Lake City, or across the desert wastes to the Owens, Mojave, and Colorado rivers.[42] In 1861 the transcontinental telegraph line was extended from San Francisco to Los Angeles.[43]

For many years Los Angeles, San Diego, Santa Barbara, and San Luis Obispo were the chief centers of population south of Monterey. But every large hacienda or rancho, like its counterpart in Mexico, served as the nucleus of a small, self-sustaining community, which, in some cases, ultimately developed into a prosperous town.[44]

A few immigrants coming into California over the southern route in 1851 founded the town of El Monte, approximately twelve miles east of Los Angeles, on the San Gabriel River. The following year about fifty additional families joined the original colonists, and the "Monte" soon became known as one of the most productive agricultural regions in the state. The settlers, usually spoken of as the "Monte Boys," were southern Democrats of the fire-eating type, who brought with them the turbulent traditions and independent spirit of the Texan frontier.[45]

A few months after the founding of El Monte, a train consisting of 437 persons, 150 wagons, and a considerable body of livestock came through the Cajón Pass to establish an outpost of the Mormon empire in southern California. According to Milton H. Hunter, Brigham Young intended

to build a station near the Pacific Ocean that could be used as an outfitting post for immigrants bound for Utah, and as a shipping point. It was to be the gateway settlement from the Pacific into the Mormon commonwealth—an outpost of the greatest importance. February 23, 1851, President Young selected two apostles "to take a company to southern California to preside over the affairs of the Church in that land and to establish a stronghold for the gathering of the Saints." . . . Early in April Brigham wrote:

"Amasa M. Lyman and Charles C. Rich left this place . . . with others . . . for the purpose of establishing a settlement in the southern part of California, at no great distance from San Diego, and near Williams' ranch and the Cajon Pass, between which and Iron County we design to establish settlements as speedily as possible, which Elder Lyman will commence on his route, if practicable, so as to have a continued line of stations and places of refreshment between this point and the Pacific, which route is passable during the winter months."

After President Young had sent the colonists to California in the spring of 1851, he instructed Franklin D. Richards, President of the European Mission, to "open every desirable correspondence in relation to the various routes, and rates, and conveniences, from Liverpool to San Diego, and make an early report so that if possible the necessary preparations may be made for next fall's emigration."

The Saints in the countries bordering the Pacific were instructed to travel directly to San Diego and then to San Bernardino from which place they could, if they wished, go to the Basin.

* * *

At this time [1853] Young intended to make San Bernardino a second Salt Lake City—that is, a gathering place for thousands of his followers who could best live under southern California conditions. The seaport of San Diego was looked upon by Brigham Young as the logical ending of the Mormon Corridor, but further investigation would probably have revealed to the colonizer's keen mind that San Pedro would be a better terminus.[46]

The location selected for the Mormon settlement, a tract of eight square leagues originally granted in 1842, by Governor Alvarado, to Diego Sepúlveda and the Lugo family, was well chosen. The land had excellent agricultural possibilities; thousands of acres of virgin forests in nearby mountains were available for timber; and the overland trade routes, both to Salt Lake City and Santa Fé, ran through the pass adjacent to the site.[47]

In laying out the town of San Bernardino, the colonists followed the general pattern of Salt Lake City. With characteristic energy they set about developing farms, building irrigation works, erecting flour and grist mills, and forcing the lofty mountains, which rose like a rampart above the little settlement, to supply them with lumber and various other materials. But the colonists did not find life in San Bernardino altogether an unmixed blessing. Their farms were exposed to the depredations of Indians and outlaws; and the strong anti-Mormon sentiment then prevalent in most western communities led to a measure of social and economic ostracism.

The hostility engendered by the Mountain Meadows Massacre, together with the possibililty of a conflict with the federal government, eventually led Brigham Young to summon the San Bernardino colonists back to Utah.[48] Most of those who obeyed were compelled to sell their farms at a great sacrifice, but a few of the original colonists declined to abandon their holdings and remained permanently at San Bernardino. Commenting upon the withdrawal the *Star* said:

The exodus of the Mormons from San Bernardino, is giving an opportunity to those who are desirous of fixing themselves permanently, in one of the most desirable localities in the State, to accomplish their wishes under the most favorable circumstances. That our readers may judge for themselves, we give some items of sales recently made. One tract of eighty-two acres, that cost $10.50 per acre, fenced with a good picket fence, which cost two dollars per rod, the entire tract under cultivation, with good ditches for irrigation, was sold for $500. One lot of two and a half acres, in the city, with a good dwelling house, blacksmith's and wagon maker's shops, out houses, and one hundred and fifty fruit trees, forty of which are bearing, was sold for $300. Another tract, containing 600 acres, under fence, on which were 7,500 grape vines, and was assessed last year at $10,000, sold for $1,500. A tract of 300 acres, under fence, having 500 peach trees, in fruit, and 350 young trees, assorted fruits; a good distillery, which cost $17,000; a flouring mill, with two run of stones; a saw mill; all in first rate condition, with unfailing water power, was sold for $6,000. This property cost not less than $75,000. The titles to all this property is unexceptionable.

There cannot be less than one hundred improved farms, with comfortable dwellings, now for sale in that county.[49]

Nearly nine months later, the *Star* printed a document which showed indirectly the extent of the Mormon exodus. It may be remarked, too, in passing, that the document was as typical of the old time, direct spoken, often only semi-literate frontier sheriff, as the gray-white sage bush was typical of the brushlands of that day. The article said:

A document is on file in the office of the State Controller, which may be considered a curiosity. It is the delinquent tax list of San Bernardino county for the years 1855, 1857, as furnished June 30th, 1858, by Joseph Bridger, sheriff of said county and ex officio collector. It contains twelve feet in length of delinquent names, and opposite to each, remarks designating the particular reasons why the respective taxes could not be collected of their owners. Most of the delinquents appear to have been Mormons, who found it convenient from time to time to remove their "household goods" to the Salt Lake Zion. The preparation of so voluminous a document, with the examination that was necessarily made into the circumstances of each person may be regarded as alike creditable to the industry and inventive faculty of the sheriff. We will particularize a few of the expressions which may be found in that document: "Gone to Salt Lake," "gone to glory," "gone to glory with three steers," "gone to Zion," "gone to h——, and he ought to," "under arrest for grand larceny," "got nothing, nary red," "couldn't find him," "not worth a red," "old cripple, and unable to pay," "gone crazy, in the hospital," "gone to glory and found no property," etc.[50]

In 1857 a group of fifty Germans, most of whom were residents of San Francisco, subscribed $2,500 to purchase a tract of 1,200 acres of the Rancho San Juan Cajón de Santa Ana from Don Bernardo Yorba and Don Pacífico Ontiveras, and began the experiment in co-operative community development called Anaheim.

After setting aside two hundred acres for a town, the colonists divided the remainder of the land into twenty-acre tracts, which were planted to vineyards, gardens, and fruit trees. Water for irrigation was obtained from the Santa Ana River and distributed to each plot by a series of lateral canals, or *zanjas*.

Forty thousand willow poles, planted eighteen inches apart,

were used to make a live fence about the property. The upright cuttings, which were set to project six feet above ground, were "strengthened by three horizontal poles, and defended by a ditch four feet deep, six feet wide at the top, sloping to a breadth of one foot at the bottom."[51] The barrier soon became impenetrable, even to herds of starving cattle made frantic by the drought.

Under its co-operative plan of management, the Anaheim colony planted, fenced, and cultivated the land for two years. At the end of that time, the twenty-acre plots were appraised and awarded to the individual colonists by lot. The average value of the holdings, including all improvements, was about $500. In case a plot was appraised at a higher figure, the recipient paid the difference into the common treasury; but if the value was less than $500, the owner received the difference in cash. Within a year the individual holdings had appreciated about a hundred per cent in value.[52]

In addition to the three settlements just mentioned, a number of less important towns were laid out, at least on paper, before 1860. In 1858 Banning founded San Pedro New Town, or Wilmington. Five years later J. Ross Browne wrote:

Wilmington is an extensive city located at the head of a slough in a pleasant neighborhood of sand banks and marshes. There are not a great many houses in it yet, but there is a great deal of room for houses when the population gets ready to build them. The streets are broad, and beautifully paved with small sloughs, ditches, bridges, lumber, dry-goods boxes, and the carcasses of dead cattle.[53]

Despite the successful establishment of settlements at El Monte, San Bernardino, and Anaheim, southern California made little appeal to prospective colonists until drought and bankruptcy, completing the ruin of the cattle industry, brought about the subdivision of many of the large ranchos into farms and homesteads, and led to concerted efforts to stimulate immigration and attract settlers.[54] Such changes brought about a wider distribution of wealth, the growth of diversified agriculture, a striking increase in immigration, the construction of new roads, noticeable reduction in lawlessness, and marked expansion in the number of public schools. The following chapter deals at length with these factors and the new southern California which they created.

CHAPTER IX

The Genesis of a New Social and Economic Order

RESPONSIBILITY for the economic backwardness of southern California prior to 1865, and for the prolonged lag in wealth and population from which the region suffered, was popularly ascribed to the Spanish-Mexican land-grant system, the obstinate refusal of rancheros to subdivide their immense holdings, and the obstacles placed in the way of settlers and small farmers by truculent and selfish landowners. As the editor of the *Southern News* declared:

No one who has resided in Los Angeles county for a twelve-month, is surprised at the continued repulses given to visitors and strangers who come to this section of California for the purpose of settling. ... All are told that this country is "played out," and that there are no chances, etc. The latter assertion is made too true by those who would wish to have it understood that they ... own most of the land in the form of now almost bare ranches. ... The majority of ranches in this county have been stripped of their former herds of stock at high prices ... and large tracts of land are daily becoming more and more valueless. ... The best portion of our county is covered by large grants, thus confining cultivation ... to a few points where Government land can be obtained; and which, if occupied, would in numerous instances be claimed as a portion of somebody's ranch. The reasons for the present condition of Los Angeles county, with respect to improvement, are clearly chargeable to the indisposition of grant owners. If no change is permitted, ruin must be the ultimate result.[1]

The indictment of the great landowners as economic obstructionists was by no means confined to southern California. Commenting upon conditions in Marin County, in 1863, William H. Brewer wrote:

160

The finest grazing district I have yet seen in the state is among these hills, lying near the sea, moistened by fogs in the summer when the rest of the state is so dry. But the curse of Marin County is the Spanish grant system. The whole county is covered with Spanish grants, and held in large ranches, so settlers cannot come in and settle up in smaller farms. The county is owned by not over thirty men, if we except men who have small portions near the bay or near some villages. As a consequence, there is but one schoolhouse, one post office, etc., in the whole county, although so near San Francisco.

From the County Surveyor's map I find that there are 330,000 acres of land in the county, of which less than 2,000 acres were ever public lands—in fact, only 1,500 acres besides some little islands. The rest of the county is covered by twenty-three "grants" of which seventeen are over 8,000 acres each! ... No wonder that the country does not fill up.[2]

Later in the decade the State Surveyor-General reiterated the charges made by Brewer and the editor of the *Southern News*. "The state should use every exertion to promote immigration of the industrious classes from Europe," he urged. "We want workers; we have non-producers enough already; we have doctors, lawyers, clerks, and politicians in abundance; we now want farmers, mechanics, artisans, and winegrowers; ... I deem it my duty, in connection with the foregoing to call your attention to the evil of land monopolies. This is, and has been, the great drawback to the settling of our fair State."[3]

It is not necessary to inquire how far the opinions voiced above were applicable to conditions in other parts of the state; but, after impartial examination, one is forced to conclude that the condemnation of large landholdings, as the sole cause of southern California's economic backwardness, was an oversimplification of a highly involved, many-sided problem.

The survival of the great cattle ranches of the Spanish-Mexican period was, in fact, not so much the reason for the south's retarded development as its logical result; and the landowners as a class had little more control over the fundamental causes which prevented the subdivision of the ranchos than the settlers themselves.[4] Large landholdings persisted because of a chronic dearth of capital and prohibitive interest rates; uncertainty and confusion in land titles; the Trespass Act and other legislation which favored the grazing interests at the expense of settlers; restricted markets and lack of transportation; and inadequate facilities for irrigation.

Except for moist tracts in river bottoms, most of which were subject to periodic floods, little range land in southern California could be farmed successfully without irrigation; and irrigation had made almost no advance since the secularization of the missions in 1833. Under such conditions, it was economically impossible for southern California, a land of limited rainfall and "sun-burned rivers," to support a large population; for rancheros to convert more than a small fraction of their grazing lands into farms; or for large numbers of settlers to find land suitable for diversified crops and intensive cultivation.

Stephen Powers, an intelligent, well-informed traveler, who wandered up and down the state, chiefly on foot, and visited many other portions of the semiarid Southwest during the late sixties and early seventies, summed up the situation as follows:

California is not *now* a good home for small men. More than any other State I know of, it is a theatre for pioneer operations in the large, and is no place for patches. Rich men must occupy the dry lands, and dig costly wells, and cut long trenches, and then give liberal terms to tenants, or small purchasers. . . .

Nature is obstinate here and must be broken with steam and with steel. Until strong men take hold of the State this way and break it in—I speak of southern California which I have seen—its agriculture will be the merest clod whacking. . . .

If there is one thing more than another that the State now needs, it is a class of keen, intelligent, small landowners to serve as a foil against the plutocracy to which it is inclined. Muscle is unequally pitted against drought; and gold must come generously to its succor, or the growth of the yeomanry will be stunted.... The glorious fat valleys of southern California are asking only for a drink of water, and offer in return for it immeasurable barley; but nobody gives it. Take a loose-woven cobweb, and slide a drop of dew along the threads, and you have all the farms there are.[5]

The dearth of capital, to which Stephen Powers referred, was unquestionably one of southern California's greatest handicaps. Immigrants and settlers brought little money with them; large landowners, financially prostrate since the early sixties, were in no better case; usurious interest rates foredoomed any attempt to develop farm lands with borrowed capital. Few rancheros were therefore in a position to supply their land with water, either by sinking wells or by building dams and canals; and without water the land was wholly unfit for diversified farming or large-scale settlement.

All other economic activities, as well as agriculture and immigration, felt this blight of insufficient capital. "The scarcity of money clogs the wheels of business and is an impediment to all legitimate enterprise," said a memorial to the state legislature in 1870. "Business men with the best securities find it difficult to get bank accommodation. Money for ordinary purposes cannot be obtained."[6] According to many well-informed writers, California's chief financial difficulties arose from a venal, stupid, and corrupt legislative policy which delivered the state's banking system into the hands of a group of unscrupulous aliens and allowed a few powerful monopolies to strangle all forms of business. "Every avenue of trade and travel," said the author of a popular guidebook to the West, "every branch of industry, every profession and calling . . . is monopolized by a company . . . which drives all competition away and raises the price of everything."[7]

In addition to these evils, the farmers were beset by high

freight rates, excessive commission fees, and the exactions of an
endless chain of middlemen. "Our agricultural population of
24,000 has produced $75,000,000 almost entirely without the
aid of capital," wrote J. Ross Browne in 1873.

No banks . . . have stood ready to take shares in their enterprises
and back them by heavy loans; their stock has never drawn forth
the millions hoarded on California Street. . . .[8] Let any farmer who
desires to dyke, drain, irrigate, or fence his land: to plant a fruit
orchard, a vineyard or an orange grove; to go into the business of
cotton raising, silk growing or the manufacture of beet-sugar—all
sound and legitimate enterprises, well tested on this coast—let such
a farmer undertake to raise money in San Francisco at a reasonable
rate of interest, and he will find that the money market is unusually
tight. By working at it a long time, offering ruinous rates of interest,
sharing his prospective profits liberally, and giving security to the
amount of three to one, he may possibly be accommodated, but I
would be sorry to invest largely in his chances. The fact that his
enterprise is sound and legitimate is sufficient to damn it.

The truth is, the grain merchants, the hucksters, the middlemen,
the shippers, the railroad men, the sack-makers, the law-makers, the
assessors, and the tax collectors, manage to hold the agricultural
classes in a condition of servitude unparalleled in a free country.[9]

As concrete examples of the farmers' grievances, Browne
pointed out that the consumer in San Francisco paid a dollar and
a half a bottle for wine for which the Los Angeles vintner received only eight cents; that the middleman bought grapes in
southern California at ten cents a pound and sold them in the
northern cities for seventy-five cents; and that commission
houses, not content with reasonable profits and oblivious to the
welfare of producer and consumer alike, created an artificial
market, from which they alone profited, by dumping large
quantities of fruit into San Francisco Bay.

The difficulties of the southern farmer were further increased
by lack of local demand, limited transportation facilities, and
complete financial dependence upon the bankers and money

brokers of San Francisco, who had a monopoly of the fluid capital in the state.

The evolution from grazing lands to small farms, so essential to a more advanced economic· and social order, was further retarded, as we have already seen, by the uncertainty of land titles and the difficulty of obtaining bona fide deeds, whether to homesites of a few acres or to ranches measured in square leagues.

California land titles were, in fact, so muddled and confused, even down to the close of the Civil War, that the state itself could not give satisfactory deeds to its own public lands. "The General Government," said a report of the State Agricultural Society in 1864, "has donated to this State, for various purposes, about eight million nine hundred and fifty thousand six hundred and eighty acres of land ... yet, at this late day, the State, even, has not a title to one single acre, and is not able to make good her promises [to furnish a clear title] to one of the many thousands of persons who have purchased of her in good faith nearly the whole amount of these grants."[10]

The report added that under such circumstances few settlers were willing to make permanent improvements on their lands or to plant crops which required more than a few months to mature. Many holders of state lands had consequently abandoned their holdings; while others, in an effort to anticipate the invalidation of their titles, were resorting to the most wasteful methods of cultivation, robbing the soil of its fertility and leaving it permanently impoverished.

Edward H. Hall, author of the guidebook, *The Great West*, found this confusion of land titles chiefly responsible, both for the "migrating and unsettled habits" of a large element in the state's population, and for "the unstable character of its business."[11] Southern newspapers often declared that dubious and insecure land titles discouraged immigration, destroyed the foundation of true prosperity, and constituted one of the state's most serious economic drawbacks. The fifteen-year-old settlement of El Monte, according to the *Southern News*, furnished a striking example of the hurtful effects of such confusion. Situated in the midst of one of the loveliest, most fertile regions of the state and blessed with every attraction nature could bestow, the community still remained a "lick-skillet town," conspicuously lacking in economic or cultural advantages.

The rancheros suffered, even worse than the settlers, from the confusion and long-continued uncertainty in land titles. In the expressive phraseology of the day, "nobody wanted to buy a lawsuit," and hard-pressed landowners, many of whom were on the verge of bankruptcy, were forced to throw their title-clouded, squatter-infested ranchos on the bargain counter and accept whatever they were offered. "From 1865 to 1880," said Hallock F. Raup, citing one historic case, "seventy-eight law suits, six partition suits, a dozen law suits for the ejection of squatters, three condemnation suits . . . and much other litigation over Palos Verdes lands took place."[12]

Yet, notwithstanding the handicaps mentioned above, southern California began to make rapid social and economic progress after 1865, and to lay some of the lasting foundations for its present phenomenal development. This transformation was due to many factors, one of the most significant of which was the large immigration of settlers at the close of the Civil War.

It is a truism to say that California has been the most widely and effectively publicized state in the Union. Such publicity can be traced almost to the beginning of California history, and indirectly proved the most important of many factors in bringing about the annexation of the province by the United States. The spectacular events of the Gold Rush focused the attention of the world upon the new land. After 1849 an endless stream of books, descriptive articles, and persuasive private letters continued to keep popular interest actively alive, and land and colonization companies added their contributions to the flood of seductive publicity.[13]

The release of enormous numbers of men from military service, in the mid-sixties, gave new impetus to the trans-Rocky Mountain migration; and the demoralization brought about by war and Reconstruction led hundreds of families in the former Confederate States to seek opportunity for economic rehabilitation in the Far West. "The movement of population, native as well as foreign, over this continent," said Hall in 1865, "is greater at this time than at any former period of our history. The close of the war, the demand for labor in the West, the consequent high rate of wages which prevail there, and the almost certain competence and probable wealth which is always within the reach of the enterprising laborer in the mines, all contribute to swell the tide of immigration settling into the Eldorado of the West."[14]

Hall's swelling "tide of immigration . . . into the Eldorado of the West" constituted a significant, but heretofore almost neglected, phase of the westward movement. The story of the adventures, sufferings, and day-by-day experiences of the overland parties which came to California during the colorful days of the Gold Rush appealed irresistibly to the popular imagination and became the greatest of Western epics. But the drama of the immigrant trains that crossed the continent after the mining era, though enacted on an equally heroic scale, finds little place in the histories of the West.

Until the Pacific Railroad made the Far West only a romantic memory and a name, however, thousands of settlers came annually to California by the overland routes. These later immigrants followed the same trails their predecessors had traveled, endured the same hardships, traversed the same long miles of monotony and weariness, crossed the same passes, encountered the same

danger from unseasonable autumn snows, suffered the same
thirst on pitiless, mirage-haunted deserts, encountered the same
dread pestilences that stalked the wagon trains of 1849, and
faced the same grim horror of Indian massacre. Our long failure
to recognize the dramatic quality and heroic proportions of this
post-Argonaut migration constitutes a strange case of historical
myopia.

Following the practice adopted by emigrant companies as
early as 1841, California-bound wagon trains of the fifties and
sixties left the Missouri or New Mexican frontier in early spring,
and endeavored to reach the coast before the first snowfall.
Three main roads led to California. Most popular of the three
was the route adopted by the Butterfield Overland Mail Company, running from St. Louis to Houston, El Paso, Tucson,
Yuma, Warner's Ranch, and Los Angeles. North of the Butterfield route lay the so-called Beale road. Starting at Taos, New
Mexico, this road passed the bold, historic landmark called El
Morro, crossed the Colorado River at the Mojave villages, and
thence found its way, through the Cajón Pass, to Los Angeles.
The third route was the familiar Platte River-South Pass road,
running from Missouri, via Fort Hall, to Great Salt Lake. There,
southern-California-bound emigrants usually took the old Mormon trail along the Sevier and Virgin rivers to Las Vegas and
San Bernardino.[15]

In one important respect, California immigration in the fifties
and sixties differed materially from that of the Gold Rush. The
expeditions of 1849 were composed chiefly of men; later overland parties represented the migration of households and families. The members of such companies, instead of planning an
immediate return to "the States" after making a fortune in the
mines, sought permanent homes in the new land, and brought
with them their wives, children, household effects, farming implements, livestock, and even seed.[16]

As already suggested, the economic prostration of the Confederacy and the harsh conditions imposed by the congressional policy of Reconstruction, led many families from the stricken southern states to move to California at the close of the Civil War. A typical instance of such refugee emigration was furnished by a company of fifty Mississippi families, from "among the best people of the state," who proposed to purchase 10,000 acres in California and there find an opportunity to restore their broken fortunes.[17] It was also reported that a number of families planned to move from Danville, Kentucky, to the vicinity of Los Angeles.[18] A considerable Southern migration likewise found its way, during the Reconstruction era, into the San Joaquin Valley.

"The superintendents and upper employers on the place," wrote Bishop, concerning a large ranch near Bakersfield,

are largely Southern men. California was a favorite point for Southern immigration at one time, so much that the course of the State in the war . . . was considered problematical. These that I speak of, however, are gentlemen who have come here to repair their fortunes at a later period. They have for the most part titles from the service of the extinct Confederacy, and the gentle voices and friendly courtesy characteristic of the Southern type.[19]

The publicity which carried the fame of California's climate and resources across the continent and thereby kept a constantly increasing stream of immigration flowing into the state, was almost as effective in Europe as in the United States. J. Ross Browne, one of the best-known lecturers and most prolific writers on California of that day, planned a tour of the British Isles in 1868 to advertise the fertility, cheapness, and other desirable qualities of land in Los Angeles County.[20]

To a company of Hollanders, who were thinking of emigrating to California and had requested information on the public lands in southern California, J. S. Wilson, Commissioner of the General Land Office, gave an inviting picture:

It will be observed that the good lands of Southern California are found on the Pacific . . . extending inland from twenty-five to seventy-five miles, embracing an area susceptible of cultivation and admirably adapted to horticulture, equal in extent to the State of Massachusetts.

The climate of these valleys, some little distance from the coast, is not surpassed in any portion of the world; . . . Numerous streams of water flow through these valleys—many of them permanent—furnishing the means of irrigating large bodies of land. The grape vine flourishes here luxuriantly; . . .

But the soil and climate of these valleys are equally well adapted to the growth of the orange, lemon, lime, citron, fig, walnut, olive, banana, almond, filbert, and currant; and wheat, barley, corn, potatoes, cotton, tobacco, and sugar cane thrive well. In an orange grove of 2,000 trees, near Los Angeles, the annual crop averages 1,500 oranges to each tree, some of the trees producing as many as 4,000 each. The sides and summits of the mountains contain an abundance of pine, cedar, hemlock, maple, and oak; and deposits of gold, silver, copper, tin, marble, alabaster, asphaltum, sulphur, salt and coal are numerous.

* * *

Hundreds of thousands of acres of the finest lands, blest with a climate equal to that of the fairest portions of Italy, are held under Mexican grants, and are either entirely unoccupied or devoted to grazing; the proprietors, however, manifesting a willingness to subdivide and sell their claims as rapidly as the increase of settlers creates a demand.[21]

Typical of the publications designed to attract British immigrants to the state, was Carr's *Illustrated Hand-Book of California*, published in London in 1870. Flattering descriptions of the climate and resources of the region; tables of statistics; scenes of natural grandeur; lists of products, both real and imaginary; information on steamship and railroad travel; advice to immigrants; extracts from articles, in leading London newspapers, on California—all were made available in this one small book.

"California only needs immigration to make her rank as one

of the wealthiest States in the Union," wrote Carr, in a typical paragraph.

She has room for millions, who could be most profitably engaged in developing her unrivalled resources of agricultural and mineral wealth. She needs more varied crops, more prudence in living, and industry among her people. . . . To the honest, energetic, and industrious there are opportunities to acquire wealth, either by farming, mining, or mechanics, that cannot be found in other States. With the same energy, industry, and prudence that are exercised by the population of the middle States, California would, when properly peopled, outstrip in the value of her annual crops the States of New York, Pennsylvania, Ohio, and Indiana combined. She has the area of soil, fertility, and climate, that, if taken advantage of, will make the above statement, not an idle boast, but a reality.[22]

The cumulative effect of such encomiastic publicity was enormous. California captivated the popular imagination; and southern California, especially, because of its scenery, sunshine, and flowers, came to be thought of as akin to the "island-valley of Avilion," or as a counterpart of some other fabulous land of medieval romance.

As early as 1866 the increase of population led to a mild building boom in Los Angeles, and caused "a greater demand for lots than ever before in the city's history." The next two years, thanks in part to the anticipated completion of the transcontinental railroad, witnessed an unprecedented movement of settlers to southern California. "The tide of immigration will be immense this season," wrote the editor of the Los Angeles *Semi-weekly News* in August, 1868; and his prophecy was soon justified by the arrival of a number of huge overland trains, some of which contained over five hundred persons and at least a hundred wagons.

As further evidence that the region, "so long backward and wanting in enterprise," had at last outgrown its economic swaddling clothes, the *News* later declared that more than eight hundred new names had been added during the year to the tax rolls of Los Angeles County. Thanks to the subdivision of large ranchos, reasonable prices for farm lands, a measure of clarification of land titles, and the county's unrivaled natural advantages, the editor also predicted that Los Angeles would soon outdistance every other portion of the state, except San Francisco, in wealth and population.[23]

The influx of settlers, and the consequent demand for small farms, brought about a small real estate boom, and gave southern California a slight foretaste—or solemn warning—of what the future would periodically hold in store. By 1867 owners and land agents had begun to advertise the subdivision of large ranches for the benefit of settlers and colonists. One company alone offered 100,000 acres for such purposes. Former Governor John G. Downey advertised that 20,000 acres of choice agricultural land, situated sixteen miles from Los Angeles, would be subdivided into 50-acre tracts and sold on the installment plan for ten dollars an acre, with interest on deferred payments at the low rate of ten per cent per annum. A colony of a hundred families sought to purchase a portion of the Rancho La Laguna from Abel Stearns, and his agent informed him that settlers in large numbers were "running over the ranchos," looking for choice farm sites.[24]

About this time the publicity which southern California had received in Europe began to bear fruit. Through the agency of the Danish Consul in San Francisco, a colony of Danes purchased 5,000 acres for subdivision into small farms. An English investor began tentative negotiations for 100,000 acres, or more, for settlers from the British Isles. Abel Stearns was asked to consider the sale of a large part of his holdings to immigrants from "England, Ireland, and Scotland." It was reported that German colonists were looking for a tract of land on which to establish a second Anaheim, and that French and Swiss settlers were negotiating for the ranchos Azusa and Santa Anita.[25]

Real estate prices quickly responded to this increased demand. The same type of land which sold for seventy-five cents an acre in 1866 brought twice that amount a year later.[26] By 1868 the price of ranch land near Los Angeles, as we have already seen, had risen to ten dollars an acre. Early in that year the Rancho Tujunga was sold for $3,300; four months later it brought $6,600. The Brent, or Marengo, Ranch, purchased for $10,000, was resold within a year for $25,000. The value of real estate transactions in Los Angeles County rose from $40,000 in January, 1868, to $200,000 in January, 1869.[27]

The boom in real estate, the rising tide of immigration, and the realization that a new economic era was at hand, created a lively spirit of optimism in Los Angeles and fired the highly volatile imagination of its citizens. "We doubt," said the editor of the *Semi-weekly News*, in an inspired, if slightly involved, eulogy,

if there is any city on the Pacific Coast of equal wealth and population that has more reason to be proud of the many enterprises set on foot for the improvement not only of the city but of the surrounding country than Los Angeles. Whatever is in the future for this city, and with her vast natural resources and unequalled climate, backed and supported by rich mines, broad and fertile valleys of agricultural land, with a great wealth of oranges, lemons, limes, figs, grapes and a hundred other varieties of tropical and semi-tropical fruits, with corn, wheat and barley fields, unrivalled in the amount produced per acre, already numbering far into the thousands of acres, and large numbers of mulberry trees and cocooneries and silk factories in the not distant future rivalling those of France and the East, and the thousands of immigrants that are now daily settling up and populating our fertile valleys, no man can fix a limit to the prosperity and greatness of this city in the future. Her citizens will look with pride upon the enterprises commenced in the year 1868.[28]

The chief local business undertakings which called forth the editor's panegyric were a gas plant, an ice factory, two banks, and the Los Angeles & San Pedro Railroad, which ran between Los Angeles and Phineas Banning's embryonic port of Wilmington.[29] As an item of minor interest, it may be added that before the opening of the local ice factory, ice was shipped by sea from San Francisco to Los Angeles where it sold for 15 cents a pound. According to the *Southern Vineyard* of April 15, 1858, the firm of Marchessault & Beaudry brought 200 tons of ice from Mt. San Antonio, or "Old Baldy," and placed it in storage in the city.

Los Angeles itself, at that time, was difficult to classify, for it could scarcely be called either city, town, or pueblo. Orchards and vineyards came almost to the doorways of the shops; flowers bloomed in nearly every yard; picturesque adobe houses delighted the eye of the traveler; and both stranger and householder found the community a place of tranquillity and peace. "In the suburbs, there is a beauty perceived through the droughts," wrote one of the chance visitors in the late sixties.

There is an embroidered and flowery geometry of gardens, and arbors in the vineyards and villas nested among weeping willows, and dark solemn olives, and pimientos delicate in their fringe of foliage and swinging scarlet pouches of seeds. Borne across a thousand aromatic groves of orange and citron and California walnut, the long Pacific breeze comes up; and returning, travels again along the labyrinth to the sea, swinging in the streets of the city its morning and evening censer of sweet incense.[30]

With the exception of Los Angeles, Anaheim and El Monte were the only important settlements in the county at the close of the Civil War.[31] These were supplemented by the Indian and mestizo villages that clustered about the ranchos and abandoned missions; and by 1866 the prosperous agricultural community of Los Nietos had begun to take its place beside the two older centers. Occupying a portion of the old Rancho Santa Gertrudes, the settlement grew so rapidly that three years after its foundation it had six miles of cultivated farms and 2,000 inhabitants. "As we stand on the bank of the river and gaze over the fine fields with their teeming population," mused the silver-penned editor of the *Semi-weekly News*, ". . . we cannot but wonder at the goodness of God and the power of man to redeem and civilize a country. A few years ago, the vast tract of land we now so much admire, was only a cattle Rancho, uninhabited save by a few vaqueros."[32]

Most of the settlers who came to southern California during the post-Civil War period were stable, thrifty folk; but there was one element—a distinct, easily recognized type—poorly educated, difficult to assimilate, without fixed abode, chronically inclined to wander, and accustomed to live almost wholly off the country. Members of this class of "wandering, gypsy-like poor whites" were commonly known as "Pikes." They were especially numerous in Los Angeles County, and added little to its economic or cultural advance. "The true 'Pike,'" wrote Nordhoff in 1872,

. . . often lives with his family in a wagon; he rarely follows steady industry; he is frequently a squatter on other people's lands; "he owns a rifle, a lot of children and dogs, a wife, and if he can read, a lawbook," said a lawyer describing this character to me. "He moves from place to place, as the humor seizes him, and is generally an injury to his neighbors. He will not work regularly; but he has a great tenacity of life, and is always ready for a lawsuit."

Near San Diego a Pike family were pointed out to me, who had removed from Texas to California, and back to Texas, four times. They were now going back home again to please "the old woman" who, it seems, had had a fit of homesickness. They travelled in an old wagon drawn by a pair of broncho or native horses, and would probably be six or eight months on the road.[33]

With the exception of the roving "Pikes," most of the settlers who came to southern California were small farmers. For a time, these transplanted immigrants followed their former agricultural methods and planted corn, wheat, and other crops to which they were accustomed. Later they learned the art of irrigation and took advantage of the country's semitropical climate to introduce a great variety of crops that other states could not produce.

Horticulture, though not of major importance from a commercial standpoint until the coming of the railroad, was recognized, almost from the beginning, as having almost unlimited possibilities. As noted in the preceding chapter, a considerable acreage had been planted to seedling-orange groves prior to 1865, and, by the early seventies, Los Angeles County shipped nearly 5,000,000 oranges in a single year to San Francisco. The "paper profits" of an orange grove were enormous. The cost of purchasing and developing a ten-acre grove, according to one well-known writer on California agriculture, was as follows:

Raw land, at $30 an acre	$ 300
Fencing	300
Nursery stock	125
Labor and incidental expenses	500
Total	$1,225

It was estimated that such a grove, in full bearing, would yield 750,000 oranges annually; and, at the average price of twenty dollars per thousand, the fruit would bring an annual gross income of $15,000. The care of the trees, together with the cost of picking, packing, and marketing the oranges, amounted to less than $3,300. The annual profit on a ten-acre orchard was thus, hypothetically, close to $11,700.[34]

Lemons and olives, as well as oranges, were planted on an extensive scale. Flax and tobacco were grown successfully, and large tracts of irrigable land were sown to "Peruvian grass," or alfalfa.[35] Experimentation was the order of the day in southern California agriculture; and the introduction of any new crop was likely to touch off its own private boom. Silk and cotton furnished the most spectacular examples of such feverish excitement.

Starting in an obscure way, the idea that California would soon become one of the major silk-producing centers of the world rapidly developed into an obsession. At least a score of companies were formed to engage in the venture; newspapers and magazines were filled with articles on the subject; millions of silkworms and larvae were imported from France and Japan; hundreds of acres were planted to mulberry trees; and the state legislature offered liberal bounties to encourage the experiment.

Because of climatic conditions and cheap land, southern California found itself the center of the new boom. The large and well-financed Silk Center Association sought to purchase 3,200 acres of the Jurupa Rancho, embracing the present site of the city of Riverside, for conversion into a mulberry forest.[36] J. S. Wilson, Commissioner of the General Land Office, came under the spell of the excitement and wrote from Washington:

Of late years large quantities of mulberry trees have been planted, and preparations are making to commence the rearing of silkworms on an extensive scale, experience having fully demonstrated the adaptability of the soil and climate of California to the successful prosecution of this industry; the number of trees set out in different parts of the State being already about 4,000,000, and increasing every year. Every variety of mulberry succeeds well, the tree attaining a growth in three years equal to five years in Europe, and yielding leaves in much greater abundance. The cocoons are remarkably exempt from disease, and are nearly one third larger than those of other countries. This fact has become so well known abroad that a large foreign demand has grown up for the eggs of the California worm, and orders from France, Belgium, Italy and Mexico are constantly being filled to so large an extent as to threaten to retard the manufacture of silk for several years to come.

Two crops of cocoons are raised in the year, in May and July, a season during which the atmosphere of California is almost free from clouds, there being neither thunder storms, wet nor cold spells to check the progress of the cocoons, or to injure the mulberry leaf, such vicissitudes being not only destructive of the health of the worm, but fatal to the quality of the silk it produces.

The extraordinary advantages of the climate and soil of California for the successful prosecution of the two important industries of wine and silk manufacture are already attracting a large immigration from the localities in Europe where these branches form leading industries; and with such advantages in favor of these pursuits as exist here, they cannot fail to be carried on upon an extensive scale within the life-time of many already advanced in years. The counties in the Southern part of the State in which the cultivation of the mulberry has been entered upon are Los Angeles, Santa Clara, and Santa Barbara; but many of the valleys and side hills of the remaining four counties are equally well adapted, and need only an enterprising population to develop their wonderful capacity.

The State of California, with the view of establishing the business of silk making as one of its fixed pursuits, offers a premium of $250 for every 5,000 mulberry trees, to be paid when they are two years old, and a premium of $300 for every 100,000 cocoons.[37]

Not long after Wilson's glowing account reached the American consulate in Rotterdam, the California silk boom, which had grown with the rapidity of Jack's beanstalk, died as quickly as it had sprung up, and in after years only scattered plantations of mulberry trees remained to mark the site of visionary fortunes and disappointed expectations.

Interest in cotton raising developed contemporaneously with the boom in silk. Experimental planting, undertaken during the Spanish-Mexican era and continued by a few American farmers after 1850, had shown conclusively that cotton of superior quality could be grown in many parts of California. At the time of the Civil War, newspapers, magazines, and government publications gave considerable publicity to the success of the experiments and held out the hope that California would eventually become one of the leading cotton-producing states of the Union. Southern California editors responded with characteristic enthusiasm to such stimulus and freely predicted that the new crop would revolutionize local agriculture.

Eighty acres, lying north of Jefferson Street and west of Figueroa in Los Angeles, were converted into a cotton plantation by Matthew Keller. According to J. M. Guinn, "The plants grew luxuriantly and produced abundantly. The bursting bolls whitened the fields like the snows of winter in an Arctic landscape."[38]

A cotton planter from Mississippi named Strong developed a plantation of several hundred acres near Merced, and made a contract with the Los Angeles and San Bernardino Land Company to set out six hundred acres on one of the Stearns ranchos near Santa Ana. Strong also published numerous articles to show that California could produce a better grade of cotton at a lower cost than that grown in the Lower South.[39]

Although California has since become one of the largest cotton-producing states in the Union, the boom of the sixties and early seventies ended in disappointment. The failure was due in the main to labor and transportation difficulties. J. M. Guinn explained the collapse of one of the most ambitious cotton experiments as follows:

The California Cotton Growers and Manufacturers Association purchased ten thousand acres of land adjoining, and covering part of the present site of Bakersfield. . . . To secure laborers, the members of the association imported a colony of negro cottonfield laborers from the South, built cabins for them and hired them to plant, cultivate and gin the prospective crop. The colored persons discovered that they could get much better wages at other employments and deserted. . . . The cotton crop went to grass and the cotton growers went into bankruptcy.[40]

Notwithstanding the failure of the silk and cotton booms, southern California real estate values continued to rise so rapidly that favorably situated range lands, which had been appraised as low as ten cents an acre during the drought of 1862-64, were subdivided and sold, ten years later, for $50, $100, and $200 an acre.[41]

But in the districts where such prices prevailed, the average settler was at a great disadvantage; for, in addition to the initial outlay, it was necessary to pay heavily to fence the land; and in the end drought sometimes robbed the farmer of his year's returns. "Though Los Angeles offers to men with fair capital advantages not surpassed in any other part of the State," said the author of an otherwise enthusiastic article, "to the small farmer, to whom a plentiful supply of rain is a necessity, it is more likely to bring beggary."[42]

In the meantime, while the solid foundation of future growth and prosperity was being laid in the development of agriculture, southern California experienced the seductive intoxication of its first oil boom. Prophesying better than he knew, the editor of the Los Angeles *Star* wrote on February 25, 1860: "Kerosine Manufactory.—We understand a party from San Francisco is about to start an establishment for the manufacture of kerosine (oil of coal tar,) from the bitumen abounding in this vicinity. If the enterprise succeeds, it will be of great moment to our community."

The oil excitement became acute in 1865. Under the heading, "Oil Spring, A New Feature," the *Semi-weekly News* of January 3 reported that certain petroleum seepages near Los Angeles were creating "quite a stir," and that a group of capitalists, ready to "embark on the enterprise of penetrating the earth for streams of pure kerosine," had instructed their agents to purchase "lands upon which oil springs abound." Four weeks later the same paper carried a long article on the history and prospects of the "rock oil" industry in the south. "The people of San Francisco, and the upper country," stated the editor,

have run wild on "Petroleum"; here the excitement has become intense; everybody's lot now corners in a coal-tar spring, as that substance has usually been termed here. A stranger would gather the idea . . . that petroleum was a new discovery in this section. This is not the case; it is an old story here . . . whole tracts of land are found in this region which cannot be traversed on foot, in consequence of the thick coating of soft "tar"; it has been frequently a resort for fuel. Oil was manufactured from the substance in question, near this city, by Mr. Dreyfuss—formerly of Anaheim —prior to the year 1857; the factor was successful in producing an excellent article for use in the lamp, which was attended with too great an expense, for want of facility, to make it a profitable business—in this machinery was used. . . . Oil was manufactured—nearly upon the same ground occupied by Mr. Dreyfuss—by a Mr. Gilbert, in 1860-61, with much success and profit. . . . Our citizens have slept until the present day, when all of them seem to be entering the lists of the insane on the subject of petroleum. If no better success attends the present thirst after the oleaginous fluids than that which has heretofore followed the mining excitements of this region, it will be many years before the country is relieved of its embarrassments. . . . [But] if theory . . . is to guide us here, "diving" for petroleum may not be a total failure . . . there is encouragement in the fact that in one or two localities, in the immediate vicinity of Los Angeles, pure oil is found rising to the surface in quantities—forms a stream as it flows—of a proper consistency for burning &c., and which seems to require bleaching only, to make it a first class merchantable article.[43]

As the months passed, the oil excitement grew ever more intense. A crude refinery was erected in Pico Cañon, near the present town of Newhall, to care for the petroleum produced by the "spring of Pico and Wiley." Early in February, it was reported that "a fine oil spring" had been discovered at the depth of fifty feet, near Buena Vista, in Tulare County. The oil was free from water, and gave rise to the report that a daily production of 50,000 gallons could be obtained at little cost. Oil and *brea* were produced in considerable quantities in Santa Barbara County; and wells were bored, with the primitive machinery then available, at Cañada la Brea, on the Rancho Camulos (near the present-day town of Piru), at Palos Verdes, and in various parts of the city of Los Angeles.[44] Promising as the outlook appeared, however, the oil industry was not established on a profitable basis until a later decade.

Southern California's general economic progress during the period now under discussion was reflected in the following annual assessment returns of three representative counties:

1866	*Los Angeles*	*San Diego*	*Santa Barbara*
Real Estate	$1,089,529	$133,777	$512,045
Improvements	59,738	41,250	[No return]
Personal property	1,204,000	367,798	259,816
Total	$2,353,267	$542,825	$771,861
Estimated population	8,700	2,630	5,000
1869-1870			
Real estate and improvements	$3,711,055	$1,271,937	$ 841,868
Personal property	2,086,116	971,818	626,267
Total	$5,797,171	$2,243,755	$1,468,135
Estimated population	16,000	5,000	6,000
1872			
Real estate	$5,264,888	$1,582,684	$3,404,592
Improvements	1,779,596	228,580	651,809
Personal property	3,510,108	807,664	1,943,831
Total	$10,554,592	$2,618,928	$6,000,232
Estimated population	17,400	7,359	8,400

As southern California increased its wealth and population, taxes, public debts, and governmental expenditures grew like the proverbial green bay tree. Land assessments rose almost vertically, the tax rate was also raised, and in some counties the property tax increased fully a hundred per cent during the year.[45] "Beneath the fair exterior," lamented one editor, in the midst of a glowing description of the country's resources, "are seen the agonized faces and heard the fearful groans of the tax payers. A heavy debt weighs upon the county. The taxation is appalling."[46]

But, notwithstanding the "fearful groans of the tax payers," a new economic era was at hand for southern California. Under the stimulus of rapidly increasing immigration, the great cattle ranchos, one by one, gave way to orchards, vineyards, and grain fields. Irrigation and diversified farming revolutionized the pastoral life of earlier days. Money became more plentiful and interest rates declined to saner levels. The promise of railroad connection with the outside world broke down the long-standing wall of cultural and economic isolation and focused the attention of settlers and capitalists alike upon the latent, but immensely rich and varied resources of the region.[47] By 1872 southern California's transition from Mexican cattle frontier to American commonwealth was almost complete.

CHAPTER X

Abel Stearns: The Personification of an Age

BEFORE the Mexican War, American-born land owners, most of whom were married to members of influential California families, formed an important element in the province. Abel Stearns, whose name appears with almost monotonous regularity in earlier pages of this volume, became an outstanding member of that group, and for nearly half a century made himself an inseparable part of the changing scene in his adopted country.[1]

Stearns came to Los Ángeles while the missions were still at the height of their prosperity; he died when the amazing southern California we know today was just beginning to take form. During those fifty or more eventful years, he witnessed the development of the ranchos, the annexation of California by the United States, the revolutionary changes resulting from the Gold Rush, the cattle boom of the early fifties, and the Great Drought.

Stearns's death coincided with the close of the grazing era and the opening of southern California to settlement on a large scale. In that movement, his own vast landholdings played a highly important part. More than any other man of his generation, he thus personified both the southern California of the Mexican tradition and the southern California of the American period. The brief account of his life presented in the following pages is, therefore, not so much the biography of Abel Stearns, as the epitome of an age. In a peculiar sense, the man's career was the embodiment of the eventful transition years with which this volume deals.

Stearns was born in Lunenburg, Massachusetts, February 9,

1798.[2] When the death of his father and mother left the family virtually penniless, the twelve-year-old Abel went to sea, and gradually advanced to the responsible position of supercargo in the South American and China trade. About that time, lured by curiosity, love of adventure, or fabulous tales of the "treasure chest of the world," many young Americans began to filter into Mexico; and in 1827 Stearns gave up his seafaring career to try his fortunes in that fascinating but often disillusioning republic.[3] It is probably safe to say, however, that Stearns's decision was dictated far more by a practical New England interest in making money than by any notions of adventure or romance.

His career in Mexico was brief, but eventful. He formed a lasting and beneficial association with Eustace Barron and Alexander Forbes, the two most important British merchants on the west coast;[4] became a naturalized Mexican citizen;[5] and obtained from the Mexican government a shadowy concession to an immense tract of land somewhere in the interior of California.[6] Possibly for the purpose of taking possession of this grant, Stearns left Mexico in 1829 to identify himself, for the remainder of his long life, with California. Following a temporary residence in Monterey, he established himself as storekeeper and merchant in Los Angeles. According to the custom of the time, he bartered groceries, liquors, and dry goods for hides and tallow from the neighboring ranchos, and purchased furs from American trappers who came to California on the heels of the Smith and Pattie companies.[7] Among those who occasionally visited the pueblo were Ewing Young and Joseph Reddeford Walker, two of the most famous of all the mountain men. From his camp on "Red River," or the Colorado, under date of "14 March, 1834," Young wrote to the Los Angeles merchant:

Mr. A. Stearns

Dear Sir—if Capt Cooper has not got the Mill Irons from Mr Anderson I wish you would do me the favour to precure them for me I will be in the Pueblo some time in the month of may   I am not Ketching much Beaver but doing the best I can   I would have sent you two or three pack of beaver by Pedro Cordover to pay for the mill Irons and to get some other articles I stand in need of but he was so bad of for animals that I had to Lend him some pack Mules to Carry his own baggage   I would also write to Mr Anderson but I do not know if he is yet on the Cost

Your Truly

E. Young[8]

Visiting Los Angeles in the spring of 1841, "Old Joe Walker," discoverer of the Yosemite Valley, Owens Valley, Walker Pass, and many other notable landmarks in the West, purchased some horses from Don Juan Bandini. Writing to Bandini, Stearns made the following comment on the transaction:

Don José Walker tells me that he has received from you two horses at $45 which are to be charged to his account. He also tells me that he wishes to buy some mares or horses from you and for that purpose has left on deposit with me twenty-four pesos ($24) which also (if agreeable to you) will be entered upon the current account.

Should the said gentleman buy any more animals from you or enter into any other arrangement, you can receive payment in beaver at three pesos per pound and I will receive them at the same price in goods or on account.

On the back of Stearns's letter, in Walker's handwriting, appears the following indorsement:

April 7, 1841

Mr Abel Stearns:

Sir   I had misunderstood Mr. Bandini when I was trading with him the first time   he now says he wants the cash for his Horses. I therefore make the reduction of 50cts on the pound which will be fifty eight dollars and fifty cts   you will please settle with him and oblige.

Yours,

J. R. Walker[9]

After building up a successful business in Los Angeles, Stearns bought a small adobe building (which stood on the site now occupied by Fort MacArthur) in San Pedro, and converted it into a store, warehouse, and office. The remodeled building was approximately a hundred feet long and forty feet wide.

The storage facilities of the warehouse served a double purpose: they made it possible for Stearns to buy hides and tallow at the convenience of the rancheros, and to furnish cargoes, with a minimum of delay, to the Yankee trading ships that visited San Pedro. The arrangement worked so successfully that Stearns gradually gained control of a large share of the south-coast trade. Shipmasters from China to the Horn heard of the *Casa de San Pedro*, as the establishment was called; and, like Callao in Peru, Macao in China, and Honolulu in the Sandwich Islands, it served as a depository for mail for American vessels engaged in the Pacific trade.[10]

By maintaining a substantial supply of cash, in a land where barter was almost universal, Stearns was also able to buy more advantageously than his competitors and at times to aid influential rancheros who found themselves in need of ready money. As a result of his forehandedness and Yankee shrewdness, he soon became the wealthiest merchant in southern California.

The first decade in California brought personal and political difficulties, however, as well as success. In 1831 Stearns incurred the ill will of Governor Manuel Victoria and was summarily ordered to leave the country. But before the decree could be carried out, a revolution, led by such influential politicos as José Antonio Carrillo, Pío Pico, José María Echeandia, and Stearns's future father-in-law, Don Juan Bandini, forced the hot-tempered governor out of office and sent him instead of Stearns back to Mexico.

In 1835 a half-intoxicated sailor, named William Day, quarreled with Stearns over a cask of brandy and stabbed him several times in the face and shoulder. By good luck a doctor happened to be in the store at the time and saved the wounded man from bleeding to death. But Day's attack badly disfigured Stearns's face and left his speech permanently impaired.

Some months after the Day incident, Governor Mariano Chico, "the most hated ruler the province ever had," attempted, like Victoria, to force Stearns to leave the country. But again like his predecessor, the disgruntled Chico was hoist by his own petard. The Los Angeles merchant joined a revolution, initiated by some of the leading Californians, and had the satisfaction of forcing Chico to sail for Mexico on the very ship the ousted governor had selected for Stearns's deportation.[11]

Although he was generally respected by Californians and foreigners alike, Stearns had certain influential enemies who tried from time to time to get him in difficulty with the law. They accused him of erecting the *Casa de San Pedro* without permission of the provincial government; of conniving with cattle thieves in the purchase of stolen hides; and of receiving goods smuggled at night into San Pedro from the island of Santa Catalina.

The charges against Stearns came to a head in 1840 when California customs officers found a large amount of contraband goods and a number of improperly branded hides in the warehouse of the *Casa de San Pedro*. In the face of the evidence, Stearns's conviction seemed a mere formality. But Don Abel was an old hand at the devious game of California politics and stood on such intimate terms with the dominant families in the south that presently the matter was hushed up, and instead of standing trial as a contrabandista, Stearns himself became administrator of customs—an office he reportedly filled with great fidelity and zeal![12]

In extenuation of Don Abel's admitted disregard of customs regulations, one may say that merchants and ship captains on

the west coast universally resorted to bribery, evasion, or outright smuggling to evade the high customs charges then in
effect, and that such practices were an accepted feature of all
Spanish-American trade. Stearns had been a merchant-adven-
turer too long, and had inherited too much of the New England
tradition of the Navigation and Molasses acts to run counter to
such an orthodox and profitable convention!

Soon after his arrival in Los Angeles, Stearns formed a lasting friendship with Don Juan Bandini, one of the two or three
most influential rancheros and politicos in southern California.
As time went on, Stearns found an added attraction in the Bandini household in the person of Arcadia, one of Don Juan's five
attractive daughters. Although Arcadia was little more than a
child, Stearns made formal suit for her hand, and Don Juan
gave his permission to the proposed marriage.[13] Because Stearns
was foreign-born, the wedding required the prefect's special
sanction. The wide difference between the ages of the bride
and groom constituted a further complication, and led the em-
barrassed Don Abel to present the following naïve petition:

To the very R. P. president and prefect, Abel Stearns, a native of the
United States of the north and a naturalized citizen of Mexico, and
citizen of the City of Los Angeles, before your Worship declares;
that having entered into a marriage contract with Maria Arcadia
Bandini with the approval and consent of her father, Don Juan Bandini, . . . and desiring to avoid the ridicule which the differences in
ages might arouse among thoughtless young people, she being fourteen years of age and I forty, and finding myself also occupied with
matters of business in Los Angeles and San Pedro and other affairs
which unexpectedly demand my attention, I petition your Worship
graciously to dispense on my behalf with the three proclamations or
at least with two, obligating myself to contribute to charity whatever you impose.[14]

The prefect approved Stearns's petition for the marriage and
the priest granted his request to dispense with the proclamation;

so Don Abel and Arcadia were married in the little church of Our Lady of the Angels.

Despite the wide difference in ages, the two lived happily together until Stearns's death in 1871. Their home was a large adobe building, known far and wide as *El Palacio*, which Stearns erected on the corner of what is now Main and Arcadia streets for his young and socially minded bride.[15] The house at once became a center of pueblo society, and nearly every person of distinction who came to Los Angeles prior to the Civil War enjoyed its hospitality.

A year after his marriage, Stearns purchased the well-known Rancho Los Alamitos, and thus began his career as landowner and ranchero—a career that in time made him almost a legendary figure in the history of southern California.[16] As explained in Chapter I, the Rancho Los Alamitos was originally included in the Nieto concession of 1784 and had been allotted to Juan José Nieto when the original estate was broken up by José Figueroa, half a century later. The new owner thereupon sold back the 26,000-acre ranch to Governor Figueroa, for the paltry sum of $500.[17] The price, less than two cents an acre, was ridiculously low even for that day, and subsequently led to the charge that it was merely a bribe to induce Figueroa to favor Juan José in the division of the Nieto grant.

No effort was made at the time, however, to dispute Figueroa's title to the Alamitos. Lacking sufficient resources of his own to stock the ranch, the governor formed a partnership with Nicolás Gutiérrez and Roberto Prado. The partnership was called *La Compañia Agricultura*. Figueroa and Gutiérrez each contributed 1,000 head of horned stock to the company, and Prado supplied 600 cattle and a *manada* of brood mares. The rancho's cattle brand was formed from the initial letters of the words, *Compañia Agricultura*, and remained in use for over half a century.[18] Prado was made *administrador* of the ranch and

NUMERO. 2.258. | **EL CIUDADANO GUADALUPE VICTORIA,**
Registrado á fs. 92. | *PRESIDENTE DE LOS ESTADOS UNIDOS MEXICANOS*
del Libro del ramo. | *concede libre y seguro pasaporte á* ...

*para que por el término de un año contado des-
de esta fecha permanezca y transite por el territorio de la República, observando lo preve-
nido en el Decreto reglamentario de 5 de Ju-
nio de 1826; y manda S. E. á todas las Au-
toridades así civíles, como militares de la Na-
cion, no le pongan embarazo en su permanen-
cia y tránsito, y le franqueen los aucsilios que
puedan convenirle, pagándolos por sus justos pre-
cios. Palacio del Gobierno Federal en México
á 4. de Agoso — de 1827 — 7º. de la
Independencia y 6º de la Libertad.*

De órden de su Excelencia.

El oficial mayor de la 1.ª secretaria de Estado, encargado de su Despacho.

Valga por un año. Derechos,

PASSPORT OF ABEL STEARNS ISSUED BY THE MEXICAN
GOVERNMENT, 1827
Courtesy of Historical Society of Southern California

added substantially to the profits of the partnership by contracting with the friars of San Gabriel to slaughter the mission cattle and dispose of their hides and tallow before the Secularization Act could be enforced.[19]

The death of Governor José Figueroa in 1835 necessitated the dissolution of the *Compañía Agricultura* and the distribution of its assets (consisting chiefly of some 5,000 head of cattle and a large number of horses) between Figueroa's heirs and the two surviving partners. Francisco Figueroa became administrator of his brother's estate and manager of the Rancho Los Alamitos.

Stearns began negotiations in the spring of 1840 to purchase the Alamitos:

I have been to examine the ranch of the Alamitos [he wrote José Antonio Aguirre in April], and with Señor Temple we have had a conference with Don Francisco Figueroa who has fixed the price of the ranch at 9 thousand pesos, the value placed upon it, so we are informed, by the owners. According to your list of large and small cattle and the horse herd, calculating at current prices, the value will not run much above 4,000 pesos.[20]

Contemporary accounts disagree as to the actual amount Stearns paid for the property. "I bought my rancho Los Alamitos in 1842, for $6,000, including 900 cattle, nearly 1,000 sheep & 240 horses," he later testified; "there were 6 sq. leagues of land, a small house & a few other trifling articles worth some $200."[21] But the figures cited by Stearns do not agree with an inventory made in 1842, nor with the statements of other persons who were well acquainted with the details of the transaction.

The official list of improvements on the property, at the time of the sale, included "one house of adobe with two apartments covered with pitch and others without roof with two opposite doors. One more house of adobe with three apartments covered by rushes and with one door placed therein. One other house of Adobe with two apartments covered by rushes and with one door." A table of the livestock showed 231 "cows of the plains," at $5.00 each; 134 steers, $2.00 each; a *caballada*, or horse herd, of 39 mares with colts, at the same figure; 8 horses without blemish, $8.00 each; 14 half-broken horses, $6.00 each; 4 horses, not quite half-broken, $6.00 each; and 45 young mares, $1.50 each. The total value of improvements and livestock given in the inventory amounted to $5,943.50.[22]

Most, if not all, of the proceeds derived from the sale of the Alamitos went to satisfy the debts left by Governor Figueroa. Stearns paid one creditor the sum of "$2,050, 7 shillings," in suet at "12 shillings an *arroba*," and in hides at $2.00 each, and another $1,483 in the same commodities. Out of the remainder of the purchase price, Mariano Roldán, owner of an undivided interest in the ranch, received "1,019 pesos, 5 reales, and 4 granos."[23]

Stearns subsequently filed in the Recorder's office in Los Angeles, an extraordinarily long and fully detailed list of the articles he acquired in the purchase of the Alamitos.[24] After reading the list, one might reconstruct, with considerable accuracy, the picture of life on a California ranch of that time. The items included a large pot of iron, a copper pan, a mill, three old barrels for carrying water, a carbine, a broken gun, four pairs of shearing scissors, five gunlocks, five pairs of wool cards, four spindles, one forge, ten yokes, four *malacates* or windlasses, and four branding irons.

Seven years after Stearns purchased the Rancho Los Alamitos, the Gold Rush ushered in the spectacular cattle boom described in Chapter VI. The county assessment of 1850 fixed the area of the Alamitos at 28,512 acres, and valued the ranch, on the basis of 3 reals or 37½ cents an acre, at $10,692. Two houses on the property were appraised at $1,500. The ranch pastured 10,000 cattle, 700 horses, and 1,100 sheep. Cattle and horses were assessed at $6.00 a head, sheep at $2.00 each.[25] The value of livestock was thus about six times that of the land itself, but the assessor's figures on both real and personal property represented less than a third of the actual value of the ranch. Within a year, John C. Frémont made Stearns the following proposal:

I offer to purchase his rancho [Los Alamitos] in the sum of three hundred thousand dollars ($300,000), to be paid in the following manner,—

Fifty thousand dollars ($50,000) to be paid within six months after date of purchase.

Permission to be granted me to drive off for sale during the present year three thousand beef cattle (steers or *novillas*) and the proceeds of such sale to be paid to Mr. Stearns on account of the purchase.

The remainder to be paid in three yearly equal payments, with interest at 6 pr. cent. per annum.

The privilege to be granted me of using an amount of stock equal to the yearly increase of all the stock upon the place until the purchase money is paid.

The purchase money to be secured to Mr. Stearns by lien upon the rancho and stock.

It is further understood in making this offer that Mr. Stearns will turn over all the stock, improvements, implements, &c., belonging to the place, & that no sale will be made or stock driven off, provided these terms be accepted.

Ten thousand dollars ($10,000) to be forfeited by me in the event that I fail to comply with the terms of the contract. Mr. Runkel is associated with me, and is [to] be constantly upon the place or occupied in driving up cattle, & general management of the business.[26]

Nothing tangible came of Frémont's offer, and Stearns remained in possession of the Rancho Los Alamitos for another decade and a half. In 1854 the United States Land Commission confirmed his title to the grant; and as long as the cattle boom continued, the property proved immensely profitable. But early in the fifties a cloud, considerably larger than a man's hand, appeared on the horizon. Certain inquisitive San Francisco lawyers began to challenge the validity of Stearns's purchase of the Alamitos in 1842 on the grounds that Governor José Figueroa, who supposedly died intestate, actually had three legitimate sons in Mexico to whom he left the ranch, and that Francisco Figueroa and Nicolás Gutiérrez, administrators of the governor's estate, illegally suppressed the latter's will, kept the sons in ignorance of their title to the Alamitos, and fraudulently disposed of the property of the estate.[27]

Whatever the merits of the claim, it offered lucrative possibilities to a host of lawyers and land speculators. Springing up like grass after the fall rains, self-appointed representatives of the defrauded heirs offered to furnish Don Abel a quitclaim deed to the disputed property, at prices ranging from $1,200 to $25,000. Lawyers threatened suit to vacate Stearns's title to the Alamitos and require him to render an accounting of the property. Finally, in proceedings on behalf of Manuel Mariano Figueroa, eldest of the heirs, Stearns was charged with "combining and confederating" with Francisco Figueroa and Nicolás Gutiérrez to purchase the Alamitos for a pretended consideration, to suppress José Figueroa's will, and to perpetrate "a gross fraud upon the plaintiff."[28]

By 1856 the situation had become so critical that Stearns commissioned Don Juan Temple to serve as his confidential agent in Mexico and effect a compromise with the claimants. Temple carried through the negotiations successfully; but it cost Stearns over $10,000 to secure a clear title to the Alamitos.[29]

With the Rancho Los Alamitos as a nucleus, Stearns built up the largest land-and-cattle empire in southern California. His long residence in the country and intimate knowledge of the business affairs and financial difficulties of all the large landholders, enabled him to add one ranch after another to his holdings on highly advantageous terms. He purchased the 11,000-acre Rancho La Laguna, originally a part of the celebrated San Antonio grant, from Balestro Lugo, for example, for $3,125—or less than 30 cents an acre![30] He acquired a substantial interest in the seven-square-league Rancho Las Bolsas by defending Justo Morrillo's claim to the grant before the United States Land Commission, and making a payment of fifty young cows.[31] Stearns subsequently bought further rights in the property from the Yorba and Nieto heirs and loaned money, at five or six per cent a month, to some of the other holders of undivided interests in the ranch.[32] On February 14, 1861, the Rancho Las Bolsas was sold at public auction to satisfy a judgment for $28,043 which Stearns held against María Cleofa Nieto, José Antonio Morrillo, and María Rafaela Morrillo. Stearns bid $15,000 and secured title to the ranch.[33]

During the early sixties Stearns added four or five other ranches to his already large empire. A loan of a few hundred dollars to Joaquín and Catarina Ruíz eventually gave him possession of the choice 6,800-acre Rancho La Bolsa Chica. He bought a fractional interest in the Rancho Temescal for $1,500. The Serranos, who held the grant, then deeded him one-half of their undivided interest in the property, in return for "100 cows of two years old and upwards." A $15,000 note of Pío Pico's eventually added the grant known as Los Coyotes to the list of the Stearns ranchos. The ownership of a fractional interest in the Rancho Santiago de Santa Ana enabled him to join with a minority of Bernardo Yorba's heirs in a partition suit to force a division of that large estate.[34]

The acquisition of the Rancho Jurupa, one of the largest Mexican grants in what was then San Bernardino County, grew out of the financial difficulties of Stearns's distinguished father-in-law, Don Juan Bandini. In 1851 Don Juan had "borrowed of Adolfo Savin (a Frenchman, gambler, etc.) . . . the sum of

$10,800." Unable to meet the note when it fell due, Bandini
gave Savin a mortgage for $12,800, at four per cent a month, on
all his San Diego property. In addition to this indebtedness,
Bandini had other heavy obligations. "The expenses of the family as you very well know are enormous in this town," wrote
C. R. Johnson, the husband of Dolores Bandini, to Don Abel.
Johnson added that Don Juan was "on the rancho trying to
round up cattle to meet the note," but the stock was in poor
condition and Johnson did not believe it would bring enough
to save Bandini from bankruptcy. Don Juan was sick with
worry over the whole situation. "But there is no man in California," Johnson concluded, "whose estate, under proper management would pay so handsomely."[35]

In response to Johnson's plea, Stearns gave Savin about
$13,000 for the assignment of the Bandini mortgage. During
the ensuing years Don Abel made further advances to his harassed father-in-law, until the total exceeded $24,000. In partial
satisfaction for these loans, Bandini deeded Stearns the Rancho
La Jurupa.[36]

By 1860 Stearns was recognized as the most important ranchero and landowner in the south. Although he had disposed of
his business at San Pedro, he continued until late in the fifties
to operate his store in Los Angeles, buying hides and tallow
from the rancheros, and beaver pelts, sea-otter skins, and deer
hides from the fast disappearing mountain men who occasionally straggled into the pueblo.[37]

To his activities as merchant, landowner, and ranchero,
Stearns added a wide variety of other interests. He engaged in
several costly and unprofitable mining ventures;[38] opened a
flour mill in Los Angeles; held numerous public offices and
identified himself with nearly every charitable or civic enterprise undertaken in Los Angeles. In 1858 he erected the celebrated Arcadia Building which long stood at the southwest

corner of Arcadia and Los Angeles Streets. The two-story brick building, equipped with heavy iron shutters fabricated at a foundry especially established for the purpose, was reputed to be the largest business block south of San Francisco. It contained eight stores, returned from $600 to $800 a month in rentals, and represented an investment of about $85,000.[39]

Stearns's long-established relations with the old Californians and his marriage into the Bandini family kept him socially a true *hijo del país*; but his varied economic interests also brought him in contact with influential Americans from every section of the state. In addition, he carried on a wide correspondence on the business conditions and economic opportunities of southern California, with government officials, bankers, and prospective land buyers in many parts of the United States, and even in Europe.

During the Civil War, Stearns opposed secession and served as a confidential agent for the Union party, to thwart the plans of southern sympathizers in California. He was a loyal, though not a conspicuously active, member of the Republican party; and at a time when neither state nor county government provided funds for roads, hospitals, or kindred enterprises he subscribed liberally to all such public undertakings.[40]

By 1862 Stearns had acquired over 200,000 acres of the choicest land in the Los Angeles-San Bernardino area, including all but two of the ranchos embraced in the original Juan Nieto grant. He had other properties between Santa Maria and San Diego, and owned claims to immense grants in Lower California. His financial situation, however, was highly vulnerable, and with the decline in livestock prices, he found himself land- and cattle-poor. By the spring of 1862 his obligations were out of all proportion to his income; and a number of his notes, including one for $15,000 and another for $10,000, were "long over due."[41]

The Great Drought began in the fall of that year. For at least six years thereafter it was touch-and-go whether Stearns would succumb, as so many of his contemporaries did, or survive. He lost thousands of cattle from thirst and starvation; and most of those which the drought spared, his creditors attached.

As financial and business conditions grew worse throughout southern California, demands poured in on Stearns from every quarter. One of his lawyers, unable "to get a cent from him" on account, threatened to bring suit to collect a bill for $1,800; several notes on which both principal and interest had long been in default were presented for payment; and one of his agents plaintively wrote, "There are so many demands for money . . . but I do the best I can."[42]

Early in 1864 Stearns's financial plight became even more serious. Among the most pressing of his obligations was a note for $35,000 to John Parrott of San Francisco. The relations between debtor and creditor were becoming more and more strained, and in a letter written to Parrott on August 16 Stearns vented his grievances in strong if not grammatical English:

Dear Sir—Yours of the 11th inst was handed me by your Son Don Tibursio Parott on Sunday on his arrival at this place—As Soon as I read its contents I informed him that I would give him ample Security as you desired and mentioned on what property Real and personal, and he was to See me the next morning (yesterday) but instead of doing So dispatched the Sheriff early in the morning to the different Ranchos to embargo Ranchos & Stock without advising me & in fact did not know he had done So untill late in the day— I am Sorry that he fell into the hands of the *Philistines* as his advisers, Kewen & Morrisons—As I after Saw Mr Downey and he told me he had not advised that Step—Now there is ample property and Some that has no incumbrance on it and other that has but a trifle besides all the personal property—To prevent any unnecessary disorder in the Ranchos I was obliged to [go] out last Evening to See the Sheriff & prevent the collecting or moving the Stock and have just returned 11 O.C.

Your Son with Kewen Started out to San Bernardino to attach the Ranchos of Jurapa, Sierra & Temascal unknown to me untill they were gone—

It appears the advisers of Tibursio want to make as much cost as possible both to you and me—I desire that you on the receipt of this will Telegraph to your Son to Stop the proceeding and I will give you ample and all the Security you desire on Real or personal property or write him immediately as it will Stop unnecesary Expenses—I would go up on the Steamer but think it best to remain—Shall Send you a list of all my debts—

I had arranged here with my Creditors, only one or two had attached the other day Say amt. of $8000, all of which was arranged to wait one year or before if [I] have it—I Should Say more but the Express is about to leave—Shall write more by mail—

After seeking unsuccessfully to collect the note, and alleging (perhaps with good reason) that other creditors, "mostly Jews," were about to seize Stearns's property, Parrott sued out a writ of attachment against 3,000 of Don Abel's horses and 15,000 of his cattle. Though some attempt was made to avoid a forced sale of the stock, Parrott soon grew impatient with what he called Stearns's "procrastinating system of doing business"; scolded him for refusing to accept advice; and finally instructed the sheriff to enforce the writ. As a result of this action, there was such an "awful sacrifice" of livestock that one of Stearns's representatives doubted if "anything" could be saved, either for Don Abel or his creditors.[43]

Each year Stearns added to his other debts a long list of delinquent taxes. In 1865, and again in 1866, Los Angeles County brought suit against him for unpaid levies, both on his ranchos and personal property. Taxes on his San Diego holdings were not paid after 1861 and his land in San Bernardino County was similarly in arrears.

Time after time Don Abel's ranchos were advertised for sale at public auction to meet the most inconsequential sums: $14.07

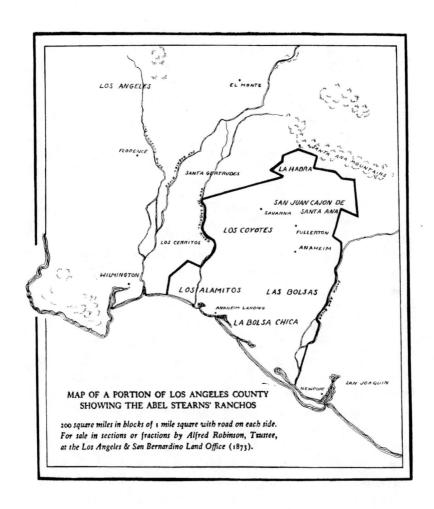

MAP OF A PORTION OF LOS ANGELES COUNTY
SHOWING THE ABEL STEARNS' RANCHOS

200 square miles in blocks of 1 mile square with road on each side.
For sale in sections or fractions by Alfred Robinson, Trustee,
at the Los Angeles & San Bernardino Land Office (1873).

on the 6,700-acre Rancho La Habra; $91.35 on the eight-square-league Rancho Las Bolsas; $12.10 on his interest in the Rancho Cajón de Santa Ana; $81.90 on the Rancho La Laguna.[44]

Even a marked business revival after the drought brought Stearns no relief. His herds had been reduced to only a few hundred head; the court had issued a decree of foreclosure for $23,625 against the Arcadia block;[45] Senator Cornelius Cole, and other attorneys whom he had engaged to defend his interests in Washington, denounced him for bad faith and threatened to bring suit for unpaid fees; and in 1868 his annual net income had fallen to less than $300.[46] But, in spite of such multiple liabilities, Stearns succeeded in keeping most of his huge landholdings intact. He lost only one ranch—Los Alamitos—his first and probably most cherished holding. There was nothing novel in the story, except that Stearns, who had profited from similar debacles on the part of so many other rancheros, now found himself the loser.

In 1861 Don Abel mortgaged the Alamitos to Michael Reese of San Francisco for $20,000, with interest at one and a half per cent a month, to complete the financing of the Arcadia block. During the barren years of the drought, Stearns was compelled to default both principal and interest on the note; and on February 18, 1865, in the "Case of Michael Reese, Plaintiff, v. Abel Stearns, Defendant," the district court of Los Angeles County issued a decree of sale against the Rancho Los Alamitos. Although Stearns obtained a year's extension on the note, he failed to raise the necessary funds; and the ranch of the "Little Cottonwoods," like so many of its kind, passed into the hands of another money lender.[47]

In 1868, in return for a mortgage on all his ranch properties in Los Angeles and San Bernardino counties, the Hibernia Loan and Savings Society of San Francisco advanced Stearns $43,000 to meet his most pressing obligations. The loan enabled him to consolidate his debts and postpone the impending threat of bankruptcy.

During the breathing spell that ensued, Alfred Robinson, Don Abel's former business associate and one of his most intimate friends, succeeded in interesting a number of San Francisco investors in a plan to subdivide and sell Stearns's holdings in southern California.[48] The group finally organized themselves into a company or syndicate commonly known as the Robinson Trust, and embarked upon one of the most ambitious real-estate programs in the history of the state.

The Trust was composed of Alfred Robinson, Sam Brannan (the former Mormon leader), Edward F. Northam, Charles B. Polhemus, Edward Martin, and Abel Stearns. Under an indenture, dated May 25, 1868, Stearns conveyed to the Trust all of his ranchos (except that of La Laguna) in Los Angeles and San Bernardino counties; and the syndicate in turn agreed to pay him a dollar and a half an acre for the properties, as fast as the land was sold; to make an advance of $50,000 for the liquidation of his debts; and to allow him an eighth interest in the Trust.[49]

The agreement involved a total of 177,796 acres, or nearly 278 square miles, and included the following ranchos: Los Coyotes, 48,825 acres; La Habra, 6,698 acres; San Juan Cajón de Santa Ana, 21,572 acres (net); Las Bolsas y Paredes, 33,509 acres (net); La Bolsa Chica, 8,272 acres; Jurupa, in San Bernardino County, 41,168 acres (net); and La Sierra, in the same county, 17,752 acres. Much of the land was extremely fertile, well adapted to diversified farming, and susceptible of irrigation at moderate cost.

The Trust next organized the Los Angeles and San Bernardino Land Company to serve as a selling agent. In its publicity and sales campaign, the company employed many of the high-pressure methods so widely used today. It distributed thousands of maps of the Stearns ranchos throughout the United States and Europe; flooded the East with literature describing the incomparable climate and agricultural advantages of southern California; and employed well-known lecturers and writers to advertise the manifold attractions of the delectable land.

Under the company's plan, the ranchos were divided into 640-acre tracts; and each tract, or section, was further broken up into farms, containing from 20 to 160 acres. The company also mapped out a number of towns which resembled the prophet's description of Jerusalem of the restoration period: "Now the city was large and great, but the inhabitants were few and the houses not yet builded." On the sites of such towns conspicuous signs indicated the locations of hotels, schools, churches, and imposing public buildings, none of which were then built and most of which have not even yet materialized.[50]

In the whimsical, humorously tolerant vein in which he described so many features of early Los Angeles, J. M. Guinn thus wrote of his encounter with the aggressive representatives of the Los Angeles and San Bernardino Land Company:

In 1868 and 1869 Southern California was in a transition state. The era of cattle and sheep raising as distinctive industries was on the decline. Grain and fruit raising were beginning to be recognized as the coming industries of that region. Los Angeles was experiencing its first real estate boom. Every steamer was crowded with immigrants seeking cheap lands for homes. The Stearns ranches in the southeast part of the county, comprising over 200,000 acres, had been subdivided into small tracts and thrown on the market at prices varying from $2.50 to $10 per acre. Just before we cast loose from the wharf at San Francisco an active young man came aboard the steamer with an armful of boom literature, the first I had seen. It was maps, plots and circulars descriptive of the lands of the Los Angeles and San Bernardino Land Company (the Stearns ranches). These he distributed where he thought they would do the most good. A map and description of the city of Savana fell to my lot. The city was described as located on a gently sloping mesa overlooking the valley of Santa Ana. Sites had been reserved by its founders for churches and schools, and a central location was held in reserve for a city hall. A few weeks after my arrival I visited the city. I found it on the western slope of the Coyote Hills, about six miles north of Anaheim. Long rows of white stakes marked the line of its streets. A solitary coyote on a round top knoll, possibly the site of the prospective city hall, gazed despondently down the street upon the debris of a deserted sheep camp. The other inhabitants of the city of Savana had not arrived, nor have they to this day put in an appearance.[51]

The Los Angeles and San Bernardino Land Company maintained agents in many cities in California, including Los Angeles, Anaheim, and San Francisco, and disposed of properties on the installment plan, with interest at ten per cent per annum on deferred payments. Although the company's sales at first were slow, the influx of settlers and speculators into southern California furnished such an ever expanding demand that the Trust was able to dispose of over 12,000 acres in a few months.

Considerable friction had developed in the meantime, however, among the members of the syndicate. Whatever the legal powers of the trustees, Abel Stearns had been his own master too long and dominated too completely the little world in which he lived, to surrender the management of his affairs to other hands. From the time the Robinson Trust was formed, he disregarded its authority, decided matters on his own responsibility, and otherwise ignored the wishes and instructions of his associates. The latter, in turn, grew more and more exasperated, both with Stearns's actions and his attitude. They criticized him especially, for substituting unauthorized land prices for those advertised by the company and quoted by its agents to prospective purchasers, and for leasing thousands of acres, covered by his contract with the Trust, for the pasturage of sheep.

Don Abel's assumption of authority in leasing the ranchos to sheep men was particularly galling to the other trustees. As Alfred Robinson pointed out, and indeed as Stearns himself very well knew, sheep ate the grass clean down to the ground, in time destroyed even the roots with their sharp hoofs, and left the land too naked and unattractive to appeal to prospective purchasers.[52] Stearns's leases thus threatened serious interference with the Trust's program of selling its holdings for farms and homesites. "The purpose of this trust," wrote Northam to Stearns, "is to lease to farmers and to induce them to buy, and sell by instruments in writing—Pasturage was not contemplated —if unauthorized by the Trust is against the trespass law, will check sales and is in every way inexpedient."[53]

As time went on, the breach between Stearns and his associates grew wider. Even Robinson finally turned against him, charged him with carelessness and procrastination in matters of grave importance, and angrily berated him for spending his time in Los Angeles, "fussing about horses," when he should have been devoting himself more vigorously to the business of the company.[54]

In an impatient bill of particulars, Robinson later pointed out that Stearns was pasturing his horses on company property, placing obstacles in the way of the sale of the land, antagonizing his associates, pursuing a "penny wise and pound foolish" policy, and permitting hundreds of squatters to occupy the ranchos. With a parting shot, Robinson bluntly advised his irritating and obstinate friend to give some serious thought to the business of the company, and "send his horses to the devil."[55]

The friction between Stearns and his associates might impede, but it could not defeat, the success of the Robinson Trust. The new era of settlement and diversified agriculture was already at hand; a seemingly insatiable demand for homes and small farms was just beginning; and in the Stearns ranchos the Trust had tens of thousands of acres with which to take advantage of that demand.

But in this new prosperity, Stearns himself was permitted to have only a fleeting share. By 1870 he had recovered from the financial debacle of the sixties and apparently was on the eve of amassing one of the greatest of California fortunes.[56] But the prospect proved illusory. On one of his rare absences from *El Palacio*, Don Abel was stricken with a sudden illness and died in the Grand Hotel in San Francisco on August 23, 1871.

Stearns's life in California, as noted earlier in the chapter, spanned four revolutionary decades. It began when Los Angeles was only a collection of simple adobe houses "on the long rim of the Mexican frontier"; it closed as the southern California of today was just beginning to take form. In that transition the orphan boy of Lunenburg played a colorful and commanding part.

CHAPTER XI

The End of a Decade and an Era

THE "Discontented Seventies," though marked by local and state-wide depressions of great intensity, constituted, on the whole, a period of unusual economic and social progress for most of southern California.

"In those years," wrote a historian of San Luis Obispo County in words that were equally applicable to southern California as a whole,

systematic roadbuilding was begun; the sea-ports utilized; railroads constructed; many of the great ranchos divided and sold to settlers; the public school system organized; the county seat incorporated and the population of the county quadrupled. . . .

Immigrants came from all points of the compass, ex-Confederates from the South and ex-Union men from the North and West, many from other parts of California. They were for the most part strangers to each other but all, with curious unanimity, inspired with the common conviction that Fortune would surely smile upon them; that the county promised rapid growth; that the climate was perfect and the country a Garden of Eden. Most of them were men of mature years and ripened judgment. All the professions and all lines of business were represented among them and while none of them were wealthy, none were without means sufficient for their business requirements. They were men of vision and enterprise, high qualities that were assuredly needed to cope with local conditions.[1]

During the Civil War, as already noted, the sheep industry underwent a sustained boom which eventually carried the price of raw wool to forty or fifty cents a pound, and allowed the sheep men to reap fantastic profits. In 1872, however, these inflated prices suddenly collapsed, and a severe drought took heavy toll of many of the flocks.

This drought, severe though it was, caused only a temporary

DON ABEL STEARNS—THE PERSONIFICATION OF AN AGE

DON JUAN TEMPLE

setback to the sheep business of southern California, but five years later the industry suffered a major disaster. The winter of 1876-77 was abnormally dry, the rains that occasionally fell were followed by hard desert winds that sucked the moisture out of the air and ground alike, and left the soil so lifeless and dry that "the barley burned in the fields, and there was nothing green to be seen in the wide stretches of country about the town." As in the historic drought that demoralized the cattle industry in 1862-64, a severe smallpox epidemic ravaged both town and countryside, the ranges again turned to barren wastes, the streams and springs dried up, and the sheep died in appalling numbers.

In one day, on the Las Posas Rancho, in what is now Ventura County, Thomas R. Bard and his herders "slaughtered 60,000 lambs as fast as they were born." Seventy thousand sheep were killed at one time on Santa Cruz Island for their pelts and tallow. Sheep were sold for twenty-five cents a head, and dressed sheep carcasses could be bought for fifty cents a piece on the streets of many southern California towns.[2] Some ranchers were fortunate enough to find grass in other parts of the state and transferred their sheep to new pastures while the animals could still travel. But contemporary accounts record many incidents similar to that of the unfortunate owner who undertook to move 18,000 starving animals from the dry ranges along the coast to the upper part of Soledad Cañon and lost every animal before the second day's drive began.

The decline in sheep raising, after the climax of the wool boom of the early seventies and the crippling losses suffered in the drought of 1876-77, proved, in the end, almost as great a blessing to southern California as the collapse of the cattle industry in the mid-sixties. In both cases, drought and disaster stimulated the subdivision of large landholding and the substitution of diversified agriculture for a large-scale grazing system.[3]

The new era that began with, or even before, the decline of sheep farming was especially noteworthy for the foundation of new towns, the coming of the railroad, and the rapid expansion of irrigated farms.

After the settlement of Anaheim, El Monte, and San Bernardino in the early fifties, almost no new towns were established in southern California for nearly twenty years. Then a period of community development began that witnessed the foundation of such important present-day cities as Pasadena, Riverside, Santa Ana, Orange, Pomona, Lompoc, and Santa Paula.

Most of these communities represented the natural outgrowth of the expansion of diversified farming. As the large land holdings were broken up and placed under cultivation, a store and a blacksmith shop were opened to meet the first pressing needs of the new settlers. A school and a church soon followed, and presently the crossroads settlement had become a town. In other cases, real estate promoters platted a townsite, laid out a few dusty streets, marked the location of pretentious but imaginary buildings, and sold lots, in the approved California manner, by means of an enticing installment plan and widely publicized auctions, to home seekers, speculators, and the stream of invalids that came from the East in ever increasing numbers to find both health and fortune in the new land.

Other towns, however, represented a different and much more carefully organized type of settlement than those just mentioned. Pasadena and Riverside, for example, were the product of a mutual colonization plan of co-operative enterprise.

Pasadena owed its origin to an association called the "California Colony of Indiana." Organized by a group of friends meeting at the home of Dr. T. B. Elliott in Indianapolis in May, 1873, the association arranged to send an advance party to California to select a suitable site for a settlement; but the financial panic of that year disrupted the group and compelled many of the prospective settlers to abandon the California venture.

Some of the representatives of the Indiana Colony, however, had already reached California before the association broke up. One member of this advance guard was D. M. Berry, the colony's secretary. After visiting a number of possible sites, Berry and a few others decided upon a part of the old Mexican grant known as the Rancho San Pasqual, lying east of the Arroyo Seco, organized the "San Gabriel Orange Association," sold shares in the new company for $250 each, and bought some 4,000 acres for the prospective owners. The new settlement was called "Pasadena," presumably from a Chippewa word freely translated to mean the Crown of the Valley.

From the very first, Pasadena enjoyed a distinctive reputation. To an unusual degree the settlers met the requirement laid down by a man of wide experience and sound judgment who answered the question, "What should the emigrant bring to southern California?" with the laconic but completely satisfactory answer, "Religion, money, brains, and industry."[4]

The holdings of the San Gabriel Orange Grove Association were divided into tracts ranging from 15 to 180 acres in size; but almost from the beginning the settlement began to assume an urban character. The settlers established a school, a church, and a newspaper called the *Chronicle*; boasted that in nine years not a single criminal case had originated in the colony; and incorporated the "Pasadena Library and Village Improvement Society," of which an early writer declared, "It is believed that the operations of this society must be highly advantageous to the community in conserving the moral and mental condition of the people, in cultivating a love and taste for the beautiful, and in beautifying and adorning the streets and public grounds."[5]

By 1880 Pasadena had a population of 391. The reminiscences of Mary Agnes Crank offer the following vivid picture of life on the old San Pasqual Rancho, while Pasadena was still in its adolescent stage:

The house was built by Mrs. Albert Sidney Johnson who on December 19, 1868, sold it together with the ranch to Judge Benj. S. Eaton—a relative by marriage—of whom we bought it. This house was the first frame dwelling house erected in the old San Pasqual Ranch and, excepting the adobe-built hacienda, was the first good house built in that part of the valley, and was very comfortable. This house was later moved to a new site where it remains at this time [1926] in excellent preservation. At the time of our arrival the outside was clapboarded and the walls inside were covered with muslin tacked to the wall and then covered with wallpaper. The ceiling of the room consisted of the floor joists and floor of the rooms above. There were two rooms above with sloping ceilings and four good sized rooms below. Large open fireplaces in the three principal rooms were all that could be desired for comfort and appealed to us very strongly. Solid wooden outside shutters with small openings cut in the upper part, closed and darkened the rooms on a hot day and, as we found later, added to the comfort. . . .

The cleared land was planted to vineyards and orchards. Orange trees, we were told, would be worth when in full bearing about forty dollars a year per tree. We had visions of future wealth as we computed the income a thousand trees would bring. In addition to the 200 seedling trees already on the place there were also some sixty acres of mission grape vines. The grapes were sold to the winery of L. J. Rose at Sunny Slope. At that time the grapes were crushed in the ancient fashion—by men who trampled them with their bare feet on gratings placed over large vats or tanks. It was not long after that when crushing machinery came into use, and the old-time picturesque method was discontinued.[6]

Riverside, like Pasadena, represented the organized or "colony" type of settlement. Its creator was Judge J. W. North, a man of wide interests and varied fortunes—lawyer, abolitionist, founder of the University of Minnesota and of the town of Northfield; Surveyor-General, Judge of the Supreme Court, and President of the Constitutional Convention, of the Territory of Nevada; pro-Negro industrialist in Knoxville, Tennessee; and California colonizer and agriculturist.

Judge North began the organization of his California colony at the close of five years of struggle and disappointment in Tennessee. Widely-distributed circulars set forth the nature of the proposed settlement and its general plan of organization. One of these, entitled "A Colony for California," contained the following persuasive statement of the founder's plans:

The undersigned, in association with personal friends and correspondents in the North and West, as well as with a considerable number of good people in different states of the South, is now engaged in organizing a Colony for settlement in Southern California, on or near the line of the Southern Pacific Railroad.

Appreciating the advantages of associated settlement, we aim to secure at least 100 good families, who can invest $1000 each, in the purchase of land; while at the same time we invite all good, industrious people to join us, who can, by investing a smaller amount, contribute in any degree to the general prosperity. We do not expect to buy as much land for the same money, in Southern California, as we could obtain in the remote parts of Colorado or Wyoming; but we expect it will be worth more, in proportion to cost, than any other land we could purchase within the United States. It will cost something more to get to California than it would to reach the States this side of the mountains; but we are very confident that the superior advantages of soil and climate will compensate us many times over for this increased expense.

Experience in the West has demonstrated that $100, invested in a colony, is worth $1000 invested in an isolated locality.

We wish to form a colony of intelligent, industrious and enterprising people, so that each one's industry will help to promote his neighbor's interests, as well as his own. It is desirable, if possible, that every one shall be consulted in regard to location and purchase; but since those who will compose the colony are now scattered from Maine to Texas, and from Georgia to Minnesota and Nevada, this seems next to impossible.[7]

In a later circular, issued from San Francisco, North pictured the advantages of the new colony in language so lush and color-ful that the real estate folders of today seem drab and prosy by comparison.

"In addition to the production of all the grains, fruits and vegetables of the East, which are here produced in double quantity," he wrote

this soil and climate are peculiarly adapted to the growth of oranges, lemons, limes, figs, English walnuts, olives, almonds, raisin-grapes, wine-grapes, peanuts, sweet potatoes, and to silk culture. The sorghum and sugar beet are said to more than double the yield in the East. The net profits per year, from the semi-tropical fruits and silk culture, are estimated at as high as one thousand dollars per acre. Mining districts, within reach, furnish a ready market for all products. Ornamental trees, and flowering shrubs and vines, grow with wonderful rapidity. It is safe to say that as much can be done in ornamental gardening here in three years, as can be done in the East in ten. The Pepper tree, one of the cleanest and most beautiful of shade trees, grows with astonishing rapidity. The orange groves, in which may always be seen both fruit and blossoms, are unrivalled in beauty. The Pomegranate, always with fresh foliage, bearing fruit and flowers; the Lemon and Lime, always ornamental, as well as profitable; the Oleander tree, wonderfully rapid in its growth, always green, and always ornamented with gorgeous blossoms; and other flowering trees and vines, easy of cultivating here, are sights very inviting to Eastern eyes. . . .

After this flow of adjectives and a paragraph devoted to irrigation and the development of the colony's prospective town, North added the following sound, practical, but most unusual note of caution:

We would suggest to our friends the policy of buying only small portions of land. The great error is getting too much, and cultivating too little; or cultivating large farms imperfectly. On large farms people must necessarily be widely separated; on small lots they can enjoy the society of near neighbors, and have all the advantages of town or city life. Besides this, ten acres of land, which can be made to yield an annual income of five hundred or one thousand dollars per acre, is enough to furnish a very reasonable income. Small farms, near neighbors, and a compact settlement are best for all.

North's company, incorporated as the "Southern California Colony Association," eventually bought the holdings which the "Silk Center Association" had originally obtained from Abel Stearns and the Robidoux estate, named the colony "Riverside," and constructed a large canal to bring necessary water from the Santa Ana River.[8]

Only a few months before North brought his first colonists to Riverside, W. H. Spurgeon had laid out the town of Santa Ana further down the Santa Ana River on part of the sixty-two-thousand acre Rancho Santiago de Santa Ana, a Spanish grant that dated back to the year 1810. It is said that the wild mustard grew so thick and tall on the fertile land that Spurgeon was forced to climb a sycamore tree to get a bird's-eye view of the proposed townsite.

East of Santa Ana, "between Gospel Swamp and Tomato City," stood the small settlement to which Columbus Tustin had given the ambitious name of Tustin City, while somewhat to the north and east lay the Richland Farm District, a tract of six hundred acres, "beautifully located, under the flow of the A. B. Chapman Canal . . . well-watered, sheltered, and above the influence of frosts."

The owners of the latter property proposed to divide the land into medium and small size ranches and lay out a town surrounding a plaza on a forty-acre site near the center of the tract. The town was originally called Richland, but is better known today as Orange.

The town of Pomona was founded in the mid-seventies by the Los Angeles Immigration and Land Cooperative Association on part of the large Rancho San José which Governor Juan B. Alvarado granted to Ignacio Palomares and Ricardo Vejar in 1837. Some 2,500 acres surrounding the town were subdivided into ranches ranging from five to forty acres in size and the land, some of which is now priced at three or four thousand dollars an acre, was sold at an average price per acre of only fifty or sixty dollars.

"In November, 1875," wrote J. M. Guinn, "the town had a hotel, a drug and provision store, a dry goods store, a grocery and meat market and eight or ten dwelling houses." A successful auction sale of town lots early in 1876 added to the population and prosperity of Pomona and rail connection with Los Angeles by means of a branch of the Southern Pacific afforded unusual opportunity for growth. The drought of 1876-77, however, seriously damaged the newly-planted farms and orchards and a great fire in the summer of 1877 almost wiped out the little town itself. In 1880 Pomona had a population of only a hundred and thirty, and it was not until the spectacular boom of the eighties that the town again came into its own.[9]

Life in the southern California towns of the seventies was characterized by what might be called semi-frontier conditions. The settlers had the advantage of roads, stores and neighbors. They were not required to fight Indians or organized bands of outlaws. Doctors, schools and churches were usually within easy reach. But most of the standard necessities of modern living were as yet unknown, and the housewife of that time, as the following description graphically attests, knew nothing of the labor-saving devices which her successor of today enjoys:

"A galvanized iron tub or two (not stationary), a washboiler and a washboard comprised the paraphernalia for the laundry. With water hauled in barrels or dipped from the ditch there were no bathrooms; the same tubs served for bathing. An out-house, built over a vault digged in the ground, was the toilet.

Washstands with bowls and pitchers stood in the bedrooms. Usually there was a 'washbench' outside the back door, with a basin and soap-dish for the use of the men when they came in from the fields. A broom, dustpan and dustcloth, supplemented by a scrubbing-brush and pail, did all—and more—that the vacuum-cleaner does now. There was no bakery, so the housewife baked her own bread. . . . She made her own butter, too. . . .

"Water was carried in from outdoors and was carried out to be emptied. . . . People went to the cañon to pick up wood for the cooking-stove. Kerosene lamps were used for lighting."[10]

In addition to the foundation of the towns already mentioned, the seventies witnessed the establishment of many other settlements and the agricultural development of large areas that previously had been used only for sheep or cattle ranges. One of the largest of the latter undertakings involved the San Fernando Valley. Much of the initiative in this venture was taken by Charles Maclay, a Methodist minister who served for some years in the sixties as a member of the California state Senate from San José. Maclay was a devout man, a past master in the art of propaganda, a recipient of Leland Stanford's favors, a benefactor both of society and himself. He enjoyed more than local reputation as a public speaker, and one of his eulogies, delivered in the state Senate in support of a bill to encourage silk culture in the state, might well serve as a classic example of the flamboyant language to which the era was so addicted. This was his tribute to California:

"Nature has designed our young queen, sitting by the sunset sea, bathing her feet in its pacific waters, her flowing hair touching our golden hills, her fairy fingers plucking the peach and the lily the year round—as one of the brightest constellations in the galaxy of stars of our never to be ruptured Union. No land so favored; none so promising."

Coming to southern California in 1874, Maclay formed a

partnership with B. F. and George K. Porter of San Francisco, borrowed some $60,000 from his patron, Leland Stanford, and bought 57,000 acres of land in the northern end of the San Fernando Valley, at a cost of about $2.50 an acre. In a subsequent distribution, Maclay acquired the eastern third of the original purchase. He subdivided part of his holdings into small ranches, laid out the town of San Fernando, advertised extensively and effectively, and made a generous fortune out of the venture. In three months after its foundation, according to newspaper reports of the time, the town of San Fernando had forty houses, two hotels, two stores, a drug store, a blacksmith and wheelwright shop, a bakery, harness shop, boot and shoe establishment, and the promise of a school and a church.[11]

With the decrease of the wool industry in the middle and late seventies, the growth of diversified farming in southern California centered in the main around citrus fruits, grapes, and grains. The orange industry, as we have already shown, was well established prior to 1870, and by 1875 there were nearly 100,000 orange trees in the state. More than five million oranges were shipped annually from southern California to San Francisco, and even before the coming of the railroad good southern California orange groves yielded remarkably large returns and occupied a prominent place in the florid advertisements of the region. In December, 1873, John Shirley Ward, a Tennessee editor, sent the following typical panegyric to the *Nashville Rural Sun*:

The future wealth of this country will be its tropical fruits. An orange, lemon, lime, or walnut orchard, is better than a gold mine. Mr. Rose, who owns one of the most delightful orange groves in the country, has five hundred bearing orange trees, and he has just sold his crop for the snug little sum of $15,000.

For the benefit of those who have money invested in bonds, or lying idle, we submit the following figures as to what can be done by an investment in the orange business:

100 acres of land	$ 6,000
7,000 five-year old orange trees	7,000
Interest on $13,000, for five years, at ten per cent . . .	6,500
Services for attention and cultivation five years	5,000
Taxes and irrigation	500
Total cost of orchard at end of five years	$25,000
Fruit of seven thousand orange trees, at $10 per tree . .	$70,000

Thus it will be seen that an investment of $25,000 will pay, in five years, after allowing ten per cent. interest, the sum of $45,000, and the yearly income, after the five years, would be $70,000. This calculation is based on $10 per tree, while Mr. Rose has just sold his for $30 per tree. At the end of five years the orange orchard would be worth $1,000 per acre, thus realizing $100,000 from an investment of only $25,000. These profits seem fabulous, yet they are not visionary, as the same results, on a smaller scale, are more than realized here, by many persons now in the business.[12]

A few years after Ward's enticing letter appeared in the Nashville paper, the California orange industry was revolutionized by the introduction of the seedless orange, later called the Washington Navel, from the Brazilian province of Bahia. Twelve trees were sent from Brazil to the Department of Agriculture in Washington, and a member of the Department later sent three of these trees—or, as an alternative, three young seedling stock budded to the new variety—to L. C. Tibbets of Riverside. From this point on, authorities differ as to whether Mr. or Mrs. Tibbets was responsible for the care of the trees and the propagation of the navel orange in California, but the weight of evidence now favors the husband rather than the wife.[13] Without entering further into the family controversy, it is enough to say that the Washington Navel was so superior in looks, taste, and marketability and proved so well adapted to California soil and climate that hundreds of acres of seedling orchards were budded to the new variety.[14]

Wheat became a commercial crop in southern California when Isaac Lankershim formed the "San Fernando Farm Homestead Association," bought 60,000 acres in the southern end of the San Fernando Valley from ex-governor Pío Pico for $115,000, and joined with I. N. Van Nuys to plant part of the land to grain. Drought and rust ruined the early harvest, but in 1876 the valley produced enough wheat to ship two full cargoes to Liverpool.[15] Two years later Lankershim and his associates built a flour mill at the corner of Commercial and Alameda streets to furnish an additional outlet for the wheat.[16]

The treeless landscape of southern California presented both a commercial and scenic liability. In the mid-seventies the "Forest Grove Association" sought to convert the barren horizons into both beauty and profit by planting eucalyptus trees on a large scale. Like the mulberry groves of the silk enthusiasts, a decade earlier, the eucalyptus forests helped materially to relieve the monotony of the bare hillsides and uncultivated wastes, but the venture proved a financial failure.

The same factors—undeveloped facilities for irrigation, insufficient capital, lack of markets, inadequate transportation, and confusion in land titles—that had retarded the growth of diversified agriculture in southern California during the fifties and sixties, remained effective if somewhat less significant obstacles during the next decade. The financial picture became a little brighter, however, when interest rates dropped abruptly from the preposterous heights at which they had remained pegged for nearly twenty years to a more sane and desirable level.

After 1868, or 1870, the three, five, or ten per cent compound interest charges a month, which had prevailed in the fifties and sixties, gave place to a going rate of ten per cent a year on well-secured loans. The "Hayward & Company Bank," opened in Los Angeles in 1868 by James Alvinza Hayward of San Fran-

cisco and John G. Downey, began the development of the banking system of southern California. In July of the same year,
Isaias W. Hellman, William Workman, his son-in-law, F. P. F.
Temple, and James R. Toberman started a second Los Angeles
bank, under the name of Hellman, Temple, and Company. The
Farmers and Merchants Bank, oldest and one of the most distinguished of present-day southern California banks, opened
for business on April 10, 1871. Five years later the Commercial
Bank, forerunner of what later became the First National Bank
of Los Angeles, was organized.

Hayward and Company, the first of the banks just mentioned,
soon retired voluntarily from the field. Hellman presently with-
drew from Hellman, Temple, and Company to form the Farmers and Merchants Bank and left his former associates to continue under the name of Temple and Workman. The venture
came to an early and tragic end. Neither Temple nor Workman
was qualified either by experience or temperament for the business. They were constitutionally unable to refuse a loan to a
friend or indeed to anyone else who came to the bank profess-
ing to be in need. They could not understand that the Los Angeles and the California of 1870 were not the Los Angeles and
the California they had known when they first came to dwell
in "the land of the large and charitable air." The cashier, who
actually ran the bank, was either incompetent or unwilling to
risk his position by insisting upon the adoption of sound financial policies.

So, in the panic of 1875, the Temple and Workman Bank
became virtually insolvent and the partners borrowed $210,000
from E. J., or "Lucky," Baldwin of San Francisco, master of a
fortune from the Comstock Lode, landowner, speculator, a hard
and ruthless man, to save them from disaster.[17]

Before making the loan, Baldwin warned the two partners
that he would expect full payment when the note fell due and

reject any plea for an extension of time or any other consideration. As security, he not only demanded a mortgage on all the
properties owned by Temple and Workman but also on a nearby ranch of 2,200 acres that belonged to their close friend, Juan
M. Sánchez. Against the urgent advice of many business men in
Los Angeles, Sánchez foolishly agreed, like the old Californian
that he was, to permit the mortgage to be placed against his
property to accommodate his friends.

A few weeks after Workman and Temple received the money,
the bank failed. Baldwin foreclosed his mortgages and thereby
acquired four separate ranches—a total of nearly 27,000 acres—
a frontage of 240 feet on Spring Street, and 80 additional acres
in Los Angeles. Sánchez was left bankrupt. Temple suffered the
same fate. The seventy-six-year-old William Workman, broken
in fortune and hope, shot himself through the head. The effects
of the panic of the mid-seventies and the Temple-Workman
failure were thus summarized by Remi A. Nadeau in *City Makers*, a historically valuable, pleasantly flavored study of early
Los Angeles:

"All over the county the panic brought a sudden collapse of
the boom. Land sales fell off abruptly, and prices of unimproved
land in the south-county region dropped from a high of $100
an acre to between $30 and $65. Los Angeles County's assessed
valuation, which had risen two or three million dollars per year
since 1868, retreated for the first time in 1876. The promoters
of Downey, Orange, and practically every new community
along the railroad soon found the influx of settlers dwindling
off. Half-a-dozen budding subdivisions—Fair Haven, Centralia,
Orangethorpe, Centinela, and others—were scuttled before they
had been fairly launched. The ambitious Los Angeles Immigration and Land Cooperative Association failed in the crisis, and
its two products, Artesia and Pomona, fell into gloomy stagnation. B. D. Wilson's Alhambra tract suffered a premature death,

while Santa Monica, San Fernando, and Pasadena languished
for want of immigrants. The spread of farm lands was so rudely
checked that the market for young orange trees fell off sharply;
orange nurserymen, riding on a high tide since '73, now found
both prices and volume skidding hopelessly."[18]

During this first half of the seventies, mining played a large
part in the prosperity of Los Angeles and the economic development of southern California as a whole. Some of the mines, discovered during the preceding decade in San Gabriel Cañon and
the San Bernardino Mountains, continued to be worked on an
extensive scale during the period, and other valuable deposits
were opened in San Diego County (notably at Julian), along
the Colorado River, and at various places on the Mojave Desert.

The largest of such developments, however, took place in the
Owens Valley-Panamint-Death Valley sectors. Here, as noted
in an earlier chapter, the Cerro Gordo became the most important center, and continued large-scale production until the
middle of the decade. Remi Nadeau's Cerro Gordo Freighting
Company, which employed a hundred men and used upwards
of 500 horses and mules, had the contract for the delivery of the
silver. Great freight wagons, each drawn by twelve or fourteen
mules, transported seventeen tons of bullion a day over the two
hundred miles of mountain and desert that lay between Owens
Lake and the terminus of the railroad at San Fernando.[19]

In 1873 paying ore was discovered in the desolate Panamint
Mountains, on the western side of Death Valley, and a year or
two later the town of Panamint began to make mining history.
John P. Jones and William M. Stewart, both former United
States Senators from Nevada, were the most important investors
in Panamint. The camp at one time had a population of 1,500
and its owners believed its silver deposits might even rival those
of the Comstock.

When interest in Panamint began to decline, a major boom

developed in the nearby district known as Darwin. The camp soon became the scene of large-scale mining and milling operations and added materially to the prosperity of Los Angeles merchants by furnishing a market for supplies and merchandise.

The development of mining and agriculture, the increase of population, and the subdivision of the great land grants into diversified farms were all indicative of a significant economic change that was taking place in the southern California of the cattle and sheep range era. But this development was greatly retarded and everywhere curtailed by the region's oldest, most serious economic handicap—the need for rapid and adequate communication. Pack trains, stage coaches, freight wagons belonged to the southern California of the semi-wilderness, the southern California of the cattle frontier. Only a transcontinental railroad could remove this greatest of all handicaps and break down the vast wall of isolation with which deserts, mountains, and distance so jealously guarded the region.

A number of small local railroads were built from Los Angeles to nearby communities before the mid-seventies. The "Los Angeles and San Pedro Railroad," sometimes called the Banning line, was opened in October, 1869; and in 1871, Major Ben C. Truman, booster extraordinary for southern California in general and the Central-Southern Pacific Railroad system in particular, pointed out that four railroad lines already centered in Los Angeles—one running to Wilmington, one to Spadra, one to San Fernando, and one to Anaheim—a total trackage of 103 miles!

In 1874 a number of local businessmen and landowners, including Downey, Temple, and B. D. Wilson, obtained a charter for the construction of the "Los Angeles and Independence Railroad" and proposed to run a line through the Cajón Pass and across the Mojave Desert to tap the rich Owens Valley mining trade. A few months later, ex-Senator Jones obtained a con-

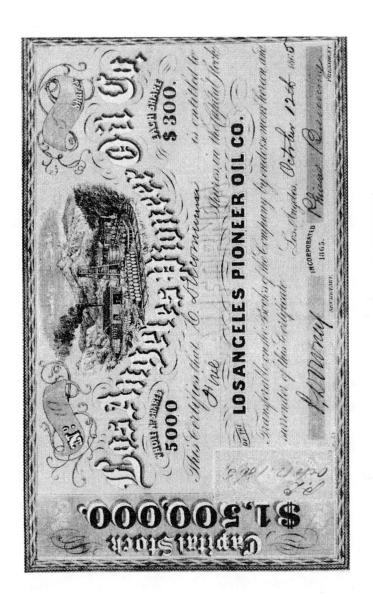

THE LOS ANGELES PIONEER OIL COMPANY

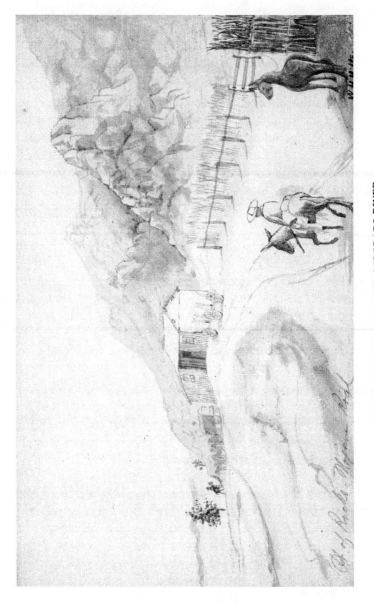

THE MOJAVE ROAD TO THE COLORADO RIVER

trolling interest in the stock of the company to provide an outlet for his new mines at Panamint.

The next year Jones laid out the town of Santa Monica, the "Zenith City of the Sunset Sea,"[20] and announced that the railroad would be built from the new harbor city to Independence without making a connection with any other road. For a time, Huntington and the other members of the "Big Four" were seriously concerned over the plans of Jones and his associates to monopolize the Owens Valley traffic and sought ineffectually to gain control of the route through the Cajón Pass for the Southern Pacific.

Though the Los Angeles and Independence Railroad failed to survive the panic of 1875 and the collapse of the Temple-Workman bank, its proposed construction hastened the completion of the Southern Pacific and played an important part in forcing the Big Four to build their transcontinental line through Los Angeles.

The story of the city's battle with the Southern Pacific began in 1872 when the voters of Los Angeles County, not without threat and pressure, agreed to provide a subsidy worth something over $600,000, if the railroad would build its main transcontinental line through Los Angeles and fulfill certain other minor requirements.

More than once during the next four years, the railroad builders were accused both of needless delay and the intention of by-passing Los Angeles and most of southern California in favor of a more direct line to the Colorado River and New Orleans.

Finally, however, the huge barrier of the Tehachapi Mountains was overcome, a difficult and costly tunnel was driven through the San Fernando range, and on September 5, 1876, Charles Crocker drove a gold spike with a silver hammer to join the rails that bridged the last gap between San Francisco and Los Angeles. The ceremony—colorful, tumultuous, and above all, historically significant—was held at the drab little station of Lang in the midst of the desolate waste of Soledad Cañon.

The long awaited coming of the Southern Pacific must have proved, for the time being at least, an acute disappointment to the hopeful citizens of southern California. For the railroad signally failed to solve the transportation problem of the region's merchants and farmers; and the Big Four's short-sighted policy of discrimination, indifference to the public, and high freight rates retarded the country's development until the coming of another transcontinental line broke the Southern Pacific's ten-year-old monopoly and brought about many welcome improvements in the transportation field.[21]

The lawlessness that characterized the fifties and sixties continued, though in a more sporadic fashion, to plague both Los Angeles and the general countryside during the early part of the next decade. Holdups, robberies, and murders seldom aroused any great outburst of excitement or sustained indignation from San Diego to San Luis Obispo; and the Owens River mines, notably Panamint, acquired a reputation for gunplay, viciousness, and murder that rivaled that of Tombstone, Arizona, a few years later.

By far the most appalling example of southern California lawlessness in the seventies, or any other decade, for that matter, was furnished by a Los Angeles mob that ran amok against the Chinese in 1871. The tragedy started with the threat of a so-called tong war, an incident common enough in any California Chinatown; but unfortunately the Chinese gunmen first wounded a Los Angeles police officer and his fifteen-year-old brother and then killed a private citizen who attempted to aid the wounded men.

As word of the shooting spread through Nigger Alley and other disreputable parts of the town, a mob of several hundred hoodlums, armed with guns, knives, and pistols, "the scum and dregs of the city," poured into the Chinese quarter. The resistance of the terror-stricken Chinese merely added to the frenzy of the blood-crazed mob. Breaking through doors and windows, they stabbed and beat the helpless victims or hanged them in groups from the corral gates at New High and Commercial streets and from makeshift scaffolds hurriedly devised by suspending a wagon tongue or heavy timber between two upended wagons.

Efforts of the sheriff and some of the better element in the population to disperse the mob or prevail on its members to spare the Chinese were futile, and the rioting continued until between twenty and twenty-five victims, nearly all of whom were innocent, had been massacred.

The episode was so horrible and altogether indefensible that public opinion in Los Angeles was sufficiently shaken out of its lethargy both to demand the punishment of the leaders of the mob and to make it highly advisable for many others to flee the pueblo. Eventually the federal government paid a considerable indemnity to the families of the murdered foreigners.

A few years after the Chinese massacre, Tiburcio Vasquez wrote his name on the list of notorious California bandits only a little lower than that of the half-mythical Joaquín Murieta. Vasquez was a specialist in cattle stealing and highway robbery, and the high sandstone outcroppings, now called Vasquez Rocks, in the wild country between Mint and Soledad cañons, served the bandit as a lookout for many of his raids upon the stages and ore wagons running between Owens Valley and Los Angeles, while the high, rough mountains of the Chilao region behind Mt. Wilson served as a secure hideout for the bandit and his stolen horses.

After a brief but spectacular career, Vasquez was captured near the western entrance to Cahuenga Pass by a posse, secretly organized by Billy Rowland, sheriff of Los Angeles County, in

May, 1873. The bandits were enjoying the hospitality of "Greek George," a native of the Levant who had come to California to serve as a camel driver in Jefferson Davis's interesting but ill-fated experiment in American desert transportation. Vasquez was shot by one of the officers, but his wounds were superficial and in a few days he was taken to San Benito County and charged with murder. Obtaining a change of venue, Vasquez was tried and convicted in San José and speedily hanged. Some of his followers continued their depredations until Cleovaro Chavez, his chief lieutenant on whose head the state had placed a price of $2,000, was killed on the Colorado River.[22]

The Chinese massacre and the death of Vasquez marked the end of the era of violence in the south. Thereafter Los Angeles and southern California as a whole began to substitute the manners and culture of older and more stabilized communities for those of an isolated cattle frontier.

In 1873 the Los Angeles Library Association, depending at first upon private subscriptions and later drawing upon public funds, laid the foundation for the great municipal public library of today. Churches of many denominations, some of whose predecessors had succumbed to the adverse conditions of the preceding decades, now multiplied rapidly, not only in Los Angeles but in the smaller communities throughout the south. Schools also expanded with the growth of population, and opportunities for education beyond the grammar school level began to be offered both by public and private institutions. The Los Angeles High School was established in 1873, and the University of Southern California, first of the southern California colleges of Protestant foundation, opened with a small enrollment in 1880.

Though the development of anything like a distinctive southern California literature did not begin until the eighties and nineties, Charles Nordhoff's *California: for Health, Pleasure and Residence* . . . and Benjamin C. Truman's *Semi-Tropical California* were interesting, informative, and vivid enough to survive the generation for which they were designed. Benjamin Franklin Taylor's *Between the Gates*, the tone of which, according to Franklin Walker, "ranged from contentment to ecstasy,"[23] was another valuable contribution to the early descriptive literature of southern California; and the same year that Taylor's book appeared, the Archduke of Austria, Ludwig Salvador, published *Eine Blume aus dem goldenen Lande oder Los Angeles*, a well and carefully written account of the country as he had seen it in 1876. Translated by Margaret Eyer Wilbur and published in 1929 under the title *Los Angeles in the Sunny Seventies: A Flower from the Golden Land*, the book is of great value to any student of the southern California of that time.

In the newspaper field the decade was one of unusual importance. The Los Angeles *Star*, the *Semi-Weekly News*, and other pioneer journals of the post-Gold Rush era, gave up the ghost before or during the early seventies; but other newspapers, direct predecessors of the large metropolitan dailies of today, came in to take their place. The Los Angeles *Evening Express*, edited first by Henry C. Austin and afterwards by James J. Ayers, appeared in March, 1871. The *Weekly Mirror* (later merged with the Los Angeles *Times*) and the Los Angeles *Herald* were both established in 1873.[24]

But Los Angeles had no monopoly of the newspaper field. There were indeed few towns or even settlements in southern California during the seventies that lacked their local journals. The list of newspapers included the Los Nietos Valley *Courier*, the El Monte *Observer*, the Santa Monica *Outlook*, the Santa Ana *Blade*, the *Chronicle* of Pasadena, the San Luis Obispo *Tribune*, and the *Weekly News* (which later gave place to the *Press and Horticulturist*) of Riverside.

Ventura had the *Signal* and the *Free Press*. Santa Barbara was called upon to support a succession of newspaper foundlings, most of which either died a-borning or merged with the able but belligerent Santa Barbara *Press*. J. A. Johnson, editor of the *Press* during the early seventies, was a former minister whose pugnacity and vituperative editorials made him the most popularly hated newspaper man on the southern coast. "When he was not being cow-hided or pummelled by the exasperated victims of his diatribes," wrote one author, "he was engaged in extinguishing incendiary fires, started with the intent of burning him out."[25]

The San Diego *Herald*, one of the oldest newspapers in the state, had given place to the *Union*, the *News*, and the *Bulletin*. The San Bernardino *Argus*, first issued in 1873, soon found competition from the *Evening Telegram* and the *Times*. The publication of the Inyo *Independent* in 1870 marked the beginning of the Chalfant family's beneficent domination of the little newspaper world of the Owens Valley.

The recreations and amusements of the sixties carried over into the next decade. An archery club, with thirty-two members and a number of "Lady Patronesses," enjoyed the support of Los Angeles society in 1879. About that time the city also experienced the first of its many roller-skating crazes. Hunting and fishing continued universally popular and neither large nor small game showed signs of serious diminution. Thousands of quail and ducks were killed each season by market hunters and shipped to hotels and restaurants by the barrelful. Flocks of geese, beyond all counting, ate up the wheat and barley in newly planted fields near sloughs and waterways. Rabbits, ground squirrels, gophers, and coyotes were major pests in nearly every farming area. Rattlesnakes were so prevalent in certain places that the ranchers found it necessary in plowing to wrap gunny sacks about their horses' hooves.

The following description of an antelope hunt, on Beale's Ranch near Fort Tejon, furnishes a typical example of the abundance of wildlife in California at that time.

The party consisted of six men on horseback, three in a light, two-horse wagon, and two well-trained hunting dogs. After driving twelve miles across a plain we were given our stations to watch for the coming herds. Two men were sent out about six miles to start them. It was not long before we saw in the distance a cloud of dust, as if an immense flock of sheep or cattle were crossing the sandy plain. From the appearance of the dust we knew the antelopes were coming our way. We kept still until they were within four or five hundred yards of us—then the shooting commenced. The Spencer and Henry rifles beat the world. It was nothing but bang, bang, bang. The antelopes became frightened and acted as if they were bewildered. Most singular, they formed a circle around us, drawing nearer every circle they made, until they were within one hundred yards of us, but still running at full speed. Quite a number dropped dead, and others went along for a short time on three legs until they were exhausted. The cartridges gave out and shooting ceased. Then they broke for the hills and ravines away beyond. I have seen people excited, but nothing to compare to this. Nothing in the hunting line can surpass it.[26]

The industrial development of southern California remained insignificant during the seventies and met only the most elementary needs of the simple society of that day. In its description of the celebration that marked the hundredth anniversary of the Declaration of Independence, the *Centennial History of Los Angeles* gave a list of the industries represented in the grand parade that served as a climax to the occasion. The account also furnished a naïve but revealing picture of the life and culture of the little city that a visitor once described as "the product of one era of barbarism, two or three kinds of civilization, and an interregnum."[27]

The long line of trades display presented itself, preceded by a handsomely decorated wagon representing the Philadelphia Brewery.

Page & Gravel followed with an immense van in which a dozen or more artisans were plying the different branches of wagon making and blacksmithing. Page & Gravel never do anything by halves, and they made the most of their opportunity. The van was surmounted by a handsome picture representing Washington and other Revolutionary worthies welding the links of the Union chain. On each side of the wagon was this legend: "He who encourages home industry is a public benefactor. Mechanics—the foundation of civilization and progress. The American mechanic—the strength of the Union, the symbol of patriotism and the bone and sinew of the nation."

Next the Asbestine Stone Company with specimens of their excellent handiwork.

Then Cameron's display, comprising fish, flesh and fowl, and on the whole, unique and amusing.

Then a wagon with specimens of B. Aphodl's cooperage, with an immense wine vat marked "A. Pelanconi, wine dealer."

Then a fine display of Halliday's standard windmills.

Next a wagon from the Grange store laden with all sorts of toothsome delicacies. Then a laundry wagon driven by a lady, whose name we did not learn. Next came a fine display by the Adams Windmill Company. Then a wagon from Coulter & Harper's hardware store containing a little of everything in the housekeeping line from a stove to a nutmeg grater. Next came Trapp's fruit wagon with the motto, "Home Produce;" a good idea. Then Reinert's cooperage made a fine display with the legend, "Show us a leak in the Union and we will tighten it." W. M. Stoddard followed with a long line of wagons, carryalls and buggies. Then the Los Angeles Soap Company with specimens of their handiwork. Dotter & Bradley followed with a very handsome canopied wagon which contained a number of elegant specimens of their own manufacture of furniture. J. T. Woodward & Co., of the Los Angeles Broom Factory, made a very fine display of broom ware, all of which is manufactured in this city. The Centennial broom was a feature of the display. Next the New York Brewery, then the Los Angeles Steam Coffee Factory, and after them the Sewing Machine Companies. A long line of citizens on horseback and in carriages followed, and the most magnificent pageant that Los Angeles has ever witnessed came to an end as far as the passing of the procession was concerned. . . .[28]

A summary of the *Los Angeles Directory* for 1875 showed the following classifications: "107 carpenters, 72 fruit dealers, 50 attorneys-at-law, 43 blacksmiths, 33 printers, 32 physicians and surgeons, 30 boot and shoe dealers and makers, 30 butchers, 28 teachers, 28 wagon and carriage makers, 27 saddle and harness makers, 23 upholsterers, 23 house and sign painters, 22 clergymen, 22 livery, feed and sale stables, 2 real estate men, 19 clothing and dry goods dealers, 19 bakers, 18 hotels and lodging houses, 18 dealers in general merchandise, 14 jewelers, 13 editors and publishers, 11 restaurants, 10 drug stores."

The growth of southern California, in the three decades following the Gold Rush, was shown by the census returns of 1880:

| | | Assessed Value | | |
Counties	Population	Real Estate	Personal Property	Total
Los Angeles	33,000	$13,800,000	$2,600,000	$16,400,000
San Bernardino	7,700	2,100,000	400,000	2,500,000
San Diego	8,600	2,400,000	1,100,000	3,500,000
San Luis Obispo	9,800	3,400,000	1,000,000	4,400,000
Santa Barbara	9,000	4,400,000	900,000	5,300,000
Ventura	5,000	2,700,000	600,000	3,300,000
Monterey	11,000	6,000,000	1,100,000	7,100,000[29]

At the time this census was made, the cattle frontier had disappeared; sheep no longer monopolized the coastal valleys; the stage coach was fighting a losing battle with the railroad; and the last of the notorious native California bandits had been hanged in a San José jail. The wealth, culture, and civilization of the East were preparing to engulf the land; and the pioneer days of southern California were slipping into the irrecoverable past as fast as the waters of a mountain stream sink into the dry sands of the Mojave Desert.

Appendixes

I

Grant of the Rancho Ensenada de Todos Santos

Although fifteen or twenty important land grants were made in California while the province was under Spanish rule, few of the early *expedientes* are still extant. Fortunately, the original *concesión* by which Governor José Joaquín de Arrillaga, who presided over the affairs of California from 1802 to 1814, conferred the well-known Rancho de Todos Santos in Lower California upon Manuel Ruíz, has been preserved among the Stearns MSS.

In form and wording the grant was typical of similar grants of the Spanish period, whether in Alta or Baja California. Mexican land grants, though differing in some particulars from their Spanish predecessors, followed the latter in all essential procedures.

The translation of the document is by Miss Haydée Noya, of the Huntington Library.

Señor: Josef Manuel Ruíz, ensign in the company of cavalry of the Royal Presidio de Loreto, and at present commandant of these frontiers of Lower California, says to Your Excellency: that, having some cattle in this neighborhood of the Mission of San Miguel for the support of my family, and there not being enough pasture land around in which to keep these cattle, I entreat Your Excellency to grant me the tract of land known as "Ensenada de Todos Santos," which is situated between the missions of Santo Tomás and San Miguel, on the Camino Real, wherein I may keep and feed my cattle, inasmuch as this will not inconvenience either mission. I beg Your Excellency to grant my request, for which I shall be most grateful. May the Lord grant you many years of life. San Vicente, March 2, 1804. Josef Manuel Ruíz. To Governor Don Josef Joaquín de Arrillaga.

Real Presidio de Loreto, May 1, 1804. Show this petition to the Reverend Fathers of the missions of San Miguel and Santo Tomás, whom I request to append a statement, in their names and those of the natives, whether the granting of the tract known as Ensenada de Todos Santos to Ensign Josef Manuel Ruíz is in any way detrimental to the interests of those missions and the property of the natives, that we may decide what is most convenient to do. Arrillaga.

I find no objection, neither do I perceive anything detrimental to the best interests of this mission (which I have administered for these twelve years), nor to the natives, in view of which I am of the opinion that the land petitioned for by Ensign Don Josef Manuel Ruíz should be granted him. San Miguel, May 26, 1804. Fray Mariano Toldí, present minister.

Concerning the granting of the site known as Ensenada de Todos Santos to Ensign Don Josef Manuel Ruíz, to be used as a ranch, it is my opinion that neither now nor in the future will it be detrimental to the best interests of this mission of Santo Tomás de Aguirio, now under my charge, or to the natives; and in order that this may serve as evidence I sign it here, in the above-mentioned mission, on the 29th day of May, 1804. Fray Juan Riban.

Loreto, July 6, 1804. Communicate the foregoing to the Reverend Father President, Fray Miguel Gallego, entreating him to append his opinion with respect to this matter, of which he is duly informed. Arrillaga.

From my own practical knowledge of the tract solicited by the ensign, gathered during my seven years of frontier service, I share the opinion of the Reverend Fathers, ministers of San Miguel and Santo Tomás; besides, I consider the above-named ensign worthy of being granted his request, in view of his good services, for so many years, rendered to the frontier missions. Loreto, July 7, 1804. Fray Miguel Gallego.

Real Presidio de Loreto, July 10, 1804. Referring to the preceding information, wherein it is established that no injury is done to the neighboring landholders, the tract known as Ensenada de Todos Santos is hereby granted, and, in order that it may be registered and possession be granted to the petitioner, I authorize Sergeant Estanislas Salgado to proceed with two witnesses to the above-mentioned place of La Ensenada, and also with two other persons, representing the missions of San Miguel and Santo Tomás, and put Don Josef Manuel Ruíz in possession of the land, with the understanding that, for every sitio he receives, he has to make acknowledgment of it to the Supreme Government, by giving one peso or one young calf to His Majesty, in accordance with established procedure; and certified copies of these proceedings are to be given him, and the original is to be kept as a record in the government archives. Josef Joaquín Arrillaga.

Ensenada de Todos Santos, jurisdiction of Old California, July 15, 1805. Estanislas Salgado, sergeant of the Loreto troop: In compliance with the foregoing order, assisted by the witnesses, two soldiers from the same troop, Ramón Agundes and Miguel Mesa, I proceeded to mark and measure two sites, for cattle raising, in the following manner: from the south, 10,000 varas, reaching up to the place called El Mancasero; from the north, 5,000 varas, up to the place called Arroyo de Carmerre; from the east, up to the Sierra Madre, 5,000 varas (no measurement being taken on the west, as the tract borders on the sea); and, having placed the corresponding marks or posts, I took Don Josef Manuel Ruíz, lieutenant of the troop at the above-mentioned presidio, by the hand and led him to the two sites; he then walked about and broke down some branches from the trees. All this I performed to give token of true, real, actual civil and natural possession granted him by His Majesty in peace and quiet, without any opposition and with the understanding that he shall acknowledge the supreme authority of His Majesty in accordance with the usual procedure; and to give evidence of this the witnesses signed with me on the same day, month, and year. Ensenada de Todos Santos, July 15, 1805. Sergeant Estanislas Salgado. Assistant witnesses: Ramón Agundes, Miguel Mesa, and Tomas, Xavier, and Nicolás, neighboring Indian landholders from the mission of San Miguel. Melchor, Juan Evangelista, and Atanacio, neighboring Indian landholders from the mission of Santo Tomás.

This is a true and faithful copy from the original, and, in order that it may be so considered, I sign this at the Presidio of Monterey, April 30, 1806.

Arrillaga.

II

Petition of the California Landowners

We, the undersigned, residents of the state of California, and some of us citizens of the United States, previously citizens of the Republic of Mexico, respectfully say:

That during the war between the United States and Mexico the officers of the United States, as commandants of the land and sea forces, on several occasions offered and promised in the most solemn manner to the inhabitants of California, protection and security of their persons and their property and the annexation of the said state of California to the American Union, impressing upon them the great advantages to be derived from their being citizens of the United States, as was promised them.

That, in consequence of such promises and representations, very few of the inhabitants of California opposed the invasion; some of them welcomed the invaders with open arms; a great number of them acclaimed the new order with joy, giving a warm reception to their guests, for those inhabitants had maintained very feeble relations with the government of Mexico and had looked with envy upon the development, greatness, prosperity, and glory of the great northern republic, to which they were bound for reasons of commercial and personal interests, and also because its principles of freedom had won their friendliness.

When peace was established between the two nations by the Treaty of Guadalupe Hidalgo, they joined in the general rejoicing with their new American fellow countrymen, even though some—a very few indeed—decided to remain in California as Mexican citizens, in conformity with the literal interpretation of that solemn instrument; they immediately assumed the position of American citizens that was offered them, and since then have conducted themselves with zeal and faithfulness and with no less loyalty than those whose great fortune it was to be born under the flag of the North American republic—believing, thus, that all their rights were insured

238

in the treaty, which declares that *their property shall be inviolably protected and insured*; seeing the realization of the promises made to them by United States officials; trusting and hoping to participate in the prosperity and happiness of the great nation of which they now had come to be an integral part, and in which, if it was true that they now found the value of their possessions increased, that was also to be considered compensation for their sufferings and privations.

The inhabitants of California, having had no choice but to dedicate themselves to the rural and pastoral life and allied occupations, ignorant even of the laws of their own country, and without the assistance of lawyers (of whom there were so few in California) to advise them on legal matters, elected from among themselves their judges, who had no knowledge of the intricate technical terms of the law and who were, of course, incompetent and ill-fitted to occupy the delicate position of forensic judicature. Scattered as the population was over a large territory, they could hardly hope that the titles under which their ancestors held and preserved their lands, in many cases for over half a century, would be able to withstand a scrupulously critical examination before a court. They heard with dismay of the appointment, by Act of Congress, of a Commission with the right to examine all titles and confirm or disapprove them, as their judgment considered equitable. Though this honorable body has doubtless had the best interests of the state at heart, still it has brought about the most disastrous effects upon those who have the honor to subscribe their names to this petition, for, even though all landholders possessing titles under the Spanish or Mexican governments were not forced by the letter of the law to present them before the Commission for confirmation, nevertheless all those titles were at once considered doubtful, their origin questionable, and, as a result, worthless for confirmation by the Commission; all landholders were thus *compelled de facto* to submit their titles to the Commission for confirmation, under the alternative that, if they were not submitted, the lands would be considered public property.

The undersigned, ignorant, then, of the forms and proceedings of an American court of justice, were obliged to engage the services of American lawyers to present their claims, paying them enormous fees. Not having other means with which to meet those expenses but their lands, they were compelled to give up part of their property, in many cases as much as a fourth of it, and in other cases even more.

The discovery of gold attracted an immense number of immigrants to this country, and, when they perceived that the titles of the old inhabitants were considered doubtful and their validity questionable, they spread themselves over the land as though it were public property, taking possession of the improvements made by the inhabitants, many times seizing even their houses (where they had lived for many years with their families), taking and killing the cattle and destroying their crops; so that those who before had owned great numbers of cattle that could have been counted by the thousands, now found themselves without any, and the men who were the owners of many leagues of land now were deprived of the peaceful possession of even one vara.

The expenses of the new state government were great, and the money to pay for these was only to be derived from the tax on property, and there was little property in this new state but the above-mentioned lands. Onerous taxes were levied by new laws, and if these were not paid the property was put up for sale. Deprived as they were of the use of their lands, from which they had now no lucrative returns, the owners were compelled to mortgage them in order to assume the payment of taxes already due and constantly increasing. With such mortgages upon property greatly depreciated (because of its uncertain status), without crops or rents, the owners of those lands were not able to borrow money except at usurious rates of interest. The usual interest rate at that time was high, but with such securities it was exorbitant; and so they were forced either to sell or lose their lands; in fact, they were forced to borrow money even for the purchase of the bare necessities of life. Hoping that the Land Commission would take quick action in the revision of titles and thus relieve them from the state of penury in which they found themselves, they mortgaged their lands, paying compound interest at the rate of from three to ten per cent a month. The long-awaited relief would not arrive; action from the Commission was greatly delayed; and, even after the Commission would pronounce judgment on the titles, it was still necessary to pass through a rigorous ordeal in the District Court; and some cases are, even now, pending before the Supreme Court of the nation. And in spite of the *final* confirmation, too long a delay was experienced (in many cases it is still being experienced), awaiting the surveys to be made by the United States Surveyor-General. The general Congress overlooked making the necessary appropriations to that end, and the people were then obliged to face new taxes to pay for the surveys, or else wait even longer while undergoing the continued and exhausting demands of high and usurious taxes. Many persons assumed the payment of the surveyors and this act was cause for objection from Washington, the work of those surveyors rejected, and the patents refused, for the very reason that they themselves had paid for the surveys. More than 800 petitions were presented to the Land Commission, and already 10 years of delays have elapsed and only some 50 patents have been granted.

The petitioners, finding themselves unable to face such payments because of the rates of interest, taxes, and litigation expenses, as well as having to maintain their families, were compelled to sell, little by little, the greater part of their old possessions. Some, who at one time had been the richest landholders, today find themselves without a foot of ground, living as objects of charity—and even in sight of the many leagues of land which, with many a thousand head of cattle, they once had called their own; and those of us who, by means of strict economy and immense sacrifices, have been able to preserve a small portion of our property, have heard to our great dismay that new legal projects are being planned to keep us still longer in suspense, consuming, to the last iota, the property left us by our ancestors. Moreover, we see with deep pain that efforts are being made to induce those honorable bodies to pass laws authorizing *bills of review*, and other illegal proceedings, with a view to prolonging still further the litigation of our claims.

The manifest injustice of such an act must be clearly apparent to those honorable bodies when they consider that the native Californians were an agricultural people and that they have wished to continue so; but they have encountered the obstacle of the enterprising genius of the Americans, who have assumed possession of their lands, taken their cattle, and destroyed their woods, while the Californians have been thrown among those who were strangers to their language, customs, laws, and habits.

The undersigned respectfully maintain that, if the promises and honor of the United States Government, so solemnly pledged, had been faithfully kept, Sonora, Baja California, and all the northern part of Mexico, seeing with envy the happy state of the Californians under their new government, would have been already anxiously clamoring to be admitted to the glorious confederation; but now, aware of the pitiful state in which the Californians find themselves, they adhere with almost frenzied despair to the feeble shadow of protection which they still enjoy under the confused, weak, and insecure government of unfortunate Mexico, looking forward with pain and dismay to an approaching conquest.

The American people and the state of California would be no less prosperous in that event. If the land titles had been confirmed to their holders, the land would not be valued higher than the price stipulated by the government; it would have been covered with houses and families, had they owned the land, and they would have given it the attention and care necessary to insure future production and value, while, actually, they consider themselves trespassers on the land and not its rightful owners, and so they have cultivated it temporarily for their immediate use, they have devastated it, exhausted its fertility, destroyed its timber without giving a thought to the future. It would have been better for the state, and for those newly established in it, if all those titles to lands, the *expedientes* of which were properly registered in the Mexican archives, had been declared valid; if those holders of titles derived from former governments had been declared perpetual owners and presumptive possessors of the lands (in all civilized countries they would have been acknowledged legitimate owners of the land); and if the government, or any private person or official who might have pretensions to the contrary, should have been able to establish his claim only through a regular court of justice, in accordance with customary judicial procedure. Such a course would have increased the fame of the conquerors, won the faith and respect of the conquered, and contributed to the material prosperity of the nation at large.

Wherefore, the undersigned, with dignified obedience and respect to your sovereignty, beg, trust, and expect the justice and equity that should characterize such honorable bodies, by giving no consideration to, and refusing, not only the before-mentioned *bill of review*, but also any other demands from the state which, as at present, may tend to work injustice and cause the destruction of the rights of the old native Californians; but they should, on the contrary, respect, protect, and uphold the treaty of Guadalupe Hidalgo, by which conduct both the honor of your august bodies, and that of the general government of the United States as well, will be insured. The undersigned so swear.

San Francisco, February 21, 1859.

Antonio M[ari]a Pico
Antonio Chavolla
Antonio Suñol
Pedro Chabya
Chrisostomo Calindo
Angel Quevedo
Atilano Hernandez
Fran[cis]co Bulo
Felipe Gongora
Albisu Mesa
Fernanda Chavolla
Joaquin Higera 2°
J. A. Archuleta
Fran[cis]co C. Muños
C. P. de la Mora
Carlos Berreyesa
Rafael Galindo
José Noriega
Joaquin Higera
Basilio Bernal
Carmen Berreyesa de
    Pinedo
Pedro Mesa
José Urridias, heir of
    Alviso Rancho
Secundino Robles

Jacob P. Leese
José G. Estudillo
Manuel G. Soberanes
Lazaro Ygera
Pedro Bernal
Pedro Garcia
Jesus Gonzalez
Fulgencio Salazar
Juan G. Geva
Juan Gonzalez
Frank Lightston
Petra Pacheco de Soto
Juana Soto de Lightston
Rafaela Soto, widow
Estevan Joaurdain
A. Mongeon
L. Ellseler
E. Agarfey (?)
B. Fernandez
Nicolás Pacheco
Ines Pacheco
Lorenzo Pacheco
C. Visente Soto (?)
Enc[a]rnasi[ón] Pacheco
Talecio (?) Higera
Francisca Pacheco

[From Stearns MS., Huntington Library]

III

Crime and Justice on the Frontier

[The most lurid of western melodramas created today in Hollywood had their grim counterparts in the actual life of southern California eighty years ago. The threatened attack upon Los Angeles by a mob of "the lowest and most abandoned Sonoranians and Mexicans," and the murder of Sheriff Barton's posse by the Flores-Daniel band, best illustrate the lawless and disorganized condition of society at that time. The following accounts of the episodes are from the Los Angeles *Star*.]

A Man Killed.
Great Excitement in Los Angeles
The Citizens in Arms—Threatened
Attack on the Town

On Saturday morning last, an attachment was issued from the Justice's Court of Alex. Gibson, and placed in the hands of Wm. Jenkins, a deputy constable, for execution on the property of a Mexican named Antonio Ruis. This circumstance, simple in itself, led to events, which have kept the town in a state of alarm and excitement during the whole of this week—the consequences of which may yet, in many cases, lead to fatal results.

On that morning Jenkins proceeded to execute the writ, and meeting with some little obstruction in the discharge of his duty, rashly pulled his pistol and fired, the ball taking effect in the breast of Antonio Ruis, causing his death on the evening of the following day, Sunday.

We shall say nothing of the circumstances connected with the shooting in this place, as they are detailed at length before the examining Judge, and will be found elsewhere.

It will be seen, by the evidence, that the conduct of the officer was wholly uncalled for, no opposition being made to the execution, requiring a forcible display, much less for the sacrifice of human life.

244

Circumstances, however, have since occurred, which have almost obliterated the offence from the public mind. These we shall now relate as briefly as possible.

Immediately after committing the rash deed, Jenkins surrendered himself to a Justice, and was admitted to bail. On the death of Ruis, a warrant was issued for his apprehension, on application by the District Attorney to Judge Hayes, and he was committed to the custody of the Under Sheriff, to await examination. That officer did not think proper to place him in confinement, but let him go at large, and to this circumstance, in our opinion, is mainly attributable the excitement that followed, the Spanish population taking offence that one who had, in their estimation, committed a murder, should be at large, and armed. Great excitement prevailed amongst them from the time of the shooting till the funeral, which took place on the afternoon of Monday and was said to be the largest procession of the kind ever seen in Los Angeles. The deceased was a quiet, inoffensive man, and was highly esteemed by his acquaintances. The feelings of his friends were not expressed in public till after the funeral, when they held a public meeting in the graveyard, to consider what should be done on the occasion. The malign influence of certain firebrands was exerted to rouse the people to an attack on the jail, in which, by order of Judge Hayes, the accused had been confined; but by the exertions of certain gentlemen, Californians and Mexicans, this was overruled, and a committee of six appointed to assist the officers in protecting the jail, and to see that the law was impartially administered. With this determination the meeting broke up, but the ring-leaders not liking this, attempted to create a disturbance afterwards in the town, and would have been arrested but for the fleetness of their horses. One of them, a Frenchman, made himself particularly obnoxious, by wholesale and violent denunciations of Americans, and was afterwards the leader of the lawless band who assembled to sack the city, and murder the inhabitants.

Arming of the People

During the proceedings in the graveyard, reports were brought to town of the nature of the speeches, and alarm began to spread among our citizens. At last, it was understood that the crowd intended to attack the jail, and the citizens began to arm in self-defence. Naturally all proceeded towards that building, and in a short time a strong guard was in readiness to give them a warm reception should they attempt to carry out their threats. The guard remained on duty all night, and no disturbance occurred.

TUESDAY—Jenkins was brought up for examination before Judge Hayes this morning, the particulars of which will be found elsewhere. A guard remained on duty all day, outside the Court House, under the orders of the Sheriff, commanded by Major Harvey and Judge Norton. There was no excitement in town during the day.

THREATENED ATTACK ON THE TOWN

About sundown, rumors began to prevail, of meetings among the lowest and most abandoned Sonorians and Mexicans, and that they were to attack the town at night. These reports were confirmed. Immediately the City Marshal and deputies, W. Getman, W. Peterson and E. Smith, mounted their horses and patroled the outskirts of the city. Crowds were detected in several suspicious places, and at last about nine o'clock, all had withdrawn to their rendezvous, a hill behind the church, from which it was intended to march in, attack the jail and sack the town. This plan had been determined during the day, and warning to that effect had been sent to certain citizens whom they did not wish to overwhelm in the general destruction. The leaders boldly avowed their intentions, and indulged in the fiercest maledictions against the Americans, stating their determination to wipe them out and sack the town. Meanwhile, our citizens were not idle. Every man who could procure a gun or pistol, went to the aid of the Sheriff, D. W. Alexander, who had his rendezvous at the jail, the point of the anticipated attack.

SEIZURE OF ARMS

Between nine and ten o'clock a party of banditti called at the residence of the Roman Catholic Priest, and while one or two engaged him in conversation, the others ransacked the house, and carried off about a dozen stand of arms and small brass cannon. No information of this outrage reached the Sheriff till next day.

ALARM OF FAMILIES

The rumors of an expected attack becoming verified, the utmost consternation prevailed among the families living in the outskirts of the town. Some left their houses and came into the city, and others congregated together for mutual protection.

REMONSTRANCES WITH THE MOB

Several gentlemen rode up from time to time, to the hill where the insurgents were drawn up, to remonstrate with them on the madness of their course; but if they succeeded with a part of the crowd their efforts were immediately counteracted by the captain, a Frenchman, who ordered them to leave on their peril. Amongst those gentlemen who endeavored to disperse the mob we have heard that Messrs. Juan Padilla, Pedro Romo, Jose Rubio and Tomas Sanchez, were conspicuous.

EXERTIONS OF THE OFFICERS

From nine o'clock, the Sheriff, the City Marshal and his deputies were unceasing in their efforts to gain information of the movements of the mob, and arranging plans for their reception. These gentlemen exposed themselves freely to ascertain who composed the mob, or by whom they were led.

RUMORS

All kinds of rumors prevailed during the night; horsemen galloping up and down the streets, carrying messages, or reconnoitering on their own hook. All their movements tended to keep up the excitement, but our armed citizens kept at their rendezvous, quietly awaiting the orders of the Sheriff. There was no provocation of the mob—there was no excuse for their premeditated attack, but the people awaited quietly the course of events; not desirous to be the aggressors, they resolved to deal out a terrible retribution.

THE ATTACK

About twelve o'clock, the moon being then up, W. C. Getman, the Marshal, and his deputy Wm. Peterson, rode towards the hill where the insurgents were drawn up, accompanied by five or six armed citizens, for the purpose of ascertaining the position and force of the mob. There were then supposed to be from two to three hundred persons, all armed; a large number were mounted. While this party were reconnoitering, the mob were put in motion towards the town, Getman directed his party to retire, the footmen first, Peterson and himself protecting them from attack by the crowd. It appears he stopped too far behind, as the scouts from the insurgents came in sight of him, recognized him and fired. He returned the fire, discharging two shots, when the horsemen came up with him and he had to retreat. The party on foot discharged their arms and also retreated. Getman and Peterson still keeping behind to protect them.

SHOOTING OF THE MARSHAL

From this cause, Getman fell behind his party when four mounted Mexicans rode up and fired, one ball taking effect in his head, which caused him to fall from his horse, which was also wounded. While on the ground, these ruffians rode past him, each firing at him, and then fled towards their crowd, which by this time had reached the Plaza. About fifteen shots were fired altogether.

ARRIVAL OF THE MILITARY

The alarm being thus given, the military company on duty at the jail, having first removed the prisoner, marched up to the Plaza, but too much time had been lost, and when they arrived the other party had marched off, to the shrill notes of a fife. It was reported the mob divided, leaving the town in different directions.

The military company remained on duty till daylight, patroling the city and suburbs, but no trace of them could be obtained.

ARREST OF PRISONERS

On Wednesday morning a number of prisoners were arrested, and lodged in the jail. Judge Hayes examined them in the evening, and discharged them all but two.

EXPRESS TO THE MONTE

Immediately after the firing, it was resolved to send to the Monte for assistance, and Mr. O. W. Childs volunteered for the service. Mounting his horse he started off alone about one o'clock in the morning and well and faithfully executed his mission.

ARRIVAL OF ASSISTANCE

WEDNESDAY.—This morning about 10 o'clock, a party of citizens from the Monte, mounted and armed, numbering thirty-six muskets, arrived in town, and were received with loud cheers. They reported themselves to the authorities, and awaited in readiness to discharge whatever duty might be required of them.

Public Meeting

At an early hour in the morning handbills were circulated calling a public meeting of the citizens, in front of the Montgomery House. At 10 o'clock the meeting was organized, a report of which will be found elsewhere.

Organization of Military Companies

The afternoon was spent in organizing military companies, in addition to the Rangers and City Guards. Judge Norton took command of the Guards; J. Z. A. Stanley led the Rangers, and Dr. Griffin the Citizens' Company. The various arrangements being completed, the military quietly moved off to the performance of their several duties. Strict watch was kept throughout the night.

Removal of Families

The excitement in town this night was more general than on the previous one, and in consequence the families in the suburbs of the city very generally moved into town and were provided for in the best manner under the circumstances.

Mounted Californians

Don Andres Pico, at the head of a party of twenty Californians, well armed and mounted, started out to scour the hills and ravines, and returned on Thursday evening, bringing in a prisoner, a Frenchman, one of those in command of the insurgents. He was seen on the road near the Mission, and immediately took to flight. He was pursued, and arrested in a house in which he had taken refuge. Don Andres and party had a most harassing duty, having ridden fully seventy miles during their search.

Attempt to Kill

A most audacious attempt to kill one of our citizens was made on Wednesday evening, by a couple of mounted Mexicans. They were passing down Commercial street, about nine o'clock, and observing two men crossing the street, one of the scoundrels fired at them, the ball striking one of the men on the ear. They then put spurs to their horses and swept out of town.

Wednesday night passed over without any occurrence tending to disturb the peace of the town.

THURSDAY.—Today the Committee appointed by the public meeting were in session. We have not heard what course of proceedings they have adopted.

During the day the country for miles around was scoured by a party of Rangers.

At night, the military were again on duty, but nothing of importance occurred. All was peace and quietness.

FRIDAY.—The town assumed its usual peaceful character today, the Rangers were out on duty, and the citizens, relieved from their alarms, engaged in their usual occupations.

At night, the usual guards were set, but no further alarm.

[Los Angeles *Star*, July 26, 1856]

The Late Murder of Sheriff Barton and Three of His Party

In our last publication we alluded to the report which had arrived here at a late hour on Friday evening, of the murder of the Sheriff and three of his party, by a gang of robbers which has infested the county for some time past. It was at first hoped, that the rumor might be exaggerated, or that some of the brave men who fell might have been only wounded and have escaped with their lives. But, unfortunately, such was not the case—the messenger was but too well informed, and we have now to deplore the loss to the county and society of four good and brave men. They fell in defence of the lives and property of their fellow-citizens—nobly discharging a duty for which all had volunteered their services, and in its execution unfortunately fell victims. Will their deaths be unavenged—will the people rise in their might, and sweep the villains and murderers from the face of the earth—or will the present deep feeling be allowed to exhaust itself in idle complainings? Time will tell. Four of our best and bravest have fallen. Their blood cries from the ground for vengeance. How long?

CAUSE OF THE EXPEDITION—OUTRAGES AT SAN JUAN

For some time past, it has been known to the city and county officers, that a gang of desperate ruffians had taken up their residence among us, and were committing depredations, but the officers were unable to come up with them.

On Sunday, a young man named Garnet Hardy, one of three brothers, teamsters of the city, left town with a load of goods for a dealer in San Juan. While there, he was advised not to drive out his team (four fine American horses) as it would be taken from him and himself probably killed, as the robbers were in that vicinity. Profiting by the advice, he wrote a letter to his brother, Alfred Hardy, called upon J. R. Barton, Esq., and gave the information. The Sheriff prepared to start—told the circumstances to Messrs. Wm. H. Little and Chas. K. Baker, constables of this township, who volunteered to accompany him; also to Mr. Frank H. Alexander and Mr. Charles F. Daly, who at once offered their services—making in all a party of six armed men, with a Frenchman (unarmed) as guide. This party left town on Thursday night.

Meanwhile, the robbers were not idle. On Thursday morning, they attacked the house of Miguel Krasazki, a Pole, robbed the store, taking out everything it contained, destroying what they did not carry off. The owner fled, and thus saved his life.

At night, they came back, and robbed the store of Henry Charles; attacked the house and robbed the store of Charles Flugard, whom they brutally killed in his own room, and then ordered his assistant to serve up supper for them on the counter, where they deliberately ate it, the dead body lying before them all the time. Afterwards, they attacked and robbed the store of Manuel Garcia who also fled and saved his life.

ATTACK AND MURDER

The Sheriff's party arrived at Sepulveda's ranch on Friday morning. The Mexicans residing there told the Frenchman (who had been a baquero on the ranch for some years) that the robbers were in among the hills, that they were at least fifty in number, and would kill the whole party, should they meet them. This report was not believed by the Sheriff—the party made light of it, and proceeded on their journey.

When about twelve miles from Sepulveda's ranch, at a spur of the San Joaquin Ranch Mountains, they observed a man galloping along the plain, for a distance of a mile, off on the left from the road, when Little spoke to Baker, saying it would be better to ride forward and see what the man meant to do. When they had advanced about 400 yards ahead of the party, they were suddenly attacked by a band of robbers, at least twenty in number, who rushed out from between the hills. There is an arroyo on the left, between them and where the man had been seen galloping, but no one came to the attack from that quarter. When the guide saw the robbers advancing, he called out, "these are the robbers, shoot them, shoot them."

Barton and the other three immediately rushed to the assistance of Little and Baker, but before they could reach them, the latter were killed. The four charged on the robbers, fired their guns, and Barton his pistols, and then fought with it clubbed. One of the robbers was heard to say to Barton "G—d d—n you, I have got you, now." To which Barton replied, "I reckon I have got you, too." Their guns were being leveled at each other during the remark, the discharge was simultaneous, but Barton fell, shot through the heart. Our informant states, that three of the robbers fell on the first discharge.

Daly, who was mounted on a mule, was cut off from his party in the charge to assist Baker and Little, was run for about three miles, and then overtaken and murdered.

Hardy, seeing Barton fall, called to Alexander, stating, also, that he had lost his pistol. There being only two left, and Hardy practically without arms, they broke and run for their lives, and effected their escape, owing to the fleetness of their horses.

The robbers pursued them for twelve miles, till they came within sight of Sepulveda's house. For the first 400 yards of the chase, the balls whistled thick and fast around the fugitives, making the dust on the road fly up before and around them. The two stopped at the ranch to get a drink of water, and while there several shots were fired in the rear, supposed to be when the robbers had given up the chase and turned back.

At the time of the attack, there was another party on the left hand hill, but they did not come down. Mr. Alexander stopped at the

Monte to inform the citizens, and Mr. Hardy came on to town with the intelligence.

THE EFFECT OF THE INTELLIGENCE

On the arrival of Hardy, the news instantly spread over the town, and the most intense excitement prevailed throughout the community. It was at once resolved to arm and equip a party to go out in pursuit of the robbers and exterminate them, and within two hours, about forty men, well armed and mounted, started off in the good cause.

RECOVERY OF THE BODIES

On Saturday morning, another party, about fourteen in number on horseback and in carriages, started out to recover the dead bodies of the murdered men, taking with them four coffins in wagons.

The bodies of Barton and Baker were found within about ten feet of the lower road to San Juan—about a mile below the Rodeo de la Laguna, on the ranch of San Joaquin, on the near side of the small hills to the right of Arroyo de los Palos Verdes—on the Sanjon del Alisal—about fifteen miles this side of the Mission of San Juan Capistrano. Barton's body was lying on the left side of the road with the head towards the road, and about 300 yards this side of Baker, who was lying on the right hand side of the road. Little's body was lying about 100 yards from Baker, at about right angles with the road. The body of C. F. Daly, the blacksmith, was found about three miles from the road, as if he had started to go to the middle Santa Ana road. Little's horse was found within ten steps of the body of Barton, shot through the heart on the off side. The pockets of all were rifled of their contents, the robbers becoming possessed of three gold watches and chains, valuable diamond pins and other jewelry. Barton's papers all torn in small pieces, which were collected and brought in.

Little's horse had the saddle on—Barton's boots were taken, his hat was near his body—the hats of Little and Baker were missing.

Barton's body had three wounds in the region of the heart, the left arm broken, and a shot in the right eye.

Little was shot in right eye, head and body.

Baker was shot in back of head when aiming at Flores, also in right eye and cheek.

Daly shot in the mouth and body. The face burned with the powder. The bodies had evidently been fired upon, after death.

[Los Angeles *Star*, Jan. 31, 1857]

The Pursuit of the Robbers

The various companies having returned from their search in the mountains, we give the following reports of their operations:

THE MONTE COMPANY—ARREST OF THE ROBBERS

This company started out on Tuesday, the 26th ult., twenty-six in number. On arriving at San Juan, it got information of the party of robbers in the mountains, and started out in pursuit. About twenty miles north of San Juan, received an express from Don Andres Pico and went to his assistance, as he was guarding a canon in which the robbers were concealed. On Friday evening, the united parties saw them on the top of a mountain, and made arrangements for their capture, which resulted in the arrest of three, Flores and two others, and the escape of three. The party remained at this place two nights and a day, then divided into three parties, Don Andres taking the Californians, Dr. Gentry one part of the American company and Mr. Copewood the other.

The parties continued the search, and at about ten miles distance from their former action, came in sight of the robbers who had escaped. They again ran for another hiding place, a chase ensued for about three miles, several shots were exchanged—there being only four men in close pursuit—finally, the balance of the party came up, surrounded the robbers, who seeing their position, laid down their arms and surrendered.

Flores had Barton's gold watch; and from the party were taken two double barreled guns, one musket, two navy revolvers, one five-shooter, two knives, and other plunder.

ESCAPE OF THE ROBBERS

Having secured the principal men concerned in the murder of the Sheriff's party, the company turned homeward, and arrived at the ranch of Don Theodocio Yorba, about five or six miles from the place of capture. Here they camped for the night, expecting to meet the remainder of the party—tied the prisoners and placed a guard over them. About twelve o'clock, from the negligence of the guard, the prisoners effected their escape. Shots were fired after them, but in vain. Expresses were sent out for the other companies who shortly after arrived, and a general search was made. The party returned to the Monte and were making preparations for another expedition, when on Wednesday evening, they received intelligence of the re-arrest of the principal prisoner.

The search was long and harassing, the men being compelled to travel or watch day and night, with little food for themselves or fodder for their horses.

THE CALIFORNIA COMPANY

On Monday, the 26th ult., Don Andres Pico started from town, with nineteen Californians, the men armed with lances. At the Rancho of Don Pio Pico obtained twenty-five other men, but not having sufficient arms for the whole number, selected thirty-five men, and started for San Juan. At the Rancho of Don Jose Sepul-veda got five more men, and at San Juan obtained eleven men, making in all, a company of fifty-one men.

On the arrival of the party from the Monte at San Juan, they joined the Californians, and Don Andres held a consultation with them as to the plan of action. His suggestions were adopted, and the two companies acted in concert throughout the whole affair. By the aid and influence of Don Andres, a party of Indians, numbering forty-three men, under their captain Manuelito, of the Potrero, was secured, by whose aid the mountain passes were effectually watched and guarded.

The first step taken was to send Indian spies into the mountains, to find the camp of the robbers. One of the runners returned before dark the same day, and reported that the camp was situated at the head of the Canada de Santiago. A second spy came in during the night, and reported to Don Andres that he had conversed with one of the band, Antonio Ma. Varelas (Chino) who sent word to Don Andres, to place his men in a certain position, and he would be sure to catch the whole gang. The moon, however, going down at an early hour, prevented the execution of the plan. Early next morning, the party marched to the place designated, but as they were taking up their position, Flores crept to an overhanging rock, observed the movement, and commenced a retreat into the mountain fastnesses.

Don Andres then charged up the mountain after him, Flores driving Chino before him, with his gun leveled on him. The Chino was
prevented by Flores from joining the Californians, till the arrival of
Dr. Gentry's party of Americans, when being engaged in arraying
his men, Chino effected his escape to Don Tomas Sanchez. Shots
were exchanged by the parties, but at too great a distance to take
effect.

Flores and his men climbed up a very high peak of the mountain
on horseback and two went up afoot. Don Andres disposed his men
along the side of the mountain, so as to guard the robbers, and dispatched a runner for the Americans who were encamped in the
Trabujo Pass. On their arrival, they divided into two parties—that
under Dr. Gentry guarding the mountain, while the other, under
Mr. B. Copewood, made the attack.

The mountain to which the robbers had fled, was almost inac-
cessible, even on foot, and while the Americans were ascending the
hill, Juan Flores, Jesus Espinosa, and Leonardo Lopez slid their
horses down a precipice to a kind of shelf about fifty feet below,
where they abandoned them and escaped down a precipitous ledge
of rocks, about 500 feet high, by aid of the brush growing on its
side. Thence, they took refuge in the adjacent mountain, making
their way through dense chaparral on foot.

Francisco Ardillero, attempting to escape down the mountain,
was captured by Gentry's party.

Juan Silvas, fearing to make the desperate leap with Flores and
his two companions, and knowing that he could not evade the
guards, gave himself up to the Californians.

When the company left the scene of the attack it was sundown;
they went to the foot of the mountain and encamped, and learned
that night from Chino that Francisco Daniel, Andres Fontes, Santos
(since shot at the Mission) and the Piquinini, had gone to Los
Angeles.

Next morning a party under Don Tomas Sanchez, started for the
city, with the Chino as a guide to point out their hiding place. The
remainder of the party kept up a strict guard on the various mountain passes.

Don Andres returned to San Juan, obtained the assistance of the
Indians and scoured the mountains.

Dr. Gentry's party discovered the trail of Flores and his associates, pursued it and came in sight of them, when the robbers attempted to evade them by hiding in a cave in the canada. From this, they fired on their pursuers, wounding one of the party, Francis Goddard. Seeing that they were at last caught, and overpowered by numbers, they made no further attempt to escape, and surrendered. They were conveyed to the rancho of Don Theodocio Yorba, where they effected their escape, as elsewhere related.

When Don Andres Pico left the camp for San Juan, he gave the charge of his troop to Don Juan Sepulveda. On obtaining the Indians, he sent an express for his own troop to unite with Copewood's command, and scour the hills and the canada of Santiago, while the Indians should climb the mountain peaks.

That night the companies united, then forming a band of 119 men, including the Indians. An express arrived from Dr. Gentry, that he had captured the fugitives.

The San Juan company were then dispatched below the San Joaquin rancho, to guard the mountains and intercept the retreat of Daniel and the Piquinini who were expected to come out there.

Next morning, the remainder of the command started to join Gentry. When on the road, they were informed of the escape of the prisoners. Don Andres, not wishing to risk the safety of his prisoners, hung Silvas and Ardillero. He then divided his forces, and diligently searched the whole country from San Juan to the Los Angeles River.

The party was out on this harassing duty eleven days, and underwent great hardships.

Don Andres Pico furnished sixty horses for the party, and procured a large number from other rancheros.

Don Jose Sepulveda drove a band of horses into the mountains, as a depot for the company, and supplied the whole force with beef.

CASUALTY

We regret to have to state, that Jose Antonio Serrano, Mayor Domo of Don Pio Pico, and a most reliable and trustworthy man, had his thigh broken by his horse falling from the precipice, when in close pursuit of Flores.

Two horses of the company were killed by falling from the cliff.

Mr. Thompson's Party

On Thursday week this party started for San Gabriel, as stated in our last publication. There were twenty-seven men in the company, under the command of James Thomson, Esq. Stopped first night out of San Gabriel Mission, and stood guard there; during the night, heard of three men; with pack animals, having gone to Rincon, and went in search of them, passing through by the back of the first range of mountains, and coming to Bodega canon. At this point received reinforcements; sent a command of ten men to San Fernando; others to Cahuenga to get forage for animals, and guarded the roads with balance. It was supposed that during the night some five or six persons had come along the road, and seeing the guard from a distance, or being informed by spies, retreated.

Next day, camped at Rancho del Encino and guarded the road. Next day marched about fifteen miles from that station, and camped. Here the company was joined by a command of U.S. troops from Fort Tejon. Mr. Thompson placed ten of the soldiers, with two of his own men at San Fernando Pass; ten soldiers with two others, at Simi Pass; ten of his own men at Scorpion Ranch, and thirteen of his own men on the main Santa Barbara road.

Arrest of Flores

On Tuesday last, Juan Flores came to the Simi Pass, in search of water; two soldiers who were placed on watch behind a rock, quietly stepped up behind him, and with their guns leveled and cocked ordered him to stop, which he immediately did, and dismounted. At this time, he was without arms, had not even a pocket knife, was mounted on a very poor horse, and had only a little dried beef on his saddle behind him. He was questioned as to who he was, where he was going, where he had come from, etc. etc. In reply to which he stated, that his name was Juan Gonzales Sanchez, that he belonged to, and had come from San Fernando Mission, that he was out hunting horses and that he was going no further. He was then carried to camp, where he was recognized by Don Pancho Johnson, who was of the guard, as Juan Flores, the noted robber and murderer. He was of course secured.

The Companions of Flores

About an hour after the arrest of Flores, two other men came up to the Simi Pass with about fourteen horses. They were challenged by the guard in front, and at once took to flight, through the Pass. Here Mr. Thompson had placed two men, telling them the fugitives must pass that spot. Neglecting the caution of the commander, the men had left the post in search of forage for their horses, unfortunately at the time when their presence was required. The Pass not being guarded, the two men, of course companions of Flores made their escape, as there were no horses to pursue them. The sergeant in command of the soldiers, fired after the fugitives, and it is supposed he struck one of them. A horse ridden by one of them, returned to camp, but he was utterly worn out and unfit for further service. It is supposed the bandit left him and climbed the mountain afoot. The other robber was well mounted and made his way easily over a most difficult and dangerous route.

RECOVERY OF HORSES

In addition to the horse with saddle and bridle, which came to camp, and the band of horses in possession of the latter fugitives, Mr. Thompson recovered six horses, which had been stolen the previous night at Cahuenga.

Flores stated to Mr. Thompson that he did not know who the men were, nor anything of the horses. That he, Espinosa, and Lopez, had escaped from the guard at Santa Ana on Sunday night—that they then separated, and he had not seen them since. That he had stolen a horse, saddle and bridle at Santa Ana, or near there, on which he escaped and reached the Mission of San Fernando, where he caught the horse he was riding when taken. He requested Mr. Thompson to bring him to town, so that he might have the benefit of a clergyman, make confession, and write to his mother—and then he was ready for his fate.

Flores stated that he was not the captain of the gang, but that Pancho Daniel was; Flores was wounded in the right arm, which he stated was done when he and the two others escaped from the Monte party, by leaping over a precipice, his own gun exploded by the shock of his fall, or by coming in contact with the rocks.

ARRIVAL OF FLORES

On Thursday afternoon Mr. Thompson arrived in town, bringing Flores along with him in his buggy. During the journey he maintained his coolness and self-possession, but when he arrived at the jail, and saw the crowd of people, his firmness gave way, and he begged Mr. Thompson not to leave him, but walk with him to the jail. His wish was complied with and he was at length lodged in prison, and heavy irons placed upon him, to await the action of the people.

PURSUIT OF DANIEL

Mr. Thompson, having heard that Daniel had been at Cahuenga on Wednesday, where he had purchased crackers and sugar, started off in pursuit and scoured the country till dark, but without meeting with him.

MORE ROBBERIES

In the early part of the week, a report reached this city, that a gang of robbers had made a descent on certain ranches in Santa Barbara county, and carried off over 100 head of horses from Moore's ranch, San Cayetano, and the Sanchez ranch, on Santa Clara river.

* * *

THOMPSON'S COMPANY

The citizens having determined to make a thorough search for the band of robbers who infested the county, enrolled several companies, as stated in our last, the command of one of which was entrusted to James Thompson, Esq. This company was intended for hard service in the mountains, and a more fitting choice of a commander could not be made. With patience and perseverance, and an untiring energy, he continued the search, until his efforts were crowned with success. The disposition of the men at his command, as will be seen from the report of his company, was such as to render the escape of the fugitives impossible; and had certain of the men remained at their posts, as they should have, the two robbers who are now missing, would be with their leader, Flores. It is much to be regretted that men who volunteer their services for duty of this nature, will not implicitly obey the orders of their commander.

Mr. Thompson's company, however, have done good service, and we think it would be well for the county if their organization were continued for some time to come. The expense of maintaining them will be more than compensated by securing protection to life and property, and establishing peace and tranquility throughout the county. By this means, travel on the roads will be rendered safe, and the cattle and other property on the ranches secured from depredation. Such a course would be highly proper—indeed, it is necessary and we doubt not will meet with the cordial approbation, the hearty support and cooperation of the people at large.

[Los Angeles *Star*, Feb. 7, 1857]

List of Executions

The people having taken the administration of justice into their own hands, the death penalty has been inflicted on the following persons:

1. Juan Catabo, *alias* Juan Sanripa, *alias* Juan Silvas.
2. Francisco, *alias* Guerro Ardillero.
3. Jose Santos.
4. Diego Navarra.
5. Pedro Lopez.
6. Juan Valenzuela.
7. Jesus Espinosa.
8. Encarnacion Berryessa.

Three others, names unknown.

Besides these, Juan Flores, the captain of the gang, is in custody, awaiting execution.

Making in all twelve persons, whose lives had been devoted to robbery and murder.

[Los Angeles *Star*, Feb. 14, 1857]

Public Meeting—Execution of Juan Flores

On Saturday last, the people of this city, and a large number from the towns of the county, assembled together for the purpose of determining what should be done with Flores and the other prisoners then in jail. After a good deal of talking, a vote was taken, and it was resolved, without a dissenting voice, that Flores should be executed forthwith.

It was resolved to hand the other prisoners over to the authorities, their crimes being only attempts at murder, burglaries, and horse-stealing. We had intended to make some remarks how this decision was secured—to notice the inference justly deducible therefrom—but we have had so much of this of late that we have no disposition to return to the subject.

When the meeting adjourned, the people marched to the jail, and took possession of Flores. He had been expecting this visit. In a short time he was led out, and was received by Capt. Twist's company who guarded him to the place of execution. These were followed by Capt. Farget's company (French) the whole escorted by a large company of mounted Californians and Americans. The Rev. Father Raho and Rev. Vicente Llover, were also in attendance, and accompanied the prisoner to his last scene. The prisoner walked with firmness and seemed as composed as any one in the crowd. The distance from the jail to the hill on which the scaffold was erected, is about a quarter of a mile. The prisoner was dressed in white pants, light vest, and black merino sack coat. He was a young man, about twenty-two years of age, and of pleasing countenance. There was nothing in his appearance to indicate the formidable bandit which he had proved himself to be.

On arriving at the place of execution, the prisoner was led to the foot of the gallows, still accompanied by his spiritual guides, the armed men forming a hollow square, supported by the cavalry in rear. His arms were then tied to his body and thus pinioned, he firmly ascended the drop. He expressed a wish to address the people, who instantly became silent. His remarks were interpreted, and were merely to the effect—that he was now ready to die—that he had committed many crimes—that he died without having ill-will against any man, and hoped that no one would bear ill-will against him. He repeated that he was now ready to die. Observing some persons among the crowd whom he had known, he called one or two towards him, and gave some final directions leaving his body to them. He then handed a white handkerchief to one of the attendants, and wished his face to be covered with it, which was done. His legs were then bound, and the rope adjusted around his neck, during which he continued in conversation with those in his immediate vicinity. The handkerchief was placed over his head, the attendants took farewell of him, left the drop, and immediately after the plank was drawn from under him, the body of Flores swung in the air. The fall was too short, and the unfortunate wretch struggled in agony for a considerable time. In his last, despairing efforts, the rope around his arms slipped above his elbows, and he grasped the rope by which he was suspended. It required considerable effort to release his hold. After a protracted struggle, very painful to behold, the limbs became quiet and finally stiff in death. Thus ended the brief but stormy life of the bandit captain, Juan Flores. After hanging some time, a physician examined the body and declared that there was no pulse. The body was kept hanging for about an hour and was then handed over to those who had engaged to take charge of it.

After which, the people dispersed. The execution took place about two o'clock P.M.

[Los Angeles *Star*, Feb. 21, 1857]

[An account of the lynching of Pancho Daniel appeared in the *Star* of Dec. 4, 1858.]

IV

Massacre on the Colorado

During the latter part of August, 1858, the Mojave Indians attacked a wagon train bound for California and killed or wounded many of the immigrants. The episode was one of the most tragic in the history of western travel.

A few weeks after the massacre, L. J. Rose, a member of the immigrant party, wrote to the editor of a newspaper in Keosaugua, Iowa, giving a detailed description of the company's experience. The letter is reprinted here as it appeared in the *Missouri Republican* of November 29, 1859.

Rose later played a noteworthy and colorful part in the development of the San Gabriel Valley. His ranch, Sunny Slope, lying east of the present city of San Marino, was known far and wide for its vineyards, wine, oranges, and race horses. Rose was the uncle of the distinguished attorney, Henry W. O'Melveny, whose life for three-quarters of a century was woven into the warp and woof of Los Angeles.

In 1868 John Udell, a member of the company mentioned in Rose's letter, published a journal describing the Indian massacre and other incidents of the expedition.

Albuquerque, N.M.,
October 28, 1858

You may have heard of several parties of immigrants who started on Beale's route for California last spring, and possibly of their return from the Colorado on account of Indian troubles. I was in all of those troubles, and a plain statement of facts connected therewith, may possibly be not uninteresting to yourself and readers.

The first company consisted of two parties: Joel Hedgpath, Thos. Hedgpath, G. Baily, Wright Baily, J. Holland Baily, John Udell, their families, and probably eighteen hands, forming one party, who

264

had with them one hundred and twenty-five head of oxen and cows, twelve wagons, and fifteen horses.—Messrs. Bentner, Alpha Brown, S. M. Jones, myself and families, and seventeen hands, the other party, with two hundred and forty-seven head of cattle, and twenty-one horses and mules. We kept our stock separate until our troubles with the Indians began, although we traveled together and camped near each other.

We left Westport, Missouri, the 1st of May, and Albuquerque, New Mexico, the 30th of June, with E. M. Savedra, as a guide, who had been the guide of Whipple and Beale. We got along reasonably well, until we arrived at what, I think, Beale names Hemp-hill spring (our guide calls it Peach tree spring,) where we saw the first Indians on the route and they, by way of introduction, stole one mare and one mule. Three of the men went in pursuit, tracking them nearly for a day, and while going through a deep cañon were shot at with arrows by the Indians, but without being hurt. Night coming on, and their animals being tired out, they gave up the pursuit and got back to camp in the night very hungry, thirsty, and tired. This according to Lieutenant Beale's report, is one hundred and twelve miles this side of the Colorado. The next evening, near dusk, while under way, Savedra espied some Indians on the side of a mountain. After much coaxing by sign and speech he succeeded in prevailing on them to come down to us. They, finding that no harm was meant them, followed us to camp.—While coming down, they kept up a continual rapid jabbering, and when near would pat their breasts, saying hanna, hanna, hanna, repeatedly; they also used the word Mojaves.—Savedra, who understands their language to some extent, said that they said, they (the Cosninos) had our horses, and had taken them from the Mojaves, who had stolen them from us, and that they would bring them to us the next day. That they were good, or hanna, hanna, and that the Mojaves were bad. We treated them kindly, gave them as much to eat as they wanted, wishing to have no trouble with them, and thinking that possibly they might return the horses, although we rather inclined to the belief that they themselves had stolen the horses, Savedra saying that the Mojaves never came out so far from their own country.

Next morning, about ten o'clock, word came up, sure enough, the Indians were bringing the horses. Of course everybody was surprised and in good humor. About eleven o'clock, A.M., we got into Indian Springs, ninety-one miles this side the Colorado, when about twenty-five Indians came up with the horses and gave them up to us. It was soon evident that they anticipated very extravagant rewards, all expecting shoes, clothing and trinkets, besides some cattle. I gave each of the two a blanket, shirt, pants, knife, tobacco and some Indian trinkets, and the balance tobacco and some trinkets, also preparing an ample dinner for them, and again a supper. I also gave the two who had returned the horses a certificate that they had voluntarily returned them, and that I believed they had also stolen them. Many remained in camp with us that night, doubtless for the purpose of stealing, but the guard kept so sharp a lookout that they found no opportunity.

Next morning, a new supply came in, numbering probably near fifty, also claiming some reward, commencing with their jabbering as soon as in sight, and keeping it up as long as breath would hold out, pointing out at the same time which way the horses had been taken when stolen, how they retook them, how they fought—wore out their moccasins running after them—wanting shoes, etc., and, to our great relief, about eleven o'clock A.M. they all left. They were becoming very annoying, assigning as a reason that the Mojaves were pursuing them. I felt some little apprehension for the safety of the cattle, but as we expected to move camp about a mile as soon as we could eat dinner, no extra precaution was taken, and it would have been useless then. When we were hitching up we found some of our oxen missing and, on counting, found six of our cattle gone. Some of the men went in pursuit, and found four of them killed. From two the meat had all been cut, nothing but the carcass remaining; the other two the Indians had had only time to kill, and being apprised by their watchers of our men coming, had left them. It being near sun-down, and the cañon becoming very narrow and rocky, the men thought it prudent to return, seeing nothing could be gained by pursuing, and not even seeing one Indian, but probably passing in thirty yards of many secreted among the rocks. From there to the Colorado we were continually harassed and shot at by them. Many of our horses and cattle were wounded, also one man, whom I sent back from Savedra's spring, to let Mr. Brown know that there was but little water. He was shot with three arrows, and only after an illness of two months was able to walk or ride. But it would be tedious to narrate all the annoyances and, compared with what followed, petty troubles.

The 27th of August, about sunset, we reached the top of the last mountain between us and the Colorado. We had toiled two nights and days incessantly. Our animals were without water, footsore and worn out; the weather had been hot. The men, too, were all worn out with incessant toil, and nothing but the verdant valley with the Colorado meandering through it, looking in the distance like a brook, and the evening mountain breeze kept them in spirits, and willing to encounter another night's toil. We halted and had supper, the first meal for the day, discussed the merits of green beans and corn, which we expected to eat when we got there; how long it would take to cross the river, and then, O then, only ten days to St. Barnardino, California and civilization. We gave one general hurrah, and again rolled on expecting to reach the Colorado before day break. Some of the Mojave Indians here met us, bringing a melon and a little corn, which were greedily purchased. They asked us how many of us there were, and whether we expected to settle on the Colorado. (Rather an unusual question I thought at the time.) We told our number, saying more were coming, and that we were going to California. They appeared very friendly all the way, showing the road and performing other service unasked during the night. Instead of getting there before morning, it was after 11 o'clock, when we got to the edge of the woods, yet a mile from the river, and our oxen being completely exhausted, we had to unyoke and drive them to the water.

On nearing the river many Indians came out, and as the number increased, their manner changed to insolence and impudence. My wife and I were walking along, the teams being unable to carry us. An Indian stepped between us, asked many impertinent questions in bad English and Mexican, and laid his hand on her bosom and shoulder. I pushed him away and shook my head, assuming as pleasant a look as possible, which must have been a ghost of a smile, for my blood fairly boiled, and nothing but the life of my wife and little ones prevented me giving him what he deserved. He merely gave a big ha, ha.

By this time we had reached the wagons. Mr. Brown's wagon was probably a hundred yards from the others. Mr. Brown himself had gone to see to the watering of the animals and to bring water to the camp. The day was very hot—the hottest I ever experienced, and Mrs. Brown and children were very much in want of some to drink. I found them all in tears and begging the Indians to bring them some, at which they only laughed and told her if she would pull off her dress and give them that, they would give her some. She offered them various articles of more worth than it, but nothing else would answer. They also would take hold of her little boy, saying that they were going to take him, and stood around, laughing and talking in a very impudent manner, judging from their manners and actions and the little English they spoke.

I had the wagon hauled near the others, and Mr. Brown returning with water, they troubled her no more. Had they attacked us then, we would have been their easy victims, for there were not five persons awake in camp. The men were so exhausted that as soon as they reached camp they lay down under the trees, and fell into a heavy sleep, and amidst gnashing teeth and distorted faces around them, were still, in their dreams, driving oxen.

The Indians killed and drove off our cattle without much opposition, and when caught in the act would laugh and treat the matter as a very good, rich joke. They troubled themselves but little about us, and would cut up animals and cook them in sight of camp. But evening came at length, and the Indians started for their homes, leaving us in the enjoyment of quiet and needful sleep.

Next morning, after a hearty breakfast, we moved camp to the river bank, and all hands feeling refreshed got things in regular working order again. Some started in search of a place to cross the river, whilst others for better grass, in the finding of which they succeeded as well as could be wished, and better than we had expected. A strict watch was kept over the animals, and we lost nothing that day.

About noon, one of the chiefs came to camp to pay us a visit. He had a number of his men with him. When told about his men stealing some of our cattle, he spoke to some of them, but evidently not very earnestly, and gave us but little satisfaction, only saying they would do so no more. He said but little, but was very attentive to all that was said or done and there was a cunning twinkle in his eye which I did not half like. He asked whether we were going to settle there, and when told that we were going to California, he gave us a very searching look, as if not half believing it. I gave him presents which I had brought for that purpose, consisting of blankets, shirts, pants, knives, tobacco, beads, rings, bells, and looking-glasses, which he distributed among his warriors, and said we could now stay and cross the river when we pleased, and none of his men would trouble or molest us. In perhaps an hour after, another chief made his appearance. He was a stout, tall Indian, with a great deal of bluster and fuss about him. He was gaily rigged out in paint, feathers, bells, and gewgaws. I made him like presents, and he made like promises, harangued his warriors, all of whom, except a few, left.

About 4 o'clock P.M. we moved our camp down the river about a mile, where we expected to cross it, and found excellent grass, also plenty of cottonwood for constructing a camp.

Our new camp was a very pleasant one. Although the sun was very hot during the day, so much so that the horses were as wet with perspiration as if they had been in the river, yet we had a pleasant breeze from the river; the water was good and cool, and the animals were fairly "rolling in clover." The evening and night was cool and refreshing, and the next morning we felt as fresh and buoyant with hope as if we had never lost sleep nor had any trouble. But in the calm the storm was brewing. Only two Indians made their appearance; they looked around awhile and then left. About 10 o'clock, A.M., we saw many Indians crossing the river, and we counted over two hundred and fifty of them. Savedra said that the Indians acted suspiciously, and I sent word to Mr. Brown to have the cattle herded near camp. Yet we had but little fear of an attack. I felt some little uneasiness on account of Mr. Bentner, who was to come that morning from the mountains.

I will here explain how he came there. The first party, with Mr. Bentner, of my party, had left their wagons in the mountains, together with their families and most of their men, fearing that the animals could not stand it to the Colorado and draw a load, and had driven their animals loose, while I had all my wagons, animals and things at the river. They expected to recruit for a few days and then return with them for the wagons. Mr. Bentner having mules did not need so long a time for recruiting, and as we would cross the river before they could, and would get some little start, and being of our company anyway, he felt anxious to be with us. I expected him early in the morning, and his not coming, as I said before, made me uneasy, and I thought I would send back to the camp we had left and possibly we might find him and family there. Dinner being nearly ready, I postponed it until after the meal. While eating dinner, one Indian made his appearance. He looked around a little while and then left. One of our boys came in and said he had seen a good many Indians in the vicinity, and they had told him that a steamboat was coming up and pointed where the sun would be when the boat would land. There was quite an excitement in camp for awhile, but we concluded that it was too good to be true. After dinner, two of my men left for the camp we had left the day previous, to see if they could find Bentner.

About half an hour after the men had left, the Indians came running from every quarter, out of the brush, completely surrounding the camp, and attacked us. They came within fifteen feet of our wagons and they evidently expected to find it easier work than they did, for I have no doubt they expected to massacre us. But we were well armed and the men that were in camp ready to receive them. A short time afterward, all of the men came in except two, whom I had sent to see if they could find Mr. Bentner and family; and some of the enemy being killed, they retired to a safe distance. They kept up a continued shooting of arrows for near two hours, and part of them having driven off all the stock except for a few near the wagons, they all left. During this time, the two men had returned and reported of having found Miss Bentner killed, her clothes torn off and her face disfigured. They knew that it was unsafe for them to make any further search, and made for the camp. From this and the fact of an Indian from the other side of the river shaking some scalps at us, which he had fastened on a pole, we supposed that they had all been killed. Mr. Brown was also killed, dying in camp without a struggle. We buried him in the Colorado, and its waters will never close over a nobler or better man, for to know him was but to like him. Eleven more were wounded, who have all since recovered, or nearly so. There were about twenty-five men in the fight.

We held a consultation, and concluded, after discussing various plans, to return the way we had come. There were cattle enough left to pull one wagon, and two mules for the carriage. We loaded these with as much provision and clothing as the oxen and mules were able to pull, leaving the loads of five wagons, undisturbed, behind. We scarcely expected to make our retreat, yet every man felt disposed to sell his life as dearly as possible. We also feared that the families with the few men left in the mountains were all killed; but we made our way back undisturbed, and found them all safe. Out of near four hundred head of cattle, we saved seventeen head, and out of thirty-seven horses, probably, ten. The cattle that were mine have all died on the road, from the fact of their feet giving out in again having to go over the rocky road which had previously made their feet tender; but they were in good condition otherwise, and with a few days' rest at the Colorado, and no rock on the other side, (Savedra says there is none) would have been as able to have gone on without difficulty.

We found, too, at the Colorado mountains, another party of immigrants from Iowa, and from the same county from whence I have come; in fact, old acquaintances to me, consisting of Messrs. Caves, Jordan, Perkins and Davis, with their families and about thirty men. They had been much troubled by the Cosninos Indians and in consequence had lost much stock. The joy in finding them was indescribable, for without their assistance I could not have gone ten miles further. They fortunately, too, had a large share of provisions, which very generously they have divided with us, but even with the assistance that they could render, it was a never-to-be-forgotten march back. Many wagons had to be left and in order to haul all the provisions, all the women and children, as well as the men, had to walk. On account of the heat of the day and the slowness of the cattle, and having to make certain distances to reach water, we had to travel mostly at night and at times night and day. A distance that we made in coming in a day now took us two and at times more. This was on account of the cattle's feet being sore and worn through by walking so long on rough rock. The Cosninos Indians troubled us all the way back, and a party of fifteen men who had been sent ahead with the loose stock to Indian Spring, were there attacked, and had to fight half a day until we all came up to their relief. When some five miles yet from the spring a man came back who had gone ahead, but not with the first party, and reported that the first party had all been killed, that the Indians had their guns and were wearing their clothing, that they were herding the cattle around the spring and were evidently expecting to keep us away from the spring.

I shall never forget the consternation this created, but as we had to have water, there was no other alternative, and get it we must or die. When we got near enough we found the report a mistake, and a very joyous one it was, many shedding tears of joy in finding a son who they had supposed dead. They, too, were as glad as we, for their situation was anything but pleasant. One of them was badly wounded with a ball, (the Indians having one rifle among them,) and one with an arrow. Both have since recovered. To give some idea how fast we traveled, making every exertion, for the provisions of many were all gone and we had to live on beef alone, and that, too, feverish and worn out, so that it made everyone sick who ate it, it took me and the others eighteen days to make ninety-one miles. I could yet write by the day of new troubles and hardships we experienced, but this account is already getting too long.

At Indian Spring we found E. O. and T. O. Smith and train, both gentlemen with warm hearts and, too, willing and determined ones to help. We are all indebted to them for many favors and acts of kindness. They divided their provisions to the last mouthful, and when that gave out, killed their cattle, hauled all the women and children, and lent their stock as long as there was any to lend. Part of us, with mule teams, have now reached Albuquerque, where are as warm and kind hearts as beat in the world. The Americans and the officers of the army stationed here have done everything in their power to help us. They have even sent a load of supplies to meet us, and have sent two more loads to those back with Smith's train, who are now expected in daily. May they never need assistance.

The lot of many is a very hard one. Some are old, who, with large families, unable to work, were going to California to a fortunate son; some honest, industrious farmers, who had what was to them an independency; some delicate in health, expecting to improve it by the climate of California, but with a sufficiency, and all have lost their all, and are now living beggars, or on the bounty of kind people, in a strange land, and among strangers.

You can publish this as it is, if you think it would be of any interest to your readers—or parts, or none of it, as you may think best but if you do not publish it as it is, then be kind enough to send it to Hon. H. K. S. O'Melveny, Central City, Illinois. I have no time to revise it, and many corrections will have to be made, which I would do were it not for my anxiety to get it off by this mail, which closes soon.

Very respectfully yours,

L. J. ROSE.

V

Vasquez

An Interview With the Noted Bandit

We interviewed Tiburcio Vasquez yesterday. He seemed but little the worse for his wounds. Sheriff Rowland has provided him with a comfortable spring mattress, and the dinner which was brought to him during our stay in his cell was good enough for anybody. He laughed and talked as gaily and as unconstrainedly as if he were in his parlor instead of the clutches of the violated law. In reply to our questions he gave the following account of himself, substantially:

"I was born in Monterey county, California at the town of Monterey, August 11, 1835. My parents are both dead. I have three brothers and two sisters. Two of my brothers reside in Monterey County—one unmarried and one married. The other resides in Los Angeles county; he is married. My sisters are both married. One of them lives at San Juan Baptista, Monterey county; the other at the New Idria quick-silver mines.

"I was never married, but I have one child in this county a year old. I can read and write, having attended school in Monterey. My parents were people in ordinarily good circumstances; owned a small tract of land and always had enough for their wants.

"My career grew out of the circumstances by which I was surrounded as I grew to manhood. I was in the habit of attending balls and parties given by the native Californians, into which the Americans, then beginning to become numerous, would force themselves and shove the native-born men aside, monopolizing the dances and the women. This was about 1852.

"A spirit of hatred and revenge took possession of me. I had numerous fights in defense of what I believed to be my rights and those of my countrymen. The officers were continually in pursuit of me. I believed that we were unjustly and wrongfully deprived of the social rights which belonged to us. So perpetually was I involved in these difficulties that I at length determined to leave the thickly-settled portion of the country, and did so.

"I gathered together a small band of cattle and went into Mendocino county, back of Ukiah and beyond Fallis Valley. Even here I was not permitted to remain in peace. The officers of the law sought me out in that remote region, and strove to drag me before the courts. I always resisted arrest.

"I went to my mother and told her I intended to commence a different life. I asked for and obtained her blessing, and at once commenced the career of a robber. My first exploit consisted in robbing some peddlers of money and clothes in Monterey county. My next was the capture and robbery of a stagecoach in the same county. I had confederates with me from the first, and was always recognized as leader. Robbery after robbery followed each other as rapidly as circumstances allowed, until in 1857 or '58 I was arrested in Los Angeles for horse-stealing, convicted of grand larceny, sent to the penitentiary and was taken to San Quentin and remained there until my term of imprisonment expired in 1863.

"Up to the time of my conviction and imprisonment I had robbed stage coaches, houses, wagons, etc., indiscriminately, carrying on my operations for the most part in daylight, sometimes, however, visiting houses after dark.

"After my discharge from San Quentin I returned to the house of my parents and endeavored to lead a peaceful and honest life. I was, however, soon accused of being a confederate of Procopio and one Sato, both noted bandits, the latter of whom was afterward killed by Sheriff Harry Morse of Alameda county. I was again forced to become a fugitive from the law-officers, and, driven to desperation, I left home and family and commenced robbing whenever opportunity offered. I made but little money by my exploits. I always managed to avoid arrest. I believe I owe my frequent escapes solely to my courage. I was always ready to fight whenever opportunity offered, but always tried to avoid bloodshed.

"I know of nothing worthy of note until the Tres Pinos affair occurred. The true story of that transaction is as follows:

"I, together with four other men, including Chavez, my lieutenant, and one Lava, who is now in jail at San Jose awaiting an opportunity to testify, he having turned state's evidence, camped within a short distance of Tres Pinos. I sent three of the party, Lava included, to that point, making Lava the captain. I instructed them to take a drink, examine the locality, acquaint themselves with the number of men around and wait until I came. I told them not to use any violence, as when I arrived I would be the judge, and if anybody had to be shot, I would do the shooting.

"When I arrived there with Chavez, however, I found three dead men, and was told that two of them were killed by Lava, and one by another of the party named Romano; the rest of the men in the party were all tied. I told Lava and his companions that they had acted contrary to my orders; that I did not wish to remain there long. Lava and his men had not secured money enough for my purpose, and I told a woman, the wife of one of the men who was tied, that I would kill him if she did not procure funds. She did so, and we gathered up what goods and clothing and provisions we needed and started for Elizabeth Lake, Los Angeles county. On the way there I seduced the wife of the man Lava. He did not discover our intimacy until we had pitched camp at the lake. He at once rebelled and swore revenge. He left his wife at Heffner's place on Elizabeth Lake, and started to Los Angeles to deliver himself up, as well as to deliver me to the authorities, if he could do so.

"Sheriff Rowland, however, was on my track with Sheriff Adams of Santa Clara county, and a posse of men endeavored to capture Chavez and myself at Rock Creek. We fired at the party and could have killed them if we had wished to. We effected our escape, and arriving at Heffner's I took Lava's wife behind me on my horse and started back in the direction I knew Rowland and Adams and their party would be coming, knowing that I could hear them approaching on their horses. I did so, and as they drew near I turned aside from the road. The sheriffs and their posse passed on, and I took Lava's wife to a certain point which I do not care to name, and left her in the hills at a sheep ranch, while I went on and made a raid at Firebaugh's Ferry on the San Joaquin River, for money to send her back to her parents' house. I did so, and have not seen her since. I provided for all her wants while she was with me. I tied ten men and a Chinaman at Firebaugh's Ferry, in the raid above referred to.

"After sending Lava's wife home, I went to King's River in Tulare county, where with a party of eight men besides myself I captured and tied up 35 men. There were two stores and a hotel in the place. I had time to plunder only one of the stores, as the citizens aroused themselves and began to show fight. The numbers were unequal and I retired. I got about $800 and considerable jewelry by this raid.

"I went from there to a small settlement known as Panama, on the Kern River, where myself and party had a carousal of three days, dancing, love-making, etc. El Capitan Vasquez was quite a favorite with the senoritas. It was well known to the citizens of Bakersfield, which is only two or three miles from Panama, that I was there, and arrangements were made for my capture; but the attack was not made until I had been gone 24 hours. Then they came and searched the house in which I was supposed to be concealed. When I left Panama I started for the Sweetwater Mountains and skirted their base, never traveling along the road, but keeping along in the direction of Lone Pine. I returned by the way of Coyote Holes, where the robbery of the stage took place. Here Chavez and myself captured the diligencia and sixteen men. Chavez held his gun over them while I took their money and jewelry. We got about $200 and some pistols and jewelry, watches, etc., also a pocketbook belonging to a Mr. James Cray, containing about $10,000 worth of mining stock which I threw away. One man was disposed to show fight; and to preserve order, I shot him in the leg and made him sit down. I got six horses from the Stage Company, two from the station. I drove four of them off in one direction and went myself in another to elude pursuit.

"I wandered around in the mountains after that until the time of the Repetto robbery. The day before this occurred I camped at the Piedra Gordo at the head of the Arroyo Seco. I had selected Repetto as a good subject. In pursuance of this plan I had adopted, I went to a sheep herder employed on the place and asked him if he had seen a brown horse which I had lost; inquired if Repetto was at home; took a look at the surroundings, and told the man I had to go to the Old Mission on some important business, and that if he would catch my horse I would give him $10 or $15. I then returned by a roundabout way to my camp on the Arroyo Seco.

"As soon as it was dark I returned with my men to the neighborhood of Repetto's, and camped within a few rods of the house. The next morning about breakfast time, we wrapped our guns in our blankets, retaining only our pistols, and I went toward the house, where I met the sheep-herder, and commenced talking with him about business; asked him if Repetto wanted herders or shearers; how many sheep could he shear in a day, etc., speaking in a loud tone in order to let Repetto hear us and throw him off his guard. I had left my men behind a small fence, and being told that he was at home, I entered the house to see if I could bring the patron to terms without killing him.

"I found him at home and told him I was an experienced sheep-shearer, and asked him if he wished to employ any shearers; told him that my friends, the gentlemen who were waiting out by the fence were also good shearers and wanted work. All were invited in, and as they entered surrounded Repetto. I then told him that I wanted money.

"At this he commenced hollering. When I had him securely tied I asked him to give me what money he had in the house. He handed me $80. I told him that would not do; that I knew all about his affairs; that he had sold nearly $10,000 worth of sheep lately, and that he must have plenty of money buried about the place somewhere. Repetto then protested that he had paid out nearly all the money he had received, in the purchase of land; that he had receipts to show for it, etc.

"I told him that I could read and write, and understood accounting; that if he produced his books and receipts and they balanced according to his statement, I would excuse him. He produced the books, and after examining them carefully I became convinced that he had told very nearly the truth. I then expressed my regrets for the trouble I had put him to and offered to compromise. I told him I was in need of money, and that if he would accommodate me with a small sum I would pay him in thirty days, with interest at 1½ per cent a month. He kindly consented to do so, and sent a messenger to the bank in Los Angeles for the money, being first warned that in the event of treachery or betrayal, his life would pay the forfeit.

"The messenger returned, not without exciting the suspicions of the authorities, who, as is well known, endeavored at that time to effect my capture, but failed.

"But you all know about the Arroyo Seco affair. After my escape I wandered for awhile in the mountains; was near enough to the parties who were searching for me to kill them if I had desired to do so.

"For the past three weeks I have had my camp near the place where I was captured, only coming to the house at intervals to get a meal. I was not expecting company at the time the arrest was made, or the result might have been different."

[Los Angeles *Star*, May 16, 1874]

Notes

CHAPTER I

[1]Franklin Walker, *San Francisco's Literary Frontier* (New York, 1939), p. 6.

[2]The population by counties was as follows: Monterey, 1,872; San Luis Obispo, 336; Santa Barbara, 1,185; Los Angeles, 3,530; San Diego, 798. (*The Seventh Census of the United States: 1850* [Washington, 1853], Table I, p. 969.)

[3]The word *rancho* was generally used throughout California instead of *hacienda*. In his testimony before the United States Board of Land Commissioners, Abel Stearns sometimes referred to the Rancho Los Alamitos as the Hacienda de Romulo, but the word *hacienda* does not appear in other documents submitted to the Board.

[4]From a translation of the papal bull, "Inter Caetera," printed in Emma Helen Blair and James Alexander Robertson, *The Philippine Islands, 1493-1803* (Cleveland, 1903), I, 100.

[5]Pueblo, mission, and presidio grants were made in accordance with general laws or decrees. Private grants were made by specific concession. A detailed statement regarding pueblo lands is given in the instructions sent to Gov. Fages in 1786. See below, n. 12.

[6]John Whipple Dwinelle, *The Colonial History of the City of San Francisco* (San Francisco, 1863), Addenda, Nos. IV, V, pp. 3-8. The U.S. Supreme Court later held that San Francisco and other presidial towns were entitled to the legal status of pueblos. (Hart *vs.* Burnett, 15 Cal. 530.)

[7]Herbert Eugene Bolton, "The Mission as a Frontier Institution in the Spanish-American Colonies," *American Historical Review*, XXIII, 42-61.

[8]The secularization of the mission lands is discussed in Chapter II.

[9]Pedro Fages was governor of California from 1782 to 1791. The *soldado de cuero*, or leather-jacket trooper, was the guardian of the frontier. Each trooper wore a sleeveless leather jacket, made of "six or seven plies of white tanned deerskin," and carried a shield of two thicknesses of raw bullhide. A leather apron hung from the pommel of his saddle to protect him against brush and thorns; he was armed with a lance, a broadsword, and a short musket which he carried in a leathern scabbard.

[10]The letter from Fages was dated Nov. 20, 1784. A copy appears in the *Proceedings before the United States Board of Land Commissioners* [hereinafter cited as Land Commission], Case No. 404, "Rancho Los Alamitos," pp. 53-54. See also Dwinelle, *op. cit.*, Addenda, No. VI. pp. 9-10.

I.e., *sitios de ganado mayor* (literally, "places for large cattle"). A sitio was the equivalent of one square league, or 4,438.464 acres. A *sitio de ganado minor*, or "place for small cattle" (i.e., sheep or other small grazing stock), equaled 1,928.464 acres. (Robert Joseph Kerr, *A Handbook of Mexican Law* [Chicago, 1909], p. 225.)

The town of Puente takes its name from the ranch, La Zanja del Puente.

[11]The word *ranchería* was the common name for a small Indian village.

[12]Instructions issued by Galindo Navarro in Chihuahua, Mexico, on Oct. 27, 1785, and transmitted to Gov. Pedro Fages in California, by Jacobo Ugarte y Loyola, on June 21, 1786. (Land Commission, Case No. 404, "Rancho Los Alamitos," pp. 47-50. See also Dwinelle, *op. cit.*, Addenda, VI, pp. 9-10, and Henry E. Wills, *California Titles*, Vol. V, "Supreme Court of the State of California in the case of Hart v. Burnett, et al.," n. 2. [Wills' *California Titles* is "a compilation of laws, titles, decrees, decisions, etc. relating to California land grants." The items are printed separately and bound in 19 volumes. No date or place of publication is given for the unique series, which is now in the Huntington Library.])

[13]Under Spanish rule California land distribution was for the most part based upon the Vice-regal Instructions "issued by Bucareli in 1771; the Regulations of Governor Philip de Neve of 1779, and an order to Governor Roméu authorizing captains of *presidios* to grant land to citizens and soldiers in the *presidios*." (Henry W. Halleck, *Report on the Laws and Regulations Relative to Grants or Sales of Public Lands in California* [Washington, 1850], pp. 14-42.)

During the greater part of the colonial era land grants were issued directly by the crown; but by a decree of Oct. 15, 1754, the authority was delegated to the viceroys and presidents of the royal *audiencias* in New Spain and Peru. By a royal order of Aug. 22, 1776, the northern and northwestern provinces of Mexico, including California, were formed into "The Internal Provinces of New Spain." Under instructions from the *Comandante General* of the Internal Provinces the governors of California were given authority to issue land grants or concessions under certain general restrictions.

Whether the Fages grants actually conferred title in fee simple, or merely constituted revocable grazing concessions, is still a debated question; but in the eyes of the Californians the passage of time and the lack of adverse claimants undoubtedly gave such grants the status of bona fide titles. Among the authorities on early land grants in California are: Halleck, *op. cit.*; Alfred Wheeler, *Land Titles in San Francisco and the Laws Affecting the Same* (San Francisco, 1852); Thomas Donaldson, *The Public Domain* (Washington, 1879).

[14]Land Commission, Case No. 404, "Rancho Los Alamitos," p. 12. Testimony of Abel Stearns and José Antonio Carrillo.

The original documents relating to the grant were lost or destroyed early in the century. Carrillo testified that in 1806 or 1807 he saw the original concession from Fages to Nieto. (*Ibid.*, Case No. 402, "Rancho Las Bolsas," p. 14. An example of an early Spanish grant is given in Appendix I.)

[15]W. W. Robinson, *Ranchos Become Cities* (Pasadena, 1939), pp. 50, 64.

[16]Deposition of Nicolás Alanis. (Land Commission, Case No. 402, "Rancho Las Bolsas," pp. 9-10.) According to Felipe Talamantes, Nieto "had great num-

bers of horses and cattle, fifteen or twenty thousand or more." (Land Commission, Case. No. 404, "Rancho Los Alamitos," p. 14.)

[17]In the distribution Josefa Cota, widow of Antonio María Nieto, and her children obtained the Rancho Santa Gertrudes; that portion of the grant known as the Rancho Las Bolsas became the property of Doña Catarina Ruíz, widow of José Antonio Nieto; the Rancho Los Cerritos was given to Doña Manuela Nieto de Cota; and Juan José Nieto received the Ranchos Los Coyotes, Los Alamitos, and Palo Alto. The last named ranch is not easily identified. Although mentioned in Figueroa's award and in the testimony of Abel Stearns, it does not appear on the map, or *diseño*, of the Nieto lands. The Rancho La Bolsa Chica, or San Miguel, was separated from the Rancho Las Bolsas in 1841. Gov. Figueroa issued a formal confirmation of title to each ranch affected by the distribution. (Land Commission, Case No. 404, "Rancho Los Alamitos," pp. 59-61.)

[18]For a full discussion of the nature, extent, and boundaries of the Domínguez grant, see Land Commission, Case No. 398, "Rancho San Pedro," pp. 8-21 (*passim*), 31-33.

[19]*Ibid.*, p. 80.

[20]Nieto claimed half the cattle and all the other livestock on the San Pedro; after his death his heirs produced a document, purportedly signed by Domínguez, acknowledging this claim. But Domínguez denied Nieto's assertion and indignantly said of the document, "And howsoever it may read it is not the truth." As a counterclaim he demanded the return of 4,000 head of cattle and much other livestock which he charged Nieto had taken from him over a period of eight years. Land Commission, Case No. 398, "Rancho San Pedro," pp. 141 ff.)

[21]José María Lugo was employed by Father Zalvidea to kill off the wild horses and thus save the pasture for the mission cattle. Lugo spent two years at the task.

[22]Domínguez had been living with his nephew, Cristóbal, since 1804 or 1805.

[23]Gutiérrez held a life interest in the rancho.

[24]Land Commission, Case No. 480, "Rancho San Pedro," (Nasário Domínguez *v.* U.S.), pp. 10-11; Robinson, *op. cit.*, pp. 19-21. Dolores Sepúlveda was killed in 1824, leaving five children, the oldest of whom was only ten years of age.

[25]A translation both of the formal arbitration agreement and of the text of Figueroa's decision is given in Land Commission, Case. No. 398, pp. 263-79.

The Sepúlvedas claimed that, when they came into possession of the Rancho Palos Verdes or Cerro de San Pablo as it was then called, the land was wholly unoccupied, and that they stocked it with cattle, added valuable improvements, and otherwise "gave life to a tract absolutely deserted." (*Ibid.*, p. 245.)

See also Hallock F. Raup, "Rancho Los Palos Verdes," in Historical Society of Southern California *Quarterly*, XIX, 13.

The boundaries of the Rancho Los Palos Verdes, under Figueroa's decision, were officially increased in 1841. In 1846 José Loreto Sepúlveda and his brother, Juan, petitioned Governor Pío Pico to reaffirm to them Figueroa's grant of 1834, because their title to the Palos Verdes was being challenged and other persons were threatening to occupy the property. Pico formally approved the request on June 3, 1846. The Sepúlveda claim to the Rancho Los Palos Verdes was confirmed by the United States Land Commission on Dec. 20, 1853. (Land Commission, Case No. 446, "Rancho Los Palos Verdes.") The area of the ranch was fixed at 31,629 acres. A detailed bibliography of the Rancho Palos Verdes is given in "Inventory of the Bixby Records Collection in the Palos Verdes Library and Art Gallery" (Los Angeles, The Southern California Historical Records Survey, 1940.)

In 1833 Nicolás Gutiérrez, who had a life use of the Rancho San Pedro, sold his cattle to Santiago Johnson and Rafael Guirado for $12,500. After his death in 1839, 4,000 head of stock, together with his brand, were sold to Juan B. Leandry and moved to the Rancho Los Coyotes. Gutiérrez left his property to the widow and children of José Dolores Sepúlveda.

Of the six children left by Cristóbal Domínguez, only five were living in 1834, when Governor Figueroa rendered his arbitration decision. Marcelina, Cristóbal's second daughter, had married the well-known New England merchant-trader, William A. Gale, and died in childbirth on a voyage to Boston in 1833. Under Spanish law, Gale was entitled to his wife's share of Cristóbal's estate; but so far as the records show, he was never made a party to the distribution of the Rancho San Pedro and his one-sixth portion was absorbed by the other heirs. Gale died, in 1842, in an asylum in New England.

[26]As defined by the Commission on Oct. 17, 1854, the boundaries ran as follows:

"Commencing at a large Sycamore tree (*Aliso*) standing on the side of the high road leading from San Pedro to Los Angeles, thence running in a Westerly direction to a stake placed near the high road above mentioned and near a small arroyo or creek, thence crossing the plain following the line of certain stones which were placed as land marks along said boundary line to a large stone placed as a monument in said line on the top of a sand hill; thence to the Sea passing by and including the salt ponds known by the name of Las Salinas, thence along the sea until it reaches a point opposite the Northern line of the Rancho of Palos Verdes occupied by and confirmed by this Commission to the Sepulvedas; thence following said line in an Easterly direction to some sand hills for about 12,000 varas; thence Southerly to a point called La Goleta on the Sea Coast; thence following the Sea Coast and doing the same in an Easterly direction to the mouth of the River San Gabriel; thence up the said river to a point where a straight line drawn from the first mentioned stone lying near the road and the Arroyo and passing the said Sycamore Tree would strike said River; thence along said line to the point of commencement. Containing 8½ square leagues a little more or less." (Land Commission, Case No. 398, "Rancho San Pedro," pp. 94-95.) The area of the ranch was fixed by the courts at 43,119 acres, instead of at the 8½ square leagues, or approximately 38,000 acres, set by the Commission.

[27]The original grant included all or part of the sites of San Pedro, Redondo

Beach, Gardena, Compton, and the Torrance, Wilmington, Domínguez, and other oil fields.

[28]Still appropriately called "Monterey Road." The Arroyo Hondo was sometimes called the "Arroyo Seco de la Piedra Gorda," or the "Dry Arroyo of the Big Rock." The present-day "Eagle Rock," even then a well-known landmark, was "La Piedra Gorda." (Testimony of Tomás A. Sánchez, in Land Commission, Case No. 403, "Rancho San Rafael," p. 16.)

[29]Land Commission, Case No. 403, "Rancho San Rafael," p. 26.

[30]*Ibid.*, p. 27. See also the statement of Nicolás Alanis, p. 8.

[31]The order was dated May 23, 1788.

[32]Testimony of José Antonio Carrillo in Land Commission, Case No. 403, "Rancho San Rafael," p. 14.

[33]*Ibid.*, p. 28.

[34]*Ibid.*, pp. 27-28.

[35]The petition was drawn up at San Gabriel and dated Dec. 4, 1794. Although the ranch came later to be called San Rafael, it was originally also spoken of as Pasaje de Zanja de Zacamutín, and by its Indian name, Haleamuepet. The word *zanja*, meaning ditch or canal, was in common use in southern California as late at least as 1900. The *zanjero*, who supervised the distribution of water and kept the ditches in repair, was one of the most important figures in a rural community.

[36]Land Commission, Case. No. 403, "Rancho San Rafael," pp. 29-30.

[37]Borica's confirmation was dated Jan. 12, 1798. (*Ibid.*, p. 30.)

[38]*Ibid.*, pp. 4, 8, 61, 64.

[39]*Ibid.*, p. 9.

[40]*Ibid.*, pp. 34-36.

[41]Verdugo's death occurred Apr. 12, 1831. He was, of course, the last of the three original land-grant holders in California, surviving his two companions, Manuel Nieto and Juan José Domínguez, by more than a score of years. In 1829 Verdugo had added a few clauses to the original will.

[42]Land Commission, Case No. 403, "Rancho San Rafael," pp. 87-94.

[43]Robinson, *Ranchos Become Cities*, pp. 38-43.

[44]Highland Park, Garvanza, San Rafael Heights, Flintridge, Montrose, La Cañada, Glendale, Eagle Rock, the campus of Occidental College, Glassell Park, and all the industrial and residential area in the Arroyo Seco-Los Angeles River triangle.

[45]Deposition of José Antonio Carrillo. (Land Commission, Case No. 403, "Rancho San Rafael," p. 13.)
The official boundaries of the ranch, according to the decision of the Land Commission, were as follows:

"Commencing at the source of the Arroyo Hondo: which arroyo crosses the old road running from the Mission of San Gabriel to Monterey at the distance of about one and a half leagues from said Mission, said boundary line running from the source of said arroyo down said stream to its mouth at the River of the Pueblo of Los Angeles, thence up the river last mentioned to the place where said river issues from the Sierra at the Mountain called Cahuenga; thence in a Northerly direction from said Mountain at the point last mentioned to the Cerrito Colorado, and from thence to the place of beginning." (*Ibid.*, p. 112.)

In confirming the grant to the Rancho San Rafael on Sept. 11, 1855, the Land Commission declared:

"In the Peralta Case (Case No. [4]) we had occasion to express the opinion of this Commission on the character and effect of concessions of land made by the early Governors of California under Spanish domination and we held such concessions to be sufficient foundation for equitable rights which the present holders were now entitled to have ripened into legal titles by confirmation under the act of Congress of March 3, 1851. No stronger case of these ancient claims has been presented than that now under consideration and the present claimants are entitled to the full benefits of the equities thus recognized." ([U.S. Board of Land Commissioners] "Record of Decisions" [MS, Huntington Library], III, 79.)

CHAPTER II

[1]See p. 25, n. 19.

[2]The earliest of the four grants was that of the Rancho Simí, or José de Grácia, authorized by Gov. Borica in 1795. The Rancho Topanga Malibu was granted by Gov. Arrillaga in 1804; and in 1810 Gov. Argüello approved the petitions for the Rancho San Antonio and the Rancho Santiago de Santa Ana. (Ogden Hoffman, *Reports of Land Cases Determined in the United States District Court for the Northern District of California, June Term 1853 to June Term 1858, Inclusive* [San Francisco, 1862], App., "Table of Land Claims," pp. 1-109 [consult Index].)

The Lugo concession, adjoining the limits of the pueblo of Los Angeles on the southeast, in time became the center of the most lavish hospitality in southern California.

[3]*Decreto del Congreso Mejicano sobre colonización*, Aug. 18, 1824; translation in Halleck, *Report*, App. 4. The report was also published as *House Ex. Doc. No. 17*, 31st Cong., 1st Sess., pp. 118-82.

Reglamento para la colonización de los territorios de la Republica, Nov. 21, 1828. (Halleck, App. 5.) This act was modified in some important particulars by the Mexican congress, on Apr. 6, 1830.

Translations of the laws are also published in Dwinelle, *op. cit.*, pp. 23-24, 25-26, and in numerous other works on California and Mexico.

[4]Confusion in the records, duplication of grants, and imperfect titles, make it difficult to fix the exact number of grants issued between the close of Spanish rule and the Secularization Act of 1833. There were probably between twelve and fifteen. See "Tabular Statement of Land Grants in Upper California," Land Commission Exhibit D, in Wills, *California Titles*, Vol. IX.

[5]*Decreto del Congreso Mejicano secularizando las misiónes,* Aug. 17, 1833. The literature on the secularization of the California missions is voluminous. For a translation of the decree itself, the measures enacted by Gov. José Figueroa, the many subsequent acts, regulations, opinions, etc., see Wills, *California Titles,* Vol. XIV, Exhibit I, pp. 3-169, and Vol. XVII, *Manifesto . . . Don José Figueroa,* pp. 1-105. The "Report of the Commission of the District and the Territories on Secularization of the Missions of Both Californias," with a foreword by Henry R. Wagner, appears in Historical Society of Southern California *Annual Publications,* XVI, 66-73.

An excellent discussion of the subject, including the early colonization project of José María Padres and José María Híjar, is found in Charles E. Chapman, *A History of California: The Spanish Period* (New York, 1921), pp. 466-72. The following chronological outline appears in the appendix of William Carey Jones, *Report on the Subject of Land Titles in California* (Sen. Ex. Doc. No. 18, 31st Cong., 1st Sess.; Washington, 1850), pp. 148-68:

> Decree of the Mexican Government, Aug. 17, 1833
> Provisional regulations of Gov. José Figueroa, Aug. 9, 1834
> Regulations approved by the California Diputación, Nov. 3, 1834
> Decree of the Mexican Congress, Nov. 7, 1835
> Regulations of Gov. Juan B. Alvarado, Jan. 17, 1839
> Instructions of William E. Hartnell, *visitador* and superintendent, 1839-40
> Regulations of Gov. Alvarado, Mar. 1, 1840
> Proclamation of Gov. Manuel Micheltorena, Mar. 28, 1843
> Decree of the Departmental Assembly, May 28, 1845
> Regulations of Gov. Pío Pico, Oct. 28, 1845
> Decrees of the Departmental Assembly, Apr. 3, Oct. 31, 1846

[6]"In 1813 the Spanish Cortes passed a law calling for the immediate secularization of all missions which had existed as such for ten years or more. This law was not published in California until 1821 .." (Chapman, *op. cit.,* p. 466.)

[7]*The Works of Hubert Howe Bancroft* (39 vols.; San Francisco, 1882-91), XXIV, 256-57.

"By law a mission was supposed to endure for a period of not longer than ten years, but in practice the term was much longer, even a century or more." (Chapman, *op. cit.,* p. 153. See also Dwinelle, *op. cit.,* pp. 19-21, 54-55.)

[8]"Record of Decisions," III, 130 (Case No. 663; Joseph J. Alemany *v.* U.S., Dec. 31, 1855.)

[9]Charles Anthony (Fr. Zephyrin) Engelhardt: *San Fernando Rey* (Chicago, 1927), p. 47; *San Juan Capistrano Mission* (Los Angeles, 1922), p. 87; *San Diego Mission* (San Francisco, 1920), p. 204; *Santa Barbara Mission* (San Francisco, 1923), p. 116.

[10]Harrison G. Rogers, clerk of the famous Jedediah Smith fur-trading and exploring expedition, left an extraordinarily vivid description of the Mission San Gabriel as it was in 1826-27. Of the head of the mission, Rogers wrote: "Old Father Sanchez has been the greatest friend that I ever met with in all my travels, he is worthy of being called a Christian, as he possesses charity in the

highest degree, . . . I ever shall hold him as a man of God, taking us when in distress, feeding, and clothing us, and may God prosper him and all such men." (Harrison Clifford Dale, *The Ashley-Smith Explorations and the Discovery of a Central Route to the Pacific, 1822-1830* [Cleveland, 1918], p. 226.)

11According to Harrison Rogers, the mission had "upwards of 30,000 head of cattle, and horses, sheep, hogs, etc., in proportion." (*Ibid.*, p. 200.)

12Land Commission, Case No. 403, "Rancho San Rafael," pp. 40-41.

13For an excellent summary of secularization in California, see *Exposition Addressed to the Chamber of Deputies of the Congress of the Union by Señor Don Carlos Antonio Carrillo*, tr. and ed. Herbert Ingraham Priestley (San Francisco, 1938), pp. xii-xiv.

14Between 1834 and 1842 the number of Indians employed by the missions declined from 30,650 to 4,450. (Jones, *Report*, p. 27, n.)

15John S. Hittell, *The Resources of California* (San Francisco, 1863), pp. 453-54. The colonization act of 1824 provided that the maximum grant of 11 square leagues (*ca.* 48,825 acres) to one person, should be composed of 1 square league of irrigable land, 4 square leagues of cultivable or dry-farming land, and 6 square leagues of pasture. In California no attention was apparently paid to this provision.

16A list of the "Private Land Grants in California," compiled by the General Land Office in 1928, is printed in Robinson, *Ranchos Become Cities*, pp. 227-34. A similar list of the 70 Spanish and Mexican ranchos in Los Angeles County appears on pp. 219-26. See also Charles C. Baker, "Mexican Land Grants in California," in Hist. Soc. of Sou. Calif. *Annual Publications*, IX, 236-43. A standard authority on the subject is *Jimeno's and Hartnell's Indexes of Land Concessions, from 1830 to 1846*; also, *Toma de Razón, or, Registry of Titles for 1844-45*, compiled by Eugene B. Drake (San Francisco, 1861.) A "Report of Spanish or Mexican Land Grants in California, Prepared by James S. Stratton," was published in the Appendix of the California Senate and Assembly *Journals* in 1881.

17The Supreme Court of the United States later held "that creeks, hills, and mountain ranges exhibited on the map or diseño, and referred to in the grant, were adequate monuments and defined boundaries of California land grants with sufficient certainty." (John S. Watts, *Land Claims under the Treaty of 1848* [Washington, 1870 (?)], p. 25.)

18The vicissitudes through which the California *expedientes* passed are described in the following statement by Lindley Bynum: "At the time of the occupation of California by the United States forces, the provincial archives came under the jurisdiction of the military governors. After the Treaty of Guadalupe Hidalgo and the beginning of land litigation, the *expedientes*, or applications for land grants, with their accompanying maps and reports, were placed in the custody of the United States Surveyor-General for California. These documents were in the Surveyor-General's office at the time of the San Francisco earthquake and fire and were generally thought to have been destroyed at that time. They were, however, in a fireproof safe which was salvaged from the wreckage; and, though scorched and brittle, the *expedientes* were intact. On July 1, 1925, the title of Surveyor-General was abolished and that official became the Cadastral Engineer. On July 1, 1932, the office was moved to Glendale, Calif. The *expedientes* were transferred with the office and remained in the Federal Building in Glendale until Sept. 29, 1937. They were then sent to the National Archives at Washington, D.C., where they are now housed."

[19] J. M. Guinn, "*Muy Illustre Ayuntamiento*," in Hist. Soc. of Sou. Calif. *Annual Publications*, IV, 207.

[20] Land Commission, Case No. 401, "Rancho La Habra," p. 15.

[21] The testimony of leading Californians before the U.S. Land Commission almost invariably maintained the governor's right to validate a petition without the sanction of the assembly. Don Juan Bandini said that he would not recall an instance in which the governor's approval was not looked upon as sufficient. Manuel Requena testified that, although the law technically required the approval of the departmental assembly, the governor's decision was final when that body was not in session, and frequently the governor did not trouble to consult the assembly even when it was available. According to Joaquín Ortega, the assembly once asked to be convened to act on land titles, but the governor said its decisions were not necessary. Agustín Olvera testified that by custom the governor decided all land cases, whether between individuals or under petition for unoccupied lands. (*Ibid.*, Case No. 404, "Rancho Los Alamitos," pp. 29-36, *passim.*)

[22] *Ibid.*, Case No. 49, "Rancho Sespe," p. 60.

[23] *Ibid.*, Case No. 49, "Rancho Sespe," pp. 57-60.

[24] *Ibid.*, Case No. 440, "Rancho San Juan Cajón de Santa Ana," p. 54.

[25] *Ibid.*, Case No. 405, "Rancho La Bolsa Chica," p. 72.

[26] Los Angeles County "Assessment Book," 1861. Before a survey was made, the owners of all contiguous ranches were notified and given opportunity to patrol their boundaries and prevent the lines of the new grant from encroaching upon their lands. Thus, in the survey of the Rancho La Habra, Antonio Machado, Judge of the First Instance, wrote in his report: "[The line] . . . terminated in a small *aguaje* in which there is a willow tree that was selected as a land mark, for which purpose, it was cut with a hatchet as a sign, at this point Don Juan Pacifico Ontiveras having appeared; who was present there as the tract belonged to him . . . and the latter not having raised any objection that could suspend the measurement I told him that I should continue." (Land Commission, Case No. 401, "Rancho La Habra," p. 33.)

[27] J. M. Guinn, "The Passing of the Cattle Barons of California," in Hist. Soc. of Sou. Calif. *Annual Publications*, VIII, 55-56.

[28] Land Commission, Case No. 398, "Rancho San Pedro," pp. 74-78; *ibid.*, Case No. 308, "Rancho San Antonio," pp. 335-36.

[29]For an excellent discussion of the nature of the *concesión* and its fundamental place in the economic life of Mexico, see H. N. Branch, "Concessions: A Brief Analysis," in *The Mexican Year Book, 1920-21*, ed. Robert G. Cleland (Los Angeles, 1922), pp. 222-38.

[30]The formula will be found in nearly every *expediente*. The quotation is from the concession of the Rancho Bolsa Chica, *op. cit.*, pp. 68-69.

[31]The claim to the Rancho San Pasqual was forfeited in the first instance by Mariné and afterward by José Pérez and Enrique Sepúlveda for failure to fulfill the conditions imposed by the *concesión*. The ranch was later denounced by Manuel Garfías and the grant was confirmed to him by Gov. Micheltorena in 1843. The circumstances were very unusual and the award to Garfías was perhaps the result of Micheltorena's favoritism to one who was both lieutenant in his command and relative. Testifying in the case, Antonio Coronel said he had never known of another instance in California in which land once awarded was denounced by another claimant. (Land Commission, Case No. 345, "Rancho San Pasqual," pp. 23-24. See also W. W. Robinson, "Pasadena's First Owner," in Hist. Soc. of Sou. Calif. *Quarterly*, XIX, 132-40.)

[32]The case of the Rancho Santiago de Santa Ana, a 62,500-acre grant in what is now Orange County, furnished a good example of the problem which often arose from the California custom of bequeathing undivided interests in a grant. Bestowed originally upon José Antonio Yorba, in 1810, by Gov. Arrillaga, a portion of the ranch was confirmed by the U.S. Land Commission to Bernardo Yorba, son of the original grantee, in 1855. Bernardo Yorba died in 1858; in the course of a few years certain of his heirs brought suit to effect a partition and distribution of the property. Nineteen plaintiffs (not including "et uxor"), and one hundred and nineteen defendants, were named as parties to the suit!

[33]Indians were also farmed out under supervision of a *jefe*, or chief. The pay was probably about 2 reales, or 25 cents, a day. (Abel Stearns Manuscripts, Huntington Library.)

[34]Hittell lists 14 prominent Californians whose children ranged from 9 to 25 in number. He adds that when Juana Cota died she left 500 living descendants. (Hittell, *Resources of California* [San Francisco, 1874], p. ix.)

[35]Quoted in Nellie Van de Grift Sánchez, *Spanish Arcadia* (Los Angeles, 1929), pp. 195-96.

[36]Promissory notes, payable three, six, or twelve months after date, in cattle, hides, or tallow, passed from hand to hand like any other negotiable instrument. See, e.g., a note of John E. Ebbetts, dated Mar. 26, 1833, for 227 hides, payable to Nathan Spears. (Stearns MSS.) On Oct. 12, 1840, Abel Stearns and A. B. Thompson agreed to pay John Dominec $5,796 in merchantable hides at $2 each. (*Ibid.*) The minutes of the *ayuntamiento* of Los Angeles record the levying of fines and the payment of many municipal obligations in the same commodities. American trappers used beaver skins instead of cattle hides.

[37]W. A. Hawley, *The Early Days of Santa Barbara, California* (Santa Barbara, 1920), pp. 95-96.

CHAPTER III

[1] Thomas O. Larkin, "Description of California," in Official Correspondence, Pt. I, No. 124, July 2, 1846. (MSS, Bancroft Library).

The relative volume of trade between 1839 and 1845 is shown by the following table:

1839	$ 85,613	1843	$ 52,000
1840	72,308	1844	78,739
1841	101,150	1845	138,360
1842	73,729		

(*Ibid.*, Pt. II, No. 32, Dec. 31, 1845.)

[2] Charles Wilkes, *Narrative of the United States Exploring Expedition* (Philadelphia, 1844, 1845), V, 163; also Robert G. Cleland, *Early Sentiment for the Annexation of California*, reprinted from *Southwestern Historical Quarterly*, XVIII, Nos. 1, 2, 3 (Austin, Tex., 1914), p. 52.

[3] Cleland, *op. cit.*, p. 53.

[4] *Ibid.*, p. 52.

[5] Wilkes, *op. cit.*, V, 152.

[6] For a detailed discussion of the annexation movement and President Polk's plans for acquiring California, see Cleland, *op cit.*, pp. 41-107.

[7] Thomas O. Larkin, Polk's confidential agent at Monterey, "repeatedly advised" some of the more influential Californians "to ask for large tracts of land by which means they will become rich." (Larkin to Stearns, June 14, 1846, in Stearns MSS.)

[8] Stearns MSS.

[9] "Treaty of Peace, Friendship, Limits and Settlement (Guadalupe Hidalgo)" [concluded Feb. 2, 1848; proclaimed July 4, 1848], Arts. VIII and IX, Protocol 1st and 2d. (William M. Malloy, *Treaties, Conventions, International Acts, Protocols and Agreements between the United States of America and Other Powers* [Washington, 1910], I, 1111-12, 1119.

[10] Many of the grants made by Pío Pico, the last of the California governors, were especially open to question. Thus, in reference to a 7-square-league ranch he was seeking to obtain from Pico, an American named Jasper Farrell wrote Abel Stearns: "I shall be proportionately obliged to you by using the utmost dispatch in this business—and if necessary to *bribe* any of the writers, do so with goods and I shall repay you in cash whatever the expense may be and to whomsoever you may give the order. A little docecente [?] does no harm to those who have the writing out of the papers; it brightens their ideas and makes them much quicker." (O'Farrell [from San Rafael] to Stearns, Apr. 23, 1846, in Stearns MSS.)

Of Pico's claim to the place called "Jamoral," the U.S. Land Commission said:

"In this case he has taken upon himself the responsibility of donating to himself two leagues of the land belonging to the government without bringing himself within any of the provisions of the colonization laws by settling upon the same or improving it in any manner or paying to the government anything in consideration therefor.

"We think that the act of Pío Pico in the premises in donating to himself the lands of the government is without precedent, without authority of law and consequently void." ("Record of Decisions," III, 83.)

¹¹*Report on the Laws and Regulations Relative to Grants and Sales of Public Lands in California* (House Ex. Doc. No. 17, 31st Cong., 1st Sess.). The report was also published separately, in Washington, in 1850.

¹²Jones was advised, in his instructions, that the American government was bound, both by public law and the terms of the Treaty of Guadalupe Hidalgo, to "respect the valid and *bona fide* titles of individuals." His instructions were very detailed, and called for a search of the archives of Mexico City and the provincial archives of California for material relating to land titles; the preparation of an abstract showing: first, the private grants in California under Spanish rule; second, those made by the Mexican government prior to the outbreak of the Mexican War; and third, those made during the "revolutionary" period of 1846. The abstract was also to include the date of each grant included in the three classifications; give its area, dimensions, and natural landmarks; the name of the original grantee; the date of the survey, if a survey had been made; the name of the official responsible for the grant; and the government's action on it.

Jones was also instructed to separate the bona fide grants from those which, in his judgment, were of a fraudulent or questionable nature and to include in his report copies of the various forms used in Mexican land-grant procedure, such as the petition, order of survey, *concesión*, etc., a description of the different types of allotments, from the *sitio de ganado mayor* to the town lot; and a comparative table of the units of land measurement employed in Spain, Mexico, and the United States.

Jones was further instructed to make a study of mission holdings, mineral concessions, Indian lands, and claims of individuals to islands or sites along the coast that were suitable for fortification and other military purposes, and, finally to make a similar study of New Mexican land titles. See Butterfield (Commissioner of the General Land Office) to Jones, July 12, 1849 (*House Ex. Doc. 17*, 31st Cong., 1st Sess., pp. 113-17).

¹³Jones classified and described the land-grant material in the provincial archives at Monterey as follows:

"1. 1828. Cuaderno del registro de los sitios, fierras, y senales que posean los habitantes del territorio de la Nueva California.—(Book of registration of the farms, brands, and marks (for marking cattle) possessed by the inhabitants of the territory of New California.)

"This book contains information of the situation, boundaries, and appurtenances of several of the missions, as hereafter noticed; of two pueblos, San Jose and Branciforte, and the records of twenty grants, made by various Spanish, Mexican, and local authorities, at different times, between 1784 and 1825, and two dated in 1829. This book appears to have been arranged upon information obtained in an endeavor of the Government to procure a registration of all the occupied lands of the territory.

"2. Book marked 'Titulos.'

"This book contains records of grants, numbered from 1 to 108, of various dates from 22d May, 1833, to 9th May, 1836, by the successive governors, Figueroa, Jose Castro, Nicholas Gutierrez and Mariano Chico. A part of these grants (probably all) are included in a file of *expedientes* of grants, hereafter described, marked from No. 1 to No. 579; but the numbers in the book do not correspond with the numbers of the same grants in the *expedientes*.

"3. Libro donde se asciertan los despachos de terrenos adjudicados en los anos de 1839 and 1840.—(Book denoting the concessions of land adjudicated in the years 1839 and 1840.)

"This book contains a brief entry, by the secretary of the department, of grants, quantity granted, and situation of the land, usually entered in the book in the order they were conceded. This book contains the grants made from the 18th January, 1839, to 8th December, 1843, inclusive.

"4. A book similar to the above, and containing like entries of grants issued between 8th January, 1844, and 23d December, 1845.

"5. File of *expedientes* of grants—that is, all the proceedings (except of the Assembly) relating to the respective grants secured, those of each grant in a separate parcel, and marked and labelled with its number and name. This file is marked from No. 1 to No. 579, inclusive, and embraces the space of time between 13th May, 1833, to July, 1846. The numbers, however, bear little relation to the dates. Some numbers are missing, of some there are duplicates —that is, two distinct grants with the same number. The *expedientes* are not all complete; in some cases the final grant appears to have been refused; in others it is wanting. The collection, however, is evidently intended to represent estates which have been granted, and it is probable that in many, or most instances, the omission apparent in the archives is supplied by original documents in the hands of the parties, or by long permitted occupation." (*Report on the Subject of Land Titles in California* [Washington, 1850], p. 7.)

¹⁴*Ibid.*, p. 38.

Nearly three-quarters of a century later, Judge William W. Morrow, of the U.S. Circuit Court of Appeals, said of this report: "In some respects it is a remarkable document. The material was gathered at distant points under rather unfavorable conditions, and, considering its scope and detail, it was obtained in an incredibly short time. The report, itself, was carefully prepared, concise in form, and accurate in detail, and has always been referred to as an authority for the subject with which it deals." (William W. Morrow, *Spanish and Mexican Private Land Grants* [San Francisco and Los Angeles, 1923], p. 11.)

William Carey Jones was the father of Dean William Carey Jones, long identified with the School of Jurisprudence of the University of California.

¹⁵The bill was entitled, "An Act to ascertain and settle the private land claims in the State of California." (*Laws of the United States . . . upon Which the Public Land Titles in Each State and Territory Have Depended* [Washington, 1884], II, 1019-22.)

[16]The question later arose as to the right of Congress to compel the holder of a perfect title to submit his claim to the Commission. In two instances the Supreme Court of California decided against the clause; but in Botiller *v.* Dominguez (130 U.S. 238), and again in Barker *v.* Harvey (181 U.S. 481), the U.S. Supreme Court held that "the United States were bound to respect the right of private property in the ceded territory, but that it had the right to require reasonable means for determining the validity of all titles, within the ceded territory, to require all persons having claims to present them for recognition, and to decree that all claims which are not thus presented, shall be considered abandoned." According to Morrow, "A different law was provided for New Mexico with respect to perfect titles."

[17]A preliminary meeting was held in Washington in September.

[18]Eight hundred and thirteen cases are listed in Hoffman, *California Land Cases,* the standard authority on the subject, but some of those represent duplicate claims for the same tract. In Wills, *California Titles,* Vol. IX, *Land Commission Exhibits,* p. 6, appears a "Tabular Statement of Land Grants in Upper California presented before the Board of Land Commissioners," containing a list of 803 grants. These covered 2,706.8929 square leagues, about 19,000 square miles, or 12,160,000 acres.

[19]According to Morrow, 604 cases were affirmed, 190 were set aside, and 13 were withdrawn. (*Op. cit.,* p. 14.)

[20]An example of the criticism of the Board is furnished in the following excerpt from a letter from C. R. Johnson to Abel Stearns, under date of Dec. 17, 1850:
"The Land Commission are acting disgracefully; every one is down on them, with the exception of the Squatters, in whose favor as you will see by the papers they are working." (Stearns MSS.)
Unfortunately, the continuity of the work of the Board was affected by all-too-frequent changes in personnel. There were seven different Commissioners in five years.

[21]*Organization, Acts and Regulations of the United States Land Commissioners for California* (San Francisco, 1852), p. 5.

[22]Los Angeles *Star,* Feb. 28, 1852. The rancheros met in the house of Ignacio Coronel.

[23]John S. Hittell, "Mexican Land Claims in California," *Hutchings' Illustrated California Magazine* (1857-58), II, 447.

[24]Unsigned, undated draft. (Stearns MSS.) Stearns added that there were some 12 or 15 claims of a suspicious nature but the rest were perfectly legitimate, and that fraud and forgery were encouraged by the Land Act and its method of enforcement. He also added that the law imposed a direct tax upon landowners, and that often the cost of defending the title far exceeded the value of the land.
According to William Heath Davis, José Joaquín Estudillo spent over $200,000 defending his title to the 7,010-acre Rancho San Leandro. ("The

Sunshine and Shadows of San Leandro," William Heath Davis MSS. Huntington Library.)

25Dated Mar. 22, 1855. (Stearns MSS.)
Subscriptions totaling $3,150 were made to the fund. Pío Pico subscribed
$300; William Workman, $300; Juan Forster, $300; José Sepúlveda, $300;
Enrique Dalton, $100; and Abel Stearns, $500.
A series of seven articles on land titles in California, written, presumably,
by Don Juan Bandini, appeared in successive issues of the *Southern Californian*
from Mar. 7 to Apr. 18, 1855.

26*Hutchings' Illustrated California Magazine*, II, 447.

27The quotations are taken from Cleland, *Early Sentiment*, pp. 27, 57-60.
The volume deals at length with the extent and nature of the pre-Gold Rush
immigration and the effective advertising California received at the hands of
self-appointed publicity agents. See also *idem, A History of California: The
American Period* (New York, 1923), pp. 91-127.

28*Hutchings' Illustrated California Magazine*, II, 445.

29Stearns MSS.

30Quoted in Joseph Ellison, *California and the Nation, 1850-1869* (Berkeley,
1927), p. 22. For many years the settler-landowner controversy constituted an
important issue in California politics. Because of the manifest injustice often
suffered by legitimate settlers when court decisions deprived them of land
which they had occupied and developed in good faith, a law was passed, in
1856, declaring all lands in California for which title had not judicially been
confirmed, part of the public domain. If the courts subsequently held such
land to be part of a bona fide grant, the grantee was required either to permit
the settlers to remain on the land or to compensate them for buildings, improvements, and growing crops. The act was declared unconstitutional by the
State Supreme Court. (*Ibid.*, pp. 20-21.) As one objection to the law, landowners complained that juries invariably awarded exorbitant compensation to
the ejected settlers.

31For a description of the vicissitudes which the provincial archives suffered
during the American conquest, see W. W. Robinson, "Abel Stearns on the
California and Los Angeles Archives," in Hist. Soc. of Sou. Calif. *Quarterly*,
XIX, 141-42.

32Hoffman, *Reports of Land Cases*, p. 451. The Limantour case occupies
pp. 389-451.
See also "Record of Decisions," III, 150-55. Limantour appealed to the French
traveler, Duflot de Mofras, to assist him in recovering compensation for his
goods from the California government. Vols. IV, VII, and IX of Wills,
California Titles, are devoted exclusively to the Limantour claims. Many
additional items relating to the case are included in other volumes of the series.

33The fraudulent documents submitted by Limantour bore the signatures of
a former Mexican governor and a Mexican secretary of state; they were
sworn to by a high Mexican official who came to California, with official

permission, to testify on behalf of Limantour and as the bearer of a personal letter from the president of Mexico to the governor of California and the Land Commission. (Jeremiah S. Black's *Report* [House Ex. Doc. 84, 36th Cong., 1st Sess.], p. 30. Printed in Wills, *California Titles,* Vol. XVI.)

See also Wills, Vol. VII (District Court of the United States for the Northern District of California, No. 429, "Transcript of Record").

To avoid arrest, Limantour fled to Mexico. His son, José Limantour, later became secretary of the treasury (hacienda) under Porfirio Díaz and is generally regarded as the most capable financier in Mexican history.

[34]For additional grants of this type see H. H. Bancroft, *History of California,* VI, 548-60, n.

In 1835 the heirs of the Emperor Agustín Iturbide received a grant of 400 square leagues in Texas. The grant was afterward transferred to California. The Land Commission disallowed the claim, and the claimants failed to file notice of appeal within six months, as the law required. The grant was generally regarded as fraudulent; but Judge Ogden Hoffman, though forced to deny the claim because of the expiration of the time limit, said in his decision: "We are very sensible of the hardship of this and similar cases. We regret that we have no power to relieve them." (Hoffman, *Reports of Land Cases,* p. 278.)

The cases of the Mariposas grants (confirmed to John C. Frémont by the Supreme Court) and of the famous New Almadén quicksilver mine are too long and intricate to be discussed in these pages. It is interesting to note, however, that the New Almadén grant gave rise to a futile damage claim for $16,000,000, against the United States. This was presented by Barron, Forbes & Co., to the British-American Claims Commission meeting at Geneva after the Civil War. (Bancroft, *op. cit.,* p. 511, n.)

[35]Black, *Report,* p. 31. For a violent and detailed criticism of Black and Stanton, see *Letters of William Carey Jones in Review of Attorney General Black's Report* (San Francisco, 1860). Jones did not deny the spurious nature of many California claims, but ridiculed Black's exaggerated statements regarding their extent and the importance of Stanton's activities.

For an excellent survey of the subject, see Alston G. Field, "Attorney-General Black and the California Land Claims," *Pacific Hist. Rev.,* IV, 235-45.

[36]Los Angeles *Star,* Mar. 31, 1860.

[37]Black, *Report,* p. 32.

[38]Los Angeles *Semi-weekly News,* Jan. 21, 1869. The *News* was published under the following titles: *Semi-weekly Southern News,* Jan. 18, 1860, to Oct. 3, 1862; *Semi-weekly News,* Oct. 8, 1862, to Jan. 11, 1863; *Tri-weekly News,* Jan. 12, 1863, to Nov. 12, 1863; *Semi-weekly News,* Nov. 17, 1863, to Dec. 24, 1869.

[39]The troublesome carry-over, from the Spanish-Mexican system, called the "floating grant," added further uncertainty and confusion to the vexed question of California land titles. As the name indicated, a floating grant was an overriding claim to a certain amount of land within a larger grant. Until the owner of the floating grant elected to designate the land of his choice, his

claim made it impossible to alienate any portion of the parent tract, under unencumbered title, and also discouraged its improvement.

Because of the manifest impossibility of relying upon the original surveys of Spanish-Mexican grants in California, or upon their vague and ill-defined boundaries, the Act of 1851 required that a certified plat or survey of a confirmed grant must be submitted to the General Land Office in Washington for its approval. The procedure was further systematized by the Act of June 14, 1860, which required a survey, by the Surveyor-General's office, of all validated grants, and authorized the U.S. District Court to "order the survey of a private land claim into court for examination and adjudication." These and all other federal statutes affecting the public domain in California, down to 1880, will be found in *Laws . . . upon which the Public Land Titles . . . Have Depended*, Vol. II.

Although the Act of 1860 helped in some measure to bring order out of the growing confusion of disputed and overlapping boundaries, it was by no means a final answer to a much-vexed and muddled question. The Surveyor-General's office was frequently charged with abusing its wide discretionary powers, either to protect the interests of the great landholders as a class or to enlarge the boundaries of some particular ranchero's grant, at the expense of the public domain or of less-favored neighbors. Long delays frequently attended the surveys of legally validated grants, thereby leaving the ownership of disputed areas undetermined and creating a legal no man's land out of which all manner of controversies and uncertainties arose. Rejection or modification of the original surveys by the District Court, misunderstandings between the Surveyor-General and the General Land Office, appeals to the Supreme Court, and many other factors of a legal or technical nature, served still further to prevent the expeditious surveys contemplated by the Act of 1860, and thereby added to the general confusion.

[40] Jones, *Report*, pp. 38-39.

[41] Henry George, *Our Land and Our Land Policy, National and State* (San Francisco, 1871), p. 14.

In 1948, W. W. Robinson published, through the University of California Press, a comprehensive survey called *Land in California* that materially supplements the contents of this chapter.

CHAPTER IV

[1] California State Surveyor-General, *Annual Report, 1855*, pp. 226-27.

[2] Stephen Powers, "On the Texan Prairies," *The Overland Monthly*, II, 372-73.

[3] *Up and Down California in 1860-1864: The Journal of William H. Brewer*, ed. Francis P. Farquhar (New Haven, 1930), p. 48.

[4] Don Meadows, "Bernardo Yorba Hacienda of Rancho Cañada de Santa Ana." MS, Charles W. Bowers Memorial Museum, Santa Ana, Calif.

[5] *List of Acts Passed by the Legislature of the State of California at Its First Session* [in 1849 and 1850] [San José, 1850], No. 48. See also *Compiled Laws of the State of California, Containing All the Acts of the Legislature of a Public*

and General Nature, Now in Force, Passed at the Sessions of 1850-51-52-53, compiled by S. Garfielde and F. A. Snyder (Benicia, Calif., 1853), pp. 337-39, 866-68.

[6]For the facsimiles of representative cattle brands in Los Angeles County, see p. 73.

[7]Testimony of Don Juan Forster in "Don Juan Forster *vs.* Pío Pico" (Orange County, Calif., WPA, 1936, Project No. 3105; 4 vols., typescript), II, 39.
A full account of this celebrated case, together with voluminous excerpts from the court records, is given in Terry E. Stephenson, "Forster *versus* Pico, a Forgotten California *Cause Celebre*," in Hist. Soc. of Sou. Calif. *Quarterly*, XVII, 143-47, and XVIII, 22-30, 50-68.

[8]Charles Nordhoff, *California: For Health, Pleasure, and Residence. A Book for Travellers and Settlers* (New York, 1873), p. 241.

[9]*The Antonio F. Coronel Collection* (Los Angeles, 1906), Item 18, p. 21.

[10]"Forster *vs.* Pico," I, 128.

[11]Statement of Abel Stearns before the U.S. Land Commission, Case No. 398, "Rancho Dominguez," p. 22. An *orejano* was defined as an unbranded calf without a mother. (Testimony of Robert Ashcroft, in Hist. Soc. of Sou. Calif. *Quarterly*, XVIII, 29.) The question of who had taken the *orejanos* in the rodeos on the Rancho Santa Margarita was an important point in determining whether Forster or Pico owned the ranch.

[12]Land Commission, Case No. 398, "Rancho Dominguez," pp. 21-22.

[13]See "Laws Concerning Rodeos." The quotation is from a supplementary act of the state legislature, Apr. 30, 1855.

[14]Mr. Dan S. Hammack, Jr., of the law firm of Hammack & Hammack, of Los Angeles, has courteously supplied me with the following data regarding the subsequent history of the office of Judges of the Plains, or *Jueces del Campo:*
"According to Henning's General Laws, Hyatt's 3rd Edition, 1920:
" 'This act provided for the appointment of judges of the plains. They were required to attend rodeos of cattle and also to settle disputes as to the owner-ship of animals. The act was continued in force by the codes, and has never been superseded or expressly repealed. It is probable, however, that the provi-sions of the county government acts relating to powers of supervisors, with the general repealing sections of the acts, operate as an implied repeal, by leaving no power to appoint these very useful officials of a time that is past. Their activities have left little or no mark upon the judicial records of the state, even in those which relate to the early days. They are referred to in some of the early cases on trespassing animals, estrays and animals running at large. Beyond that there is practically nothing.'
"When codes were adopted in California in 1872, sec. 19 of the political code expressly kept the acts in force regarding Judges of the Plains, but in 1933 all agricultural laws were revised in California and incorporated into a newly formed Agricultural Code. The original act of 1851 was expressly repealed by

this code, and a terse note by the Code Commission which drafted the new Agricultural Code finally eliminated the Judge of the Plains from California law as 'obsolete.' (See Deering's *General Laws*, Act 3908, 1933 supplement.)"

[15]"Forster *vs.* Pico." It was customary for wealthy rancheros to live in the pueblo and leave the management of their estates to *mayordomos.*

[16]Judge J. E. Pleasants, in Luther A. Ingersoll, *Ingersoll's Century Annals of San Bernardino County, 1769 to 1904* (Los Angeles, 1904), pp. 120-21.
In a report on the *caballada* of the Rancho Los Alamitos, one of Stearns's employees classified the 53 animals under 11 heads. (Miguel Gonzalez to Abel Stearns, Aug. 5, 1850, in Stearns MSS.)

[17]C. H. Brinley to Abel Stearns, Nov. 13, 1852, *ibid.* In one of the cattle drives to northern California, described elsewhere in this volume, a number of cattle were lost in the mustard near Castaic.

[18]See Chapter V for a detailed account of crime in Los Angeles during this period.

[19]The ordinance, adopted Aug. 16, 1850, read: "When the city has no work in which to employ the chain gang, the recorder shall, by means of notices conspicuously posted, notify the public that such and such a number of prisoners will be auctioned off to the highest bidder for private service; and in that manner they shall be disposed of for a sum which shall not be less than the amount of their fine for double the time which they were to serve at hard labor." (James M. Guinn, *Historical and Biographical Record of Southern California* [Chicago, 1902], p. 148.)

[20]C. H. Brinley to Abel Stearns, Aug. 30, 1862. Stearns MSS.

[21]Los Angeles *Semi-weekly News,* Feb. 11, 1869.

[22]*Ibid.*

[23]Horace Bell, *Reminiscences of a Ranger; or Early Times in Southern California* (original ed., Los Angeles, 1881; Santa Barbara, 1929), pp. 35-36.

[24]Two-year-old bulls could be bought from the Mormons for $25 each. (S. A. Pollard to Abel Stearns, May 4, 1855, in Stearns MSS. See also H. F. Teschermacher to Stearns, May 17, 1862, *ibid.*) Three thoroughbred bulls and seven grades were valued at $2,000. In 1855 Alexander S. Taylor sent "Alfalfa Grass" seed from Peru, and blue grass and timothy from the United States, for Stearns to plant. (Taylor to Stearns, Monterey, Calif., Mar. 19, 1855, *ibid.*)

[25]California cattle were much smaller than the Hereford stock now raised on western ranges. Describing a herd of "large steers" in 1861, Abel Stearns wrote, "The cattle are large and fat [and] will weigh from six hundred to eight hundred pounds." (Stearns to Don José P. Thompson, May 26, 1861, in Stearns MSS.)
During the time of the hide-and-tallow trade, native California hides averaged from 22 to 24 pounds; South American hides were 6 to 10 pounds heavier. (Adele Ogden, "Hides and Tallow," *California Historical Quarterly,* VI, 261, n.)

In northern California the State Agricultural Society and the annual State Fair at Sacramento were important factors in stimulating public interest in the production of finer cattle, and in aiding stock growers to improve the quality of their herds; but the influence of these agencies did not extend to the southern ranges.

²⁶*List of Acts Passed by the Legislature of the State of California at Its First Session*, No. 53, pp. 328-29. See also *Compiled Laws of the State of California*, p. 793.

In 1852 a memorial signed by 140 citizens sought the repeal of the Trespass Act and the enactment of a law giving damages to the owner of unfenced cultivated land for injuries suffered from trespassing cattle. The memorial was rejected by the Committee on Agriculture of the State Assembly, as "extremely prejudicial" to the interests of the agricultural sections of the state. (*Assembly Journals*, 7th Sess., 1856, pp. 360-61.)

As stated in the text, the Trespass Act remained in effect until 1872. On Mar. 27 of that year the legislature brought about its repeal by approving "An Act to protect Agriculture and to Prevent the Trespassing of Animals upon Private Property." (*The Statutes of California Passed at the Nineteenth Session of the Legislature*, 1871-72 [Sacramento, 1872], chap. 307, pp. 563-66.) For contemporary discussions of the Trespass Act, see the Los Angeles *Star*, July 1, 1863, Mar. 26, Apr. 26, 1871; and California State Agricultural Society *Transactions, 1870-71*, pp. 15 ff.

²⁷J. W. North to B. D. Wilson, Riverside, Jan. 29, 1872, in B. D. Wilson MSS, in the Huntington Library.

²⁸About 10 acres of land was required, year in and year out, to support each head of stock. Barbed wire was not patented until 1868; it was placed on the market in 1874.

²⁹Ezra Cornell, founder of Cornell University, estimated that board fencing in New York, at the time of the Civil War, cost 30 cts. a rod, or $96 a mile. The cost of the same type of fencing in California came to $700 a mile. (Calif. State Agr. Soc. *Transactions, 1864-65*, p. 68.)

Statistics were even compiled to show that all the range cattle in northern California were not worth the cost of the fences that the settlers built to protect their orchards and grain fields; and that if the farmers had put the money required to build such fences into a common fund, the interest would have been sufficient to pay the rancheros an annual subsidy of three million dollars to slaughter their cattle and go out of business. (*Ibid.*, 1863, pp. 150-51.)

A standard fence in 1859 consisted of seven-foot redwood posts, set six feet apart; four boards, the lowest eighteen inches or two feet from the ground; and a ditch and bank on either side of the fence. Lumber then cost $30 per thousand. (J. W. Osborn to Hobbs, Gilman & Co., Dec. 21, 1859, in Stearns MSS.) In 1860 "F. P. F. Temple, at a cost of about forty thousand dollars for lumber alone, fenced in a wide acreage." (Harris Newmark, *Sixty Years in Southern California* [Boston and New York, 1930], p. 274.)

The author of an article on California farming spoke of the settlers' fences as "light and temporary, but costly beyond conception." (J. S. Silver, "Farming Facts for California Immigrants," *Overland Monthly*, I, 176.)

[30]The estimate was based on the following figures: hide, $2.00; 200 lbs. of tallow at 4 cts. per lb., $8.00; 50 lbs. of dried beef at 5 cts. to 6 cts. per lb., $2.50 or $3.00.

[31]Memorandum, of 1862 [?], in Stearns MSS. Banning & Hinchman, of San Pedro, operating under a contract with a number of large rancheros, expected "to stew up" 10,000 animals during the summer of 1861. (Banning & Hinchman to R. L. Raimond, June 1, 1861, in Stearns MSS; also an unsigned letter addressed to Handy & Hoadley, New York, Dec. 22, 1862, *ibid.*) It was reported that Stearns planned to manufacture soap and other animal by-products. (James Bowden to Stearns, Apr. 12, 1862, *ibid.*)

At the beginning of the great drought of 1862-64, a San Francisco firm agreed to build four iron tanks for Abel Stearns, for melting tallow. Each was to be 14 feet long and 5 feet in diameter. (Coffey & Ridoux to Stearns, Dec. 22, 1862, *ibid.*)

[32]John Kelly, "Life on a San Diego Cattle Ranch" [MS in Huntington Library], p. 8; R. C. Raimond to C. J. Couts, June 10, 1861, in the Cave Couts Collection of MSS, in the possession of Mr. Cave Couts, Rancho Guajome, San Diego County. In 1861 Stearns sent three large tins of dried beef to Major S. H. Carlton, of San Francisco, asking him to try it for army use. (Stearns to Carlton, Aug. 16, 1861, in Stearns MSS.)

[33]Stearns to Col. I. B. West, Oct. 7, 1861 (*ibid.*).

[34]George William Beattie and Helen Pruitt Beattie, *Heritage of the Valley* (Pasadena, 1939), pp. 126-27.

[35]Most of the horses were used for food; in some instances, however, the stolen animals were sold to Mormon settlers or even to California-bound emigrants.

[36]Los Angeles *Star*, Apr. 2, May 7, 1853.

[37]Don Luís Zamorano to Abel Stearns, May 2, 1849, in Stearns MSS. It is probable that these Indians came into the valley by way of San Gabriel Cañon, which opened out just above the Rancho Azusa.

For an interesting and detailed account of two punitive expeditions against renegade Coahuila and Mojave Indians, before the American conquest, see the narrative of Benjamin D. Wilson, published in Robert Glass Cleland, *Pathfinders* (Los Angeles, 1928), pp. 385-91.

[38]José de G. Lugo to Abel Stearns, June 16, 1849, in Couts MSS. The name of Horse Thief Cañon, opening into the Cajón Pass, perpetuates the record both of Indian and of white raiders.

[39]H. M. Nimmo to Stearns, Feb. 11, 1850, Stearns. A company of nearly fifty men, sent in pursuit under Deputy Sheriff Hodges, followed the Indians for three days but failed to overtake them. (Benjamin Hayes to Stearns, Jan. 25, 1850, *ibid.*) A notice of Chief Walker's death appeared in the *Southern Californian*, Apr. 4, 1855.

[40]Lewis Granger to Stearns, Feb. 4, 1851, *ibid.*

[41]Guinn, *Historical and Biographical Record of Los Angeles*, p. 439.

[42]Cave Couts to Abel Stearns, Jan. 11, 1852, in Stearns MSS.

[43]Dec. 10, 1851, *ibid.*; Newmark, *op. cit.*, p. 52; Beattie and Beattie, *op. cit.*, pp. 184-85, 187.

In 1859 the Mojaves were particularly troublesome. A successful campaign was carried out against them by United States troops under Colonel Hoffman. (H. D. Barrows, "Reminiscences of Los Angeles," in Hist. Soc. of Sou. Calif. *Annual Publications*, III, 57.)

[44]Los Angeles *Semi-weekly News*, June 28, 1866.

Notices of threatened Indian depredations and of horses stolen by Indian raiders in San Bernardino appear in the *Southern Vineyard* for Sept. 25, 1858. In January, 1860, a man named Robert Wilburn, seeking to recover twenty head of stolen cattle, was shot to death with arrows by Paiute raiders. (Newmark, *op. cit.*, p. 275.)

[45]Los Angeles *Semi-weekly News*, July 10, 1866. The Los Angeles *Star* of Apr. 26, 1862, contained a report of an attack on a party of immigrants near Elizabeth Lake by Indians from the Owens Valley. Nine men were killed, and 60 horses and 30 oxen were stolen.

[46][Peter H. Burnett] *Annual Message of the Governor of California, Delivered to Both Houses of the Legislature, January 7, 1851* [San José, 1851].

For early instances of cattle rustling in Los Angeles County, see Lewis Granger to Abel Stearns, Feb. 4, 1851; Brinley-Stearns correspondence, 1852; Abel Stearns to A. Randall, Oct. 14, 1853—all in Stearns MSS.

The Los Angeles *Star*, Nov. 13, 1852, cited 14 cases of horse stealing in one night.

In 1856 Cave Couts wrote Stearns, from the Rancho Guajome in San Diego County, that he was killing his cattle to keep them from being stolen, and that "The like in stealing as goes on at present we hardly ever knew of." Two years later Couts was greatly concerned over the safety of his family during his absence from the ranch, because of the "withdrawal of troops, the number of Indians in the country, and the reckless and vagabond population." (Couts to Stearns, Nov. 9, 1856, and July 17, 1858, in Stearns MSS.)

[47]Pedro López, *juez de campo*, to Stearns, Apr. 10, 1858, *ibid.*; *Southern Vineyard*, Apr. 17, 1858.

[48]*Southern Vineyard*, Sept. 20, Oct. 18, 1861.

[49]Los Angeles *Star*, Sept. 28, 1861.

[50]C. R. Johnson to Abel Stearns, July 24, 1862, in Stearns MSS.

[51]Johnson to Stearns, Oct. 2, 1862, *ibid.*

[52]Johnson to Stearns, Feb. 23, 1863, *ibid.*

[53]Los Angeles *Star*, Dec. 12, 1863. Two weeks earlier five prisoners had been taken from the Los Angeles jail and hanged by the same committee. (*Ibid.*, Nov. 28, 1863.)

⁵⁴Los Angeles *Semi-weekly News,* Feb. 7, 1865.

⁵⁵*Ibid.,* Oct. 20, 1868.

⁵⁶C. H. Forbes to Abel Stearns, Sept. 3, 1862, in Stearns MSS.

⁵⁷Guadalupe Vallejo, "Ranch and Mission Days in Alta California," *The Century Magazine,* XLI, 187.

CHAPTER V

¹Sir George Simpson, *Narrative of a Journey Round the World, during the Years 1841 and 1842* (London, 1847), I, 402.

²The first number of the Los Angeles *Star* (*La Estrella de Los Angeles*) appeared on May 17, 1851.

A few weeks before the *Star* was issued, John A. Lewis wrote to Stearns from "Alta California," outlining a plan for starting a paper in Los Angeles and publishing in it advertisements, laws, and other material, both in English and in Spanish and Stearns favored the idea. (John A. Lewis to Abel Stearns, Apr. 4, 1851, in Stearns MSS. See also D. H. Mason to Stearns, Feb. 1, 1851, *ibid.*)

³*The Seventh Census of the United States: 1850,* pp. 960-80, *passim.*

⁴Unfortunately for the cause of historical research, the early southern California newspapers devoted comparatively little attention to local happenings, but gave most of their space to articles, copied from eastern newspapers, dealing with national and international affairs, and to scientific and literary items.

The following newspapers were published in Los Angeles County prior to 1865: the Los Angeles *Star* (*La Estrella de Los Angeles*), May 17, 1851, to Oct. 1, 1864, and May 16, 1868, to 1879 (issued June 1, 1870, under the name *Daily Star*); *The Southern Californian,* July 20, 1854, to Jan., 1859; *El Clamor Público,* June 8, 1855, to Dec. 31, 1859; the *Southern Vineyard,* May 20, 1858, to June 8, 1860; the Los Angeles *Semi-weekly News* (see Chap. III, n. 38); the Wilmington *Journal,* Nov., 1864, to 1868. (J. M. Guinn, *Coast Counties & History of California* [Chicago, 1904], pp. 354-61, hereinafter cited as *History of California*); *An Historical Sketch of Los Angeles County,* prepared by Col. J. J. Warner, Judge Benjamin Hayes, Dr. J. P. Widney [Los Angeles, 1876; repr., Los Angeles, 1936 (commonly known, and hereinafter cited, as *Centennial History of Los Angeles County*)], pp. 84-86).

Other papers in southern California during the period were the San Diego *Herald* (to which for a time Lieut. George H. Derby, better known as "John Phoenix," contributed); the Santa Barbara *Gazette*; and the San Bernardino *Herald* (the *Patriot* was also published in San Bernardino for a brief time).

In one issue of the San Diego *Herald,* "John Phoenix" wrote: "Very little news will be found in the *Herald* this week. The fact is there never is much news in it and it is well that is so. The climate here is so delightful that residents in the enjoyment of the *dolce far niente* care very little about what is going on elsewhere and residents of other places care very little about what is going on in San Diego. . . ." (Quoted in Guinn, *History of California,* p. 265.)

The editor of the *Southern Californian* during 1854-55 was Col. William Butts, an adopted son of Thomas H. Benton. (Bell, *Reminiscences,* p. 258.)

[5]Los Angeles *Star*, July 30, 1853.

[6]All the Los Angeles newspapers of the time carried Hellman's advertisement. As early as 1853, a reading room was established in the Armory used by Capt. A. W. Hope's Los Angeles Rangers. "We believe this is the first attempt made in our city to institute a reading room," said the *Southern Californian* of Jan. 4, 1853.

[7]*Southern Vineyard*, May 27, 1859. In the state as a whole there were 32 public libraries, containing over 65,000 volumes, and 91 different newspapers. (*State Register and Year Book of Facts, 1857*, p. 152.) Fourteen counties in the state had no newspapers.

[8]For an interesting suggestion concerning the effects of geographic isolation upon creative writing and literary taste in California before the railroad, see C. H. Shinn, "Social Changes in California," *Popular Science Monthly*, Apr. 6, 1891.

[9]An ordinance adopted by the first Common Council of the city, July 3, 1850, required every citizen "to sweep in front of his habitation on Saturdays, as far as the middle of the street, or at least eight varas." Another clause read, "No filth shall be thrown into Zanjas carrying water for common use, nor into the streets of the city, nor shall any cattle be slaughtered in the same." (Quoted in Guinn, *History of California*, p. 313.)

[10]Quoted in Cleland, *History of California*, p. 314; also in Guinn, *op. cit.*, p. 313.

[11]Los Angeles *Star*, June 16, 1855.

[12]Bell, *op. cit.*, pp. 5-6.
The Los Angeles newspapers announced, in June, 1940, that the last remnant of the original Bella Union Hotel was about to be demolished to make way for a parking lot.

[13]*Report of the Auditor of the City of Los Angeles, 1904*, p. 226. (Quoted in Robert Stewart Cleland, "A Glimpse at Southern California Medicine before 1870" [MS].)

[14]*Southern Vineyard*, Dec. 24, 1858.

[15]R. S. Cleland, *op. cit.*, p. 10 (from George Henry Kress, *History of the Medical Profession of Southern California* [Los Angeles, 1910], p. 8). The physicians were Charles R. Cullen, A. I. Blackburn, J. W. Dodge, and William B. Osbourne.
Los Angeles apparently had no resident dentist until the late fifties. (*Southern Vineyard*, Jan. 4, 1859.) It was the custom at that time to fill teeth with tinfoil as well as gold. (Charles Rowe, Diary [MS in Huntington Library], July 23, 1853.)

[16]R. S. Cleland, *op. cit.*, p. 9.

[17]H. D. Barrows, "Memorial Sketch of Dr. John S. Griffin," in Hist. Soc. of Sou. Calif. *Annual Publications*, IV, 183-85.
Dr. Joseph P. Widney, widely known for nearly 60 years in Los Angeles and

one of the founders of the University of Southern California, came to the pueblo in 1868 and opened an office in the Downey Block.

[18]Newmark, *Sixty Years in Southern California*, pp. 107-9.

[19]*Southern Vineyard*, July 10, 1858.

According to an "Outline of the History of Development of Social Welfare and Related Events in Los Angeles," submitted by Walter Chambers, Chairman of the Council of Social Agencies of Los Angeles, July 13, 1939, the following fraternal and charitable institutions were organized in Los Angeles prior to 1865: Hebrew Benevolent Society, Masonic Lodge, Odd Fellows Lodge, Sisters of Charity (1856), French Benevolent Society, and German Turnverein. The "Orphan's Fair" was held annually to raise funds for the Orphan's Home, established by the Sisters of Charity where the Union Station now stands. The fair usually raised several thousand dollars for the Home.

[20]C. H. Johnson to Abel Stearns, Feb. 6, 1863, in Stearns MSS. See also the Los Angeles newspapers during the last of January and all of February of that year. The effects of the epidemic in the rural districts are described in Chapter VII.

[21]*El Clamor Público*, May 21, 1857, quoted in R. S. Cleland, *op. cit.*, p. 13.

[22]Los Angeles *News*, Oct. 20, 1868.

[23]The bull ring was on the site now occupied by the French Hospital, at Castelar and College Streets. Castelar was then called *Calle de Toros*, the Street of the Bulls.

[24]Los Angeles *Star*, Apr. 7, 20, 1860.

[25]J. M. Guinn speaks of Nigger Alley, or the *Calle de los Negros*, as the "wickedest street on earth." It ran some 500 feet from the corner of Los Angeles and Arcadia Streets to the Plaza. It was absorbed by the extension of Los Angeles Street in 1886. (Guinn, *op cit.*, p. 310.)

[26]*El Clamor Público*, Apr. 5, 1856. I am indebted to Mrs. F. E. Coulter, Curator of the Bowers Memorial Museum in Santa Ana, for the reference and its translation.

[27]Los Angeles *Star*, Aug. 3, 1859.

[28]Ineffectual efforts were made by various Protestant denominations early in the fifties to organize churches in Los Angeles. James Woods, a Presbyterian minister, came to the pueblo in 1854, and in March of the next year organized a Presbyterian church of 12 members. Woods's successor left Los Angeles in disgust and the church died. Another Presbyterian minister, the Rev. W. E. Boardman, came to southern California in 1858 because of ill health, started a Sunday school, and organized the First Protestant Society, a union of the members of various Protestant faiths. Boardman also preached in El Monte (distinctly a Protestant, if not a godly, community), and perhaps elsewhere in the county. After starting a church building in Los Angeles in 1862, Boardman returned to the East. The unfinished building was later completed and became the St. Athanasius Church of the Protestant Episcopal

denomination. Dr. Matthew Carter was licensed to act as lay reader for this congregation, by the Rt. Rev. W. Ingraham Kip, first Protestant Episcopal Bishop of California.

No Protestant services were held in Los Angeles during 1863 and 1864. In 1867 the Methodist Episcopal Church, which had first carried on services from 1850 to 1858, re-established its ministry, and the First Congregational Church was also organized. Jewish services were held in Los Angeles as early as 1854, but the congregation of B'nai B'rith was not formally organized until 1862.

The Rt. Rev. Thaddeus Amat, of Barcelona, Spain, was consecrated Bishop of Monterey in 1854, and established his see in Los Angeles in 1859 as Bishop of Monterey and Los Angeles. Bishop Amat exerted a marked influence upon the educational as well as the religious life of the south. Two of his most notable achievements were the reorganization of St. Vincent's College—the first institution of its kind in southern California—and the foundation of St. Vibiana's Cathedral. (Bishop William Ingraham Kip, *A California Pilgrimage* [Fresno, Calif., 1921], *passim; Centennial History of Los Angeles*, pp. 89-92; J. M. Guinn, *Historical and Biographical Record of Los Angeles* [Chicago, 1901], pp. 147-54.) The Los Angeles *News* of June 3, 1865, contained a notice of the organization of a college by Bishop Amat.

[29]Los Angeles *Semi-weekly News*, Feb. 20, 1869.

[30]The following statistics on public education in Los Angeles County were supplied by the Los Angeles County Superintendent of Schools, Division of Research and Guidance, Dec. 19, 1939.

"EARLY STATISTICS ON PUBLIC EDUCATION IN LOS ANGELES COUNTY
(Based on Annual Reports of County Superintendent of Schools Office)

	Year	No. of Public Schools	No. of Teachers	No. of Pupils	Yearly Avg. All teachers
Unofficial	1855	8	9	180	
Official	1865	16	16	581	$577.00
"	1866	16	16	743	653.00
"	1867	24	27	960	454.00
"	1868	28	28	1,314	487.00
"	1869	36	36	1,760	565.00
"	1870	43	43	2,324	562.00

"We have no official records in our files which date earlier than 1865, and very little unofficial data. Los Angeles County itself came into official existence in 1850 and it was several years before statistics on public education were summarized into uniform and comparative records."

According to the Los Angeles *Star* of Nov. 11, 1860, there were three grammar schools and four primary schools in the county, with a total enrolment of 460 out of a juvenile population (4 to 8 years of age) of 2,353. The state contributed $2,433.98 to the county schools; county taxes produced $1,326.96 for the same purpose, and district taxes and private subscriptions added $3,507.64. Total, $7,268.58. Of this amount $4,827.19 went for salaries.

The *Star* of Aug. 1, 1863, gave the following list of schools, and their enrolment, in Los Angeles County for that year: Old Mission, 163; El Monte, 189; San Gabriel, 138; Santa Ana, 181; Dos Cueros, 40; Los Nietos, 150; Los Angeles, 1,026. Total, 1,887.

[31]Robert G. Cleland, *The Place Called Sespe* (Chicago, 1940), p. 113. As late as 1859 the public schools of Los Angeles were closed in February for lack of funds. (*Southern Vineyard*, Feb. 8, 1859.) The burden imposed on the taxpayers by an unexampled increase in the city debt accounted for this debacle. In May, 1858, Los Angeles had obligations amounting to $6,000; one year later the indebtedness had risen to $15,000—an amount just equal to the city's annual revenue. (Message of Damien Marchessault, mayor, printed in the *Southern Vineyard*, May 10, 1859.)

In 1860 the state appropriated $2,482.07 for the support of the schools of Los Angeles County, basing the amount on school attendance. The corresponding appropriations for the remote mountain counties of El Dorado and Nevada were $2,710.04 and $2,118.71, respectively. (*Annual Report of the Controller of the State for the Year 1860*, pp. 9-10.)

[32]Nordhoff, *California*, p. 146.

[33]Los Angeles *Star*, Mar. 10, 1860.

[34]Los Angeles *Star*, Oct. 2, 1858.

[35]Isaac Graham to Abel Stearns, Mar. 23, 1840, in Stearns MSS.

[36]*Centennial History of Los Angeles County*, p. 73. Harris Newmark says, "Twenty-five thousand dollars, in addition to five hundred horses, five hundred mares, five hundred heifers, five hundred calves, and five hundred sheep were among the princely stakes put up." (*Op. cit.*, p. 160.)

[37]Wagers amounting to $20,000 were laid on a race in Santa Barbara, in 1851, between Alfred Robinson's horse, "Old Breeches," and Francisco Norriega's "Buey de Tango." During the rest of the decade, before the lean years of the cattle industry devoured the patrimony of the old-time rancheros, stakes for even minor races frequently ran as high as $10,000 and seldom fell below $3,000.

California horses were bred for stamina even more than for speed. Riders, too, were capable of great endurance. Using 31 horses, Ramón Pico once rode 150 miles in 6 hours, 16 minutes, 15 seconds, for a wager of $2,500. (*Hutchings' Illustrated California Magazine*, V [1860-61], 285.)

Judge J. E. Pleasants, one of the earliest pioneers in what is now Orange County, cited many examples of the stamina of California horses, and said that he himself had known horses "to be ridden a hundred miles a day without injury, and fed entirely upon grass." California saddle horses were never shod. (*Ingersoll's Century Annals*, pp. 120-21.)

[38]*Southern Vineyard*, Mar. 25, 1859; see also the issue for Dec. 4, 1858.

[39]Los Angeles *Star*, Feb. 25, 1860.

[40]Terry E. Stephenson, "A Horse Race Goes to Court," *Westways*, Jan., 1940, p. 23.

[41]The depredations of horse and cattle thieves have been treated at some length in Chapter IV.

The studies made by Josiah Royce and C. H. Shinn of crime and law enforcement in the mining camps of 1849-52 might well be supplemented by similar studies of conditions in southern California down to 1865.

[42]The literature on each of the notorious bandits mentioned in the chapter is voluminous. The following references are representative: Joseph Gregg Layne, *Annals of Los Angeles from the Arrival of the First White Men to the Civil War, 1769-1861* (San Francisco, 1935); Bell, *Reminiscences;* Guinn, *Historical and Biographical Record;* Cleland, *History of California.* For a firsthand account of the Flores band see Don Maquel (Michael) Kraszewski, "Juan Flores in San Juan Capistrano," in *Orange County History Series,* III (Santa Ana, Calif., Apr., 1939), pp. 22-32. Contemporary newspaper accounts of the affair are printed in Appendix III.

[42a]Forster to Griffin, Jan. 30, 1857, in Stearns MSS.

[43]Los Angeles *Star,* Oct. 11, 1851.

The issue for Sept. 27, 1851, said, "During the past year no less than 31 murders have been committed in the city of Los Angeles and its vicinity, and who today can name *one* instance in which a murderer has been punished?"

[44]*Ibid.,* Oct. 9, 1852.

A prominent citizen, Joshua H. Bean, was murdered in San Gabriel in November, 1852, or, as the *Star* tactfully put it, "He died suddenly on the 7th instant." (*Ibid.,* Nov. 13, 1852.)

[45]Bell, *Reminiscences,* p. 38.

[46]Forster to Stearns, Feb. [?], 1852, in Stearns MSS.

[47]Los Angeles *Star,* Feb. 26, 1852; see also Bell, *Reminiscences,* pp. 80-82.

[48]James Woods's Diary (MS, Huntington Library), Nov. 12, 1854.

Woods belonged to the dogmatic, soul-flagellating theological school of that day. His comments on Los Angeles, and many of the incidents he records in his Diary, however, are of genuine historic value.

[49]Kip, *California Pilgrimage,* pp. 30-31; *idem, The Early Days of My Episcopate* (New York, 1892), p. 213.

[50]J. M. Guinn, "The Story of a Plaza," in Hist. Soc. of Sou. Calif. *Annual Publications,* IV, 247-56.

For further accounts of murder or other crimes in Los Angeles during the early fifties, see the Los Angeles *Star,* July 31, 1852 (gives an account of the murder of two Americans and the execution of the murderers by a citizens' committee); *ibid.,* May 7, 1853 (describes lawless conditions in Santa Barbara and crime in Nigger Alley); *ibid.,* Feb. 12, 1853 (contains an account of the trial, by a citizens' court, of a horse thief named Smith, resulting in a judgment of 78 lashes, and the mobbing, with nearly fatal results, of the unfortunate youth who undertook to carry out the sentence).

[51]In 1856 a Californian named Ruíz was killed by a deputy constable. A race

war almost resulted, and a mob of Californians and Mexicans for a time controlled the city and killed the city marshal. A summons for aid was sent to El Monte, and thirty-six of the "Monte boys" responded. The city was under guard for several days. A contemporary newspaper account of this episode is printed in Appendix III.

[52]*Up and Down California,* p. 14.

[53]Los Angeles *Star,* Nov. 29, 1862.

[54]Ramón Carrillo himself was arrested and released on $13,000 bail. (Cave Couts MSS.)

[55]Los Angeles *Star,* Nov. 28, 1863. Five persons, in all, were lynched, including a lad charged with nothing more serious than stealing chickens.

[56]*Ibid.,* Dec. 19, 1863.

[57]*Semi-weekly Southern News,* Oct. 18, 1861.

[58]*Semi-weekly News,* Jan. 8, 1864.

[59]*Ibid.,* May 6, 1865. There seems to be no reason to question the authenticity of the report.

In July of the same year the celebrated duel between Robert Carlisle and the King brothers took place in the Bella Union Hotel. See the Los Angeles *News,* July 8, 1865.

[60]The conditions existing in Owens Valley, after 1870, in many ways resembled those characteristic of Los Angeles County a decade earlier. See W. A. Chalfant, *The Story of Inyo* (Chicago, 1922), pp. 233-47.

CHAPTER VI

[1]An interesting and authoritative biography of Hugo Reid, based on his correspondence and other documentary sources, has recently been published by Susanna Bryant Dakin, under the title *A Scotch Paisano* (Berkeley, 1939).

[2]Hugo Reid to Abel Stearns, May 22, 1849, in Stearns MSS. A few weeks later, Stearns was offered $7 a head for large, fat bullocks. (D. W. Alexander to Abel Stearns, June 4, 1849.)

[3]The subject is mentioned by only a few contemporary writers, and then in the most casual and incidental way. See, e.g., William Heath Davis, *Seventy-five Years in California* (San Francisco, 1929), p. 322.

[4]In 1857 a drover named McPike delivered 1,920 head of cattle at San José, losing en route only 20, "lame Sick & Give out and Runaway." (John McPike to Abel Stearns, May 13, 1857, in Stearns MSS.)

[5]Payments for such leases were often made in cattle. Abel Stearns at one time thought of buying a number of ranches in Monterey and Contra Costa counties, but decided against the venture because of the lack of reliable men to supervise the properties. Even near at hand he found "the greatest difficulty in getting the proper kind of men to manage & take the proper kind of care of

my ranches." (Stearns to David Spence, Dec. 2, 1852, in Stearns MSS.) The subject of grazing leases is mentioned in the following correspondence in the Stearns collection: Jacob P. Leese to Stearns, Nov. 26, 1852; Stearns to A. Randall, Oct. 14, 1853; Stearns-F. D. Atherton correspondence, 1856-62; Samuel Brannan to Stearns, Dec. 5, 1856; C. R. Johnson to Stearns, July 21, 1856.

[6]Henry Miller, founder of the firm of Miller & Lux, was one of the principal purchasers of southern cattle.

[7]There were 800 head of cattle and 100 horses in the drive.

[8]Cave Couts to Abel Stearns, June 15, 1852, in Stearns MSS.

[9]W. B. Couts to Abel Stearns, July 17, 1862, in Stearns MSS.

[10][————] Blunt to his brother, Apr. 11, 1862, in Couts MSS.

[11]Davis, *op. cit.*, p. 323.

[12]The Los Angeles *Star* of Oct. 18, 1852, reported the sale of 500 steers at $25 a head. The cattle were to be driven to the mines via the "Tulare valley." *The Governor's Message and Report of the Secretary of State on the Census of 1852* (San Francisco, 1853) placed the value of beef cattle at $25 a head— a price "on the average much below the market value." See also Cave Couts to Abel Stearns, Feb. 14 and Dec. 6, 1852, in Stearns MSS. Fat cattle sold at 18 cts. on the hoof. (Abel Stearns to Louis Belcher, Apr. 28, 1852, in Stearns MSS.) Stearns cited the advantage of buying from one owner, because "cattle used to each other will not wander." Belcher considered himself lucky to secure 1,125 head for $21,300. (Belcher to Stearns, Sept. 10, 1852, in Stearns MSS.) Even heifers and mixed herds frequently brought over $30 a head on the ranges.

[13]Nordhoff, *California*, p. 153.

[14]Robert G. Cleland, "The Mining Industry of Mexico," *Mining and Scientific Press*, CXXIII, 16.

[15]Bell, *Reminiscences*, p. 10.

[16]Stearns to A. Randall, Oct. 14, 1853, in Stearns MSS.

[17]The Los Angeles *Star*, Sept. 18, 1852. During the summer and early fall of 1852 a cattle buyer estimated that at least "50,000 head of loose cattle," besides large numbers of oxen, had crossed, or were crossing the plains to California, and the major immigrant body had not yet arrived. (Belcher to Stearns, Sept. 10, 1852, in Stearns MSS.)

[18][John Bigler] *Governor's Annual Message to the Legislature of the State of California, Assembled at Sacramento, Jan. 1, 1855* (Sacramento [1855]), p. 25.

[19]Joseph G. McCoy, *Historic Sketches of the Cattle Trade of the West and Southwest* (Glendale, Calif., 1940), pp. 25-27. Some 8,000 to 10,000 cattle were driven annually from Texas to California in the mid-fifties. A detailed account of a cattle drive from San Antonio to the Rancho Cucamonga is given in "A Log of the Texas-California Cattle Trail, 1854, [by] James G. Bell," ed. J. Evetts Haley, *The Southwestern Historical Quarterly*, XXXV, 208-37, 290-316, and XXXVI, 47-66.

According to Frederick Law Olmsted, 4 men were used for each 100 head of cattle on the Texas-California drive. Five or six months were required for the trip. California-bound emigrants, who were willing to serve without pay for the sake of the protection afforded by the company, usually acted as drovers. (Frederick Law Olmsted, *A Journey through Texas* [New York, 1857], p. 274.)

²⁰Los Angeles *Star*, Jan. 21, 1859.

²¹*Ibid.*, Feb. 26, 1859.

²²*Ibid.*, Nov. 12, 1859.

²³*Southern Vineyard*, Jan. 21, 1859. Of this number 20,000 belonged to Parrea and 10,000 to the Armijos. The Armijos were probably the most important figures in the New Mexico-California trade. They owned, e.g., more than half of the 40,000 sheep sent to California during 1852. (Los Angeles *Star*, Nov. 13, 1852.) For further references to the overland cattle and sheep drives into California, see *Southern Vineyard*, Sept. 25, 1858; Lorenzo Dow Chillson, Diary (MS in Huntington Library); Thomas Flint, "Diary," in Hist. Soc. of Sou. Calif. *Annual Publications*, XII, 109 ff.; and S. I. Hensley to Abel Stearns, Feb. 19, 1857, in Stearns MSS.

F. L. Olmsted told of a Texas drover who reputedly made $100,000 by buying sheep in Mexico at $1 a head and selling them in California at $20 a head. (*Op. cit.*, pp. 274-75.) The price said to have been received in California was probably exaggerated.

²⁴William P. Reynolds MS, June 28, 1859 (MS HM 4221). The *Southern Vineyard* of Apr. 8, 1858, quoted three-year-old steers at from $18 to $22; two-year-old, from $11 to $15; and yearlings at $9 to $12. See also Cave Couts to Stearns, Apr. 20, 1856; C. R. Johnson to Stearns, July 21 and Aug. 11, 1856; John McPike to Stearns, May 13, 1857—all in Stearns MSS.

²⁵The Picos sold their best steers for $15 a head. (Abel Stearns to Cave Couts, Feb. 21, 1858, in Couts MSS.)

²⁶Los Angeles *Star*, Apr. 7, 1860. The article asserted that there were 800,000 head of cattle and 700,000 sheep in the state, and that the number was multiplying with amazing rapidity. The editor saw no remedy but to slaughter the cattle for hides and tallow.

²⁷The communication was from former Gov. John G. Downey. (*The Eighth Census of the United States*, "Agriculture of the United States in 1860" [Washington, 1864], p. clxxi.)

²⁸As explained in Chapter I, the Rancho Los Cerritos was part of the original Manuel Nieto grant of 1784. In the partition of the Nieto property in 1833-34, Gov. Figueroa awarded the Cerritos to Doña Manuela de Cota. She in turn left it to her twelve children. From these heirs it was purchased by Don Juan Temple, husband of Rafaela de Cota, for $3,300, in 1843. In 1853 the ranch was confirmed to Temple by the United States Land Commission, for five square leagues. In 1866 it was purchased by Flint, Bixby & Company for $20,000, gold. Temple, in the meantime, had made a considerable fortune under

a contract with the Maximilian government for the operation of the Mexican mint. He died about a year after the sale of Los Cerritos.

[29]Los Angeles *Star*, Apr. 27, July 20, Aug. 3, 1861. The firm of Banning & Hinchman erected reduction works at San Pedro and contracted with Temple and other ranchers to slaughter their cattle. For further discussion of this subject see Chapter VII.

[30]San Francisco *Bulletin*, Mar. 31, 1860; see also Los Angeles *Star*, Apr. 7, 1860.

[31]As early as 1854 an observant visitor in southern California wrote, "The Americans have got nearly all the vineyards from the Spaniards and a large part of their cattle though there are some farms or ranches with ten thousand head of cattle on them." (James Clarke to his brother, Dec. 6, 1854, in Clarke Letters [MSS in Huntington Library]. The Clarke letters, edited by David Davies, are printed under the title, "An Emigrant of the Fifties," in Hist. Soc. of Sou. Calif. *Quarterly*, XIX, 99-120. The reference above appears on p. 113.)

[32]In 1849 Pedro Domínguez borrowed $2,000 from Juan Temple, to liquidate existing debts and "to clothe and leave provision for his family before his departure for the bonanza." In return he agreed to pay Temple 200 ounces of gold, "in good grain (en bueno grano) clean and of good quality"; and as surety gave a mortgage on his undivided interest in the Rancho San Pedro.

[33]C. R. Johnson to Abel Stearns, May 25, 1857, in Stearns MSS. See Chapter X for further reference to this incident.

[34]Benjamin D. Hayes, *Pioneer Notes from the Diaries of Judge Benjamin Hayes, 1849-1875* (Los Angeles, 1929), p. 193. Twenty-year public-improvement bonds of the city of Los Angeles, issued in 1859, bore interest at 1% a month; merchants customarily charged 3% a month on unpaid balances. (*Southern Vineyard*, Feb. 25, 1854; Miscellaneous Papers of B. D. Wilson [MSS in Huntington Library]. See also A. F. Coronel to Don Diego Bowman, Mar. 21, 1862, in Stearns MSS.) An agent of Benito Juárez came from Mexico to San Francisco to negotiate a $250,000 loan, hypothecating the revenues and mortgaging the customhouses and other government property at Manzanillo and San Blas. The loan was to bear interest at 2% a month. (Cornwall to Stearns, Oct. 18, 1859, in Stearns MSS.)

[35]Los Angeles *Star*, July 17, 1852.

[36]The mortgage, dated Sept. 18, 1854, is in the Stearns MSS.

[37]*Ibid.* The mortgage was dated Sept. 6, 1852, and recorded Feb. 4, 1854, in Book I, Deeds and Mortgages of Los Angeles County, pp. 383-84.

[38]Sepúlveda's obligations, according to a rough memorandum in the Stearns MSS, were as follows:

B. D. Wilson	$1,175	3 mos. @ 6% a month
Timothy Foster	1,000	6 mos. @ 5% a month, compounded
Joseph Rosenbaum	1,000	2 mos. @ 7% a month, compounded
McFarland & Downey	4,697	7 mos. @ 4% a month, compounded

There were 8 other debts, ranging in amount from $300 to $1,300, with interest at from 4% to 7% a month.

³⁹Robinson, *Ranchos Become Cities*, pp. 41-42.

⁴⁰C. R. Johnson to Abel Stearns, Oct. 18, 1862, in Stearns MSS. Lugo's chief indebtedness was to Bachman & Co. There was evidently collusion between the buyers at the auction, to keep the cattle prices as low as possible. See the testimony of C. Ayers, in "Forster vs. Pico," III, 26, 27.

⁴¹*Ibid.*, II, 5, 6. John Forster's full statement was as follows: "Some time, I don't exactly recollect the day, during the winter of 1859, Don Pío Pico was very much pressed with many liabilities. His notes were scattered out all over Los Angeles, in the city particularly, and he had no means immediately at his disposal, to meet the liabilities. . . . He asked me at that time to help him pay up his liabilities and he would sell me one-half of the Santa Margarita ranch for $20,000. . . . He never did pay me or pass that deed, but remained indebted to me in the amount of nearly $25,000. . . ."

⁴²Testimony of Don Juan Forster. Forster came to California from Mexico in 1833, and later married Ysidora Pico. The controversy between Forster and the Picos over the Santa Margarita is admirably described, as previously noted, by Stephenson, in Hist. Soc. of Sou. Calif. *Quarterly*, XVII, 143-47, and XVIII, 22-30, 50-68. According to Forster, Pico's notes were outstanding in the amount of $1,481 and $4,720 to James H. Forster; $2,700 to D. Sepúlveda; $2,500 and $1,100 to Juan Temple; $2,480 to Alexander Bell; $3,000 (plus $1,450 overdue interest) to Abel Stearns; and $3,500 to Señora Guadalupe Argüello. The Argüello debt was paid by the delivery of 500 heifers. ("Forster vs. Pico," II, 8, 9.)

⁴³*Southern Vineyard*, Nov. 19, 1859; Los Angeles *Star*, Jan. 29, 1859.

⁴⁴Ernest Seyd, *California and Its Resources* (London, 1858), pp. 8-9. Seyd stated that European speculators sent large sums of money to California, in the early days of the Gold Rush, to be loaned at the high interest rates then obtainable. In time, made reckless by interest of 5% to 10% a month, the moneylenders overextended themselves, and lost heavily in the panic of 1854. As a consequence, capital had been withdrawn and money was even scarcer than before. The chief lending agencies in California were of French, Swiss, and German origin. (*Ibid.*, pp. 94, 96-67.)

⁴⁵[Peter H. Burnett] *Annual Message of the Governor of California. . . . January 7, 1851*, pp. 16-17.

⁴⁶Edward Hepple Hall, *The Great West: Railroad, Steamboat and Stage Guide and Hand-book for Travellers, Miners and Emigrants. . . .* (New York, 1866), p. 166.

⁴⁷*Southern Vineyard*, Mar. 22, 1859.

CHAPTER VII

¹Maurice H. Newmark and Marco R. Newmark, *Census of the City and County of Los Angeles for the Year 1850* (Los Angeles, 1929), p. 120. The Los

Angeles County "Assessment Book" for 1851 listed the largest taxpayers as follows:

Name	Real Estate (acres)	Personal Property (including livestock)
Eulogio de Celís	100,000	$13,000
José Sepúlveda	102,000	83,000
John Temple	20,000	79,000
Bernardo Yorba	37,000	37,000
Ricardo Véjar	—	34,000
Antonio M. Lugo	29,000	72,000
Isaac Williams	—	35,000
John Forster	21,000	13,000
Abel Stearns	14,000	99,000
Pío Pico	22,000	21,000
John Rowland	29,000	70,000
William Wolfskill	1,100	10,000
Antonio Ignacio Ábila	19,000	14,000

The names of many important landowners were omitted entirely from the list. In other cases, the figures were woefully inaccurate.

[2]Thirty-one of the fifty were Spanish-Californians; and at least half of the remainder were *paisanos* by marriage. Within another decade most of the Spanish names had disappeared from the higher brackets. The largest taxpayers were Juan Temple, $912; José Sepúlveda, $725; Abel Stearns, $718; and Antonio María Lugo, $676. (Los Angeles *Star*, Feb. 17, 1852.)

[3]*Southern Vineyard*, Sept. 18, 1858. Forty-five persons were each assessed $10,000 or more. In order to save their constituents as much as possible on the *state* tax, county assessors uniformly kept the assessment figures at least 50% below their normal value.

[4]Los Angeles *Star*, Feb. 2, 1859; Los Angeles County "Tax and Assessment List," 1859, 1860, etc. The city of Los Angeles was at that time fiscally an integral part of the county, and hence had no separate tax or assessment lists of its own.

[5]*Appendix to Assembly Journals for the Eighth Session of the Legislature of the State of California* (Sacramento, 1857), "Report of the Controller," pp. 30-31.

[6]From the "Annual Report of the State Treasurer" (for each of the years in question; published in the Appendixes of the Senate and Assembly *Journals*).

[7]Los Angeles County, "Tax Book," 1857.

[8]Los Angeles County, "Duplicate Assessment Roll," 1862.

[9]Los Angeles County, "Tax Book," 1863. The assessed value of the county's land and improvements amounted to $617,668.25; personal property was appraised at $669,515.50—making a total of $1,287,183.75. The state tax came to $8,195.02 and the county tax to $18,240.44, or a total of $26,435.46. The county assessment rolls listed 1,218,705 acres.

10Santa Barbara County, "Assessment Roll," 1860.

11Los Angeles *Star*, Dec. 15, 1860.
According to the state controller, a law passed by the legislature, in 1856, entitled, "An Act for the Protection of Actual Settlers, and to quiet Land Titles in this State," unintentionally enabled many of the large landholders to reduce the tax payments materially, or escape them entirely. (*Appendix to Assembly Journals for the Eighth Session,* "Report of the Controller," p. 7.)

12Alexander W. Hope to Abel Stearns, Dec. 22, 1849, in Stearns MSS.

13Los Angeles *Star*, Sept. 16, 1851.

14*Annual Message of the Governor . . . January 7, 1851,* p. 19.

15"Call for a Convention to Divide the State of California, 1851," in Hist. Soc. of Sou. Calif. *Annual Publications,* Vol. X, Pt. 3, pp. 77-78.

16*Annual Message of the Governor, 1856* (Sacramento, 1856), p. 241.

17The *Star* of Dec. 13, 1856, remarked that the despised "cow counties" were thought of by the rest of the state only when a revenue bill was under consideration.

18Assembly Joint Resolution, No. 22, Feb. 15, 1859. Copy transmitted to Abel Stearns by Andrés Pico, in letter of Feb. 9, 1859, in Stearns MSS. The passage of the resolution, said Pico, will provide "the only salvation of our properties and of our happiness."
See also *Southern Vineyard,* Feb. 18, 1859, and numerous subsequent issues. J. J. Warner, editor of the *Vineyard,* ardently supported the plan of state division. The Los Angeles *Star,* on the other hand, was opposed to it. See the issue of Mar. 10, 1860.

19Pedro C. Carrillo to Abel Stearns, June 6, 1861, in Stearns MSS.

20Quoted in Cleland, *California,* p. 307.

21Brewer, *Up and Down California,* p. 246. A valuable study of rainfall and drought in southern California, together with comparative tables and indices, is contained in H. B. Lynch, *Rainfall and Stream Run-off in Southern California since 1769* (Los Angeles, 1931). According to Lynch, the period from 1842 to 1883, as a whole, was one of rainfall deficiency, but floods occurred during the winters of 1849-50, 1851-52, 1852-53, 1859-60, 1861-62, 1867-68, 1873-74, and 1875-76.

22Brewer, *op. cit.,* p. 244.

23*Ibid.,* p. 249.

24Los Angeles *Star*, Jan. 25, 1862. In Imperial Valley, the steamer came up New River as far as Pilot Knob. (G. P. Tibbetts to Cave Couts, [?] 26, 1862, in Couts MSS.)

25Hayes, *Pioneer Notes,* p. 270.

26Los Angeles *Star*, Feb. 1, 1862.

27See Los Angeles *Star*, Feb. 8 and Mar. 8, 1862. Rainfall figures for the Los

Angeles area before 1870 are unavailable. San Diego received between fifteen and seventeen inches during the season of 1861-62, but the precipitation was much heavier from that point northward.

[28]As early as February, the San Francisco market was swamped by thousands of head of cattle from the debt-ridden owners of Santa Barbara County. The following list, prepared for Abel Stearns, showed the number of head disposed of by the more important Santa Barbara rancheros:

"N. Den and Hill .... 1,000 head
Forster and Pico 1,000
Noriegas 4,000
Arellanes 5,000
More 2,000
Sparks 1,000
                                    ————
                                    14,000 head" (Pedro Carrillo to Abel Stearns, June 6, 1861, in Stearns MSS.)

In the spring, Stearns refused $8.00 a head for picked cattle but let them go the following November for $7.00 a head, payable in greenbacks worth 60 cts. on the dollar. He also threw in 40 or 50 saddle horses at the same figure. (Testimony of Robert Ashcroft in "Don Juan Forster *vs.* Pío Pico.")

[29]Rainfall figures for the Los Angeles basin were not recorded. San Diego received 3.87 inches in 1862-63 and 5.14 inches the next year. Describing a storm which brought about four inches of rain to Los Angeles in Dec., 1864, the *News* remarked that the amount was "an eighth to a quarter of an inch more than fell during the whole of last winter." (*Southern News*, Dec. 3, 1864.)

[30]C. R. Johnson to Abel Stearns, Feb. 6, 1863, in Stearns MSS. An unknown disease had also done some damage to Abel Stearns's herds during the preceding fall. (Johnson to Stearns, Oct. 2, 1862, *ibid.*)

[31]Johnson to Stearns, Mar. 4 and 12, *ibid*. The *recogida* was a roundup of horses. It was held about a month earlier than the rodeo.

[32]Johnson to Stearns, Mar. 14, 1863, *ibid*. On Mar. 18 Johnson wrote to Cave Couts that the stockmen would lose half their cattle before the close of the year. (Johnson to Couts, Mar. 18, 1863, in Couts MSS.)

[33]Juan Forster to [?], Jan. 8, 1863, *ibid.*

[34]Cave Couts to Abel Stearns, Mar. 8, 1863, *ibid*. See also Couts's letters, to Stearns, of Nov. 23 and Dec. 21, 1861, expressing grave concern over both drought and smallpox. (*Ibid.*)

[35]In Stearns MSS. The agreement was dated Jan. 10, 1863. The cattle were to be delivered to the purchasers, 45 miles north of Los Angeles.

At that time, cattle were also being sent to the Washoe silver camps and to the newly opened mines on the Colorado.

Stearns and Temple paid $4.00 for picked cattle and slaughtered them for their hides and fat. (Testimony of Robert Ashcroft, *op. cit.*)

[36]C. R. Johnson to Abel Stearns, June 1, 2, 13, 1863, in Stearns MSS. Stearns found pasturage, 30 miles from Temécula, capable of supporting several thousand head. The chief of the Indian tribe to which the land belonged agreed to rent the range, for 100 head of cattle, 25 mares, merchandise to the value of $100, and one bullock a month, to be used as food for his people. (Johnson to Stearns, June 13, 1863, *ibid.*) As early as Oct., 1862, the Yorbas were reported to have sent 3,000 head of cattle to Lower California. (Johnson to Stearns, Oct. 11, 1862, *ibid.*) Forster saved perhaps 50% of the cattle on the Santa Margarita Ranch by driving them into the mountains. Because of the rugged character of the mountains from the Cajón Pass northward, and an almost complete lack of meadows, the starving herds of Los Angeles County found no such refuge.

[37]Some of the rancheros contracted with doctors from Los Angeles to vaccinate their Indians. In one case, 78 Indians were thus treated, at a cost of $60. It will be recalled that James Ohio Pattie, the Kentucky fur trader, described at length the vaccination of several thousand California-mission Indians in a similar smallpox epidemic in 1828. (*The Personal Narrative of James O. Pattie, of Kentucky,* ed. Reuben Gold Thwaites [Cleveland, 1905], pp. 264 ff.)

[38]Cave J. Couts to Abel Stearns, Jan. 4, 1863, in Couts MSS. As a result of Couts's efforts to keep the Indians from burying smallpox victims in the cemetery of Mission San Luis Rey, one of his relatives shot and killed the leader of an Indian burial party. The incident is described in letters from both Couts and C. R. Johnson to Stearns.

[39]The first rain fell in November. It was just enough to start the grass, which, in the absence of subsequent moisture, soon dried up and died. (Los Angeles *Star*, Nov. 23, 1863.)

[40]"Don Juan Forster *vs.* Pío Pico," II, 27.

[41]In 1863 Stearns agreed to sell "large, prime hides" for $2.75 each, delivered at San Pedro. (Stearns to I. Rich & Bros., in Stearns MSS.)

[42]*Southern News,* Apr. 6, 1864.

[43]Testimony of Robert Ashcroft, *op. cit.,* II, 27. "I saw 25 or 30 carcasses as I was crossing Coyote Creek all in one spot," Ashcroft added. Cave Couts said that cattle were offered at from $1.50 to $2.00 a head but no one would buy them, even at those prices. (*Ibid.,* pp. 143-44.)

[44]*Southern News,* Jan. 22, Mar. 9, 1864. To take the place of the ruined cattle industry, the editor urged the development of mines, and the planting of such crops as cotton, flax, tea, tobacco, hops, etc.

[45]*Ibid.,* Feb. 12, 1864.

[46]*Ibid.,* May 21, 1864. By midsummer, hay was selling for $45 a ton in Sacramento; beef had fallen to 2 cts. a pound; and Indians as well as cattle were starving to death in some parts of the state. (*Ibid.,* Aug. 28, 1864.) In July, Stearns complained to Julian Workman and William Rowland, of the Rancho

Puente, that their cattle were grazing on his land. He urged them to follow his example and kill off a large portion of their stock, because "the more the number is reduced the more chance for saving some." (Abel Stearns to Julian Workman, July 31, 1864, Stearns MSS.)

⁴⁷Ninth Census, Vol. III, *The Statistics of the Wealth and Industry of the United States*, p. 75. (According to the Director of the Ninth Census, no credence could be given to the statistics published by his predecessor in 1860.)

Hide exports from California to New York and Boston—a fairly good barometer—rose from about 178,000 in 1861 to over 315,000 in 1862, and to nearly 330,000 in 1864. (State Agr. Soc. *Transactions, 1864-65*, p. 382. See also *Southern News*, Aug. 28, 1864.) The *Sacramento Union* of Jan. 7, 1865, estimated that from 50% to 75% of the cattle in Los Angeles County had perished in the drought.

During the drought, cattle owners of northern and central California began the practice, still widely followed, of driving their herds into the Sierra Nevada Mountains in the spring and pasturing them there until fall. Many ranchers also sowed alfalfa, and other hay crops, to supplement range feed, so that later droughts never again took such devastating toll as that exacted in the middle sixties. (State Agr. Soc. *Transactions, 1870-71*, p. 4.)

⁴⁸Los Angeles County, "Assessment Book," 1863, pp. 112-16. The original assessment, made before the full effect of the drought became evident, was on the basis of 25 cts. an acre, but the Board of Equalization reduced the valuation by half.

Official records of the time were often humorously informal. One of the items in the assessment of Augustín Olvera's property in 1863 read, "Two fine daughters. No price—value cannot be computed. Great! Great!" (*Ibid.*, p. 90.)

⁴⁹At that time, as already explained, the city of Los Angeles did not make a separate municipal tax levy, but in all fiscal matters was an integral part of the county. How much of the property represented by the above assessments lay within the municipality and how much in unincorporated territory is therefore difficult to determine.

⁵⁰Los Angeles County, "Assessment Book," 1864.

⁵¹Los Angeles County, "Delinquent Tax List," 1864. A curious case of the confusion of justice was cited by the Los Angeles *Star* of June 7, 1862. The District Court of San Joaquin County ordered the sale of the real and personal property of Andrés Pico, to meet delinquent taxes on the Rancho Moquelumnes. Under the decree, Pico's horses and cattle were sold at from $3.00 to $5.00 a head. The court also ordered the sale of the 110,000-acre Rancho San Fernando, belonging to Pico, to meet the deficiency. But both the Federal District Court and the U.S. Supreme Court had declared that Pico did not and never had owned the Rancho Moquelumnes!

⁵²Los Angeles County, "Assessment Book," 1864 (fiscal year ending Mar. 1, 1865), p. 343. The assessment was made as of Aug. 15, 1864. This appraisal was less than one-fourth that of 1854. The "Subsequent Assessment Roll," compiled much later in the year, increased the valuation of county property to $1,922,-176.40. See also the *Southern News*, Nov. 26, 1864.

⁵³The following were typical of the names which appeared on the delinquent list: Pío Pico, John Forster, José Sepúlveda, Phineas Banning, Henry Dalton, John G. Downey, Manuel Domínguez. Two pages were required to list and describe the delinquent properties of Abel Stearns.

CHAPTER VIII

¹*Seventh Census of the United States: 1850*, p. 969.

²Los Angeles County retained its new boundaries less than two years. In 1853 two-thirds of the territory was absorbed by the creation of San Bernardino County. Orange County remained a part of Los Angeles County until 1889. Riverside County, formed largely out of territory belonging to San Bernardino and San Diego counties, was established in 1893. See Owen C. Coy, *California County Boundaries* (Berkeley, 1923), pp. 140-56; Guinn, *History of California*, I, 293.

³The figures given in the text are taken from the California state census of 1852. According to that report, whites numbered 4,091, and domesticated Indians 4,193. Wild tribes of the interior were not included. By an unprecedented act of Congress, the returns of the state census were printed as an appendix to the federal census of 1850. The figures of the two returns differ widely and in many cases cannot be reconciled; nor is it possible to determine which is the more reliable. The federal census was carried out in California in the midst of the confusion of the Gold Rush and was necessarily incomplete and unscientifically compiled; but the state census two years later was probably no more accurate.

The federal census made no mention of Indians, whether wild or domesticated, but gave Los Angeles County a white population of 3,530. Los Angeles city contained nearly half of this number, or 1,610.

See "Statistics of California," in *Seventh Census of the United States: 1850*, pp. 965-80; and "Population and Industry of California by the State Census for 1852," *ibid.*, pp. 981-85. See also M. H. and M. R. Newmark, *Census of the City and County of Los Angeles*, p. 21, *et passim*.

⁴The figures are again from the state census of 1852. The federal census gave the state's population as 92,597. The state census, therefore, showed an increase of nearly 180% in two years—a striking manifestation, even at that early date, of the true California spirit!

⁵Eighth Census, *Agriculture of the United States in 1860*, p. 10.

The Los Angeles *Star* of Feb. 28, 1863, estimated that there were 325,000 sheep in Los Angeles County. The *Star* of June 2, 1860, printed the following livestock statistics from the San Francisco *Bulletin*. The table was compiled from Forbes's History of California, material in the state's Spanish archives, annual returns made by the several county surveyors to the office of the state surveyor-general, the United States census reports, the *State Register and Year Book of Facts* for 1859, and other sources.

STOCK IN CALIFORNIA

	Cattle	Horses	Sheep
1770	200	300	—————
1790	20,000	—————	18,364
1791	24,858	—————	24,436
1802	67,782	2,187	107,172
1822	152,179	20,508	200,646
1827	194,187	—————	214,704
1831	216,727	32,201	153,455
1850	262,659	21,719	17,554
1852	448,796	67,773	82,867
1855	530,000	78,000	140,000
1856	694,000	106,991	253,312
1857	722,374	137,142	298,343
1858	814,642	160,804	417,909
1859	1,000,000	200,000	1,000,000

The federal census reports for horses and cattle from 1850 to 1870, by decades, were as follows:

	Cattle	Horses
1850	262,659 (partial)	21,719 (partial)
1860	1,180,142	173,379
1870	669,280	241,146

(Ninth Census, III, 75.)

The corresponding figures for sheep were:

1850	17,574	(Eighth Census, *Agriculture*, p. cxxii.)
1860	1,088,002	(*Ibid.*)
1870	2,768,187	(Ninth Census, III, 105.)

[6]Statistics of California wool production vary widely. The following table, whose figures for 1870 and 1871 are entirely out of line with the federal estimates, is taken from John Hayes, "Sheep-Farming in California," *Overland Monthly*, VIII, 489-97:

Year	Pounds
1854	175,000
1858	1,428,350
1862	5,530,000
1866	6,546,750
1870	19,472,666
1871	22,181,188

A communication from former Governor Downey, in the federal census for 1860, contained this paragraph: "Our wool clip will claim, in order of importance, the second rank as a product, adding largely to the material wealth of the State and nation at large, giving to large numbers pleasing and profitable employment, and adding much to our carrying trade. From a few thousand coarse-wooled and inferior Mexican sheep, our flocks will now number three millions of improved stock, yielding this year a clip approximating to 12,000,000 pounds; and at the close of the present decade, it will not be unreasonable to expect that California will produce an amount equal to the entire product of this staple in the United States in 1860—say 60,000,000 pounds." Even the maximum figures given above show to what degree Downey drew on his imagination!

⁷Circular, issued by Christy & Wise, wool dealers of San Francisco. (In Stearns MSS.) Merino sheep were probably brought into California from Honolulu as early as 1846, by Abel Stearns. (William French to Abel Stearns, Feb. 25, 1864, *ibid.*)

The Bixby Papers, in the Huntington Library, contain a wealth of material on the sheep industry of California. The most detailed single item is the "Moore and Bixby Wool Book from 1860 to 1870," which contains annual figures of wool production, flock increases, prices, grazing, and weather conditions, and furnishes a minute account of the operations of the partners for the years in question.

⁸Mr. Socrates Hyacinth [pseud.], "A Flock of Wool," *Overland Monthly,* IV, 141-46.

⁹Augustus Bixby, in the employ of Flint & Bixby of Monterey County, drove a flock of sheep into the mountains, in May, 1858, and returned in October. (Augustus Bixby, "Diary," in Huntington Library.) For a description of the sheepherder's life, see Stephen Powers, "The California Ranch," *Atlantic Monthly,* June, 1865, pp. 691-92.

Rattlesnakes constituted another very real danger to the sheepherder. A remedy against the poison, which apparently had some vogue, consisted of equal parts of onion, tobacco, and salt, made into a poultice and applied to the wound. See Bixby, "Diary," 1863, n.

¹⁰According to John S. Hittell, W. W. Hollister introduced the practice of breeding sheep for wool into California. Dr. Flint and two of the Bixbys had driven a flock of sheep overland from Illinois to California in 1853. In 1855 the firm of Flint, Bixby & Co. purchased the Rancho San Justo, of 54,000 acres, near San Juan Bautista, in Monterey County, and began raising sheep on a large scale.

¹¹W. W. Hollister to Abel Stearns, Oct. 2, 1861, in Stearns MSS. The following year Pío Pico permitted John G. Downey to pasture sheep on the Rancho Los Coyotes, of which Stearns was joint owner, and was reported ready to sell his interest to Hollister or Downey for $12,000. (C. R. Johnson to Abel Stearns, Oct. 2, 1862, *ibid.* See also the statement of Don Juan Forster, in "Forster vs. Pío Pico," III, 42.)

¹²Stearns, however, did not have the proverbial cattleman's contempt for sheep. He pastured sheep regularly on the Rancho Alamitos; occasionally rented land for sheep pasturage; and in 1870, after he had lost most of his cattle through the ravages of drought and foreclosure, leased pasturage on the ranchos Los Coyotes, La Habra, San Juan Cajón de Santa Ana, and Las Bolsas to various sheep owners, including Moore & Bixby and Domingo Bastanchury. The leases (in Stearns MSS) averaged about 10 cts. a head during the season. In 1854 Stearns himself had paid $15 a month for 2,200 acres of the Rancho La Brea, for sheep pasturage.

¹³This was at the rate of about 75 cts. an acre. (Sarah Bixby-Smith, *Adobe Days* [Cedar Rapids, 1925], p. 40.)

[14]James Irvine, a merchant of San Francisco of Scotch-Irish parentage, bought the remaining half interest in the Ranchos San Joaquin and Lomas de Santiago as well as a half interest in that portion of the Rancho Santa Ana that Flint, Bixby and Company acquired. Later he bought out his partners and combined all three of the properties into the present huge Irvine Ranch of Orange County.

[15]The sheep industry enjoyed great prosperity until 1876. A severe drought in 1871-72 caused heavy losses to individual growers, but the high price of wool brought about a swift recovery. A much worse drought in 1876-77, coupled with lower prices, reduced the sheepmen to the same straits the cattlemen had passed through during the drought of the mid-sixties.

[16]John S. Hittell, "Sheep Farming in California," *Overland Monthly*, VIII, 490-91; R. G. Cleland, *The Place Called Sespe*, pp. 116-17; R. G. Cleland and Osgood Hardy, *The March of Industry* (Los Angeles, 1929), p. 70. According to Stephen Powers, sheep raising in California normally yielded nearly 100% annual net profit. He based his estimate on the following figures:

Expenses		Income	
Interest on investment	$14,400	Fat sheep	$24,000
Herding	2,520	Spring clip	9,750
Shearing	900	Fall clip	2,730
Hauling wool	750		$36,480
Miscellaneous	250		
	$18,820	(*Overland Monthly*, VI, 146.)	

Unoccupied government lands furnished an enormous amount of free pasture to the sheep owners of the time.

[17]*Centennial History of Los Angeles County*, p. 113; Reid to Abel Stearns, June 1, 1844, in Stearns MSS.

[18]*Report of the Surveyor General of California*, 1854, p. 66.

[19]Los Angeles County assessment figures for 1862, quoted in the Los Angeles *Star*, Feb. 23, 1863.

[20]*Report of the Surveyor General of California*, 1866. (Quoted in Carr, *Illustrated Handbook of California*, p. 72.) According to the federal census of 1870, the state wine production was 1,814,656 gallons, of which Los Angeles County supplied 531,710. (Ninth Census, III, 106.)

In 1851 fresh grapes from southern California sold for 20 cts. a pound in San Francisco. In 1857 nearly 1,000,000 pounds of grapes were shipped from San Pedro to the northern markets. Among the pioneer wine producers of the county were William Wolfskill; Louis Vignes, and his nephew, Jean Louis Sansevaine; Benjamin D. Wilson, of the Lake Vineyard Ranch; Matthew Keller; and L. J. Rose, who began the development of the widely known "Sunny Slope" vineyards in 1861. (See *Centennial History of Los Angeles County*, pp. 113-14; also Los Angeles *Star*, Sept. 24, 1859.) The papers of B. D. Wilson, now in the Huntington Library, furnish basic material for a thorough study of the early southern California grape and wine industries.

[21]Bixby, "Diary."

[22]"The Tropical Fruits of California," *Overland Monthly*, I, 263-68. For interesting comments on early horticulture in Los Angeles, see "An Emigrant of the Fifties: The Letters of James Clarke," ed. David Davies, in Hist. Soc. of Sou. Calif. *Quarterly*, XIX, 111-19. William Wolfskill, Louis Vignes, and Matthew Keller were the pioneer commercial citrus growers in California. In 1841 Wolfskill set out two acres of seedling trees, obtained from the Mission San Gabriel, on a tract of land now occupied by the Arcade Station of the Southern Pacific Railroad. His orchard eventually covered 70 acres. In 1851 Louis Vignes advertised the sale of "two orange gardens that yield from five to six thousand oranges in the season." (*Centennial History of Los Angeles County*, p. 113.)

Grapes and oranges were the only fruits which could be shipped in large quantities by boat to San Francisco. The total value of California orchard products in 1870 was only $1,384,430; of Los Angeles County, $74,000. (Ninth Census, III, 106.)

[23]In 1870 California produced 16,676,702 bushels of wheat, and only 1,221,222 bushels of corn. Los Angeles County, running counter to the general trend, produced 454,896 bushels of corn and only 12,210 bushels of wheat. (*Ibid.*, p. 105.) The state production of wheat on so large a scale strikingly fulfilled the predictions of Waddy Thompson and other pre-Mexican War enthusiasts for the annexation of California, that the fertile valleys of the San Joaquin and Sacramento would one day become the "granary of the world." The extent and ramifications of the great wheat boom are well described by J. S. Silver, in the *Overland Monthly*, I, 176-83.

[24]The assessment rolls for 1862 listed 73,787 acres. (Los Angeles *Star*, Feb. 23, 1863.)

[25]Nordhoff, *California*, pp. 155, 150-51.

[26]The discovery was made by Francisco Lopez.

[27]Abel Stearns to Messrs. Pierce and Brewer, via the "Farma," Apr. 25, 1842, in Stearns MSS. Another letter, describing the first shipment of gold from the California placers to the Philadelphia mint, is also in the Stearns MSS.

[28]H. M. Nimmo to Stearns, Feb. 11, 1850, in Stearns MSS.

[29]*Southern Californian*, Feb. 8, 1855. Quoted also in Cleland, *History of California*, p. 25. Other enthusiastic reports of the Kern River mines are found in the *Southern Californian* of Feb. 15, 22, Mar. 7, *et seq.*

[30]*Southern Vineyard*, June 28, 1859.

[31]*Ibid.* The issue of Oct. 14 contained a long account of a fatal shooting and knifing affray at Welch's Bar in the cañon.

[32]Some seventy years later, several hundred persons, thrown out of employment in the depression of 1929, sought to make a living by placer mining in that part of the San Gabriel Cañon mentioned in the *Star*. See also W. W. Robinson, *The Forest and the People*, (Los Angeles, 1946), pp. 17-21.

[33]Guinn, *Historical and Biographical Record*, p. 137. Contemporary Los

Angeles newspapers also contain frequent references to the placers, especially to the equipment and operations of the Santa Anita Mining Company. See, e.g., the Los Angeles *Star*, Feb. 19, May 14, 1859. A body of mining laws for the district appeared in the *Star* of Aug. 14.

[34]Cleland, *History of California*, p. 311.

[35]C. H. Brinley to Abel Stearns, May 2, 1862, in Stearns MSS. A description of the mines appears in the Los Angeles *Star* of Jan. 31, 1863.

[36]The Stearns collection contains a large amount of material relating to the Temescal tin mines, and a smaller file on Stearns's copper mine in Soledad Cañon. For further reference to the Temescal mines, see Chapter X.

[37]In 1864 William Brewer wrote to his brother: "Mines of silver and gold were discovered in the Inyo mountains some two or three years ago. They made some excitement, a few mills were erected, and three villages started Owensville, San Carlos and Bend City." (*Up and Down California*, pp. 536-37. See also the Los Angeles *Star*, July 3, 1858.)

An interesting account of an early expedition to Owens Valley, led by Capt. Davidson, and the discovery of "Mammoth Springs" at the head of the Owens River, is found in the *Star* of Aug. 27, 1859.

[38]Chalfant, *Story of Inyo*, pp. 252-53. The famous Panamint district was not discovered until 1873; see also Remi A. Nadeau, *City Makers* (New York, 1948), pp. 31-44.

[39]The carriage and wagon works operated by Goller & Baldwin in Los Angeles furnished a good example of the Los Angeles business enterprises which depended largely on the mines. Early in 1859 the firm was operating seven blacksmith's forges, employing thirty men, and had on hand material for fifty large freight wagons. (*Southern Vineyard*, Feb. 4, 1859.)

[40]The development of transportation in southern California has been the subject of frequent studies. See Cleland, *History of California*, pp. 359-68; *idem*, "Transportation in California before the Railroads, with Special Reference to Los Angeles," in Hist. Soc. of Sou. Calif. *Annual Publications*, XI, 60-67; Rockwell Dennis Hunt and William Sheffield Ament, *Oxcart to Airplane* (Los Angeles, 1929), chaps. 4, 5; William Banning and George H. Banning, *Six Horses* (New York and London, 1930), *passim*.

Before the era of the transcontinental railroad, the Butterfield Overland Mail Company was the most famous transportation organization in the West. Its stages ran on regular schedule and required only about three weeks to make the trip between St. Louis and San Francisco. From the standpoint of southern California, especially, the Overland Mail was far quicker and more dependable than the Pacific Mail Steamship Company. In 1859 the stage fare from Los Angeles to Memphis, Tenn., was $150, and to San Francisco $30. The route from Los Angeles to the north ran by way of Fort Tejón, White River, Visalia, Gilroy, and San José. (*Southern Vineyard*, July 8, 1859.)

One of the chief figures in the development of stage and freight lines in early southern California was Phineas Banning. Born Aug. 19, 1830, near Wilmington, Del., Banning came to California, via Panamá, in 1851, and obtained a position with Douglas & Sanford, who, with the use of six horses and two mules, were then handling all freight and passenger business between San Pedro and Los Angeles. Banning later entered the employ of Temple & Alexander, and finally bought out Temple's share of the business.

After building up a large freight and passenger business, Banning opened lines to San Bernardino and Yuma. He also entered the Salt Lake trade, but claimed that the opposition of Brigham Young forced him out of that enterprise. Banning founded the town of Wilmington, built up a large marine transportation business, and initiated the first railroad, between Wilmington and San Pedro, in southern California. (Phineas Banning, "Biographical Sketch" and "Settlement of Wilmington"—MSS in the Bancroft Library of the University of California.)

[41]Some thirty citizens subscribed to the enterprise. Abel Stearns contributed $500; Alexander & Banning, $100; B. D. Wilson, $40; Juan Temple, $40; Henry Dalton, $20; etc. The contract for grading and construction was given to W. T. B. Sanford. (Stearns MSS.)

[42]The freight business out of Los Angeles reached large proportions: On Apr. 27, 1855, 15 ten-mule teams left Los Angeles for Salt Lake City, with 15 tons of merchandise. (Los Angeles *Star*, May 2, 1855.) As much as 100 tons of goods sometimes awaited shipment from Los Angeles to Salt Lake City. The rate was from 18 cts. to 25 cts. a pound. (*Ibid.*, Nov. 2, 1861.) Banning dispatched 7 ten-mule teams to Yuma on Mar. 24, 1858. Each wagon carried 5,000 pounds of freight. (*Southern Vineyard*, Mar. 24, 1858.)

[43]The first messages were sent on Oct. 9. For an account of the celebration, see the Los Angeles *Star*, Oct. 13, 1860. Seven years later it cost $9.00 to send a message of 44 words between the two cities. (A. B. Pohlemus to Abel Stearns, Dec. 6, 1867, in Stearns MSS.)

[44]The federal census of 1860 gave the following list of settlements in Los Angeles County:

Name	Population
Assuza (Azusa)	363
El Monte	1,004
Los Nietos	605
San José	463
San Gabriel	586
Santa Ana	756
San Juan	661
San Pedro	359
Tejón	920

(Eighth Census, *Population*, p. 29.)

[45]Cleland, *History of California*, p. 322.

[46]Milton R. Hunter, "The Mormon Corridor," *Pacific Historical Review*, VIII, 179-200, *passim*. Hunter's article adds new significance to the place of San Bernardino in Brigham Young's carefully devised plan for the development of a Mormon empire.

[47]G. W. and H. P. Beattie, *Heritage of the Valley*, p. 171. The Beatties' account of the settlement of San Bernardino, and the subsequent history of the Mormon colony, is so detailed and authentic that little can be added to it.

In 1848 Isaac Williams reportedly offered the Mormons the 8-square-league Rancho del Chino, 8,000 head of cattle, and a large number of horses, for "five hundred dollars down" and the balance on the purchasers' own terms! (*Ibid.*, p. 127.)

Amasa M. Lyman and Charles C. Rich, who purchased the land for the colony, paid $77,500 for 8 square leagues, or about 35,000 acres. It was their understanding that they were to receive from 75,000 to 100,000 acres under the contract. (*Ibid.*, pp. 183-84.)

One of the best of the earlier accounts of San Bernardino is found in Guinn, *History of California*, pp. 437-42. For a very recent account, written especially from the standpoint of geographic factors, see Hallock F. Raup, *San Bernardino, California: Settlement and Growth of a Pass Site City* (Berkeley, 1940).

[48]California newspapers devoted much space to the Mountain Meadows massacre. See, e.g., the Los Angeles *Star*, Oct. 10 to Nov. 14, 1857.

For the withdrawal of the San Bernardino colonists, see G. W. and H. P. Beattie, pp. 258-98; Hunter, in *Pacific Hist. Rev.*, VIII, 197-99.

[49]Los Angeles *Star*, Dec. 5, 1857. Some 25,000 acres of the original 35,000 acres purchased by Lyman and Rich were sold for $18,000. (G. W. and H. P. Beattie, pp. 291-92.)

[50]*Ibid.*, Aug. 28, 1858.

[51]*Ibid.*, Jan. 30, 1858.

[52]For contemporary accounts of the Anaheim colony, see the Los Angeles *Star*, Jan. 30, 1858; *Southern Vineyard*, Apr. 8, 1858; etc.

Excellent articles on the Anaheim settlement and personal reminiscences of the early colonists are also to be found in the volumes of *The Orange County History Series*, published by the Orange County Historical Society.

[53]Quoted in Guinn, *History of California*, p. 405. The Los Angeles *Star*, of Oct. 2, 1858, contains an article, of some length, entitled "Inauguration of New Town San Pedro."

[54]Ineffectual attempts were made by Henry Dalton to colonize the Rancho Azusa in 1851, and by John O. Wheeler, to subdivide the Rancho San Francisquito, near El Monte, in 1852. (*Centennial History of Los Angeles County*, p. 111.) In 1855 Dalton advertised the drawings for a lottery, prizes for which consisted of real and personal property to the value of $84,000. Tickets were a dollar each. Included in the real estate were "two hundred and forty elegant lots in the town of Benton," and "twenty-four superb forty-acre farms on the Rancho of Azusa." (Los Angeles *Star*, Mar. 1, 1855.)

CHAPTER IX

[1]*Semi-weekly Southern News*, July 25, 1862.

[2]Brewer, *Up and Down California*, pp. 257-58.

[3]*Report of the Surveyor-General of California from Nov. 1, 1867, to Nov. 1, 1869*, p. 13. The report was concerned both with the evils arising from the Spanish-Mexican grants, and with the land monopolies created by the federal and state land laws.

[4]Prior to the Homestead Act of 1862, private land could be bought in southern California at a much lower price than the $1.25 an acre fixed for government land by the Pre-emption Act of 1841.

An examination of actual cases shows that most rancheros, though cordially disliking squatters, were willing to sell to bona fide settlers at a fair price. Isaac Williams offered the Rancho Chino to the Mormons for a pittance; the Anaheim colonists paid a dollar an acre for 1,200 acres of some of the best agricultural land in the state. Don Juan Forster, of the Rancho Santa Margarita y Las Flores, offered to give forty acres to every settler who would spend $1,000 on the tract. (William H. Bishop, *Old Mexico and Her Lost Provinces* [New York, 1883], p. 464.)

In seeking to carry out the land distribution which formed so large a part of the Madero revolutionary program, the Mexican government some years ago encountered the same difficulty in the semiarid regions of northern Mexico that prevented the breakup of the ranchos in southern California. Without water, enormous grazing areas in Sonora, Chihuahua, and Coahuila cannot be cultivated, and consequently are totally unfit for subdivision into small holdings.

[5]Mr. Socrates Hyacinth [pseud.], "Wayside Views of California," *Overland Monthly*, II, 229-30.

[6]Petition to the State Senate and Assembly, Jan., 1870. (In Stearns MSS.)

[7]Hall, *Great West*, pp. 126-27. With the true California spirit, however, Hall concluded that, notwithstanding all these drawbacks, "California gains in population and solid matter every day. Her inexhaustible resources carry her forward in spite of herself."

[8]At this point Browne bluntly criticized San Francisco banks and capitalists for speculating wildly in mines and mining stocks and lending money recklessly on such volatile and often worthless securities, while refusing to finance constructive enterprises in agriculture or business.

[9]J. Ross Browne, "Agricultural Capacity of California," *Overland Monthly*, X, 297-314.

[10]Calif. State Agr. Soc. *Transactions*, 1864-65, p. 76.

[11]Hall, pp. 120-22.

[12]Hist. Soc. of Sou. Calif. *Quarterly*, XIX, 21.

[13]As early as 1856 a group of New York merchants and shippers, with commercial connections on the Pacific Coast, formed an organization to advertise the resources of California and to encourage the migration of settlers to that state. The organization collected information on California agriculture, methods of farming, conditions of employment, status of land titles, and the terms on which land could be bought. It was especially interested in all that per-

tained to the grape industry in southern California, and in a report, received from Alfred Robinson, that the city of Los Angeles was offering free land to settlers. (New York Committee on California Emigration to Abel Stearns, Dec. 4, 1856, in Stearns MSS. For the action of the *ayuntamiento* on free land, see the Los Angeles *Star* of July 17, 1852.)

[14]Hall, p. 31.

[15]A road also led from Santa Fé, via Green River, and intersected the Mormon Trail at Provo, Utah. Many of the immigrants who came through New Mexico carved their names on the greatest of all American historical directories—El Morro. Most of the names are still legible and furnish an invaluable aid to a study of the expeditions.

[16]A contemporary account of one of the most tragic episodes of these post-Gold Rush expeditions to California—the Mojave massacre of the Rose-Udell company of 1858—is given in Appendix IV.

[17]G. L. Mix to Volney E. Howard, Oct. 10, 1867; Mix to Stearns, Dec. 9, 1867—both in Stearns MSS.

[18]Samuel McKee to Stearns, July 5, 1869, *ibid.*

[19]Bishop, *Old Mexico*, p. 413. Many southern families also moved to California in the late sixties and early seventies to escape the recurrent plagues of yellow fever that extended as far north as Philadelphia.

[20]G. L. Mix to Stearns, Dec. 6, 1867, in Stearns MSS.

[21]Jos. S. Wilson to Albert Rhodes, United States Consulate, Rotterdam, Holland, May 13, 1869 (printed in the San Francisco *Bulletin*, May 25, 1869), the Huntington Library. The letter is also printed in Benjamin Fabian, *The Agricultural Lands of California* (San Francisco, 1869).

[22]A. Carr, *Illustrated Hand-book of California* (London, 1870), pp. 90-91.

[23]*Semi-weekly News*, Aug. 18, Sept. 1, 1868.

[24]See the correspondence of Charles H. Forbes with Abel Stearns for 1868, in Stearns MSS. Real-estate advertisements, similar to those referred to in the text, are to be found in nearly every Los Angeles newspaper of the time.

[25]Correspondence of G. L. Mix and Stearns for the year 1868; also an unsigned, undated memorandum on the subject—all in Stearns MSS.
By Oct., 1868, 12,000 acres of the Stearns ranchos had been sold, on time, for $10 an acre. (Alfred Robinson to Stearns, Oct. 19, 1868, in Stearns MSS.) On Sept. 20, 1869, Robinson wrote Stearns that recent sales had amounted to $25,000. "The fall business is commencing and I look for active sales." (In Stearns MSS.)
In July, 1868, the San Fernando Homestead Association bought 116,000 acres from Pío and Andrés Pico for $180,000. (Fabian, *Agricultural Lands*, p. 8.)

[26]In 1860 John Forster was offered $20,000 for 26,000 acres of the Rancho Santa Margarita; in 1866 Flint, Bixby & Co. bought the Rancho Los Cerritos for 75 cts. an acre; in Apr., 1868, the Rancho Sausal Redondo sold for $1.33 an

acre. See Hayes, *Pioneer Notes*, p. 204; Bixby-Smith, *Adobe Days*, p. 55; *Semi-weekly News*, Apr. 21, 1868; and Forbes to Stearns, Mar. 7, 1868, in Stearns MSS.

In 1867 W. S. Rosecrans proposed to Abel Stearns to organize a company to sell 114,000 acres of the Stearns ranchos. Stearns was to contribute the land, on the basis of a dollar an acre, while Rosecrans and his associates would supply $114,000 in cash for advertising and selling expenses. (Rosecrans to Stearns, Nov. 4, 1867, in Stearns MSS.)

[27]*Semi-weekly News*, Jan. 20, Apr. 3, 1869.

[28]*Ibid.*, Apr. 3, 1869.

[29]Los Angeles *Star*, Aug. 3, 8, 1868.
One of the Los Angeles banks, conducted under the name of Hayward & Co. and capitalized at $100,000, was organized by Alvinza H. Hayward and John G. Downey. The Bank of Hellman, Temple & Co. was founded by I. W. Hellman, William Workman, and F. P. F. Temple. (Guinn, *History of California*, p. 318.)

[30]Mr. Socrates Hyacinth [pseud.], "On Foot in Southern California," *Overland Monthly*, II, 23.

[31]In 1869 William H. Spurgeon laid out the town of Santa Ana on a portion of the Rancho Santiago de Santa Ana. The town of Compton was founded in the same year.

[32]*Semi-weekly News*, Sept. 8, 1868, Mar. 16, 1869.
Los Nietos College was opened in Mar., 1869. Classes at first were held in the home of the founder, John C. Ardis. A public sale of lots provided $2,743 for the erection of a building. Tuition was $4.00 a month. Parents were assured that the president of the college would "forbid attendance at all parties or amusements which he thinks will retard the advancement of his pupils." (*Ibid.*, Mar. 15, 18, 1869.)

[33]Nordhoff, *California*, p. 138. See also Clarence J. King, "Wayside Pikes," *Atlantic Monthly*, Nov. 7, 1871. The reader will recognize in the roving immigrants of the sixties and early seventies a certain similarity to the migrants from the "Dust Bowl" area of the mid-thirties.
The term "Pike" was derived from the Missouri county of that name.

[34]Taliesin Evans, "Orange Culture in California," *Overland Monthly*, XII, 235-44. For other accounts of orange culture in southern California, see *Overland Monthly*, I, 263-68; XII, 560-62.

[35]In 1870, according to the federal census, Los Angeles County had 43 wineries and led the state both in the production of grapes and the manufacture of wines and brandies. The wineries represented a cost of $350,000 as against $136,000 invested in all other forms of manufacture.

[36]The Los Angeles and San Bernardino Land Company, selling agent for the Stearns ranchos, offered to sell the land for a commission of $2.50 an acre. The agreement, in the Stearns MSS, is dated Apr. 2, 1870.

For a typically enthusiastic account of the industry, see Henry de Groot, "Silk Culture in California," *Overland Monthly*, IV, 453-56. De Groot cited the case of one rancher who, in two months, realized a profit of a thousand dollars an acre from his mulberry trees, through the sale of silkworms and their eggs.

[37]Wilson to Albert Rhodes, May 13, 1869.
For a typical newspaper account of the industry in its early stages, see Los Angeles *Star*, Aug. 8, 1868.

[38]J. M. Guinn, "From Cattle Range to Orange Grove," Hist. Soc. of Sou. Calif. *Annual Publications*, VIII, 148.

[39]John L. Strong, "Cotton Experiments in California," *Overland Monthly*, VI, 326-35. The Stearns MSS contain many letters referring to the cotton boom and speaking with great enthusiasm of the new crop.

[40]Guinn, in Hist. Soc. of Sou. Calif. *Annual Publications*, VIII, 149.

[41]John Hayes, "Skilled Farming in Southern California," *Overland Monthly*, VII, 448-51. There were then 25,000 acres under irrigation in Los Angeles County.
In 1871 the California Immigrant Union, managed by William H. Martin, established its "agencies all over the Atlantic States and Europe" and began the subdivision of large southern California properties. Martin disposed of the Rancho Lompoc, in Santa Barbara County, in small tracts; organized the Centinela colonization project; and proposed the "subdivision of nearly all the important ranchos throughout southern California." (*Overland Monthly*, XIV, 191.)
The following prices, per acre, of land situated near Los Angeles, are given in Ludwig L. Salvator, *Los Angeles in the Sunny Seventies: A Flower from the Golden Land*, tr. Marguerite Eyer Wilbur (Los Angeles, 1929), p. 77:

Inferior pasture land	$2.75
Grain and farm land	$5.88
Grain and farm land, near Los Angeles	$25 to $100
Orchard and vineyard lands with water	$25 to $50
Land suitable for semitropical fruits	$40 to $60
Select fruit land	$75 to $200
Olive land	$100 to $150

[42]Hayes, *op. cit.*, p. 448.

[43]*Semi-weekly News*, Jan. 31, 1865.
The Pioneer Oil Company, composed of many of the leading citizens of Los Angeles, was organized early in 1865. It acquired drilling rights on a number of ranchos, and purchased part of the old pueblo lands still belonging to the city of Los Angeles. The president of the company was Phineas Banning; among the stockholders were John G. Downey, B. D. Wilson, John S. Griffin, Matthew Keller, Volney E. Howard, W. S. Hancock, Charles Ducommun, and George Hansen.

[44]*Ibid.*, Feb. 4, 18, Mar. 21, Nov. 11, 1865.

[45]These statistics and the tables preceding were compiled from the Statistical

Tables contained in the *Reports of the State Surveyor General of the State of California*, 1866, 1869-70, 1872.

⁴⁶*Semi-weekly News*, Jan. 28, 1869; Alfred Robinson to Abel Stearns, Oct. 13, 1869, Jan. 27, 1871, in Stearns MSS. Stearns's taxes in San Bernardino County increased from $396.47, in 1869 to $1,446.06, in 1871.

⁴⁷The Southern Pacific Railroad was completed to Los Angeles on Sept. 6, 1876.

CHAPTER X

¹Except for necessary background material, this chapter deals primarily with Stearns as a part of the southern California of 1850-70.

For an excellent, but by no means definitive, biographical account of Abel Stearns, see Pearl Pauline Stamp, "Abel Stearns: California Pioneer," *The Grizzly Bear Magazine*, May-Aug., 1926.

A shorter biographical sketch was written in 1899 by Henry D. Barrows. (Hist. Soc. of Sou. Calif. *Annual Publications*, IV, 197-99.)

Stearns was universally known among his contemporaries as Don Abel. He was also called by the less complimentary nickname of *Caro del Cavallo*, or Horse Face.

²Stearns's own statements regarding his birth are inconsistent. In 1841, when he was seeking to marry the fourteen-year-old Arcadia Bandini, he said he was forty years of age; but when he appeared as a witness before the U.S. Land Commission he testified that he born in 1798.

³Stearns was granted a passport by the Spanish vice-consul at Charleston, S.C., on Jan. 22, 1822. For a reproduction of his passport of 1827, see p. 191.

According to a statement in a letter to his sister, Stearns did not return to New England after 1824. (Stearns to Theresa Warren, Sept. 16, 1868, in Stearns MSS.)

⁴From certain memoranda and correspondence between Forbes and Stearns (in the Stearns collection), it appears that Stearns furnished much of the descriptive material which Forbes later embodied in his well-known *History of California*.

⁵The motive for this act, so unusual on the part of an American citizen, is still obscure.

⁶Stearns was associated in this venture with George Washington Eayrs, a pioneer New England trader on the California coast.

⁷Stearns also outfitted expeditions to hunt sea otter, and purchased sea-otter skins.

⁸Ewing Young to Abel Stearns, March 14, 1834, in Stearns MSS.

⁹Abel Stearns to Don Juan Bandini, April 5, 1841, *ibid.*

¹⁰Mariano G. Vallejo, "Documentos para la Historia de California," XXXI,

74, 78 (in Bancroft Library, University of California); also a biographical note on Abel Stearns by John T. Gaffey, in Stearns MSS.

[11]For the Victoria, Day, and Chico episodes, see Stamp, *op. cit.*; the Stearns MSS in the Bancroft Collection; and the Stearns MSS, Huntington Library. The last-named collection contains two interesting letters on the Chico affair: Timoteo Murphy to Stearns, July 29, 1836, and B. Stark to Stearns, June 30, 1836.

[12]Both the Stearns collection in the Huntington Library and the Abel Stearns papers in the Bancroft Library contain interesting material on Stearns's smuggling operations. Good secondary accounts are given in Stamp, *op. cit.*, and in Dakin, *A Scotch Paisano*, pp. 89-93.
A reasonable explanation for the so-called stolen hides may be found in the following note from Juan Forster, who at the time was in charge of the *Casa de San Pedro* and later became the owner of the Rancho Santa Margarita:
"Please explain to the authorities that you ought not to be responsible for hides that are vented when their vents don't accord with the brand, as it is impossible to tell what iron there is on one half of the hides received here." (Forster to Stearns, Jan. 7, 1841, in Stearns MSS.)

[13]The other daughters were Ysidora, Josefa, Dolores, and Margarita. Ysidora married Cave Couts, Josefa married Pedro C. Carrillo, Dolores married Charles R. Johnson, and Margarita, the youngest, married Dr. James B. Winston.

[14]Stearns Marriage Papers, in Stearns MSS. The petition was signed by Abel Stearns and dated Apr. 29, 1841.

[15]In 1834 Stearns purchased most of the ground on which *El Palacio* was built for $150. Robert S. Baker, second husband of Arcadia Bandini de Stearns, later built the celebrated "Baker Block" on the site of *El Palacio*.

[16]Wishing to be "a farmer instead of a Marchant," Stearns requested Governor Alvarado in 1839 to give him a grant of land in Santa Ana del Chino. (Vallejo, "Documentos," XXXII, 292.)

[17]Land Commission, Case No. 404, "Rancho Los Alamitos." The grant was confirmed May 22, 1834. The deed from Juan José Nieto to José Figueroa was dated June 30, 1834. Juan José acknowledged the receipt of $500 as payment in full for the ranch.

[18]The brand was issued May 23, 1834, by José Figueroa. Abel Stearns recorded it in Los Angeles County on Apr. 15, 1853. A contemporary drawing of the original brand (1834) is in the Stearns MSS.

[19]Brief filed by Morton and Morton, of San Francisco, on behalf of Manuel María Figueroa, plaintiff, Apr. 21, 1855. (Stearns MSS.)

[20]Abel Stearns to José Antonio Aguirre, Apr. 9, 1840, in Stearns MSS. Señor Temple was Don Juan Temple, husband of Rafaela Cota, one of the Nieto family, and owner of the adjacent Rancho Los Cerritos.

[21]Statement of Abel Stearns in Benjamin Hayes, "Miscellaneous," No. 31, Bancroft Library.

22Land Commission, Case No. 404, "Rancho Los Alamitos."

23*Ibid.*

24The document was dated Mar. 3, 1859, and filed Dec. 14, 1860. Stearns made the inventory a matter of record because of the claims of José Figueroa's heirs. (Book 4 of Deeds of Los Angeles County, pp. 80-81.) The deed to the ranch, given to Stearns in 1842, was recorded in Book B, pp. 70-75.

25Assessment Returns for 1850, in Stearns MSS.

26J. C. Frémont to Abel Stearns, Apr. 24, 1851, in Stearns MSS.

27Morton and Morton, attorneys for Manuel María Figueroa, Apr. 21, 1855. (Stearns MSS.)

28The details of the controversy over the title to the Alamitos are too involved to be given here. They furnish excellent material for a more extended study. In addition to the sources already quoted, including the proceeding before the Land Commission relating to the Rancho Los Alamitos, there are numerous letters and documents, in the Stearns collection, that bear on the subject. Important correspondence will be found in the files of C. R. Johnson, Cornelius King, Samuel Beatty, and Juan Temple.

29Juan Temple to Abel Stearns, Nov. 10, 19, 22, Dec. 25, 1857.

30A copy of the deed is in the Stearns MSS. See also deed of Louis Phillips to Arcadia Bandini de Stearns, Nov. 5, 1857, recorded in Book 3, Deeds of Los Angeles County, pp. 762-63. Stearns gave the Rancho Laguna to Arcadia. With the expansion of Los Angeles after 1900, the property became immensely valuable; and when Doña Arcadia died, in 1913, her estate was the most valuable probated up to that time in Los Angeles County.

31Stearns MSS.

32The story may be traced, step by step, in the records and documents preserved in Stearns's miscellaneous financial papers in the Stearns MSS.
Consult also the indexes of the books of deeds and mortgages of Los Angeles County.

33Los Angeles *Star*, Jan. 15, 1861; Stearns MSS.

34*Ibid.*

35For the various letters cited, see C. R. Johnson to Abel Stearns, under date of 1851, in Stearns MSS.
Johnson also wrote Stearns that one of Bandini's household had fallen into the hands of professional cardsharps in San Diego, and had "made mighty bad business out of his gambling speculation." Johnson did not know the exact amount involved, but estimated that the victim had lost between $8,000 and $10,000, while "he was locked up alone with those men."

36In addition to the principal, there was accumulated interest of $7,300. (Statement of Account, Juan Bandini to Abel Stearns, Jan. 28, 1856, in Stearns MSS.) In Feb., 1856, Bandini executed a mortgage to Stearns for $15,000 on the Rancho La Jurupa. The deed conveying the ranch to Stearns was dated Aug.

19, 1859. Bandini died in *El Palacio*, at "four o'clock in the morning," on Nov. 4, 1859.

[37]In 1856 Moses Carson, Kit Carson's brother, wrote Stearns about the possibility of making Los Angeles the chief fur depot on the coast. (Stearns MSS.)

[38]Stearns attempted to develop a copper mine in Soledad Cañon and spent large sums on the celebrated tin mines at Temescal. From the material in the Stearns collection alone, a volume might be written on the latter venture. William H. Brewer wrote of the Temescal tin excitement in 1861, "Every man has from one to fifty claims, while poor devils with ragged clothes and short pipes talk as they smoke of being the wealthy owners of one hundred or two hundred tin claims, each in turn to rival Cornwall or Banca ... we rode to the principal tin mine ... [and] found it a splendid humbug." (*Up and Down California*, pp. 34-35.)

Stearns succeeded in interesting the Phelps Dodge Company, of New York, in his ventures and eventually sold part of his holdings to a syndicate. This group, under the name of the San Jacinto Tin Company, issued a prospectus offering 10,000 shares of stock at $10 a share to provide working capital for the mine. The circular also said that 3½ tons of ore, which had been shipped to the Revere Copper Company of Boston, yielded 20% pure tin and that the supply of ore was said by experts to be inexhaustible. (Printed circular, signed by H. W. Carpenter, president, and S. F. Butterworth, treasurer, of the San Jacinto Tin Co., San Francisco, Jan. 18, 1868, in Stearns MSS.)

For a full report of the title angles to the Temescal property, see James O. Wilson, Commissioner of the General Land Office, to O. H. Browning, Secretary of the Interior, May 22, 1867, *ibid.* An English syndicate later purchased the property, and at one time there was a report that the mine was purposely kept idle to prevent competition with the tin production of Cornwall! Some twenty years ago the property was acquired by an American company and later sold to the Metropolitan Water District of Southern California.

[39]Unsigned, undated memorandum, in Stearns MSS.

[40]References have been made in earlier chapters to some of Stearns's contributions.

[41]H. F. Teschemacher to Stearns, June 13; Stearns to Poett, Apr. 17; C. R. Johnson to Stearns, Oct. 7, 1862; Andrew Cassidy to Stearns, Apr. 4, 1863—all in Stearns MSS.

[42]C. R. Johnson to Stearns, Oct. 7, Nov. 8, 1862, in Stearns MSS. Johnson's letters make repeated reference to overdue notes, unpaid taxes, etc.

Between May 19 and Aug. 16, 1864, Stearns gave eleven separate mortgages on his various properties. See Book 4 of Mortgages of Los Angeles County, pp. 351-89, *passim.*

[43]For the Stearns-Parrott affair see: C. R. Johnson to Stearns, Aug. 8, 11, 22, Oct. 22, Nov. 11, 1864, and Mar. 24, June 12, 1865; Delaney and Booraem to Stearns, Oct. 3, 11, Dec. 12, 1864; M. G. Cobb to Stearns, Jan. 15, 1865—all in Stearns MSS. Parrott was associated with John G. Downey, whom Stearns had been warned to regard as a "bad neighbor." "He is not unfriendly toward you," wrote Parrott to Stearns, "on the contrary, you will find him the best friend

you ever had. I would like you to place your affairs in his hands. He will do more for you in these times of trouble than any one else"

The letter from Stearns to Parrott, quoted in the text, is in the Stearns correspondence in the Huntington Library.

The Los Angeles *Semi-weekly News* of Apr. 15, 1865, contained an advertisement of the proposed sheriff's sale of the personal property of Abel Stearns, in the amount of $36,760.08, plus interest, in favor of John Parrott, doing business under the name of Parrott and Company. The sale was scheduled to take place on Apr. 22. It involved 7,000 head of cattle, 3,000 head of horses, 200 gentle horses, and 40 head of mules. The sale was to begin on the Rancho Los Alamitos and move in turn to the other Stearns ranchos. The same newspaper carried advertisements of the sheriff's sale of the Rancho Los Alamitos and the Rancho Cajón de Santa Ana.

From the following letter it appears that Stearns transferred some of his cattle to Juan Bandini, his brother-in-law; but the sheriff later discovered the cattle and attached them also.

"Juanito:

The sheriff has laid various attachments on your animals (those bought of Don Abel) on account of debts of Don Abel. He gave orders to begin gathering them up on Saturday last, but has postponed until my return to the ranch next Wednesday.

You must get your lawyer to attend this immediately. We have *no lawyer* in San Diego. . . . You must be quick.   Cave J. Couts.

To Don Juanito B. Bandini, Feb. 6."

[44]On Apr. 20, 1867, the state brought suit against Stearns for delinquent state-and-county personal property taxes, amounting to $6,013.61, and for taxes on realty amounting to $3,344.23 (Stearns MSS. See also the *Southern News,* Dec. 17, 1864; Apr. 15, Nov. 12, 14, Dec. 12, 1865; Mar. 2, 27, 1866.)

[45]Dated Feb. 4, 1867. (Stearns MSS.)

[46]See the correspondence between Isaac Hartman, A. Chester, and Stearns; Cole to Cobb, Oct. 24, 1867; Hartman to Stearns, Oct. 29, 1868; Brannan to Stearns, Sept. 21, 1867; Benjamin Hayes (Receiver for Stearns) to Poett, Feb. 25, 1867—all in Stearns MSS. Stearns included the following items in his income tax for 1868:

Rent from the Arcadia Block, $5,043.50; from two Los Angeles houses, $585.72; sale of cattle, $360.00; sale of horses, $4,902.50. Total, $10,891.72. Expenses included care of ranchos and stock, $6,178.51; taxes, $4,428.53. Total, $10,607.04. Net income, $284.68.

In 1870 Stearns' tax return, according to a copy in the Stearns MSS, was as follows:

Income from the sale of horses	$10,867.00
Income from the sale of cattle	250.00
Income from the sale of dry hides	57.50
Rent, Arcadia Block	10,751.62
Rent, houses in Los Angeles	920.00
Orchard	660.00
Total	$23,506.12

Deductions
Interest

Hayward & Co.	$730.90	
G. Oreña	500.00	
Temple & Co.	167.97	
A. Robinson	394.50	
I. Johnson	75.00	
		$ 1,868.37
City and county taxes		3,786.82
Allowed by law		2,000.00
Loss in trade		7,500.00
125 head of horses, died of disease, at $20		2,500.00
23 head of cattle, died of dry murrain, at $25		575.00
Total		$18,230.19

[47]The mortgage is recorded in Book 4 of Mortgages of Los Angeles County, pp. 146-48. Copies are in the Stearns collection.

[48]Robinson is best known as the author of the widely read and authoritative volume *Life in California*, published anonymously, in New York in 1846. His nephew, Charles R. Johnson, married Dolores, a daughter of Don Juan Bandini. In 1849 Robinson persuaded Stearns to join in outfitting a vessel, named the "Arcadia" in honor of Doña Arcadia, to engage in the California trade. Thanks to the rascality or incompetency of a third partner, the enterprise resulted in a heavy loss to Stearns. (See the Robinson-Stearns correspondence, in Stearns MSS.) Announcement of the arrival of the "Arcadia" at San Pedro, on Apr. 18, appeared in the *Southern Californian* of Apr. 25, 1855.

[49]I am indebted to Mr. Palmer Conner for a copy of the indenture. The original is on file in the Recorder's Office of Los Angeles County. A preliminary draft of the agreement, dated Apr. 17, 1868, is in the Stearns MSS. The *Semi-weekly News* of June 23, 1868, published a full account of the Trust and estimated that Stearns would receive $268,000 for his land—a figure substantially correct.

[50]For a map of the Stearns ranchos in 1873, see p. 201.

[51]J. M. Guinn, "Los Angeles in the Later Sixties and Early Seventies," Hist. Soc. of Sou. Calif. *Annual Publications*, III, 63-64.

[52]Alfred Robinson to Stearns, July 7, Aug. 20, 1868, in Stearns MSS.

[53]Edward F. Northam-Stearns correspondence, *ibid*. In 1870 Stearns rented pasturage on the ranchos Los Coyotes, La Habra, San Juan Cajón de Santa Ana, and Las Bolsas y Paredes to various sheep owners, including Moore & Bixby and Domingo Bastanchury. The rate averaged 10 cts. per head, and the net receipts amounted to $2,765.32. Copies of the leases are in the Stearns collection.

[54]Robinson to Stearns, Nov. 15, 1870, *ibid*. Always a lover of horses, Stearns was now devoting most of his time and interest to them. He still had some 1,500

head. In the spring of 1870 Don Abel suffered a critical illness, which may have accounted in part for the lack of energy and interest he showed in business affairs. (See the Robinson-Stearns correspondence in May, 1870, *ibid.*) Stearns's physicians sent him a bill for $1,000, for medical treatment between Feb. 14 and Apr. 22, 1870, and urged "immediate payment." (Drs. Griffin and Widney to Abel Stearns, July 21, 1870, *ibid.*)

⁵⁵Robinson to Stearns, Dec. 31, 1870, *ibid.* Martin and Northam were especially critical of Stearns.

⁵⁶On June 1, 1871, Stearns's account showed a balance in his favor of $155,992. (Robinson to Stearns, June 3, 1871, in Stearns MSS.)

CHAPTER XI

¹C. M. Gidney, Benjamin Brooks, Edwin M. Sheridan, *History of Santa Barbara, San Luis Obispo and Ventura Counties California* (Chicago, 1917), I, 200.

²Sol N. Sheridan, *History of Ventura County* (Chicago, 1926), I, 343.

³In regions susceptible of cultivation and settlement, indeed, the repeal of the No-Fence Law and the use of barbed wire had doomed the old California system of the open range, even before the drought of the mid-seventies. See *ante*, p. 62.

⁴See Robert G. Cleland, *The Twilight Cavalcade* (Pasadena, 1945) p. 5.

⁵*Ibid*, p. 6.

⁶"Ranch Life Fifty Years Ago," MS in Huntington Library.

⁷Dated Knoxville, Tenn., March 17, 1870.

⁸North was first offered four-sevenths of the stock of the Silk Center Association, which owned 8,000 acres of the Jurupa Ranch, for $34,000. He eventually bought the same stock for $8,000. North to his wife, Aug. 12, 1870. (MS, Huntington Library.)

⁹Bakersfield, in the southern end of the San Joaquin Valley, was founded in 1868 and acquired considerable notoriety during the seventies. The land on which the town was built belonged to Colonel Thomas Baker and a field which he had enclosed with a fence gave the place its name.

¹⁰Margaret Gardner, "The Community of Orange," *Orange County History Series*, II, 167.

¹¹In 1885 Maclay built the Maclay College of Theology in San Fernando for the use of the Methodist Church. In 1894 the college was merged with the University of Southern California.

¹²Quoted in Major Ben C. Truman, *Semi-Tropical California* (San Francisco, 1874), p. 43. See also *supra*, pp. 169-70. According to Judge North, B. D. Wilson sold an average of 1,200 oranges from each of his 600 trees at 3 cts. each, a total of $21,600. Wolfskill sold the fruit from 1,500 trees at $40 a thousand. North to his wife, May 29, 1870. MS.

In 1872, Nathan W. Blanchard and E. L. Bradley acquired a large tract of land in Ventura County that had the water rights of Santa Paula Creek and laid out the townsite of Santa Paula. The next year the two planted a hundred acres to "Havana Seedling Oranges."

[13]See Minnie Tibbets Mills, "Luther Calvin Tibbets," Hist. Soc. of Sou. Calif. *Quarterly*, XXV, 127-161. Eliza Tibbets, formerly looked upon as the patron saint of the navel orange industry, was L. C. Tibbets' second wife.

[14]In subsequent years, the so-called "Valencia Late," an orange marketed in the spring, summer, and early fall, came to rival the Navel in popularity.

[15]*I. N. Van Nuys, 1835-1912* (Los Angeles, 1944), pp. 11-12.

[16]Harris Newmark, *Sixty Years in Southern California* (Boston and New York, 1930), p. 493.

[17]The collapse of the Comstock mining boom and the disastrous failure of Ralston's Bank of California precipitated a depression that eventually affected all the state.

[18]Remi A. Nadeau, *City Makers* (Garden City, New York, 1948), p. 220.

[19]There were twelve watering and resting stations between the rail terminus at San Fernando and the lower end of Owens Lake.

The borax deposits of San Bernardino County were discovered in the early sixties and extensively mined a decade later. By 1873 they were yielding about 1,000,000 pounds annually. Searles Lake furnished the chief supply.

[20]The phrase was coined by Thomas Fitch, orator and auctioneer extraordinary, and was obviously an adaptation of Senator Proctor Knott's ironic eulogy of Duluth in 1871 as the "Zenith City of the Unsalted Sea."

[21]The failure of Tom Scott's plans to complete the Texas Pacific Railroad to the coast was a bitter disappointment to San Diego and retarded the growth of that city and its harbor for many years.

[22]For Vasquez' own story see Appendix V.

[23]*A Literary History of Southern California* (Berkeley and Los Angeles, 1950), p. 97.

[24]The first issue of the Los Angeles *Times* appeared on December 4, 1881.

For a comprehensive list of early California newspapers, see Muir Dawson's *History and Bibliography of Southern California Newspapers, 1851-1876,* (Los Angeles, 1950).

[25]*History of Santa Barbara, San Luis Obispo, and Ventura Counties, op. cit.,* I, p. 98.

[26]Undated clipping from the San José *Patriot*, Vol. XVIII, Maclay Scrapbook (Huntington Library).

[27]Benjamin F. Taylor, *Between the Gates* (Chicago, 1878), p. 261.

[28][Prepared by Col. I. J. Warner, Judge Benjamin Hayes, Dr. J. P. Widney] *An Historical Sketch of Los Angeles County California* (Los Angeles, 1876), pp. 145-46.

[29]*Compendium of the Tenth Census of the United States* (Washington, 1883), I, 16-17, and II, 1561. The figures are in round numbers.

Bibliography

MANUSCRIPTS

Antonio F. Coronel Collection, *Los Angeles County Museum.*

Banning, Phineas: Biographical Sketch: Settlement of Wilmington, *Bancroft Library*, University of California, Berkeley, California. *Microfilm, Huntington Library.*

Bixby Papers: Diaries of Augustus S. Bixby (1857-1868), 6 vols. *Huntington Library.*

Chambers, Walter: Outline of the History of the Development of Social Welfare and Related Events in Los Angeles, July 13, 1939.

Chillson, Lorenzo Dow: Diary, *Huntington Library.*

Clarke, James: Letters, *Huntington Library.*

Cleland, Robert Stewart: A Glimpse at Southern California Medicine before 1870. MS in possession of the author.

Couts Manuscripts. A large and unsorted collection of letters, business papers, and documents, originally belonging to Cave J. Couts, owner of the *Guajome Ranch, San Diego County.*

Crank, Mary Agnes: Ranch Life Fifty Years Ago, *Huntington Library.*

Davis, William Heath: The Sunshine and Shadows of San Leandro, *Huntington Library.*

Don Juan Forster *vs.* Pío Pico (*Orange County, Calif., WPA, 1936, Project No. 3105*; 4 vols., typescript), II.

Hayes, Benjamin: Notes, *Bancroft Library.*

Kelly, John: Life on a San Diego Cattle Ranch, *Huntington Library.*

Larkin, Thomas O.: Description of California, Official Correspondence Pt. I, *Bancroft Library.*

Los Angeles County Deeds, Mortgages, Tax Assessments, etc., *Hall of Records, Los Angeles, California.*

Maclay, Charles: Papers, *Huntington Library.*

Meadows, Don: Bernardo Yorba Hacienda of Rancho Cañada de Santa Ana. *Charles W. Bowers Memorial Museum, Santa Ana, California.*

Reynolds, William P.: Letters, 1848-59, *Huntington Library.*

Rowe, Charles: Diary, *Huntington Library.*

339

Stearns, Abel: Manuscripts, *Huntington Library*. (Referred to in original edition as Gaffey MSS. For description see Preface p. xiv.)

U. S. Board of Land Commissioners, Record of Decisions, Vol. III. *Huntington Library*.

Wilson Papers, *Huntington Library*. A large collection of letters, business and family papers of Benjamin Davis Wilson, a prominent figure in the business and political life of California from 1841 to 1878.

Woods, James: Diary, *Huntington Library*.

NEWSPAPERS

Alta California, Dec. 12, 1853.
El Clamor Público, Los Angeles, 1855-1859.
Los Angeles *Star*, 1851-1864; 1868-1879.
Missouri Republican, Nov. 29, 1859.
Sacramento *Union*, Jan. 7, 1865.
San Francisco *Bulletin*, Mar. 31, 1860; May 25, 1869.
Southern Californian, 1854-1856.
Southern Vineyard, Los Angeles, 1858-1860.
The News, Los Angeles (for frequent changes of name see footnote 38, Chap. III), 1860-1869.
Wilmington *Journal*, Nov. 1864.
[See footnote 4, Chap. V for list of papers published chiefly in Los Angeles County before 1865.]

PERIODICALS

BAKER, CHARLES C.: "Mexican Land Grants in California," Historical Society of Southern California *Annual Publications*, IX, Pt. III, 236-43.

BARROWS, HENRY D.: "Abel Stearns," *Ibid.*, IV, Pt. III, 197-99.
———: "Reminiscences of Los Angeles," *Ibid.*, III, Pt. I, 55-62.

BARROWS, R. S.: "Memorial Sketch of Dr. John S. Griffin," *Ibid.*, IV, Pt. II, 183-85.

BARTLETT, W. C.: "The Tropical Fruits of California," *Overland Monthly*, I, 263-68.

BOLTON, HERBERT EUGENE: "The Mission as a Frontier Institution in the Spanish-American Colonies," *American Historical Review*, XXIII, 42-61.

Browne, J. Ross: "Agricultural Capacity of California," *Overland Monthly*, X, 297-314.

California State Agricultural Society *Transactions, 1864-65.*

California State Agricultural Society *Transactions, 1870-71.*

[Documents furnished by Mary M. Bowman]: "Call for a Convention to Divide the State of California, 1851," Hist. Soc. of So. Calif. *Annual Publications*, X, Pt. III, 77-78.

Cleland, Robert G.: *Early Sentiment for the Annexation of California*, reprinted from *Southwestern Historical Quarterly*, XVIII, Nos. 1, 2, 3.

——: "The Mining Industry of Mexico," *Mining and Scientific Press*, CXXIII, 13-20.

——: "Transportation in California before the Railroads, with Special Reference to Los Angeles," Hist. Soc. of So. Calif. *Annual Publications*, XI, Pt. I, 60-67.

Davies, David: "An Emigrant of the Fifties," [The Letters of James Clarke], Hist. Soc. of So. Calif. *Quarterly*, XIX, 99-120.

De Groot, Henry: "Silk Culture in California," *Overland Monthly*, IV, 452-57.

Evans, Taliesin: "Orange Culture in California," *Ibid.*, XII, 235-44.

Field, Alston G.: "Attorney-General Black and the California Land Claims," *Pacific Historical Review*, IV, 235-45.

Flint, Thomas: "Diary," ed. by Waldemar Westergaard, Hist. Soc. of So. Calif. *Annual Publications*, XII, Pt. III, 53-127.

Gardner, Margaret: "The Community of Orange," *Orange County History Series*, II, 149-93.

Guinn, J. M.: "From Cattle Range to Orange Grove," Hist. Soc. of So. Calif. *Annual Publications*, VIII, Pt. III, 145-57.

——: "Los Angeles in the Later Sixties and Early Seventies," *Ibid.*, III, Pt. I, 63-68.

——: "Muy Illustre Ayuntamiento," *Ibid.*, IV, Pt. III, 206-12.

——: "The Passing of the Cattle Barons of California," *Ibid.*, VIII, Pts. I, II, 51-60.

——: "The Story of a Plaza," *Ibid.*, IV, Pt. III, 247-56.

Haley, J. Evetts, ed.: "A Log of the Texas-California Cattle Trail, 1854, [by] James G. Bell," *The Southwestern Historical Quarterly*, XXXV, 208-37.

HAYES, JOHN: "Skilled Farming in Los Angeles," *Overland Monthly*, VII, 448-54.

————: "Sheep Farming in California," *Ibid.*, VIII, 489-97.

HITTELL, JOHN S.: "Mexican Land Claims in California," *Hutchings' Illustrated California Magazine*, II, 442-48.

HUNTER, MILTON R.: "The Mormon Corridor," *Pacific Coast Historical Review*, VIII, 179-200.

HYACINTH, MR. SOCRATES [STEPHEN POWERS]: "A Flock of Wool," *Overland Monthly*, IV, 141-46.

————: "On Foot in Southern California," *Ibid.*, II, 19-24.

————: "Wayside Views of California," *Ibid.*, II, 224-30.

KING, CLARENCE J.: "Wayside Pikes," *Atlantic Monthly*, XXVIII, 564-76.

KRASZEWSKI, DON MAQUEL (MICHAEL): "Juan Flores in San Juan Capistrano," *Orange County History Series*, III, 22-32.

MILLS, MINNIE TIBBETS: "Luther Calvin Tibbets," Hist. Soc. of So. Calif. *Quarterly*, XXV, 127-61.

"Monthly Record of Current Events," *Hutchings' Illustrated California Magazine* (1860-61), V, 285.

OGDEN, ADELE: "Hides and Tallow," *California Historical Quarterly*, VI, 254-64.

POWERS, STEPHEN: "On the Texan Prairies," *Overland Monthly*, II, 369-74.

RAUP, HALLOCK F.: "Rancho Los Palos Verdes," Hist. Soc. of So. Calif. *Quarterly*, XIX, 7-21.

ROBINSON, W. W.: "Abel Stearns on the California and Los Angeles Archives," *Ibid.*, XIX, 141-44.

————: "Pasadena's First Owner," *Ibid.*, XIX, 132-40.

SHINN, C. H.: "Social Changes in California," *Popular Science Monthly* (Apr. 6, 1891).

SILVER, J. S.: "The Coming Season," *Overland Monthly*, I, 415-18.

————: "Farming Facts for California Immigrants," *Ibid.*, I, 176-83.

STAMP, PEARL PAULINE: "Abel Stearns: California Pioneer," *The Grizzly Bear Magazine* (May-Aug., 1926).

STEPHENSON, TERRY E.: "A Horse Race Goes to Court," *Westways*, XXXII, No. I, 23.

————: "Forster *versus* Pico, A Forgotten California *Cause Celebre*," Hist. Soc. of So. Calif. *Quarterly*, XVII, 143-47; XVIII, 22-30, 50-68.

STRONG, JOHN L.: "Cotton Experiments in California," *Overland Monthly*, VI, 326-35.

VALLEJO, GUADALUPE: "Ranch and Mission Days in Alta California," *The Century Magazine*, XLI, 183-92.

WAGNER, HENRY R. foreword by: "Report of the Commission of the District and the Territories on Secularization of the Missions of Both Californias," Hist. Soc. of So. Calif. *Annual Publications*, XVI, 66-73.

GOVERNMENT DOCUMENTS

Annual Report of the Controller of the State for the Year 1860.

"Annual Report of the State Treasurer," Appendixes of the Senate and Assembly *Journals*, 1850 to 1870, *passim.*

Appendix to Assembly Journals for the Eighth Session of the Legislature of the State of California, Sacramento, 1857.

[Bigler, John]: *Annual Message of the Governor, 1856*, Sacramento, 1856.

[————]: *Governor's Annual Message to the Legislature of the State of California, Assembled at Sacramento, Jan. 1, 1855.* Sacramento [1855].

Black, Jeremiah S.: *Report*, House Ex. Doc. 84, 26th Cong., 1st Sess.

[Burnett, Peter H.]: *Annual Message of the Governor of California, Delivered to Both Houses of the Legislature, January 7, 1851* [San José, 1851].

California State Surveyor-General, *Annual Report, 1855.*

Governor's Message and Report of the Secretary of State on the Census of 1852, The. San Francisco, 1853.

Halleck, Henry W.: *Report on the Laws and Regulations Relative to Grants or Sales of Public Lands in California.* Washington, 1850.

Hoffman, Ogden: *Reports of Land Cases Determined in the United States District Court for the Northern District of California, June Term 1853 to June Term 1858, Inclusive* [San Francisco, 1862].

"Inventory of the Bixby Records Collection in the Palos Verdes Library and Art Gallery," Los Angeles, The Southern California Historical Records Survey, 1940.

Jones, William Carey: *Report on the Subject of Land Titles in California*, Sen. Ex. Doc. No. 18, 31st Cong., 1st Sess.; Washington, 1850. [Also separately published in Washington, 1850.]

"Laws Concerning Rodeos," from supplementary act of the state legislature, April 30, 1855.

Laws of the State of California, Containing All the Acts of the Legislature of a Public and General Nature, Now in Force, Passed at the Sessions of 1850-51-52-53 (compiled by S. Garfielde and F. A. Snyder), Benicia, Calif., 1853.

Laws of the United States . . . upon Which the Public Land Titles in Each State and Territory Have Depended. Washington, 1884, II.

List of Acts Passed by the Legislature of the State of California at Its First Session [in 1849 and 1850] [San José, 1850].

Malloy, William M.: *Treaties, Conventions, International Acts, Protocols and Agreements between the United States of America and Other Powers.* ("Treaty of Peace, Friendship, Limits and Settlement [Guadalupe Hidalgo]"). Washington, 1910.

Proceedings before the United States Board of Land Commissioners (Photostats, Huntington Library):

RANCHOS	CASE NO.
Domínguez	398
La Bolsa Chica	405
La Habra	401
Las Bolsas	402
Los Alamitos	404
Los Palos Verdes	446
San Antonio	308
San Juan Cajón de Santa Ana	440
San Pasqual	345
San Pedro	398 and 480
San Rafael	401
Sespe	49

Report on the Laws and Regulations Relative to Grants and Sales of Public Lands in California, House Ex. Doc. No. 17, 31st Cong., 1st Sess. [Also separately published in Washington, 1850].

"Report of Spanish or Mexican Land Grants in California, Prepared by James S. Stratton," Appendix of the California Senate and Assembly *Journals* in 1881.

Report of the Surveyor-General of the State of California from Nov. 1, 1867, to Nov. 1, 1869.

———: Statistical Tables for the years 1866, 1869-70, 1872.

Santa Barbara County, Assessment Roll, 1860.

State *Assembly Journals,* 7th Sess., 1856.

Statutes of California Passed at the Nineteenth Session of the Legislature, 1871-72, Sacramento, 1872.

United States Census Reports, Washington, D. C.; Seventh, 1850; Eighth, 1860; Ninth, 1870; Tenth, 1880.

United States Commission for Ascertaining and Settling Private Land Claims in California. San Francisco, 1852. *(Organization, Acts and Regulations of the United States Land Commissioners for California).*

Wills, Henry E.: *California Titles.* A collection of items bound in 19 vols. relating chiefly to land titles and the decisions of the U. S. Land Commission, Huntington Library.

BOOKS

Bancroft, Hubert Howe: *California Inter Pocula.* San Francisco, 1888.

———: *California Pastoral.* San Francisco, 1888.

———: *History of California,* 7 vols. San Francisco, 1884-1890.

Barker, Charles, ed.: *Memoirs of Elisha Oscar Crosby.* San Marino, 1945.

Banning, William, and Banning, George H.: *Six Horses.* New York and London, 1930.

Beattie, George William, and Beattie, Helen Pruitt: *Heritage of the Valley.* Pasadena, 1939.

Bell, Horace: *Reminiscences of a Ranger; or Early Times in Southern California.* Los Angeles, 1851; Santa Barbara, 1929.

BISHOP, WILLIAM H.: *Old Mexico and Her Lost Provinces.* New York, 1883.

BIXBY-SMITH, SARAH: *Adobe Days.* Cedar Rapids, 1925.

BLAIR, EMMA HELEN, and ROBERTSON, JAMES ALEXANDER: *The Philippine Islands, 1493-1803.* Cleveland, 1903.

CARR, A.: *Illustrated Hand-book of California.* London, 1870.

CARRILLO, CARLOS ANTONIO: *Exposition Addressed to the Chamber of Deputies of the Congress of the Union*; tr. and ed. by Herbert Ingraham Priestly. San Francisco, 1938.

CHALFANT, W. A.: *The Story of Inyo.* Chicago, 1922.

CHAPMAN, CHARLES E.: *A History of California: The Spanish Period.* New York, 1921.

CLELAND, ROBERT GLASS: *A History of California: The American Period.* New York, 1923.

———: *Pathfinders.* Los Angeles, 1928.

———, and HARDY, OSGOOD: *The March of Industry.* Los Angeles, 1929.

———, ed.: *The Mexican Year Book, 1920-21.* Los.Angeles, 1922.

———: *The Place Called Sespe.* Chicago, 1940.

———: *The Twilight Cavalcade.* Pasadena, 1945.

COY, OWEN C.: *California County Boundaries.* Berkeley, 1923.

DAKIN, SUSANNA BRYANT: *A Scotch Paisano.* Berkeley, 1939.

DALE, HARRISON CLIFFORD: *The Ashley-Smith Explorations and the Discovery of a Central Route to the Pacific, 1822-1830.* Cleveland, 1918.

DAVIS, WILLIAM HEATH: *Seventy-five Years in California.* San Francisco, 1929.

DAWSON, MUIR: *History and Bibliography of Southern California Newspapers, 1851-1876.* Los Angeles, 1950.

DONALDSON, THOMAS: *The Public Domain.* Washington, 1879.

DRAKE, EUGENE B., comp. by: *Jimeno's and Hartnell's Indexes of Land Concessions, from 1830 to 1846; also, Toma de Razón, or, Registry of Titles for 1844-45.* San Francisco, 1861.

DWINELLE, JOHN WHIPPLE: *The Colonial History of the City of San Francisco.* San Francisco, 1863.

ELLISON, JOSEPH: *California and the Nation, 1850-1869.* Berkeley, 1927.

ENGELHARDT, CHARLES ANTHONY (FR. ZEPHYRIN): *San Diego Mission*. San Francisco, 1920.
———: *San Fernando Rey*. Chicago, 1927.
———: *San Juan Capistrano Mission*. Los Angeles, 1922.
———: *Santa Barbara Mission*. San Francisco, 1923.
FABIAN, BENJAMIN: *The Agricultural Lands of California*. San Francisco, 1869.
FARQUHAR, FRANCIS P., ed.: *Up and Down California in 1860-1864: The Journal of William H. Brewer*. New Haven, 1930.
GEORGE, HENRY: *Our Land and Our Land Policy, National and State*. San Francisco, 1871.
GIDNEY, C. M., BROOKS, BENJAMIN, SHERIDAN, EDWIN M.: *History of Santa Barbara, San Luis Obispo and Ventura Counties California*. Chicago, 1917.
GUINN, J. M.: *Coast Counties & History of California*. [Chicago, 1904].
———: *Historical and Biographical Record of Los Angeles*. Chicago, 1901.
———: *Historical and Biographical Record of Southern California*. Chicago, 1902.
HALL, EDWARD HEPPLE: *The Great West: Railroad, Steamboat and Stage Guide and Hand-book for Travellers, Miners and Emigrants....* New York, 1866.
HAWLEY, W. A.: *The Early Days of Santa Barbara, California*. Santa Barbara, 1920.
HAYES, BENJAMIN D.: *Pioneer Notes from the Diaries of Judge Benjamin Hayes, 1849-75*. Los Angeles, 1929.
HITTELL, JOHN S.: *The Resources of California*. San Francisco, 1863; *Ibid.*, 1874.
HOFFMAN, OGDEN: *Reports of Land Cases Determined in the United States District Court for the Northern District of California, June Term 1853 to June Term 1858, Inclusive*. [San Francisco, 1862].
HUNT, ROCKWELL DENNIS, and AMENT, WILLIAM SCHEFFIELD: *Oxcart to Airplane*. Los Angeles, 1929.
INGERSOLL, LUTHER A.: *Ingersoll's Century Annals of San Bernardino County, 1769 to 1904*. Los Angeles, 1904.
I. N. Van Nuys, 1835-1912. Los Angeles, 1944.

JONES, WILLIAM CAREY: *Letters of William Carey Jones in Review of Attorney General Black's Report*, San Francisco, 1860.

KERR, ROBERT JOSEPH: *A Handbook of Mexican Law*. Chicago, 1909.

KIP, BISHOP WILLIAM INGRAHAM: *A California Pilgrimage*. Fresno, Calif., 1931.

———: *The Early Days of My Episcopate*. New York, 1892.

KRESS, GEORGE HENRY: *History of the Medical Profession of Southern California*. Los Angeles, 1910.

LAYNE, JOSEPH GREGG: *Annals of Los Angeles from the Arrival of the First White Men to the Civil War, 1769-1861*. San Francisco, 1935.

Los Angeles City Directory, 1875.

LYNCH, H. B.: *Rainfall and Stream Run-off in Southern California since 1769*. Los Angeles, 1931.

McCOY, JOSEPH G.: *Historic Sketches of the Cattle Trade of the West and Southwest*. Glendale, Calif., 1940.

MORROW, WILLIAM W.: *Spanish and Mexican Private Land Grants*. San Francisco and Los Angeles, 1923.

NADEAU, REMI A.: *City Makers*. Garden City, New York, 1948.

NEWMARK, HARRIS: *Sixty Years in Southern California*. Boston and New York, 1930.

NEWMARK, MAURICE H., and NEWMARK, MARCO R.: *Census of the City and County of Los Angeles for the Year 1850*. Los Angeles, 1929.

NORDHOFF, CHARLES: *California: For Health, Pleasure, and Residence. A Book for Travellers and Settlers*. New York, 1873.

OLMSTEAD, FREDERICK LAW: *A Journey through Texas*. New York, 1857.

RAUP, HALLOCK F.: *San Bernardino, California: Settlement and Growth of a Pass-Site City*. Berkeley, 1940.

[ROBINSON, ALFRED]: *Life in California*. New York, 1846.

ROBINSON, W. W.: *Land in California*. Berkeley, 1948.

———: *Ranchos Become Cities*. Pasadena, 1939.

———: *The Forest and the People*. Los Angeles, 1946.

SALVATOR, LUDWIG L.: *Los Angeles in the Sunny Seventies: A Flower from the Golden Land*, tr. by Marguerite Eyer Wilbur. Los Angeles, 1929.

Sánchez, Nellie Van de Grift: *Spanish Arcadia*. Los Angeles, 1929.

Seyd, Ernest: *California and Its Resources*. London, 1858.

Sheridan, Sol N.: *History of Ventura County*. Chicago, 1926.

Simpson, Sir George: *Narrative of a Journey Round the World during the Years 1841 and 1842*. London, 1847.

State Register and Year Book of Facts, 1857; Ibid., 1859. San Francisco, 1857, 1859.

Taylor, Benjamin F.: *Between the Gates*. Chicago, 1878.

Thwaites, Reuben Gold, ed.: *The Personal Narrative of James O. Pattie, of Kentucky*. Cleveland, 1905.

Truman, Major Ben C.: *Semi-Tropical California*. San Francisco, 1874.

Walker, Franklin: *A Literary History of Southern California*. Berkeley and Los Angeles, 1950.

———: *San Francisco's Literary Frontier*. New York, 1939.

Warner, J. J., Hayes, Judge Benjamin, and Widney, Dr. J. P.: *An Historical Sketch of Los Angeles County*. Los Angeles, 1876. [Also called *Centennial History of Los Angeles County*.]

Watts, John S.: *Land Claims under the Treaty of 1848*. Washington, 1870(?).

Wheeler, Alfred: *Land Titles in San Francisco and the Laws Affecting the Same*. San Francisco, 1852.

Wilkes, Charles: *Narrative of the United States Exploring Expedition*, 5 vols. Philadelphia, 1845.

Index

Abilene Trail (of Kansas), 104
Adams Windmill Company, 232
Agriculture, 143, 144, 145, 163-4, 177-80, 206, 209, 217, 218, 219, 220
Agua Caliente (ranch), 68
Agua Mansa, 129
Aguilar, Cristóbal, 28, 80
Aguirre, José Antonio, 192
Alameda Street, 78, 220
Alcatraz, 97
Alhambra, 222
Alta California, 5
Alta California (newspaper), 46
Alvarado, Francisco, 66
Alvarado, Governor Juan B., 25, 155, 216
Alvarado, Ysidro, 132
"Amagossa" (Amargosa), 148
American fur hunters, 34, 185
Anaheim, 128, 143, 157, 158, 173, 174, 205, 210, 224
Anderson, Mr. [?], 185-6
Antonio, Juan, Chief of Cahuilla Indians, 67, 68
Apache Indians, 108
Aphodl, B., firm of, 232
Arcadia Block, 202
Arcadia Building, 120, 197-8
Arcadia Street, 198
Argonauts, 45, 102, 168
Argüello, Jose Anto[nio], 105
Arguillas, José Ma[ría], 16
Arizona, 64, 109
Arroyo Hondo, *see* Arroyo Seco
Arroyo Seco, 13, 15, 17, 21, 128, 211
Artesia (town), 222
Asbestine Stone Company, 232
Austin, Henry C., 229
Australia, 114-15
Ávila (Ábila), Don Juan, 87, 88, 89
Ayers, James J., 229

Ayuntamiento, 58
"Azulejo," Pico's race horse, 88-9
Azusa, 97, 173
Azusa (ranch), 65

Bakersfield, 169, 179
Baldwin, E. J. ("Lucky"), 221-2
Ballado, 72
Bancroft, [Hubert Howe], 20
Bandini, Dolores, 197
Bandini, Don Juan, quoted on land title claims, 41-2; borrows money, 111; Stearns's letter to, 186; against Gov. Victoria, 187; relationship with Stearns, 189; bankrupt, 196-7
Bandini family, 198
Bandini, Maria Arcadia, marriage to Stearns, 189-90
Banks, 220-22
Banning line (railroad), 224
Banning, Phineas, 63, 158, 174
Bard, Thomas R., sheep owner, 209
Barron, Eustace, British merchant, 185
Bartlett, W. C., 143
Barton, James R., Sheriff, murder of, 91
Beale (landowner), 118
Beale road, 168
Beale's Ranch, 231
Bean, General J. H., 67
Bear Valley, 150
Beckwith (Beckwourth) Pass, 108
Belarde, Ignacio, 66
Bell, Horace, 59, 93, 107
Bella Union Hotel, 78, 95, 99
Benton (town), 151
Benton, Senator Thomas H., 37
Berry, D. M., 211
Bessie Brady, Owens Lake steamer, 152

351